STUDIES IN COMMONWEALTH POLITICS AND HISTORY

No. 5

General Editors: Professor W. H. MORRIS-JONES
Institute of Commonwealth Studies
University of London

Professor DENNIS AUSTIN
Department of Government
University of Manchester

SOLDIERS AND OIL

About the Series

Legatee of a vast empire, the Commonwealth still carries the imprint of its past. And in doing so it may be said to have a collective identity which, in a very varying degree, each of its members exhibits. This, we believe, can sustain a collective inquiry into the political history and institutions of countries which were once governed within the British Empire and we note signs of a revival of interest in this field. In recent years 'area studies' have been encouraged, but there is also a sense in which the Commonwealth is itself a region, bounded not by geography but history, and imperial history in particular. Seen thus the region cannot exclude areas into which empire overspilled as in the Sudan, or areas now outside the Commonwealth such as South Africa and Burma, or the unique case of Ireland. No account of the dilemmas which face the government of Canada or Nigeria or India—or indeed of the United Kingdom—which examines the present in relation to the past can be complete which omits some consideration of this 'imperial dimension'. Without in any sense trying to claim that there is a 'political culture' common to all Commonwealth countries it is certainly the case that some of the institutions, some part of the political life, and a certain element in the political beliefs of many Commonwealth leaders, can be said to derive from the import of institutions, practices and beliefs from Britain into its former colonies.

Nor is the Commonwealth merely a useful category of study. It is also a community of scholars, many of them teaching and writing within the growing number of universities throughout the member countries who share an interest in the consequences of imperial experience and have common traditions of study.

The present series of books is intended to express that interest and those traditions. They are presented not as a guide to the Commonwealth as a corporate entity, but as studies either in the politics and recent history of its member states or of themes which are of common interest to several of the countries concerned. Within the Commonwealth there is great variety—of geographical setting, of cultural context, of economic development and social life; they provide the challenge to comparative study, while the elements of common experience make the task manageable. A cross-nation study of administrative reforms or of legislative behaviour is both facilitated and given added meaning; so also is an examination of the external relations of one or more member states; even a single country study, say on Guyana, is bound to throw light on problems which are echoed in Sri Lanka and Jamaica. The series will bring together—and, we hope, stimulate— studies of those kinds carried out by both established and younger scholars. In doing so, it can make its distinctive contribution to an understanding of the changing contemporary world.

The present volume exactly fits the pattern. It explores the difficulties faced by an independent Nigeria in the aftermath of civil war when the country was enriched by oil and governed by soldiers. The transformation of its political life was effected not ony by the pulling down and re-building of constitutional structures, but by the search for different modes of political control. The attempt to transmute a divided colonial territory into a federal nation state is still being made, and the present volume is necessarily a study of change in progress: but it is all the more interesting on that account in its analysis of the politics of oil and of the attempt by the military to disengage from politics.

DENNIS AUSTIN
W. H. MORRIS-JONES

List of books in the series:

SOLDIERS AND OIL

The Political Transformation of Nigeria

Edited by
Keith Panter-Brick

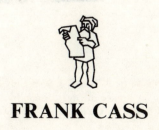

FRANK CASS

First published 1978 in Great Britain by
FRANK CASS AND COMPANY LIMITED
Gainsborough House, Gainsborough Road,
London, E11 1RS, England

and in the United States of America by
FRANK CASS AND COMPANY LIMITED
c/o Biblio Distribution Center
81 Adams Drive, P.O. Box 327, Totowa, N.J. 07511

ISBN 0 7146 3098 5

Filmset by A. Brown & Sons Ltd., Hull.
Printed in Great Britain by
Billing & Sons Ltd, Guildford, London and Worcester

Contents

Part Five—CONSTITUTIONAL REFORM

Contributors

Abubakar Yaya Aliyu, Institute of Administration, Zaria

Valerie P. Bennett, Boston University

Henry Bienen, Princeton University

Ian Campbell, University of Warwick

Martin Dent, Keele University

Alex E. Gboyega, University of Ibadan

A. H. M. Kirk-Greene, St. Antony's, Oxford

Keith Panter-Brick, London School of Economics

Oyeleye Oyediran, University of Ibadan

S. Egite Oyovbaire, Ahmadu Bello University, Zaria

Douglas Rimmer, University of Birmingham

Terisa Turner, London School of Economics

Ali D. Yahaya, Ahmadu Bello University, Zaria

Preface

This volume is very much a co-operative enterprise on the part of the Nigerian, American, Australian and British colleagues who have contributed the chapters and of institutions which have assisted both financially and otherwise at crucial moments. Separate acknowledgements are made by several of the contributors. I myself wish to thank first and foremost all those who responded so well to the idea of a collective work. I trust that they will find the result both pleasing and rewarding. I am also grateful to Martin Dent for his very helpful criticism of my own chapter on the draft constitution.

I also thank the University of London, the British Academy and the Nuffield Foundation for their generous assistance. When my two much esteemed colleagues and dear friends W. H. Morris-Jones and Dennis Austin first suggested a sequel to the earlier volume *Nigerian Politics and Military Rule: Prelude to the Civil War* I had some doubts, mainly because of an eight-year absence from Nigeria. The University of London and the British Academy resolved that problem, the first by making me a grant from the Hayter Travel Fund for an exploratory visit in December 1975 and the second by awarding me an Overseas Visiting Fellowship which took me to Nigeria in December 1976. There was also the problem of bringing the contributors together so that we could benefit from each individual's knowledge and experience. A full gathering of so many so far apart was not possible but, with the assistance of the Nuffield Foundation, a working party was held in June 1976 at the Institute of Commonwealth Studies, London at which some preliminary drafts were discussed and views exchanged. I am grateful to all who participated, especially to Dennis Austin who chaired these sessions with so much grace and skill and to David Williams who so kindly agreed to lead the opening discussion.

I have referred in the title of this book to a transformation, for reasons which are set out in the Introduction. To revisit Nigeria was, however, to re-experience the unchanging warmth of greetings from old friends and the ever courteous reception of those whom I was meeting for the first time. I am particularly grateful to colleagues in the Universities at Zaria, Ibadan, Nsukka, Ife and Lagos, especially Alaba Ogunsanwo, Ali Yahaya, Suleiman Kumo and Billy Dudley, and to members of the Constitution Drafting Committee, especially Professor S. A. Aluko, Dr. Ibrahim Tahir, Dr. Y. B. Usman, Alhaji Nuhu Bamali, Dr. Diejomaoh, Dr. Edozien, Alhaji Aminu Kano, Bola Ige, Professor Ikime, Dr. S. Osoba and Dr. O. Oyediran.

I would like to express once again my gratitude to the London School of Economics for contributing in so many ways—not least for the indispensable and never failing secretarial services of the Government Department and the help of the Geography Department in the drawing of maps and figures.

Finally I acknowledge what gave me the greatest joy—to have had throughout the intellectual stimulus and companionship of Dennis Austin. He sponsored the idea, encouraged us all and was tireless in his scrutiny of my own contribution. He was always more realistic than I about the timing of things but remained incurably optimistic about the outcome. May his faith be justified.

K. P.-B.

London
September 1977

Introduction

Keith Panter-Brick

The period since January 1966, when the Nigerian army first came to power—a period due to be brought to a close by a return to barracks in 1979—is too long to be treated simply as a military interregnum. Even if a civilian government takes over in 1979, the intervening years already amount to twice as long as that initial period of independence under civilian rule: nor will it be a case of the one resuming where the other left off. Far too much has changed for the perspective to be that of transition. There has also been transformation and the period needs to be assessed from that point of view, irrespective of what may follow. Since the military has never pretended to be more than a corrective regime, preparing the way for its own replacement, any examination of its rule is bound to some extent to be a study of military disengagement. But the Nigerian military can scarcely be said to have been in a hurry to relinquish office, even if Gowon's departure in July 1975 freed a log-jam. Time is still needed for the army to put its own house in order and doubts have been expressed, as recently as May 1977, whether 1979 allows sufficiently for this to be accomplished.[1]

Meanwhile the military has governed, through and with the assistance of the civil service, police and courts of law and has had at its disposal, thanks to oil, federal revenues amounting to an estimated 7,650 million naira in 1977/78 compared with £170 million in 1966/67, a twenty-two fold increase. The 1975-80 National Development Plan envisaged a capital expenditure of 30 billion naira compared with 3 billion and 2.2 billion in the two previous Plans. Even allowing for inflated prices—running at 35% per annum in 1975/76 alone—the volume of public expenditure has been quite unprecedented. The military has also had charge of foreign affairs and in several respects given them a new direction.[2] Nigeria is now more clearly and aggressively identified with causes which are placed at the heart of the Panafrican movement, as exemplified by its support for the MPLA in Angola. Although the military has also shown its impotence (as in the conduct of a reliable census) and although oil revenues have aggravated rather than removed some problems (notably corruption) these two factors, soldiers and oil, have in combination quite transformed the Nigerian scene.

A volume which aims to analyse recent trends and to picture the contemporary scene in a country as large, as diverse and as dynamic as Nigeria is best written by many hands, especially if the contributors are themselves diverse, some Nigerians, others British or American or Australian. Each writes from a position of advantage, Nigerians having the immediacy of local and often personal knowledge, the others the detachment of distance. Together they cover a broader canvas more quickly, offering information and views that are both many-sided and fresh. Even so, not every aspect of contemporary Nigerian politics could be covered adequately in a single volume. Priority is therefore given to the record of the military in office, to interactions between government and the economy, to changes (structural and financial) affecting the pattern of government and proposals for a more viable political system in the future. There is inevitably some slight overlap in the ground covered by the four chapters that deal specifically with the military, but each has a different approach. The two contributions on the political economy start from very different standpoints but are not so divergent in their analysis: they both emphasize in a parallel fashion the dangers inherent in too great a politicisation of the economy. The remaining chapters consider the manner in which the military has dealt with highly contentious issues partly out of necessity, as in the matter of revenue allocation, partly from a belief that they were issues that needed to be settled authoritatively in the interests of stable and effective government, such as an increase in the number of states or a reform of local government, and partly in preparation for a return to a more legitimate form of constitutional government, as in the drafting of a new constitution.

To suggest that there has been a transformation of the Nigerian political scene is to have in mind not simply the easily observable alterations to governmental structures but developments in the more complex field of political power—not least the emergence of large numbers of persons qualified by education to claim a place in the civil service, the army, and the professions or, having access to the necessary financial resources, to thrust their way forward in business enterprises. The relationship between groups such as these and the new governmental structures is a matter of conjecture but, in an introduction to chapters that outline some of these changes, one may sensibly indulge in a mixture of observation and reasoned speculation.

First to be noted is the impact of the wealth from oil. The oil industry has become by far the greatest single source of public revenue. It is moreover located mainly in two of the States or off-shore (Map 3). Thus the only national custodian of the oil revenues—for Nigeria as a whole—is the federal government. The only way in which the other states, and the vast majority of the population, can share in the revenue from oil is through action taken by the central authority. As Sam Oyovbaire makes abundantly clear this is a very different situation from earlier years, when the four Regions considered themselves largely self-sufficient. The change is epitomised by the marked departure from the rule of derivation, whereby revenues are apportioned to the areas in which they originate. This rule was never fully applied but it was the main feature of revenue allocation until the early 1970s. Once the revenue from oil became dominant the principle of derivation had obviously to be abandoned, so as to avoid a blatant disparity in the revenues of the oil-producing states and those of the rest of the country. Today most of the oil revenue accrues to the federal government or is distributed to the state governments, partly on an equal basis and partly in proportion to population.

The outcome is two-fold. First the governments of the non-oil-producing states have been able to raise their levels of public expenditure far beyond what could be sustained by revenues derived from local resources. Secondly, the federal government has a vastly increased spending power, available for financing investment, for the provision of services and as grants to state or local governments. Thus, for most Nigerians, the central authority has become, either directly or indirectly, the fountain of unprecedented public wealth far in excess of any local resources. But in order to partake of the wealth a price has been paid, namely, a loss of the financial autonomy so jealously preserved as long as local resources remained reasonably balanced.

The magnitude of the change can best be appreciated by consulting Table VII on p. 236.

No less striking are the consequences of creating nineteen states, each with considerable financial resources. It is a structure which makes for a more diffuse correlation between units of government and ethnic or cultural solidarities. Nigerians will of course continue to regard themselves as culturally and ethnically diverse, much as they have done in the past, because they use distinct languages, observe different customs and have separate recollections of the past. But the breakup of the four regions into twelve states in 1967 and the further sub-division into nineteen states in 1976 acted like a kaleidoscope. The particular pattern of cultural solidarity that had been able to express itself politically through the regional governments has been scattered—except in the Mid-West, now called Bendel. This does not mean an end to ethnicity in politics, only that the large-scale regional identifications which threatened Nigerian unity in the past are no longer so sharply focused through governmental institutions.

For instance, one may still refer to the North, meaning the Fulani or Hausa-speaking peoples, over whom Emirs and a traditional ruling class still exercise some administrative as well as religious authority. But the northern regional government, through which their collective interests could be enforced, was abolished in 1967. Although it continued for a time a shadowy existence in the form of an Interim Common Services Council, many doubts and hesitations concerning the demise of the old North were dispelled by the decisive outcome of the civil war. The region then gave way to a new set of state authorities, each of which is the focus of smaller scale solidarities and interests. Thus the Kanuri are no longer part of a Northern Region aggregate but identify with the state of Borno, in which they predominate. Likewise, regional governments no longer exist in the West and in the East to act as rallying points for Yoruba and Ibo sentiments. Subordinate identities within each of these ethnic groups have now been brought to the forefront of government activity by the sub-division of the Western State (former Region) into the three new states of Oyo, Ogun and Ondo and by the splitting of the East Central State into two, Anambra and Imo. Or, to put it differently, governmental institutions have been scaled down, bringing into relief a different configuration of identity and interests. There may still be scope, through informal combination, for political action that evokes the more comprehensive ethnic or cultural solidarity of northern muslims or of Yorubas or of Ibos. But the governmental arena in which this takes place will not in future be centred at Kaduna, Ibadan and Enugu, the former regional capitals, but at Lagos, the national capital. There is, moreover, much less likelihood of this long-standing three-cornered conflict persisting as the most salient of divisions within that national arena. While it is difficult to predict what party alignments might emerge, it is conceivable that the abandonment of the Westminster form of parliamentary government in favour of a presidential structure which is also a federal one, will permit the development of a political system in which alliances are fluid and fluctuating and in which the federal government becomes more sharply differentiated, more assertive and more autonomous: in short, it may become a centre of authority capable of mobilising support in its own name, instead of representing or acting as surrogate for some particular part of the country or ethnic dominance. There is no certainty of this but the multiplication of states makes it possible.[3]

It is interesting to note the role of both oil revenues and military in the multiplication of states. Having asserted a claim to most of the revenue from oil (100% in the case of off-shore oil) the Federal Military Government then decided to distribute a large part of that revenue to the states on an equal basis. The decision immediately put a premium on further devolution, especially in those parts of the country where the demand for services of one kind or another was most intense. A greater share of the federally distributed revenues could be obtained simply by multiplying the number of units of government, each of which could then claim its equal share of the national cake. For instance, the intense demands on the Western State government to provide more and more schools, dispensaries, roads, houses and employment could be satisfied more fully by splitting the state into three and increasing its share of federally distributed revenues from 1/12th of the total to 3/19ths. There is of course an increase in overheads but it is not seen as a loss, since (as Ali Yahaya explains) an increase of employment in administration is one of the objectives of the exercise.[4]

One may also note the parallels in the matter of local government. Recent reforms brought in by the military government, not without some difficulty because of the implications for traditional authority especially in the North, are designed to make local authorities a third tier of government. The intention is to build up an effective system of local self-government.

But that entails access to the necessary resources which can only come from the federal and state authorities. Large federal grants are being made available and the state governments obliged to do likewise. Much the same calculations operate as in the distribution of revenues to the state; smaller authorities can benefit disproportionately to the extent that part of the grant (25%) is distributed on an equal basis. It is noticeable that where the overriding consideration is to increase the amount of resources locally available—as in many parts of the South—the new local councils are relatively small-scale. Elsewhere, especially in the North, where the overriding concern of traditional rulers is to maintain some consonance between their own councils and the new style elected councils, there tends to be less fragmentation. It is a process commented on in the chapters by Abubakar Yaya Aliyu, Oyeleye Oyediran and Alex Gboyega.

A new and radically different federal pattern of smaller units and of financial dependency upon a much more powerful central authority is the more easily observable part of the story. The facts largely speak for themselves. It is an impressive edifice, but it has to be inhabited and maintained in being by some agreement about the purposes and interests which it should serve. Nationalism or patriotism is one such sustaining force and it would be wrong to deny its place in present day Nigeria. It reached a quite high pitch under the brief leadership of General Murtala Muhammed, expressing itself most strongly in the conduct of foreign policy but also in the widespread demand for a national ideology which would point the way for all to follow. But the rallying cry of nationalism needs constantly to be supplemented by an appeal for the steady support of those who see in the state the means of securing their own particular ends.

The interest that state and local governments (and the diverse ethnic groups) have in a balanced distribution of the oil revenues is vital in this respect but it is insufficient. Wealth is distributed not only on a territorial but also on a social basis. There are the rival claims of farmers, civil servants, entrepreneurs, land owners and factory workers. The support of some at least of these categories is essential to the stability of a regime, not simply on an ad hoc or day-to-day basis but on what might be called, if it did not sometimes mislead, a class basis. There is in any stable political system a mass of critical support, which may be provided by men of status or of wealth, or by sheer numbers. In theory, where elections are held, numbers count, but it is well known, and Nigerians certainly believe, that the critical support is more often that of an elite or rather of elite groups. It is their aggregated or consolidated support, exchanged for public employment, patronage and the opportunity to prosper as a class which is most likely to be the decisive factor.

At the same time, there is invariably a degree of competition among various elite groups and the struggle for place has certainly been a principal cause of instability in the Nigerian political system. Whether there is now a greater degree of intra-elite cohesion and whether this is sufficient to outweigh the claims of the more numerous but less powerful urban and rural poor are questions which one may pose but to which as yet there is no certain answer. It is conceivable that the country now has a sufficiency of resources to satisfy the most pressing of the competing claims but to take that view is to make an assumption, the validity of which can only be properly assessed in retrospect: one will only know in due course whether the regime has indeed consolidated itself by a successful accommodation of the most pressing claims or, on the contrary, has collapsed because of a failure in this respect.

One can perhaps be a little more informative about the present situation, even if it may only be in somewhat hypothetical terms. There are, in the broadest terms, two different conceptions of what is afoot in a country such as Nigeria, where the economy is dominated by oil, or rather by the export of crude oil. The one sees the economy as externally dependent, without very much feed-back into the domestic economy, except in the form of imports, primarily for the benefit of an elite engaged in conspicuous consumption. There is said to be relatively little domestic entrepreneurial activity of a productive nature and the peasantry is seen as static in its ways. It would therefore (it is argued) be illusory to think of the state and its economy as anything more than a fragile construction lacking local foundations and sustained only conditionally by the external forces of the international market. This is the conception which prompts Terisa Turner's portrayal of the relationship between the Nigerian government and the foreign oil companies, and the reason for her use of the term 'a commercial political economy'.

One might alternatively stress the emergence of indigenous social forces, the linkages which are being established internally, and the process of social stratification which is expressed politically, for or against a regime seeking to consolidate itself. Decisive importance may be attributed to the growth of the manufacturing sector, the growing numbers of Nigerians with a technological training, the fostering of intermediate technology suitable for local markets, the enforced transfer into Nigerian hands of equity holdings in existing firms, the reservation of whole sectors of the economy for enterprises owned and managed by Nigerians, and the steps taken to control the oil industry more effectively. More and more typical of the Nigerian economy is said to be the medium-sized firm in activities such as construction, transportation and services; also the farmer who supplies a sizeable local market with produce once exported. The levels of wealth, education and skills which were once the preserve of a small minority have now been attained by a sizeable proportion of the population. Their personal interests link them closely to the centres of governmental administrative authority, to those who hold the public purse and have the power to regulate, tax and license. Here is perhaps the making of a viable policy, to be created in ways analogous to those which contributed to the making of a state political system in England at the turn of the 17th century, a process that J. H. Plumb has described in his 1965 Ford lectures.[5]

Parallels of this kind are merely suggestive of potentialities and there is one obvious difference between the society of which Plumb was writing and present day Nigeria—quite apart from the distance of time. Plumb was concerned with an established monarchy and the consolidation of a party in office under the dominance of Walpole. We are dealing, in Nigeria, with military rule and with soldiers who, not unlike colonial masters, are in only temporary possession of an authority that is contested. The connexions that have been made—as for instance with civil servants and politicians as described by Henry Bienen and Ian Campbell—are at best provisional and indeed reversible, as many found to their cost when purged by the Murtala Muhammed government in the second half of 1975. If stability is the concomitant of a long period of effective government—be it that of an oligarchy, a party or a class—it can scarcely be the work of military officers who say that they will be returning to barracks, unless of course that day is infinitely postponed till it is no longer believed. It has to be the work of their civilian successors. There was a brief period around 1973-74 when, as noted by Ian Campbell, some adjustments began to be made to the prospects of a military more permanently in office, under some form of military-civilian dyarchy. Gowon's removal and the steps subsequently taken in the direction of restoring full civilian rule have tended to restore earlier expectations and calculations. What the soldiers may have achieved is the structural transformation of the administrative and financial system: what remains to be accomplished, and by other hands, is the gathering of the necessary political support from those who wait in the wings, ready to come onto the political stage as soon as the new constitution is promulgated and elections are held. Intimations of what may be in store can be seen in the very interesting accounts of recent local government elections by Drs. Aliyu, Oyediran and Gboyega.

The probability that there is now an undisputed centre of authority (to be symbolised by a re-location of the capital to a more central position—see Map 2) and the possibility—for it is no more than a supposition—that those powerful enough to claim a place in the new setting may manifest sufficient awareness of a common interest to function as governing class, leaves out of account two forces, each of which is a still more unknown factor— the poor and the army.

It might be possible to disregard the poor on the grounds that they are powerless. There are, among the elite, some aspirants to leadership who champion the cause of the working class and the rural poor, but they themselves do not rate very highly their chances of dislodging in the near future the large number of Nigerians who enjoy a new found wealth and who allow enough of it to filter down to their less fortunate brethren, producing in them a state of tempered acquiescence. This is not to say that a sense of injustice may not spark off protests, such as the 1968-69 Agbekoya riots mentioned by Henry Bienen. These were, however, no more than protest movements, inspired by hitherto unknown local leaders. They are not the socialist revolution which would endanger the fabric of the regime.

What may be said of the poor, cannot be said of the military, and especially of an army which has grown 20-fold, tasted power, enjoyed unrestricted access to the means of satisfying its own corporate and personal interests, and which might consider itself the guarantor of good behaviour on the part of those who take over the reins of office. The poor may be shut out; the military cannot be dismissed so easily. There are various proposals for promoting a stable identity between the civil and military powers, e.g. conscription and/or employment of the armed forces on public works and in socially useful activities, but the army leaders seem to prefer the conception of a professional body, with its own specialised function of attending to external defence and internal security. None the less, its acceptance of civil authority may require an ex-general as President, or a general as Minister of Defence or—to revert again to a 17th/18th century analogy—mutual recognition as being part of a ruling class, wherein officers are assured a place and personal preference or family circumstance largely decide whether one takes one's place in the social and political order wearing uniform, sitting in the legislature or presiding over part of the administration. It may be more of an oligarchical than a democratic solution but it could be a stable one, and might be considered better, even by the population at large, than a situation in which the new regime and the military are thought of as alternative powers, the one on probation, the other in reserve. The only certain return to barracks therefore may be one that might be portrayed by two photographs. They are of the same set of people, the ruling class: but one is taken at the time of military control, and the other after a return to civilian rule. In the second of the two photographs those in uniform have been arranged in their proper place. They are in the back row.

NOTES

1. *New Nigerian* 27 May 1977.
2. See for instance, Olajide Aluko. The 'New' Nigerian Foreign Policy in *Round Table* October 1976.
3. See below Ch.11, especially p. 00
4. Adedeji records that 4,327 posts were established in the Midwest Regional civil service during the three years following its creation in 1963. (The Quarterly Journal of Administration V.1. 1970 p. 10)
5. The Growth of Political Stability in England 1675-1725. London 1967.

Part One

THE MILITARY IN OFFICE

1

Back to the Barracks:
A Decade of Marking Time

Valerie P. Bennett and A. H. M. Kirk-Greene

An orderly transition to civilian rule—typified by a time-schedule for the appointment of preparatory commissions, the promulgation of a new constitution and the choosing of new representatives—can be of two kinds. First, there can be a swift return, based on the belief that the former civilian regime was uniquely ruinous, that the military is incapable of long-term rule and 'that coexistence with a new set of political leaders is possible. The necessary institutional improvements are made, the former politicians screened and elections held. The other type of transition involves a lengthy period of military rule before power is transferred back to civilians, on the grounds that comprehensive systematic reforms are required which only the military can achieve. The return to civilian rule must be slow and sure.[1] In the first case the military is more of a caretaker: in the second case, it acts more as a corrective regime.

In the Nigerian case, early beliefs in a caretaker administration and a speedy transition proved illusory. At the time of the military take-over of January 1966, a quick return to barracks was generally taken for granted. The outbreak of the Civil War dampened this initial optimism, until it was revived by Gowon's 1970 nine-point programme with its promise of a hand-over by 1976. Some regarded this date as unnecessarily remote, but the military were now much more securely in the saddle, a fact which came to be confirmed by Gowon's 1974 announcement that the return to barracks was postponed indefinitely. His own deposition in July 1975, and the action taken by his successor,

General Murtala Mohammed, to set in motion the process of handing over 'not a day later than October 1st 1979,' restored some of the earlier optimism. Indeed, this new promise has signs of becoming a reality if only because, in the meantime, the military show signs of having tired of the burden of office.

Thus, from the perspective of a return of civilian rule, the period after the civil war and the period of military rule that preceded it are both parts of a single politico-constitutional continuum. In the course of the last ten years, Nigeria's military rulers periodically reformulated the steps to be taken and re-set the target-dates. The result was an ebb and flow of expectancy and scepticism. Yet, under the exercise of emergency powers and as an outcome of civil war, some important changes did take place and certain options for the future tended to be foreclosed.

The successive blueprints for the return to civilian rule reveal a pre-occupation with a fairly constant set of issues, very similar to those which had faced the Nigerians and the departing colonial power in the late 1950s. Nigeria emerged in 1960 as a Federation of three (later four) Regions governed, on the British model, by a Head of State with formal powers and by Ministers collectively responsible to Parliament. But the party system was dominated by the Regions and by the major ethnic groups, to the detriment of national considerations and Federal authority. Proposals for reform, widely discussed prior to the coup of January 1966, consisted almost entirely of structural rearrangements—the choice between a unitary, federal or confederal form of government, the creation of more states, the powers of the President and the number of political parties (if indeed any).

Such concerns may be thought a little surprising, given the tendency in recent political studies to look not at the constitutional and institutional structures but at patterns of political behaviour, the political culture and sub-cultures, and informal group politics, as well as those underlying processes of 'modernisation' and 'social mobilisation' which entail changes in political behaviour, together with any economic relationships which may predominate. There has been some awareness in Nigeria that political behaviour may be more decisive than, and largely independent of, formal structures and procedures but this realisation has not been the general assumption underlying plans for a new political system free of the defects of the 1960-66 Republic.

The Ironsi Government January-July 1966[2]

The initial period of military rule, under General Ironsi, was notable for his unilateral attempt to bring about a unitary form of government by decree, an attempt which, by its very lack of success, merely reinforced the divisions institutionalised by colonial rule in 1954, 1914 and as far back as 1899.[3] Although perceptive enough to see that the federal structure had encouraged regional-based parties, thus favouring a Northern-based government at the centre, Ironsi failed to grasp that the beneficiaries of those structures were likely to fight, and fight determinedly, to preserve them. Perhaps Ironsi might have been more successful had his methods been different. There was little consultation with important political interest groups. Within a week of taking power, he was making known his own thinking on the political future of a New Nigeria. Although promising to consult the people ('the constitutional changes, which are a pre-requisite to the re-establishment of a parliamentary system of government, will be undertaken with the consensus of various representatives of public opinion') he left no doubt where his own hopes lay: abolition of the Regions. His statement 'All Nigerians want an end to Regionalism', made in his very first policy broadcast to the nation, revealed the capacity for self-delusion which was to contribute to his downfall. His 'remedy' was a strong, centralised, unitary form of government.

Even before the completion of Ironsi's Hundred Days there were unmistakable signs that a unitary system was not going to meet with the general approval he sought. Particularly was this so in the old North. Contributions to the *New Nigerian,* and in the vernacular *Gaskiya ta fi Kwabo,* played a key role in rallying the shell-shocked, rather than somnolent, public of the North in resistance to what was seen as a threat from the South. Articles headed 'Federalism *Is* Good for Nigeria', 'Unitary System Not For Us', 'Leave the North As It Is' and 'Smouldering Fires', along with warnings that 'to force a unitary type of government on people without an impartial referendum is setting the clock backward' were all messages, as clear as the Bauchi highlands after a rainstorm, to those who cared to read them.[4] Nevertheless, Ironsi persevered insensitively with his plans for constitutional change. His broadcast of May 24 with its blunt obituary, 'The Regions are abolished', needs to be read alongside Decree 34, the constitutional measure to which the broadcast was but a layman's explanatory gloss: 'Nigeria ceases to be what has been described as a federation'. This precipitate declaration of unitary government was cut short by the July 1966 Army mutiny, which also cost Ironsi his life.

The Gowon Government: August 1966-May 1967

Gowon, Ironsi's successor, in his very first address to the nation, made within 48 hours of his coming to power, offered Nigeria another constitutional about-turn. Ironsi's move towards a unitary government was to be reversed and a federal system restored. 'The basis of trust and confidence in a unitary system of government,' Gowon declared, 'has not been able to stand the test of time'.

In those anxious days of 1966 the new leader displayed little of the indecision sadly characteristic of later days. On August 8, he announced plans for military disengagement. Though no time-table was yet stated, all Decrees entailing 'extreme centralisation' were to be rescinded and an Advisory Committee, charged with making recommendations 'as to the form of constitution best suited to Nigeria' was to pave the way for a Constitutional Review Assembly, whose recommendations would be submitted to a referendum. Accordingly, on August 31 Ironsi's Decree 34 was revoked by Decree 59, 'taking back the Republic to the position it was prior to May 24, 1966', and in early September delegates from the four Regions met in what came to be called the Ad Hoc Constitutional Conference.

A return to a federal-type administrative structure had been decreed, but the reality of the next eight months was more of a free-for-all. The Regions, speaking through both military and civilian leaders, negotiated the terms for continued association, while Gowon endeavoured to assert the remnants of Federal authority. The open-ended nature of the negotiations can be seen in the set of alternatives which Gowon set before the Ad Hoc Constitutional Conference in September 1966:

(a) a federal system with a strong central government,
(b) a federal system with a weak centre,
(c) confederation, or
(d) 'an entirely new arrangement which will be peculiar to Nigeria and which has not yet found its way into any political dictionary'.

Only a unitary system was ruled out of consideration.

The Conference met in very difficult circumstances and adjourned without result, but it did bring to the agenda an issue which some would have preferred to suppress, namely the sub-division of at least the Northern and Eastern Regions. This was not a new proposal. It had been considered by the Willink Commission which enquired into the fears of minorities in 1957, but the concept had an even longer history.[5] Long denied satisfaction, these minority demands now resurfaced, first in meetings of Leaders of Thought which were held at Regional level, then in the Ad Hoc Constitutional Conference. They received the open blessing of Gowon in a speech made at the end of November 1966 when he declared that 'without a definite commitment on the States question, normality and freedom from fear of domination by one Region or the other cannot be achieved.' Nigeria, he suggested, should be divided into 'not less than eight and not more than fourteen states.'

This same speech acknowledged the gravity of the situation brought about by the Army's own fragmentation and by the massacre of civilians at the end of September. But it also made clear Gowon's opposition to any arrangements of a confederal nature, thus closing, as far as he was concerned, one of the options the Ad Hoc Constitutional Conference had been asked to consider. His list of conditions for a return to barracks now included not only the ever elusive constitutional settlement but also the reorganisation and 'long-term re-integration of the Army', the resettlement and rehabilitation of displaced persons, the preparation of the Second National Development Plan and, for good measure, the eradication of corruption. No terminal date was specified: understandably so, since little real progress could be made until Gowon and Ojukwu (who had become the *de facto* spokesman for the Eastern Region) settled their differences in a full meeting of the Supreme Military Council.

Such a conference was eventually held on January 4-5, 1967 at Aburi, in Ghana, under the fatherly eye of General Ankrah. The official minutes of the meeting recorded a series of quite explicit but limited agreements, notably on army organisation and the control of weapons, the question of displaced persons, and the procedure to be followed for appointment to senior posts in the Civil Service, Armed Forces, Police and Diplomatic Service. The precise 'form of Government best suited to Nigeria' was discussed, but it had not been intended, nor was it feasible in the time available (2 days) and in the absence of legal advisers, to work out a detailed constitutional draft. This task was to be resumed in the Ad Hoc Constitutional Conference. In the meantime the 'legal boys' were to identify all the Decrees of the Federal Military Government which had 'detracted from the previous powers and positions of Regional Governments' so that they might be repealed 'not later than 21 January, if possible.' In many ways the vital decision was that which confirmed the Supreme Military Council's sovereign authority in all legislative and executive matters but appeared to give the Regional Governors a veto. 'Any decision affecting the whole country must be determined by the Supreme Military Council. Where a meeting is not possible such a matter must be referred to Military Governors for comment and concurrence.' This decision proved to be the major constitutional stumbling block in the ensuing months. It prevented full agreement when the official representatives of the Federal and Regional Governments met in Benin in mid-February to produce a draft constitutional decree, and the manner in which it was unilaterally spelt out in the Federal Military Government's Decree No. 8 of 17 March still proved unacceptable to Ojukwu, despite very considerable concessions to the power of veto.[6]

The relatively open-ended negotiations continued for a little while longer but as Gowon and Ojukwu began to go their separate ways, the ultimate resort to force was not far off. A Communique issued from Lagos in the name of the Supreme Military Council in late April set out 'the political and administrative programme of action for preserving the Federation of Nigeria as one country' and, for the first time, gave a definite date for a return to civilian rule, sometime in 1969. States were to be created (on the recommendation of a Committee), civilians were to be made full members of the Federal Executive Council and of Regional Executive Committees and a Constitution Drafting Committee was to be appointed, all by the end of 1967. A Constituent Assembly was to draw up a new constitution and party politics were to resume in the course of 1968.

The halting of this programme by the brute fact of secession of the Eastern Region was coupled with Gowon's virtually simultaneous creation of States. Just as the country had earlier been surprised by Ironsi's abolition of the Regions in favour of unitary government, so was it again a year later, almost to the day, by Gowon's division of Nigeria into twelve states. It was another 'one-man coup d'état,' carried out, said Ojukwu, 'by the stroke of the pen.' It was to prove as historic a pen as that used by Lugard to draft the Amalgamation Decree in 1914.

The Gowon Government January: 1970-July 1975

Throughout the civil war, and during all the exploratory peace talks, the Federal Military Government stood firm on the question of the multi-state structure. Right from 'The conditions to avoid war' announced by Lagos a few days before fighting broke out, through the formal peace talks held at Kampala, Addis Ababa and Niamey, down to Gowon's victory address to the nation, unswerving insistence was placed on the inviolable acceptance of this principle.

The Federal victory put it beyond doubt and, by implication, legitimised the kind of federal-state relationship that had developed administratively in a de facto manner during the war. Thus in the new programme of October 1970 which was 'to usher in a period of lasting peace and political stability'—two qualities hitherto in short supply— Gowon listed much the same items as before, with only two additions, but by now circumstances had changed considerably. The extreme decentralisation of the short-lived Decree No. 8 had been left far behind. The Federal Military Government now enjoyed an unprecedented measure of acceptance, respect and authority and any future constitutional arrangements would undoubtedly have to reflect that fact. Moreover, the pace set in 1967 could be slackened. The two years that Gowon had allowed himself for a return to civilian rule was now extended to six years, making the target date 1976.

The new October 1970 programme listed nine items:—

(i)   Reorganisation of the armed forces
(ii)   Implementation of the National Development Plan and repair of war damage
(iii)   Eradication of corruption from national life
(iv)   Settlement of the question of more States
(v)   Preparation and adoption of a new constitution
(vi)   Introduction of a new revenue allocation formula
(vii)   Conducting a population census
(viii) Organisation of 'genuinely national' political parties
(ix)   Organisation of elections of popularly elected governments in the States and at the centre.

When assessing the post civil-war period of Gowon's regime it is helpful to consider these items as falling into three categories. The first, second, sixth and seventh were administrative measures on which some action was unavoidable: the end of a war is invariably followed by demobilisation and reconstruction; Development Plans and censuses have fixed dates; the growth in oil revenues, the centralisation of responsibilities and the quite arbitrary redistribution of Regional revenues among the 12 states in 1967 made a review of revenue allocation indispensable. The third and eighth items formed a second category which may also be considered indispensable, but they are moral imperatives, ideals to be realised if at all possible and in this sense perhaps timeless. The remaining three items (fourth, fifth and ninth) were integral steps in the restoration of civilian politics, to be undertaken as and when the time seemed ripe.

Gowon came to be blamed for procrastination in taking the necessary steps for a return to civilian rule and for tolerating an increase, rather than effecting any decrease, in corrupt practices. But he also lost support because of the inability to carry out any reorganisation of the Army and by mismanagement of the census. The standing of the regime was very much at stake in both cases and it suffered a double set-back.

The Army had recruited close on a quarter of a million troops and the need for partial demobilisation was undeniable. From the Army's point of view, many men were poorly equipped, inadequately trained (including many too rapidly promoted to the officer corps) and forced to live in make-shift accommodation. From the civilians' standpoint they were indisciplined, a threat to normal daily life, and a drain on public funds. The imposition of the death penalty for armed robbery was a palliative that only underlined the gravity of the situation. In any case it did nothing to stop the more minor, but daily, vexations, nor to halt the very large military expenditures decreed by the military unto themselves in uncontrolled fashion. The problem, of course, was how to demobilise without simply increasing the urban unemployed and the number of armed robbers. The most that the Gowon administration could propose was to transfer men to more productive, and less dangerous, public employment by retraining them as policemen, firemen, prison warders and customs officials—an expedient bristling with its own difficulties. Nothing much was done; retirement through old age and the image of the Army as a social service became a joke; and the regime's credit in the eyes of the public declined.

The 1973 census provided an opportunity for a military government to succeed where a civilian government had already failed, and it was seen as just such a test. It was a highly necessary exercise, not only because of the widely believed unreliability of the 1963 census figures— the first count made in 1962 was annulled because the outcome was disputed, and the final adjustments were considered to be the result, not so much of statistical expertise as of compromise—but also because so many matters would remain contested in the absence of an accurate enumeration, notably the allocation of revenues on a per capita basis, the redrawing of state boundaries, and the determination of parliamentary constituencies. Yet despite the elaborate precautions that were taken to ensure a valid count in 1973—eg a soldier accompanied every enumerator—the figures were obviously inflated in many areas, indeed to a level that, demographically, was beyond the range of probability. Inevitably such figures were denounced, and no amount of subsequent adjustment could restore credibility to the figures that were eventually published.[7] With the change of regime in 1975 they were shelved and the 1963 census figures have been brought back into use. The discredit to the regime brought about by the failure to conduct an effective census was damaging. Yet it was, for Gowon, a clear example of the lingering political sickness—the centrifugal pull of rampant ethnicity. The failure of the census was attributed to forces of the kind which had brought down the First Republic. It demonstrated the immensity of the problems still facing the nation, and so the impossibility of any demilitarization in the foreseeable future. The same kind of deadlock was reached on two other items, the creation of additional states and the formation of parties.

The creation of the twelve states in 1967 had been an emergency measure, a last minute effort to offset the Eastern Region's secession. While the division was not entirely arbitrary—there had been discussion behind the scenes during the preceding months on the optimum number of states and their boundaries—it had been declared to be provisional. Perhaps inevitably the demand for revision, unleashed at the end of the civil war was like Oliver Twist's asking for more. Indeed, so great was the flood of demands when the Irikefe Committee set to work in 1975 that it appeared as if Donne's noble belief that 'no man is an island, entire of itself' had in Nigeria given way to a conviction that every man might be his own State. The prospect of demands impossible to satisfy was sufficient to deter Gowon from taking any action at all. He seems to have been particularly apprehensive of the suggestion that one of the criteria for the creation of states be 'ethnic and linguistic affinity.' It aroused in his mind the spectre of '250 such states'. 'We would,' he said, 'be destroying the essence of our nation.'[8]

The 1970 programme was the first to mention political parties. The requirement that they be 'genuinely national' was unobjectionable but vague, and very possibly impracticable. In any case, until the ban on party political activity was lifted, the desire for nationwide parties could not be put to the test. Gowon never did this. He was deterred perhaps by the kind of Old Boys' Association which began to emerge in anticipation of the lifting of the ban, for example the Barewa

Association in the Hausa-speaking areas. The risk of sectional and particularistic parties re-emerging was not one he was prepared to take; it was simpler, and indeed seemed more prudent, to continue the ban on all party political activities.

The outcome of all these issues, the census, the demand for more states and for the lifting of the ban on political parties, was the same: government paralysis in the face of unreformed political behaviour. Gowon, having been primarily responsible for holding the nation together in the difficult days of 1966–70, was presumably in no mood to see his handiwork threatened by the 'old politics.' Yet expectations had been aroused and the inevitable disillusionment merely emphasised two different perceptions concerning the whole process of a return to civilian rule. On the one hand, a large number of people were unquestionably sceptical about the ability of the military either to redress corruption or to remove factionalism, particularly of an ethnic nature. In their view, the Military Government should resume the role of caretaker, deal with the question of creating more states, prepare a constitution, hold elections and return to barracks. On the other hand, there were those, and Gowon must be included among them, who had come to invest the Military Government with the much wider and more arduous responsibility of transforming thoroughly and dramatically Nigerian political culture, a conversion to be brought about by a sort of 'civil renewal' akin to the Christian doctrine of being born anew. The speech made by Gowon on October 1, 1974, is very revealing in this respect.

Four years ago when I gave 1976 as the target date for returning the country to normal constitutional government, both myself and the military hierarchy believed that by that date, especially after a bloody civil war for which there had been a great deal of human and material sacrifice and from which we had expected that every Nigerian would have learnt a lesson, there would have developed an atmosphere of sufficient stability.

We had thought that genuine demonstration of moderation and self-control in pursuing sectional ends in the overall interest of the country would have become the second nature of all Nigerians. Regrettably, from all the information at our disposal, from the general attitude, utterances and manoeuvres of some individual groups and from some publications during the past few months, it is clear that those who aspire to lead the nation on the return to civilian rule have not learnt any lesson from our past experiences.

In spite of the existence of a state of emergency which has so far precluded politcal activity, there has already emerged a high degree of sectional politicking, intemperate utterances and writings which were deliberately designed to whip up ill feelings within the country to the benefit of the political aspirations of a few. There is no doubt that it would not take them long to return to the old cut-throat politics that once led this nation into serious crisis. We are convinced that this is not what the honest people of this country want.[9]

This speech illustrates the extent to which Gowon held the widely-held perceptions and motivations of military leaders who take over the responsibilities of government. They are attributed with three related attitudes. They perceive government in an administrative rather than in a bargaining and coalition-building context; they see politicians as divisive—as creators rather than reflectors of societal conflict: and they yearn for the national unity that prevailed in the nationalist era prior to independence.[10]

The first two attitudes are consonant with Gowon's tenure of office but in Nigeria there never was a golden age of nationalist politics free of conflict. Gowon looked instead to the future, to an entirely fresh start. The military, he went on to say in that same October 1974 speech, had 'the responsibility to lay the foundation of a self-sustaining political system which can stand the test of time in such a manner that each national political crisis does not become a threat to the nation's continued existence as a single entity and which will ensure a smooth and orderly transition from one government to another.'

But while the objective was clear, the manner of arrival was beset with insuperable difficulties. He saw at every turn the old-style 'sectional politicking' and the spectre of unreformed political behaviour. Since the substance was too difficult to handle, Gowon increasingly occupied himself with the form. The plea for more time was a substitute for the resolution of long-outstanding issues. The target date of 1976 was declared to be 'unrealistic' since rigid adherence to it would be 'a betrayal of trust': it would 'throw the nation back into confusion.' The idea of returning to civilian rule was not abandoned, merely postponed. Various promises were made—definitely more states, a continued fight against corruption, advisory councils at Federal and State levels, new Federal Commissioners, a revised formula for allocating the Distributable Pool Account, and a panel to draw up a new draft constitution. But no new target dates were fixed.

Immediately after the speech, commentators were quick to point out that Gowon's position was both unrealistic and irrational. The *New Nigerian* noted that 'the kind of peace and stability which the Commander-in-Chief seemed to want . . . . is impossible in a huge and diverse country with a fairly well developed political culture and with the political power prize being the privilege to dispense vast resources.'[11] Tai Solarin, a columnist with the Nigerian *Daily Times,* commented that after 'eight years of experimental government, with only three of its nine-point program accomplished, the Army is pretty well spent and it would be inhuman to expect it to pull out a new trick to save the nation within two years or the next two hundred years.'

Perhaps the only new trick would have been one already much debated-some form of civilian/military dyarchy—but even that offered little hope as it merely perpetuated in another form much the same set of military governors and civilian commissioners. Gowon's continued inaction—despite his firmly declared intention to appoint a new set of Federal Commissioners and to reassign the State Governors— prompted the inescapable conclusion; short of a change of leadership at the highest level, the country would simply continue to drift in a sea of corruption. After having held office too long to be considered a caretaker government, Gowon discovered that he lacked any accomplishments to merit the title 'corrective.'

The Murtala Mohammed Government: August 1975—February 1976

The next change of administration was brought about by the coup of July 29, 1975. It removed Gowon, all officers of the rank of General, the twelve State Governors and most of the Federal and State Commissioners. It was virtually a clean sweep made by the Brigadiers and Colonels who, according to the new Head of State, had 'suffered in silence lack of consultations, indecision, indiscipline and even neglect.' Having become inaccessible, insensitive 'to the true feelings and yearnings of the people' and responsible for trends 'incompatible with the philosophy and image of our corrective regime', Gowon was removed to give the nation 'a new lease of life.'[12]

The change, so far as the return to civilian life was concerned, was one of pace rather than of method or direction. A new target date was fixed, 'not a day later than October 1st 1979', but the steps were to be the same. A Panel was appointed to examine the question of creating more States and no time was lost in acting on its recommendations.

Another Committee investigated the question of transferring the capital out of Lagos; the site of a new capital was designated and preparatory work begun. A Constitutional Drafting Committee was appointed in September 1975 and in 1976 discussions were started in the reorganisation of local authorities, an essential step for the indirect election of the Constituency Assembly. The change of pace was quite remarkable and when General Obasanjo took over as Head of State, on Murtala Mohammed's assassination on February 13, 1976, there was no slackening of tempo.

Conclusion

The removal of Gowon July 29, 1975 echoed that of the civilians in January 15, 1966. Both Ironsi and Murtala Mohammed took over from regimes which had failed. Yet the latter did not simply start from where the former had left off nearly ten years earlier. The decade of military rule, despite no apparent advance toward civilian rule, had in fact clarified a number of fundamental questions concerning the future:

1. The abolition of the four Regions in 1966, their division into twelve States in 1967 and the increase from twelve to nineteen in 1976, is the manifestation of a strong preference for a multi-state federation.
2. The considerable de facto expansion in the jurisdiction of the Federal Government, brought about by military decree and edict— the concomitant of an unsuccessful bid to break up Nigeria and of the division into nineteen states—is probably irreversible.
3. Future political parties will be required to be different in name, power-base, recruitment, function and leadership from those which operated prior to 1966. Nor will political competition be allowed to follow the practice of 'winner-takes-all.'

Thus, there has been no standing still. In three basic respects the Nigerian political system has been given shape, not by the prescription of a Constitutional Assembly but through an historical evolution— something which any future constitutional settlement can scarcely ignore.

NOTES

1. Valerie Plave Bennet, 'Patterns of Demilitarization in Africa,' *Quarterly Journal of Administration,* October 1974, pp 9–14.

2. S. K. Panter-Brick (ed) *Nigerian Government and Military Rule* (1970) and A. H. M. Kirk-Greene, *Crisis and Conflict in Nigeria* (1971) 2 Vols may be referred to for a fuller analysis of the events of the period from January 1966 to January 1970. Most of the documents cited in this chapter can be consulted verbatim in these two books.
3. Cf. the recommendation by the Selborne Committee for a demarcation between 'the Soudan region governed by Mohammedans and the Pagan regions of the Niger Delta' until such time as a single colonial administration was practical—*Report of the Niger Committee,* 4 August 1899. C.O. 446/3.
4. See, in particular, *New Nigerian* 5, 7 and 19 April; *Gaskiya ta fi Kwabo,* 28 March and 18 April; *Morning Post,* 9 May and *Nigerian Opinion,* May 1966.
5. *Report of the Commission appointed to enquire into the fears of the Minorities,* Cmd, 505, 1958. For a valuable survey of the long, articulate demand for more States, see T. N. Tamuno, 'Separatist Agitations in Nigeria since 1914,' *Journal of Modern African Studies,* 1970, 8, 4, 563–583.
6. For Decree No.8 see A. H. M. Kirk-Greene op.cit. Vol.1 p 401–2 and S. K. Panter-Brick op.cit. p 45–48.
7. The 1973 census gave Nigeria a population of 79·76 million—an increase of 43% over the 1963 figure of 55·7 million. But in some of the States eg Kano, North-East, Kwara, the population had practically doubled.
8. Gowon was not alone in adopting an attitude of 'let sleeping dogs lie.' It was recommended by a group of senior civil servants and academics at a conference at Zaria in August 1970—Mahmud Tukur, ed., *Administrative and Political Development: Prospects for Nigeria* (Zaria, 1971) Part II, especially pp 120–121.
9. Broadcast 1 October 1974, reproduced verbatim in *Nigeria Today,* No 50 October 1974.
10. See, for example, Edward Shils, 'The Military in the Political Development of the New States,' in John Johnson, ed., *The Role of the Military in Underdeveloped Countries* (Princeton, 1962); and A. H. M. Kirk-Greene, 'The Soldiers and the Second Chance Syndrome,' *Culture et Développement,* December 1974, pp. 775–798.
11. *New Nigerian,* October 2, 1974.
12. Broadcast, 30 July 1975, reproduced in *Drift and Chaos Arrested* (Lagos 1975).

2

Soldiers, Politicians and Civil Servants

Henry Bienen with Martin Fitton

Introduction

Early writings on the military in Africa overlooked the role of civilians in military regimes. These writings tended to examine the military's intervention and to focus on the internal characteristics of armed forces.[1] Subsequently, analysts became concerned with the relationship of the military to society and with the broad effects of the military on the development process.[2] But processes of government were on the whole neglected. It is of course much more difficult to get the necessary information. The way decisions are made by military regimes, the nature of deliberation processes, the ways factional and institutional alliances are formed—all these usually remain closed to the outside observer.

Recently, however, some attention has been given to civilian activities in military governments and increasingly observers have abandoned the dichotomy between civilian and military regimes. They have focused instead on civilian-military relations. The two categories of civilians most obviously involved are politicians and civil servants.

Civilians often have been called upon in advisory capacities and have been placed on consultative committees or advisory groups. Sometimes, formal arrangements have been made to institutionalise civilian input into a military regime. Civilians, including many former politicians from the old civilian regime, have been brought back as ministers or as members of special commissions. Since many African militaries have come to power explicitly promising a return to civilian rule, and have continued to reiterate these promises even a decade after military rule, demilitarisation commissions have proliferated and civilian politicians have placed prominent roles on such groups. Most attention has been given to the role of civilians at national levels and national institutions; cabinets, commissions, consultative commissions, civil services.[3] Less studied have been the roles played by former politicians and would-be new entrants into political life who reconstruct old political networks or who try to build new networks outside of the formal institutions the military creates for civilians. We know relatively little about the operation of politicians under a military regime at middle levels or at local levels.

The role of civil servants in military regimes has also begun to be examined and some observers refer to military regimes as coalition regimes of military personnel and civil servants. Edward Feit referred to African armies as the 'apotheosis of administration' and saw them as reconstructing an administrative-traditional order. Because countries are more complex than armies, the soldiers' solution was to abrogate political activity and to rule by administrative fiat in alliance with civil servants. Feit saw the military-civil service coalition as one without a consensus or basic legitimacy in which both military officers and civil servants often have a reluctance to assume responsibilities through direct involvement in politics even after a military-civil service alliance has been established. Soldiers look to civil servants to help them establish legitimacy while the latter look after their own personal and institutional interests.[4]

Anton Bebler also has called attention to the sharing of norms with the civilian bureaucracy and to the fact that African military governments often have been unwilling to commit the officer corps to active involvement in administration. He states that in Mali when a military government dismissed civilian mayors and *commandants de cercle* for being too closely connected with the former civilian regime and appointed officers formally to fill those positions, actual business was carried out by civilian administrators.[5] African military governments rarely have used military personnel to fill more than a few public corporation posts and a limited number of regional and ministerial posts. When military governments have replaced traditional authorities, they have, as Feit points out for Nigeria, replaced them with administrative cadres, not with military officers.[6]

Bebler concludes for Dahomey, Ghana, Sierra Leone and Mali that:

Regardless of the formal organisation of power the real impact of military rule on state administration seems to have been an increase in its autonomy . . . The military removed or minimised party and 'political' pressures on the bureaucrats without bringing in their own system of effective control.[7]

Bebler goes on to argue that the military juntas in these four countries espoused notions of the civilian administration's corporate autonomy and apolitical nature. While sometimes relations were not cordial between military juntas and civilian administrators, 'in the long run no junta changed anything of substance in the organisation and functioning of the civil administration.'[8]

The civil service has been seen as a net gainer from military rule in Africa. It is said that civil servants are glad to be free of political interference in their day to day work. It is said that civil servants share values with military men because they are like them in origin and education. Insofar as the military centralises authority, the civil service benefits from the top down. But military regimes put heavy burdens on civilian administrators. The military devolves on civil servants many tasks and decisions that it itself does not want to take. Then it reproaches, or in the Ethiopian case, does much worse things, to civil servants with whom military officers are unhappy. We can see African militaries both underinvolved and overinvolved with government as we examine civil service-military relationships.

Nigeria provides a particularly interesting example of civilian-military relations. Although all political offices were abolished in January 1966, thus making the civil service directly accountable to the military, the need for some sort of auxiliary role of a political nature was recognised, especially after the upheavals of May-July 1966. Informal advisory bodies known as 'Leaders of Thought' were formed in each of the Regions and the delegates to the Ad Hoc Constitutional Conference which met in September 1966 were all civilians. Later, in June 1967, after the division of the four Regions into twelve States and the secession of the Eastern Region, civilians were appointed as Commissioners in charge of Ministries or Departments with a seat in the Executive Council. This was done at both Federal and State levels and it may be said to have given formal expression to a whole variety of linkages, largely of an informal nature, which came to be established between military governors and the civilian population.

This was the context in which it was decided to interview a number of politicians so as to learn of their adaptation to a military regime and their continued involvement in public affairs, either at the behest of the military or on their own account. The experience of some of them as

Commissioners also provided an insight into the role of senior civil servants.

After a brief indication of the category of persons selected for interview, we divide this account of civil-military relations into two parts. We discuss first the role of politicians and then in a second section focus mainly on the role of civil servants. The analysis is not based entirely on the interview material; other sources of information are used to provide a more complete picture.

The politicians were former members of the Western House of Assembly (MHA). Although this limited our enquiry to a single State, it made it more thorough. We were able to conduct in-depth interviews, usually of around two hours' duration, with 54 of the 128 surviving MHAs.[9] Most of them were in the 40–60 age group (80%), had secondary or post-secondary but not university education (57%) and their main activity before entering politics had been in education (46%), in law (22%) or in trade (18%). After 1966 more of them turned to trade, fewer to teaching. A very high proportion of them had held office as Minister, Whip or Speaker (two-thirds).

Although all parties had been banned under Decree No.33 of 1966, the opportunity and indeed readiness to continue some form of political activity depended on previous party affiliation. The NNDP members, having been in power at the time of the January coup, were the most numerous, but the most discredited. Deprived of their official salaries and allowances, faced with the Somolu Commission's enquiry into their assets, they sought refuge in private life.[10] The AG members, on the other hand, saw in military rule a possible opportunity of recovering ground lost to the NNDP after the 1963 crisis and the imprisonment of their leader, Awolowo. His release by Gowon in August 1966 reinforced this hope. Table I shows, for the 54 members interviewed, their original party identification and any subsequent changes. It is to be noted that many AG and NCNC members 'crossed the floor' to join the ranks of the government party, a familiar phenomenon in Nigerian politics.

Section I   The role of politicians

The intense factionalism of politics in Western Nigeria made civilian-military cooperation as difficult as it was necessary.[11] The regional civilian-military leaders needed each other's support on many issues, especially that of maintaining Nigerian unity in some form or another

TABLE 1
RESPONDENTS BY PARTY IDENTIFICATION

	Number	Per Cent
AG	14	25·9
AG–NNDP	11	20·4
AG–UPP–NNDP	8	14·8
NNDP	1	1·9
UPP–NNDP	1	1·9
NCNC	5	9·3
NCNC–NNDP	8	14·8
NCNC–UPP–NNDP	3	5·6
NCNC–AG–UPP–NNDP	2	3·7
Unknown	1	1·9

AG: Action Group
NNDP: Nigerian National Democratic Party (formed in 1964)
UPP: United People's Party (formed in 1963 by Chief Akintola after the split in the AG
    and later absorbed by the NNDP)
NCNC: National Council of Nigerian Citizens

after the events of July-September 1966. But mutual cooperation was hard to achieve because civilian factionalism spilled over into the military. The head of the military Government of the West, Colonel Adebayo, thus had special problems. He was part of the military chain of command and so had to relate to the Supreme Military Council. But he also felt himself responsible, as a Yoruba Head of Government, for the welfare of the Western Region. From his vantage point, it was necessary to unify a divided Western Region, link military and civilian elites, and mobilize support from the populace. This meant for the military creating institutions in which the energies of politicians could be both used and controlled. For the civilian leaders it meant using these institutions to build a base of power independent of the military which would give them leverage in a political system they no longer controlled. In the Western Region from August 1966 until May 1967, when civilians were brought into cabinets headed by military men, politicians had to operate as a group out of power; but they were a group essential to military leaders.

The military instituted a number of bodies in which policies could be explained and discussed and essential civilian support secured. We consider, in turn, the Leaders of Thought, local bodies such as school boards, local advisory councils and self-help committees and, finally, informal representation.[12]

(a) LEADERS OF THOUGHT

It has been suggested that the military leadership in the Western Region faced a mobilised population and a divided elite. While Awolowo remained in jail, large numbers of the Yoruba remained unhappy and not completely reconciled to the national military regime or to the military government in the Western Region. Thus General Gowon released Awolowo and greeted him on August 3, 1966 with the remark, 'We need you for the wealth of your experience.'[13] Within a few days, Awolowo had become 'Leader of the Yorubas'[14] and head of the Leaders of Thought in the West. The Leaders of Thought were not confined to the West. They were groups co-opted by military and civilian leaders and summoned by Yakubu Gowon to debate issues involved in forthcoming constitutional reviews.[15] The Leaders of Thought in the West became a political group whose debates were to range beyond constitutional issues. It was a forum which allowed civilian politicians to meet under the auspices of a military regime.

About two hundred attended the large gatherings held in Ibadan. They included, besides many former MHAs, some former members of the Federal Parliament, local politicians and civil servants. There were restricted meetings attended by Obas (Chiefs) and in 1967 a group of twenty met occasionally in the house of a civilian commissioner. One of the former MHAs claimed to have been a member of an 'inner caucus' or advisory group, which had influence on matters due to be discussed in Cabinet. Invitations came in a circular from the Governor's office, from the Governor personally, or from a high civil servant. Forty-five of the fifty-four former MHAs interviewed had been invited to attend and of these twenty-nine actually participated. Of the sixteen invited but never present, all but one were NNDP. Some NNDP remarked that they used to get invitations the day after the meeting. One recalled attending a meeting of about sixty-five, of whom ten were NNDP. Another estimated three-quarters were AG or NCNC and added that thirty percent of the Leaders of Thought were Ijebu Yoruba. This was not true but some non-Ijebu Yoruba certainly thought that the meetings were dominated by Ijebus (Awolowo is an Ijebu). Asked whether the meetings were useful twelve MHAs thought not, seven thought the contrary and twenty replied that they were AG dominated.

It was Awolowo who dominated the Leaders of Thought. Awolowo made the first of a number of key addresses to the Western Leaders of Thought in August 1966. At that time he talked about reuniting the country and stressed the need for unity in the Western Region. He mentioned that Leaders of Thought throughout the land must eschew self interest. He never mentioned the military in this address.[16] The term 'dyarchy' describes the Western Region after Awolowo's release from jail. However, it is difficult to reconstruct the relationship of Awolowo to the military leaders and it is hard to describe with certainty the military leaders' attitudes towards the Leaders of Thought. One high Yoruba military officer felt that it was stupid for Awolowo to show his face and be the Leader of the Yorubas. 'This should have been the Governor's position.' This officer asserted that the Leaders of Thought meetings were useless and merely an AG forum.[17] But Adebayo himself used the Leaders of Thought as a forum; in October 1966 he addressed them in Ibadan and called on the Western Region to remain calm. The Leaders of Thought constituted a gathering which caught the public eye.

How important were its deliberations is another matter. Luckham asserts that it was the military leaders and their civil service advisers who took the final decisions at the end of 1966 and through 1967 which led up to the civil war.[18] This may be true at the national level. It is hard to know what the weight of individual opinion was. In the Western Region, however, the Leaders of Thought discussed the critical issues and the civilians played a major role in these meetings, just as they did in the meetings of the Ad Hoc Constitutional Conference which met in Lagos in September-October 1966. Kirk-Greene, at one point, describes the function of the Ad Hoc Constitutional Conference as being to consider resolutions of all the regional Leaders of Thought.[19] The delegates to the Conference were selected, according to Luckham, by military governors and by the Leaders of Thought.[20]

Awolowo used the Leaders of Thought as a forum in which to make important policy pronouncements. He announced to the meeting in November 1966 that the Western Region had been victimised by the loss of the Yoruba people with the excision of Lagos, Ilorin, Kabba and Akoko-Edo from the homeland.[21] It was Awolowo who, at a meeting in Ibadan on May 1, made the famous announcement that if the Federal Government, by 'acts of commission or omission,' brought about the secession of the East, then the West would secede too.[22] At this time, Awolowo stated his responsibility for the physical, mental, and spiritual well-being of the Yoruba people in particular and Nigerians in general. He announced his opposition to the use of force to keep Nigeria one. He also announced his opposition to the disintegration of the Federation. When he made this address, he was flanked by Colonel Adebayo, Lt. Col Olutoye, and Major Sotimi.[23] Adebayo was Governor, Olutoye was Area Commander of the West and Sotimi was Commanding Officer, 3rd Battalion, Ibadan. The military command in the Western Region appeared to be giving its support both to Awolowo and to his use of the Leaders of Thought as a forum.

From November 1966 on, Awolowo exercised control over the composition of meetings.[24] Here was a military regime in which civilians had a great deal to say, publicly, about policies and appointments and where civilian factional conflict remained an important factor for military regime strategy.

In the Western State, the Leaders of Thought meetings had legitimating functions and they were also arenas in which Awolowo could consolidate his authority. They probably produced some give and take on policy questions but do not appear to have been a place where policies were thrashed out. They were arenas in which civil servants, officers, and politicians came together. Officers addressed meetings and made their views known there.

The Leaders of Thought met most frequently between August 1966 and August 1967. Most of our respondents agreed that meetings fizzled out in 1968. Indeed, according to the man who had been in charge of the arrangements for meetings, they were then terminated. Yet a member of the Governor's cabinet affirmed in 1973 'We still meet. We were called up to Agodi or Mapo Hall (meeting places in Ibadan) and while the permanent secretaries and commissioners pretend they are telling us about new policies, they are really asking for our help.'[25] The confusion probably arises because informal groups of leaders were still called together in the early 1970's and some seemed to think of these as convenings of Leaders of Thought. But the introduction of the civilian commissioners into the military Governor's cabinet in mid-1967 made the Leaders of Thought less necessary for the mobilising of both elite and mass support.[26] Governor Adebayo was not reluctant to see the Leaders of Thought meetings, dominated by Awolowo, replaced by a cabinet system in which non-AG leaders offset Awolowo's authority in the Western State.

(b) LOCAL CHANNELS FOR POLITICAL PARTICIPATION

Some of the typical problems of civilian-military cooperation are well illustrated by events and procedures at the more local level. The local councillors had been displaced in 1966 by 'sole administrators' who were civil servants, but functional bodies such as education committees and school boards had been left in place. The military hoped to tap local information and harness local energies without giving local politicians the means of re-establishing for themselves positions of power and influence. However the need and opportunity for political activity inevitably arose over questions such as reform of local government areas, designation of new administration centres and chieftancy disputes, the serious discontent engendered by one particular issue, tax collection, manifestly required the mediatory role of the politicians, even though the military suspected them of complicity. Over a third (35%) of the MHA's interviewed were members of some local school board, education committee or local advisory council.

(i) *Agbekoya and the establishment of local advisory councils.*

The large scale tax riots which broke out in the Western Region in 1968 and 1969 came to be known as the *Agbekoya* riots. *Agbekoya* means in Yoruba, literally, 'farmers reject suffering.' The *Agbekoya* movement was one of the most significant uprisings in contemporary African politics. In the Western Region, there was a long history of peasant unrest associated with areas which had suffered swollen shoot disease of cocoa plants. But the riots of 1968–69, to use the words of Christopher Beer, 'possessed distinctive characteristics which set them aside from many such earlier manifestations. First, they were essentially based on support of the peasantry . . . the riots were without doubt caused by the rise of specifically *agrarian populism* . . . . the 1968–69 riots were large in scale, materialised widely in dispersed geographical locations, whilst occurring almost simultaneously in time.'[27] Indeed the *Agbekoya* riots seemed to have been a rebellion with overtly class manifestations.

During the riots, farmers refused to pay taxes, and tax collection virtually ceased in many areas until July 1969. When the authorities tried to resume tax collection, riots broke out again and well into the 1970's tax collection had not been restored in all places. Traditional leaders were attacked and the Shoun of Ogbomosho, Oba Laji Layode, was murdered. Alhaji Adegbenro, a major AG leader and at the time Commissioner of Finance in the Adebayo Government, was attacked on the road from Abeokuta to Ibadan. Farmers entered Ibadan in September 1969 and attacked the Federal prison in daylight, freeing its occupants. The prison is in the Agodi area which adjoins the headquarters of the Ibadan Garrison of the Nigerian army and is about one hundred yards from the State House, the residence of the military Governor. At this time, police disappeared from many of the towns, including Ibadan, which were affected by rioting. Pitched battles occurred between army, police and farmers in certain areas. But for the most part, the military Government seemed paralyzed. It did not attempt to crush the dissidence with overwhelming force. And it lacked political institutions at the local levels through which conflict could be mediated. Thus the military Government had to rely on *ad hoc* meetings between politicians and dissident leaders while it occasionally used and more often threatened to use force.

One of the most striking things about the tax revolts of 1968–69 was the presentation of a coherent political program by organised movements such as the *Egbe Agbekoya* in Ibadan. While some major politicians were involved in a few localities, many of the leaders had not been prominent in Yoruba politics prior to the revolts.[28]

The man who emerged as a folk hero, 'Tafa Adeoye, was not a well-known figure prior to *Agbekoya*. Nonetheless, the military Governor, Commissioners, and other important politicians went to Adeoye's headquarters to meet with him. As the violence escalated in 1969 Awolowo set out to portray himself as the saviour of the peasantry and he met with Adeoye in early October on Adeoye's home ground. Awolowo endorsed most of the peasants' demands in his recommendations to Governor Adebayo although Awolowo did not agree to the abolition of the district councils, then run by the Sole Administrators and he favoured a higher flat tax rate than the farmers wanted. It is not clear what kind of mandate, if any, Awolowo had from Adebayo but there was no doubt the negotiations during a crisis situation were in civilian and not military hands.[29]

Many former NNDP MHAs thought that *Agbekoya* had been incited by the AG to embarrass the military Government once Awolowo's close connection to Adebayo had been broken. But the AG had not been identified with low status and low income elements in Yoruba politics although it had a wing of younger members who saw themselves as socialists. In Ibadan, the major leaders of lower class elements had come from the Mabolaje Grand Alliance (MGA) and later from the NCNC. According to one MHA who was extremely important in Ibadan politics, Governor Adebayo at first appealed to Awolowo and Adegbenro to head off the peasant movement. They replied that it was NNDP fomented. Indeed, in 1968, the government ordered the closure of publications that were reputedly organs of the banned NNDP.

The Governor himself, at least in retrospect, came to see *Agbekoya* as an AG plot. At least one commissioner agreed with him, saying

> *Agbekoya* was hatched by politicians. They were in back of it to discredit the military regime. They tested the strength of the military. Then they arrested it and nipped it in the bud. Then they confirmed their own authority.

Another commissioner held the old Mabolaje Grand Alliance and the NCNC politicians from Ibadan responsible for *Agbekoya*. Perhaps the most accurate assessment was from the commissioner who felt that AG and NCNC politicians had all been trying to use farmers' cooperatives and unions for political purposes. Politicians in the Governor's Cabinet were included in his indictment. He said, however, that '*Agbekoya* was not a party thing. People wanted to use *Agbekoya* but they couldn't control them.' Politicians had no liking for the violent methods and lack of political sophistication of the *Agbekoya* farmers.

One commssioner, A. Adisa, who had responsibilities for Lands and Housing and who also headed the Western State Marketing Board, believed that the ·Governor once thought him to be the head of *Agbekoya*. Adisa was a major Ibadan politician who had been in the MGA and in the NCNC. He insisted that the Governor, after meeting with *Agbekoya* leaders, came to understand that he, Adisa, had refused to support *Agbekoya*.[30] Adisa, among other politicians, went on tour with the Governor to disaffected areas. Mojid Agbaje, another old MGA politician in Ibadan who had opposed Adisa over the succession to leadership of the MGA after Adelabu's death, also toured with the Governor. Yet Agbaje was offering legal advice to farmers from Ibadan and many politicians considered him one of the town politicians with extremely ciose ties to *Agbekoya* groups.

Politicians in the Cabinet, and some outside of it, like Awolowo and Agbaje, appeared to fill a political vacuum. The Government looked to established politicians to make contact with and possibly coopt the leaders of the farmers' movement. Thus it is no surprise to find out that a number of MHAs were approached by the Government to help it deal with *Agbekoya*.

The military government had not been sensitive to the farmers' plight having tried to raise taxes at a time when farmers' incomes had fallen and Government services to famers had declined. But the Governor considered the rebellion to be politically instigated and

TABLE 2

RESPONSES OF MHAS APPROACHED BY GOVERNMENT ON AGBEKOYA

	Number	Per Cent
No	10	18·5
There was no *Agbekoya* in my area	11	20·4
Yes	14	25·9
Yes, I would not help	4	7·7
I was approached by farmers	4	7·4
I told farmers it was wrong	1	1·9
I kept away from my area	1	1·9
No answer	9	16·7
	54	

spoke of 'unprovoked and premeditated attacks on police.' He refused to recognise the protest as one directed against unjust taxation, arguing that tax agitation was most rife in areas where people had basic services such as water and electricity, although he did reproach Obas and Leaders of Thought for not showing more concern about their areas.[31] The politicians were more sensitive to the real grievances and it was clear both to them and to the Commission which inquired into the disturbances, that there had been a failure in the representative function of Government.

The Commission reported as follows:

The sole administrators appreciating that they could not by themselves discharge their functions without local aid have sometimes used their own initiatives to surround themselves with a body of advisers . . . . It is not clear to the Commission how these bodies of advisers were selected . . . They had no statutory locus nor functions. Their power and duties are not defined. Their identities are sometimes unknown to the local populace, and it would appear that they held their offices at the pleasure of the particular sole administrator who selected or made use of them. Without definite criteria to guide him, other than his own absolute discretion, the body so selected sometimes reflected a leaning towards this or that banned political party . . . . Where inconvenient measures are introduced, the sole administrator and his body of advisers . . . . are accused of having brought them about by the local populace acting under the increased propaganda of the dissatisfied Party adherents . . . . The so-called ban which had been placed on political activities becomes a sham or dead letter.[32]

The suspension of locally elected councillors had clearly created a communication gap. Governor Adebayo acknowledged this when he said 'Although this is a military regime, I strongly believe in the ability of members of the community to assist the Military Government in the affairs of the state.'[33] He thus set about establishing local advisory councils insisting, however, that politics be kept out. Not party identification but only merit was to be the criterion for appointment to advisory councils. No consultation with political leaders was to take place nor was lobbying for posts on the councils allowed. Appointments were reviewable every six months. The councils were to meet every three months or during emergencies. The district council officer was still to make decisions, but he was also supposed to take advice from the advisory councils. The military Government was caught in a problem: it wanted nonpartisan representatives to carry out representative tasks in a highly partisan and conflict-ridden local environment. The politicians saw this conflict. Some said that local advisory councils fell into disuse as the farmers' revolt deepened in 1969 because farmers would have taken politicians' participation in advisory councils as a sign of support for Government.

The military got the worst outcome. It continued to lack a set of institutions through which cleavage and conflict could be mediated at the divisional and district levels. At the same time, politicians did come back into local political life, notably through the local advisory committees. For example, ten of the MHAs who were interviewed had been appointed to local advisory councils.

(ii) *Self-Help Committees*

Self-help committees constituted another sphere of activity open to politicians. In July, 1968, Adebayo addressed the Obas, Chiefs and Leaders of Thought on the subject of economic development through self help.[34] The following September the Western State Self-help Council was launched and in each of the 25 administrative divisions of the State, a 15-man divisional self-help committee was set up. These committees were supposed to raise capital and to organize people for cooperative self-help activities. When they were established, Adebayo warned against politicians' 'spreading the tentacles of political activities.'[35]

Political figures became involved in self-help committees. Of the MHAs we interviewed, at least half had had some involvement with them. How political the self-help programs became depended on specific politicians and the politics of particular areas. Some MHAs said that they avoided self-help schemes because they were political and the MHAs did not want to get into difficulties with government.

Some individuals avoided them because they were expensive, not for political reasons. Others said the self-help schemes were a call to service, not an opportunity for political contacts.

Self-help schemes provided an opening for politicians to be involved in local politics just as they also provided an opening for some military personnel. However, there was no systematic development of civilian political networks through self-help committees. They were localised in the same way as school committees. Insofar as civilian political networks did extend beyond quite local levels, they depended on the old party and personal alignments, although new factions continued to be formed out of old factional arrangements.[36] The local networks were pulled together insofar as they were pulled together at all, by major leaders who, except for a few prominent NNDP leaders, operated as Leaders of Thought.

(c) INFORMAL REPRESENTATION

Our interviews with the former MHAs provided information about more informal ways of 'nursing a constituency' in a period of military rule. Table 3 sets out their answers to two questions.

TABLE 3
DO YOU STILL TRY TO REPRESENT YOUR PEOPLE?

	Number	Per Cent
Yes	29 (AG 11; NCNC 3; NNDP 14; No identification 1)	53·7
No	18 (AG 1; NCNC 1; NNDP 16)	33
NA	7 (AG 2; NCNC 1; NNDP 4)	13

DO YOU DO MANY FAVOURS NOW?

	Number	Per Cent
Yes	29 (AG 11; NCNC 4; NNDP 14)	53·7
Yes, but less than before	14 (AG 3; NNDP 10; No identification 1)	25·9
No	9 (NCNC 1; NNDP 8)	16·7
NA	2 (NNDP 2)	3·7

When it came to doing favours and continuing to represent people, AG MHAs were more active on both counts than NNDP MHAs. Overwhelmingly, the AG respondents said that they continued to represent their people but NNDP were about evenly split. This reflected the forcing out of politics of some NNDP MHAs and it also reflected the greater activity of AG MHAs. Doing favours meant and means many things. It means giving money for gifts, handouts, and school fees. A number of our respondents said that people understood that politicians could not give money now but that they could still intercede for individuals and groups. The range of these intercessions was great with respect to intensity and scope. Some MHAs helped groups to organize petitions; some would lead groups to lobby civilian commissioners but they would not go to military people. Others were willing to deal with former contacts among civil servants, both technical personnel such as engineers and high level administrators, but they were unwilling to go to military personnel. Others said they would go to military officers if they knew them personally or if they were from their home area. There was more reluctance to go to military men than to civil servants. This was partly a matter of pride, but it also reflected the fact that many MHAs did not know military officers. Yoruba officers tended to come either from outside the Western State, that is, they were Yoruba speakers from what is now Kwara State, or they came disproportionately from certain Yoruba areas like Ekiti. Thus, there were large parts of the Western State which did not have many officers as native sons. In a system which relies heavily on personal contacts through which representations are made, MHAs were cut off from officers. This was clear from responses to direct questioning about the contacts MHAs had with officers as compared to contacts with civil servants and other MHAs. We asked: Do you see officers, civil servants and MHAs?

TABLE 4

MHA CONTACTS WITH MILITARY OFFICERS, CIVIL SERVANTS AND OTHER MHAS*

	Other MHAs	Military Officers	Civil Servants
Often	23 (42·6%)	9 (16·7%)	24 (44·4%)
Seldom	14 (25·9%)	16 (29·6%)	12 (22·2%)
Never	3 (5·6%)	19 (35·2%)	6 (11·1%)
As friends only	11 (20·4%)	8 (14·8%)	7 (13·0%)
NA	3 (5·5%)	2 (3·7%)	5 (9·3%)

*Out of 54 respondents

Section II The role of civil servants

The role of civil servants under military rule is illustrated in three ways: first, by presenting in summary form the manner in which it was perceived by the MHAs whom we interviewed, secondly by presenting in extenso the perceptions of thirteen MHAs who served as civilian commissioners, and finally by reference to a number of statements made by civil servants themselves.

(a) MHA PERCEPTIONS

We ask the MHAs: Who gained most from the military regime? Do most civil servants want a return to civilian rule? Do civil servants have different relationships with officers than they had with civilians in the past? The answers were all self-supplied; we made no suggestions regarding individuals or groups. There was a strong belief that civil

TABLE 5
MHA'S PERCEPTION OF CIVIL SERVANTS

	Number	% out of 54[a] respondents
Who has gained most from the military regime?		
The military	10	19
The civil servants	13	24
The North	6	11
The West	1	2
The people	3	6
Women Contractors	3	6
Minorities	1	2
No answer	21	39
	58	
Do most civil servants want a return to civilian rule?		
Yes	5	9
No	31	59
They can say	3	6
Don't know	3	6
No answer	12	12
	54	
Do civil servants have different relationships with officers than they had with civilians in the past?		
No	4	7
Yes[b]	6	11
They have more power	29	54
They had more power at first, not now	3	6
They have less power	1	2
Can't tell	1	2
No answer	10	19
	54	

[a]More than one answer was sometimes given.
[b]Most of the 'Yes' responses seemed to indicate that civil servants were more influential under the military regime, but the response was not clear-cut so we made a distinction between 'Yes' and 'more power.'

servants had gained in power almost as much as the military and that they did not want a return to civilian rule. Some MHAs suggested that the civil service had struck a bargain with the military. The military would get what it wanted on interest group demands, eg barracks, salary and hardware. The civil service would determine substantive policy in areas outside of narrow military interest group concerns. Senior Federal and State civil servants were prepared to be vetoed on some issues in order to get what they wanted most of the time.

(b) CIVILIAN COMMISSIONERS' PERCEPTIONS

Those appointed to serve in the Governor's Cabinet were naturally in a closer position to assess the role of senior civil servants. Some stressed the personal aspects of their own relationships with civil servants rather than any change in basic system-wide authority relationships with the coming of a military regime. It is best to let them speak for themselves on their relationships. One said:

> It is not easy to categorize the civil servants. If commissioners were weak they took over. It all depended on how one dealt with civil servants. Mine were loyal to me. They did not go without my knowledge to the Governor. The Governor would occasionally see them. He was a clever and efficient man and could see people personally. Once I took exception to this [seeing civil servants directly] and he never did it again. In fairness to Adebayo, he did not bypass me. I stood by my civil servants too.

Another commissioner offered:

> The old ministers had much more power. Civil servants could do things to commissioners and get away with it. They were careful though in the way they dealt with us. They could go to the Governor. It was an invisible Government. If a commissioner was strong he could override them. Real civil servants went to Odumosu [the Civil Service Head in the Western State]. When other civil servants went to the Governor, Odumosu called them to order.

One commissioner felt that the civil service was important but that this was more of a personal problem than one of general application:

> Civil servants tasted power before the commissioners were appointed, and did not want it taken back. I had experience of this. When I came in, I wasn't briefed. I took the initiative. I asked for a total review of my Department. I worked from 8:00 a.m. to 9:00 p.m. Within a weekend I had made the queries. I wanted briefs in 48 hours on 48 items. The civil servants tested you. The permanent secretary might go to the governor. It depended

on his personal relationship to the Governor. But the governor would not act without a commissioner. Adebayo dealt with you decently and on a cabinet basis.

Yet another commissioner said:

The civil service relationships were different. Before the appointment of commissioners, the government had been by permanent secretaries. Some did not feel that they needed civilian commissioners. They had been there from January 1966 to July 1967. They had power and ministerial responsibility too. But some felt that a revolt against government would hurt them. They saw the commissioners as buffers. They readjusted to commissioners. They knew the real power was with the governor and they could go to him directly. He encouraged this but not in writing. They could also go to the Secretary to the Military Government [Odumosu]. There were many cabinet reshuffles and conflicts and resignations. But the civil service will obey any master. I can't speak for them but they prefer the present setup. They like the inexperience of military leaders.

And another commissioner:

Civil servants were far more powerful than in the civilian regime. If you could not master your subject, they ruled you. Civil servants played havoc on the Alafin issue [the appointment of a new Alafin of Oyo]. The Commissioner for Local Government did not even see the file. Permanent secretaries went to the head of the civil service or even the governor if he called them without the commissioner's permission. But the commissioner had real power. It wasn't easy to wield it. The governor could overrule you, and even overrule the cabinet. But he was cautious. He would advise you. We had frank and open cabinet meetings.

Another commissioner:

Civil servants felt they had to keep clearing with the governor, not just their commissioner. In a civilian government only a major issue went to the cabinet as a whole. The civil servant is responsible to you as a commissioner, but all the same they work to the governor. Many commissioners are young and inexperienced. [The commissioner was referring to the regime of Brigadier Rotimi, governor of the Western State from 1971 to 1974, not to the Adebayo regime, which has experienced commissioners.]

One commissioner when asked who was influential in the cabinet, responded by saying:

I think it all depends on the issue; it all depends on the subjects. One would not say that any commissioner was the most influential . . . . I remember now when we first went into the cabinet, it was said that Adebayo was leaning too much on the senior civil servants, not even permanent secretaries, civil servants, the people lower down, and that he had his own purposes [for doing so]. So you can see the grievances of the commissioners now, and as a result of it we began to hold our meetings to see to it that what were our privileges were not taken away from us.

When this commissioner was asked whether the governor tended to take advice directly from permanent secretaries or from the commissioners, he said:

It all depends on which ministry and which permanent secretary. As a whole we have a team of brilliant civil servants. There's no doubt about it and they are aware that their influence depends on the value of their advice, and if they give advice which proves wrong in the long run, they will lose influence. At the same time, I don't think the civil servants are easily affected by the circumstances and factors which affect a commissioner's actions. They [civil servants] don't have that element of distraction that this thing should be done as quickly as possible. This is where the commissioner undoubtedly sits on top. The only difference between a commissioner and a minister in the civilian regime is that the premier would hardly ever call on the permanent secretary. Information would always come through the minister. But with the governor this is not necessarily so. If he feels that the commissioner would happen to know more about it or if he feels it would be better to go through the channel of the commissioner he would. But nothing inhibits him from approaching the permanent secretary directly.

When asked if this caused friction, the commissioner answered:

No, I don't think so because the first few months we spent there we made it clear that the information we gave the governor and the permanent secretary was one and between them they could do whatever they liked with it. But between us and the governor is preeminence [vis-a-vis civil servants] and we would not like it usurped.

This commissioner also stated that civil servants did not attend cabinet meetings and that therefore if a civil servant wanted to send a proposal to the cabinet and the commissioner did not agree, that was the end of it. 'He could go to the governor but the governor could only say that the commissioner had better bring this matter to the cabinet with the permanent secretary's view and his own.'

It appears from the above that personal relations with permanent secretaries were very important. At the same time, the commissioners believed that they had to master their civil servants. Of course this is a feeling that ministers in civilian regimes often have too. But the fact that a military regime existed meant that commissioners did not have a direct constituency base and they felt this even though some of them believed that political criteria counted for their appointment. They felt that they had a lessened authority because they were not elected and lacked a mandate. They also knew that civil servants acted differently under the military and felt freer in going to the Governor directly. This was especially true of the three powerful permanent secretaries who attended Cabinet meetings.

Some of the civilian commissioners had been ministers in a civilian Government. Two had been Federal ministers; some were ministers in the old Western Region. One had been a junior minister in the Western Region. Thus they could compare Cabinet Government in civilian and military regimes. Only one of those we interviewed thought the relationship was the same under both military and civilian regimes. For the rest, their words speak for themselves.

(c)   CIVIL SERVANTS SPEAK FOR THEMSELVES

The testimony of senior civil servants confirmed that there had been an expansion of their power or at least a more open manifestation and recognition of it under military rule. One Federal official whom we interviewed summarised the relationship with Commissioners in these terms. The civil servants worked to the commissioner. A strong commissioner could dominate. A senior civil servant could go to the head of the civil service, but a permanent secretary could not go directly to the Head of State or to one of his military secretaries or aides. If he did that and lost, the civil servant would be finished. Civil servants used to formulate policies under the civilian regime. 'Many ministers were uneducated. Who used to write their memos?' But under a military regime they had acquired new roles. They had more operating leeway and they were more independent on state corporations and boards.

In another interview, a senior civil servant from the Western State reported that Permanent Secretaries could go to Colonel Adebayo, but he contended that it had also been possible under civilian rule to by-pass Ministers and go straight to the Premier. He regarded Adebayo as a cunning politician, but someone with whom one could talk frankly. His own view of the commissioners was complex.

> The worse they were the better because you could do things then. Some were brilliant but wouldn't concentrate. It was an individual matter between a civil servant and the commissioner. Although the styles are

different between Adebayo and Rotimi, in a way Government functioned the same. It was a hybrid regime. It was military up to July 1967. But they appointed commissioners because they could not rule by themselves. Cabinet discussions were frank although sometimes Adebayo had made up his mind already. The Cabinet was advisory to the Government. It is wrong to say otherwise. Three civil servants were in the Cabinet as such. [These were the permanent secretaries for Finance, the political administration in the Governor's Office and the Secretary to the Military Governor.] Sometimes a commissioner had his permanent secretary present for discussions. A Cabinet meeting was for enlightenment and thus a commissioner should not be embarrassed to have a permanent secretary present. Permanent secretaries were members of the executive councils but did not swear allegiance.[37] Some permanent secretaries talked as Cabinet members although they were discreet on certain political things. They sometimes just kept asking and asking questions.

He attributed to key civil servants in the Federal Government much greater power.

If you went to Lagos you could speak to civil servants there. The key ones run things. It is frightening they have so much power. If Gowon says something and Ebong or Ayida [former permanent secretaries for Economic Development and Finance respectively] don't agree, next day he changes it.

We were told in another interview that the civil servants and the military had entered into a marriage of convenience.

The military goes along with the civil servants. It wants to stay in. When the army wants something for itself it is adamant. It says, 'That's it.' But generally they do not come into policy matters. They don't want to administer and they can't. The military wants to be in politics but it is inept; it doesn't know how. It has no talent for politics. Adebayo was rare; and the army can't administer anything. So it makes a marriage of convenience with the civil service. It gives them substantive power and administration in exchange for being able to stay in. The military doesn't want to rule with the gun so it needs the civil service.

This civil servant affirmed his abhorrence of military Government and claimed that this was a sentiment shared by many of his 'liberally educated' colleagues, even the key civil servants in Lagos, although he added 'Maybe power has gone to some of their heads.'

The above views were expressed privately and must therefore remain anonymous. But some of the highest ranking Federal officials have expressed their views quite openly, and not only on the general question of their position in Government but also on specific questions of public policy, which is itself evidence of a change in their position.

Mr Phillip Asiodu, for many years Permanent Secretary to the Ministry of Mines and Power, addressed a conference in August 1970 as follows:

> The members of the civil service are often the only concrete manifestation of government for the citizens . . . The effectiveness of a government is to a very great extent determined by the efficiency and competence of the civil service. The Higher Civil Service indeed plays a crucial role in that it participates fully in the formulation of policy and at the same time is responsible for the execution of agreed policy. This was always the case under the Civilian Regime. To some extent, moreover, it can be argued that the policy formulating role of the Higher Civil Service has expanded, or has been given greater recognition, under the Military Regime.[38]

Alhaji Yusufu Gobir, another of the top Permanent Secretaries who spoke at this conference, added:

> . . . . when the military took over the politicians were regarded with some suspicion and the only alternative source of advice they had was the civil servant. And because of this, one finds that in many of the states' executive councils, probably in all, the Head of the Civil Service is a member of the Executive Council.[39]

Two years later, senior civil servants joined a number of academics and civilian commissioners in another conference, this time on the topic 'Institutional and administrative perspectives for national development'.[40] They took an active part in discussing the most controversial of constitutional questions and associated themselves with the conclusions reached by the Conference. For example, the Conference was in favour of maintaining the ban on political parties during the transition from military to civilian rule. It also advocated executive Governors in the States and a modified presidential system at the centre. An 'extensive debate' regarding the 'concept of accountability' and their own role in any future civilian regime yielded the hopeful, or perhaps evasive, conclusion that 'there should be no conflict of interests because the two groups (civil servants and Ministers) should be equally committed to national objectives.'[41]

The most striking instance of a high level civil servant speaking out publicly on major issues was the address of A. Ayida to the Nigerian Economic Society's Annual Meeting in 1973. Mr Ayida spoke on 'The Nigerian Revolution 1966-1976.'[42] He was at the time the Permanent Secretary to the Federal Ministry of Finance. He spoke in his capacity as President of the Nigerian Economic Society.

After some deep reflection, I have decided to share some of my inner thoughts on the past, present and future of Nigeria with you, by analysing the social and economic forces which have determined the course of events in this country since 1966. One cannot analyse meaningfully economic and social determinants without making explicit one's assumptions about the future pattern of politics in the country . . . . Every Nigerian has the right to predict the likely course of events on the basis of knowledge at his disposal .

In addition to speaking out on the sensitive issue of creation of more states and on allocation of revenues as between states and the Federal Government, Mr Ayida stressed the supremacy of the military. He distinguished five categories of advisers and pressure groups associated with the determination of policies since January 16, 1966: (1) public officers, notably senior civil servants; (2) political appointees, notably civil commissioners; (3) members of the armed forces; (4) the private establishment such as church leaders, trade unionists, and captains of industry and employers; and (5) personal friends and confidants. Mr Ayida came to the conclusion that, 'Unfortunately, there is abundant evidence that the basis of civilian participation in the military administration is not abundantly clear even to some Civil Commissioners.'

If Civil Commissioners appear to exercise less power than the former Ministers, it is not because their functions have been usurped by Permanent Secretaries and other Senior Servants. It is because authority now resides in the military. Commissioners and senior civil servants are fellow advisers to the powers-that-be who sometimes receive their advice from outside the two groups, to their mutual frustration and suspicion. Commissioners were not appointed to run the Government as political masters but as servants of the military, the new political masters.

He went on to say that it was the barrel of the gun that determines the outcome of political controversy or personality conflict and even speculated that the ultimate distribution of power in a future civilian Government may not be significantly different. 'The political reality in Africa today is that the fact of the elective basis of government will not, *ipso facto,* remove the ultimate sanction in the hands of the military.'

At the same time he argued that modern governments depend on professional and technical advice in the formulation and execution of public business. The military recognised this by permitting permanent secretaries and professional experts to participate in meetings of the Federal Executive Council. It was a role that civilian rule had obscured.

The viability of the few politically determined ideas, such as free primary education, had to be worked out by the civil service machinery. The material difference between then and today is that there is no parliamentary forum under the military for Honourable Ministers to deliver speeches and appear to be seen to originate new ideas and policy measures.

We have cited at length from Mr Ayida's address becuase it showed clearly the disposition of a high level civil servant to comment on political matters, including the civil service's relationship with politicians and the military in a most striking fashion. While Mr Ayida specifically stated that the civil service should not be politicised and that it should not compose the vanguard he saw as necessary for the survival of the military revolution, he nonetheless cast the civil service in a critical policy formulation and implementation role. He saw civil servants involved in sensitive political matters in the past, present and future. In one part of his speech, Mr Ayida stated that at the time of the July 1966 coup, civil servants volunteered to go to Ikeja barracks to advise against secessionist threats from northern troops.

> It was gratifying to note that while we were driving to the barracks, the troops in battle order, and hidden in the bush, stood up in a column subsequently known as the Rising Grass, to ask our escort in Hausa, 'What is their tribe or nation?' Apparently our escort replied, 'They are civil servants.' There could have been no greater compliment to the public image of the Federal Civil Service in those dark days. That intervention probably had a decisive impact on the pattern of political events in the country.

In assessing the role of Nigerian civil servants under military rule we should distinguish on the one hand senior civil servants at Federal and State capitals and on the other hand local administrators. The former were often aggressive in moving to fill political vacuums. At the local levels, where civil servants had both to administer and to represent, the tax riots of 1968 showed the breakdown of the system.

The civil servants' greater freedom of action in administrative and political spheres have made them more vulnerable to charges of corruption. Margaret Peil states that senior civil servants have used their freedom of action to provide decisions in the national interest but some lower executive officers and clerks have found the opportunities for corruption too good to miss.[43] But Nigerian civil servants probably have no greater opportunity for corruption than they had under civilian regimes. Rather, the civil servants are no longer seen to be under politicians' orders and they are more visible and perceived more as independent actors.[44] Indeed, this holds true more for senior civil servants than for junior ones. And large numbers of senior civil servants became victims when Gowon fell.

We are not on very solid ground when we speculate about mass opinions or the views of political groups concerning civil servants. It does appear that both military officers and civil servants came to be seen by significant political groups as representing various political and ethnic configurations. This was evident when different groups petitioned for the breaking up of the Western State into more states. Civil servants and military were identified with particular subdivisions within the Yoruba. Many high level civil servants were either Ijebu or Ekiti Yoruba and many Yoruba officers were from the Ekiti areas. Thus when the Alafin of Oyo and the Chief of Oyo submitted a petition to General Gowon for the creation of more states they wrote: 'Since the Army take-over, the harsh hands of neglect have gripped our area and we are choking under the throes of a ruthless Ijebu and Ekiti officialdom.'[45]

There is some evidence that there has been fairly widespread dissatisfaction with civil servants at local levels especially. The military regime in Nigeria is perceived as not trying to be representative. Peil reports that respondents in a survey made in 1971-72 were largely in favour of civilian commissioners on the grounds that military severity must be moderated by some representation of the people.[46] Our own interviews with civilian commissioners established that they saw their appointments as designed to link military and civil service to the people. Only 5 of the 54 members of the Western House of Assembly whom we interviewed felt that the military had been more successful in representing the people than had civilian government.

Conclusion

From the very inception of a military regime in the Western Region/State there was a sharing of authority between civilians and military although ultimate power rested with military leaders. Between 1967-1971, authority was shared between Adebayo, the military governor, and Awolowo, the civilian leader. Awolowo could call on his past party supporters and large numbers of people in the Western State who looked upon him as a martyr and great leader, although he also had the liability of having made party and personal enemies. Adebayo himself had liabilities as well as advantages. He had to take account, more than Awolowo, of the sensibilities of his colleagues in the Armed

Forces. He had to deal personally with enlisted men and officers. This was both an advantage and a constraint. While some old politicians saw Adebayo as partisan, he played the game in such a way that he could not easily be identified with a particular factional group. He tried, after June 1967, to create more of a balance between the old parties so that there would be among the civilian leaders those who did not support Awolowo. Adebayo's own personality and political alignments thus came to be important factors in the politics of the Western State.

The evolution of the dyarchy in the Western State took place within the context of the civil war. The war influenced the ways that civil-military relations evolved. The army rapidly expanded. The very expansion of the army made the recruitment of Yorubas into the armed forces easier. While actual fighting allowed the military leaders to rule without feeling pressure for a return to civilian rule, the civil war made it necessary to mobilize civilian support. In order to do this, the military had to rely on old political and civil service networks. Most officers did not have the time, nor did they appear to have had the inclination, to forge their own political networks, although a few individual officers did become involved in civilian factions.

There was widespread agreement about the expanded role of the civil servants and what was true of the Western Region/State was no doubt still more true at the Federal level and in other States. The civil servants in Ibadan, while highly trained, had to contend with party politicians still able to assert themselves quite vigorously. In Lagos and most State capitals there was more of a political vacuum. Moreover some States had few native sons in high level military positions.

Civil servants however became more intimately linked in factional alliances with military officers from 1966 to 1975. Individual military leaders and senior police officers undoubtedly had grievances against some of the politicians all along.[47] But the increasing visibility of the civil service and the perception among elites and nonelites in Nigeria that the civil service was a political actor made the civil service more vulnerable to the housecleaning that a new military leadership undertook in 1975. The civil service was now part of the political fray and thus fairer game. As some civil servants feared, the political activity of civil servants weakened the civil service as an institution. Some high level civil servants who were closely linked with the Gowon regime were not tolerated by the Mohammed regime. Low level civil servants and high level ones too became convenient scapegoats for a military regime itself vulnerable to charges of corrupt practices. True, some military personnel were removed after the Mohammed coup, including the Military Governors of the States, but civil servants constituted the overwhelming number of public officials who were removed. By the time General Mohammed was himself assassinated in February, 1976, as many as 11,000 civil servants were reported to have been removed.

This examination of civilian participation—of ex-politicians, of Commissioners, of newly aspiring politicians, of civil servants—suggests that military rule is a term which needs redefining. What kinds of decisions are made by which groups and through which processes? What political networks exist outside the military and in what ways do they relate to the military's own factional alliances? How do civil servants fit into these civilian and military networks?

These kinds of questions can only be answered on the basis of empirical research still to be undertaken. That they are pertinent questions to ask should however be clear from what we have been able to discern by this limited enquiry into civilian military relations in the Western Region/State in the period 1966-71.

NOTES

1. For a review of the literature see Samuel Decalo, 'Military Coups and Military Regimes in Africa,' in *Journal of Modern African Studies,* 11, 1, 1973, pp. 105-127; Henry Bienen, 'The Background,' in Henry Bienen (ed.), *The Military and Modernization* (Chicago, 1970).

2. See Samuel Huntington, *Political Order in Changing Societies* (New Haven, 1968); Claude Welch, *Soldier and State in Africa* (Evanston, 1970); Robert Dowse, 'The Military and Political Development,' in Colin Leys (ed.), *Politics and Change in Developing Countries* (Cambridge, 1969), pp. 213-246; Henry Bienen, 'Military and Society in East Africa,' in *Comparative Politics,* 6, 4, July 1974, pp. 489-518.

3. For a discussion of civil-military ties see: Thomas S. Cox, *Civil-Military Relations in Sierra Leone,* (Cambridge: Harvard University Press, 1976); Samuel Decalo, *Coups and Army Rule in Africa,* (New Haven: Yale University Press, 1976); Eboe Hutchful, 'Military Rule and the Politics of Demilitarization in Ghana 1966-1969' thesis submitted to the Department of Political Economy, University of Toronto, 1973; Henry Bienen and David Morell, editors, *Political Participation Under Military Regimes,* (Beverly Hills: Sage Publications, 1976).

4. Edward Feit, (i) 'Military Coups and Political Development: Some Lessons from Ghana and Nigeria,' in *World Politics,* 20, 2, January, 1968, pp. 179-193.
(ii) 'The Rule of the "Iron Surgeons": Military Government in Spain and Ghana,' in *Comparative Politics,* 1, 4, July 1969, pp. 485-497.
(iii) *The Armed Bureaucrats* (Boston, 1973), esp. pp. 1-21.

5. Anton Bebler, *Military Rule in Africa: Dahomey, Ghana, Sierra Leone, and Mali* (New York, 1973), pp. 192-4.

6. Feit, 'Military Coups and Political Development,' *op.cit.* p. 100.
7. Bebler, *op.cit.* p. 203.
8. *Ibid.* p. 204.
9. All the interviews with the 54 former Members of the Western House or Assembly were carried out by Henry Bienen or Martin Fitton singly or jointly. All interviews were conducted in English. We conducted the interviews, usually between two and three hours long, with a questionnaire in front of us, although the order of the questionnaire was not rigidly followed. All former MHAs were promised anonymity. During 1972-73 when we did the interviews, 128 MHAs were potentially interviewable. We interviewed somewhat less than half because we could not reach all the MHAs. When we did reach a person, it was extremely rare that he was unwilling to be interviewed. We have no reason to believe that the MHAs that we were able to interview were unrepresentative by age, education, or occupation as compared to those we did not reach, although we underrepresented those MHAs newly elected in 1965 as compared to those who had been elected before 1965. The MHAs who were elected for the first time in 1965 were less well known figures in the politics of the then Western Region and they were harder to track down in 1972-73.
10. A five-man tribunal headed by Justice Olujide Somolu and known as the Somolu Commission of Inquiry investigated 75 minsters, 186 corporation chairmen and directors, 51 Members of the Western House of Assembly, and 246 senior civil servants, among others.
11. For a discussion of the intense factionalism of Western Region politics see B. J. Dudley, 'Western Nigeria and the Nigerian Crises,' in Keith Panter-Brick, editor, *Nigerian Politics and Military Rule: Prelude to Civil War,* (London: The Athlone Press, 1970), pp. 94-110; also see B. J. Dudley, *Instability and Political Order,* (Ibadan: University of Ibadan Press, 1974); and Anthony Kirk-Greene, *Crises and Conflict in Nigeria: A Documentary Source Book, 1966-1970, Vol. 1,* (London: Oxford University Press, 1971).
12. Civilian activities in Cabinet Government in Nigeria have been discussed in Henry Bienen, 'Military Rule and Political Process: Nigerian Examples,' *Comparative Politics,* forthcoming; also see, Henry Bienen, 'Transition from Military Rule: The Case of Western State Nigeria,' in Bienen and Morell, *op.cit.* pp. 50-65.
13. Kirk-Greene, *op.cit.,* p. 55, citing *Daily Times,* August 4, 1966.
14. Dudley states that when Awolowo was made Leader of the Yorubas, by this the Yoruba intelligentsia (Dudley's term) meant not just the peoples of the Western Region but all Yoruba-speaking peoples. There was a territorial claim to include in a single political unit the Yoruba people of the Western Region, Lagos, Kabba/Ilorin in the North and Akoko-Edo in the Midwest; Dudley, *Instability and Political Order op.cit.* pp. 146-147.
15. In the East, an Eastern Nigerian Consultative Assembly was set up. See Robin Luckham, *The Nigerian Military* (Cambridge: Cambridge University Press, 1971) p. 311 ff. Lt.Colonel Usman Hassan Katsina, Military Governor of the North, had been meeting with the traditional ruling structure in the North for months. He himself was a son of the Emir of Katsina and moved easily within this structure.
16. Kirk-Greene, *op.cit.* pp. 202-203, reproduces this address.
17. Interview with high-ranking military officer, 1973.
18. Luckham, *op.cit.* p. 311.
19. Kirk-Greene, *op.cit.* p. 60. cf. p. 291-2.
20. Luckham, *op.cit.* p. 313.

21. Dudley, *Instability and Political Order, op.cit.* pp. 147-148
22. Awolowo's address is reprinted in full in Kirk-Greene, *op.cit.* pp. 414-418, and a report of it is reprinted in Panter-Brick, *op.cit.* pp. 200-205.
23. Luckham, *op.cit.* p. 320.
24. *Ibid.* p. 333; and Dudley, in Panter-Brick, *op.cit.* pp. 108-109.
25. Interview with former commissioner, Ibadan, 1973.
26. In 1967 twelve men were appointed as civilian commissioners in the Cabinet of the Governor of the Western State, Brigadier Adebayo. Between 1967 and 1971 some replacements were made. There were *ex officio* members of the Cabinet, including the General Officer in Command of the Western State and the Police Chief of the Western State. Three permanent secretaries attended Cabinet meetings regularly: the permanent secretaries for Finance and for Political and Administrative Affairs in the Military Governor's Office, and the Secretary to the Military Governor. Including Brigadier Adebayo, there were 22 Cabinet members between 1967 and 1971.
27. For description and analysis of the 1968-69 riots I have relied heavily on two sources: Christopher Beer's dissertation. *The Farmer and the State in Western Nigeria: The Role of the Farmers' Organisations and Cooperatives,* University of Ibadan, Department of Political Science, 1971; and the *Report of the Commission of Inquiry into the Civil Disturbances Which Occurred in Certain Parts of the Western State of Nigeria in the month of December 1968,* (Ibadan: Government Printer, 1969). This report is known as the Ayoola Commission Report after the Chairman, Mr Justice Ebenezer Olufemi Ayoola.
28. The role of traditional leaders varied from place to place. As mentioned, the Shoun of Ogbomosho was murdered. But in Egba division, the *Parakoyis,* or traditional market chiefs, appear to have organised riots. These chiefs felt that their functions were being usurped by district council officials. *Ibid,* p. 405 and *Ayoola Commission Report,* p. 25. The Alake of Abeokuta, the major Yoruba Oba there, also opposed the district council administration and was thought to have surrounded himself with NNDP people. *Ayoola Commission Report,* p. 26.
29. One commissioner said in an interview that it was Gowon who asked Awolowo to see 'Tafa Adeoye, the *Agbekoya* leader.
30. Interview with Mr Adisa, in which he allowed these views to be reported.
31. See Adebayo's 'The Truth about Tax Riots: Governor Adebayo Speaks,' (Ibadan: Government Printer, 1969). Adebayo also spoke out in a speech made to the Leaders of Thought on December 23, 1968, titled 'Why This Ado About Tax?' This speech was reproduced in R. A. Adebayo *Problems and Solutions,* Vol. 1, (Ibadan: Ministry of Home Affairs and Information, 1971).
32. See the Ayoola Commission Report.
33. From an address by Governor Adebayo to members of Advisory Commissions for Local Government Councils entitled, *A Call to Service,* (Ibadan: Information Division, Ministry of Home Affairs and Information, nd.).
34. Address of July 17, 1968. See *Face to Face with Brigadier Adebayo,* (Ibadan: Information Division of the Ministry of Home Affairs and Information, 3 September 1970), p. 11. See also, *Self Help for Social and Economic Progress,* (Ibadan: Information Division of Ministry of Home Affairs and Information, nd.).
35. See Adebayo *Problems and Solutions, op.cit.* p. 121.
36. A fascinating look into a group convened by Bola Ige, former Publicity Secretary of the AG and one of Awolowo's leading lieutenants, is provided by a list of those

who attended Chief Awolowo at the burial of his mother in February, 1970. Bola Ige sent a circular from the Ministry of Lands and Housing, of which he was commissioner, to 106 people, requesting that they join in a procession from the home of the deceased into the church. While many of the 106 were former AG leaders at the national and Western Region levels, NCNC leaders like S. Yerokun and Chief Kolawole Balogun were there. A few former AG turned NNDP were there, too, as were some NCNC turned NNDP. But these were very few indeed, whereas almost all the MHAs and MPs who stayed loyal to the AG were present. All the AG members of the Cabinet who were serving under Adebayo were present, but not all non-AG members of the Cabinet were present.

37. In the minutes of the Western State Executive Council meetings, permanent secretaries were listed as Executive Council members.

38. Phillip Asiodu, 'The Future of the Federal and State Civil Services in the Context of the Twelve State Structure,' in Mahmud Tukur (ed.), *Administrative and Political Development: Prospects for Nigeria* (Kaduna, 1970), pp. 124-146. Among the participants were the federal permanent secretaries, Mallam C. L. Ciroma, permanent secretary, Ministry of Information; Alhaji Yusuf Gobir, permanent secretary, Establishments; Mallam Ahmed Joda, permanent secretary, Education; P. C. Asiodu, permanent secretary, Ministry of Mines and Power. From the State Governments, seven other permanent secretaries attended.

39. *Ibid.* p. 161.

40. Among the participants were Mr Asiodu, permanent secretary, Mines and Power; Mr Ayida, permanent secretary, Ministry of Finance, Alhaji Gobir, permanent secretary, Establishments; Mr Ime Ebong, permanent secretary, Economic Development; Alhaji A. Ciroma, permanent secretary, Ministry of Industry; the secretaries to the Western and North Central States' Military Government, P. T. Odumosu and Alhaji Garba Ja Abdul Kadir.

41. A summary statement of the conclusions of the conference can be found in the *New Nigerian,* November 25, 1972. p. 11.

42. The quotations that follow are taken from a copy of the mimeographed version of Mr Ayida's speech.

43. Margaret Peil, 'A Civilian Appraisal of Military Rule in Nigeria,' *Armed Forces and Society,* 2, 1, Fall, 1975, p. 41.

44. Peil herself makes this point in *Ibid.* She does not cite any hard survey data from her sample on perceptions of corruption.

45. 'Petition for the Creation of More States in the West,' submitted by Alafin of Oyo and chiefs, people of Oyo, to General Gowon, June 20, 1967, published as Appendix F in Panter-Brick, *op.cit.* pp. 267-268. 'Petition for the Creation of a Yoruba Central State,' submitted by Oshun Representatives' Committee to General Gowon, June 28, 1967, published as Appendix E in *Ibid.* pp. 269-271 made similar points.

46. Peil, *op.cit.* Peil's sample consisted of 830 people, half of whom lived in Lagos. The sample was not representative of Nigeria by occupation or income.

47. The Deputy Police Commissioner of the Western State, K. O. Tinubu, has written: 'We all will recall how during the 1962-1966 crisis some of us were made scapegoats and sacrificial lambs for the inordinate ambitions and heart-rending atrocities of some of our politicians.' 'The Dilemma of the Nigeria Police under the Civilian Regime' (unpublished paper, 1972). This is an interesting account of police powers and the way that politicians interfered with the police. We are grateful to Mr Tinubu for making this paper available.

Acknowledgments

Henry Bienen has been responsible for the writing of the chapter and the analysis of interview data. Henry Bienen and Martin Fitton did interviews with politicians and civil servants. We are grateful for the comments made on a larger manuscript by Ruth Collier, Grady H. Nunn, and Colin Leys. The research was supported by the Rockefeller Foundation, Princetown University's Center of International Studies, and the Woodrow Wilson School. Final manuscript preparation was facilitated by the Center for Advanced Study in the Behavioral Sciences. We gratefully acknowledge all this assistance.

3

Army Reorganisation and Military Withdrawal

Ian Campbell

Withdrawal by the military, whether it is executed voluntarily or under pressure, is still a comparatively rare event. In Nigeria, therefore, the decision to set a firm date for the return to civilian rule, initially 1976 but later rescheduled for 1979, aroused considerable interest and has since provoked much debate about the organisation of the future polity and, in particular, the likely pattern of civil-military relations. By examining the debate we hope to be able to explore, in some detail, the complex network of interests involved in the transition from a military to a civilian regime.[1]

Until 1973, expectations that the military would withdraw probably outweighed a certain scepticism. Early in 1973, a prominent southern politician, S. G. Ikoku thought it necessary to urge the military to act in good time—lest disorder should provide "the needed excuse for a prolonged period of military rule."[2] But as the military did little or nothing to implement their nine-point programme, the real danger was soon perceived to be not that the transfer would begin too late but that it would not begin at all.

The original target date, when it was first announced in 1970, had been sufficiently remote to be reassuring to those in power: the prestige of the government and of the army was at its peak following federal victory in the civil war; pressures for military withdrawal were few and could be fairly safely ignored. The situation changed perceptibly as 1976 drew close. Memories of the war had largely receded while criticism of the military administration had grown with the rising expectations of different sectors of society.

The debate at first had an air of unreality. So long as the government seemed reluctant to move forward, even the politicians out of office found it difficult to focus on such a tenuous and hypothetical future. Debate was further hampered by the fact that Nigeria was under a state of emergency—a legacy of the civil war which the military found convenient. All organised political activities and strikes were still banned. When one of Gowon's civil commissioners suggested that the ban be lifted so as to permit a more structured, and presumably more purposeful form of debate, Gowon, anticipating a revival of civil unrest, refused. "I will not be stampeded into taking decisions that might be detrimental to the interests of the nation at this time."[3]

As discussion continued there was a growing appreciation, among soldiers and civilians alike, of the problems associated with military withdrawal. Underlying much of the debate was the fear of praetorianism: that if the army withdrew, or was excluded from government, it would only be a matter of time before it returned to power under the same or different leadership. In Nigeria, where the civilian intelligentsia is highly politicised, it was to be expected that the intelligentsia-in-uniform would be similarly motivated. The point was clearly made in April, 1973, by a prominent civil servant, Allison Ayida, permanent secretary in the Ministry of Finance and later secretary to the Federal Military Government and head of the civil service. "Nigeria no longer has a ceremonial army. We are building a large modern army of well-trained, self-conscious and intelligent young men who will not be content to be relegated to the barracks for life."[4]

One possible answer to this problem is the civilian-military dyarchy which Dr. Nnamdi Azikiwe, the country's first president, had suggested in 1970 and again in October 1972. He wanted 'a combined civil and military government' that would rule Nigeria 'on a democratic basis' for five years.[5] His opponents referred to it disparagingly as a 'mixed grill'. The national press and most other politicians were also critical of the idea and the army in any case was more concerned with the problem of its reorganisation. While civilians and the military in office chose to debate a return to barracks, senior officers preferred to discuss the size, composition and character of the army that would occupy the barracks. However, the two questions, although initially distinct, could not be kept apart and, with the approach of the target date, became almost inseparable. For it was widely believed that an incoming civilian regime should not have to face an unreformed army. It was up to the army to put its own house in order first.

Army reorganisation

The first phase of the reorganisation programme aroused little controversy and was soon implemented. The three infantry divisions were redeployed so that each stretched from North to South, straddling the old regional frontiers and incorporating several of the recently created states. This was designed to insulate them from political pressures. Here the main obstacle was insufficient and inadequate accommodation. Other aspects of the programme proved more controversial, there was delay while Gowon searched for a compromise acceptable to the various military constituencies. The main issues were firstly, the composition of the army command and the allocation of responsibilities therein and secondly, the nature and scope of demobilisation.

The leadership of the army had undergone substantial modification in the course of the civil war. Reputations fluctuated during the protracted campaign and some of the changes of command, imposed by Lagos, left a long legacy of bitterness. The war also produced marked discontinuities in career patterns and these, in turn, affected the cohesion of the officer corps. Most striking, but not untypical, was the promotion of Yakubu Danjuma and Martin Adamu. Both were middle-ranking officers at the start of the war, distinguished themselves in the hard-fought Enugu sector and ended the war among the de facto leaders of the army. Many junior officers also won accelerated promotion, further eroding existing differentials and overturning established routines. With a new generation of leaders thus brought near to the top of the army hierarchy, there arose the problem of reconciling their expectations with those of other, more senior officers.

There was also the problem of striking a new balance among the various military constituencies. By 1970 officers from the Middle Belt had reached the top of all three divisions, while the principal strength of the Yoruba and Hausa officers (who tended to be better qualified technically and, on the whole, better educated than their Middle Belt colleagues) was in the specialist services and at Army Headquarters, Lagos. Nevertheless an attempt was soon made to correct the apparent imbalance with the appointment of a Yoruba to command the Second Division.[6]

The distribution of authority and the allocation of responsibilities within the army command, always a sensitive issue, became more critical in anticipation of a return to civilian rule in 1976—amidst growing speculation that General Gowon might retire from the army in order to be President. Undecided about his own future, Gowon was determined to retain sole command of the military. Hence the appointment as Chief of Staff (Army) of Major-General David Ejoor, former military governor of the Mid-Western Region. He had not distinguished himself at the time of the Biafran invasion and his promotion in February, 1972—after a period of relative obscurity at Army Headquarters and a senior officers' course in Britain—was seen as a personal decision by the Head of State which blocked the main contenders for the post and effectively left a vacancy at the top of the military hierarchy.

Demobilisation, the other main issue to be resolved, was accorded equal priority, at least by the divisional commanders. They favoured a drastic reduction in the size of the army from a quarter of a million to around a hundred thousand, mainly on the grounds that between eighty and ninety per cent of the already substantial defence budget was absorbed by salaries alone, leaving little for the purchase of modern armaments or the replacement of obsolete and damaged equipment. A reduction in the number of soldiers would also assist the authorities in their efforts to provide urgently needed barracks and other amenities, while the retirement of former veterans, the rehabilitation of the disabled, and the transfer of those who could be usefully employed elsewhere, would facilitate an early resumption of normal recruitment.

Demobilisation was nevertheless to prove an extremely sensitive issue, as any appearance of discrimination against any section whatsoever was likely to precipitate civil as well as military unrest. Hence the decision by Gowon to entrust the exercise to prominent representatives of the main military constituencies, thus ensuring an equitable distribution of responsibilities while retaining the right to arbitrate should any serious dispute arise. [7]

Before determining where cuts could best be made there was the preliminary question of securing a measure of agreement about the role of the army in peace-time. The Inspector of Army Engineers, Olusegun Obasanjo, advocated continuing and active participation by the military in the execution of the country's major social and economic programmes. "Instead of demanding that defence expenditure be considerably reduced people are now demanding that the military should contribute in real physical terms to the development of the state". [8] This approach had little appeal for officers in the combat units who lacked specialist training and skills, and saw only limited (and not very glamorous) opportunities for the deployment of infantry battalions in developmental projects. They probably had many fewer illusions than Obasanjo about the capacity of the military to undertake such work in the light of its previous accomplishments in this field. Theirs was a more traditional conception of the role of the army. Thus whereas combat officers tended to see the exercise as a means of releasing additional credits for the purchase of arms and military hardware, the specialist took the opportunity to press for improved communications (Signals), greater mobility (Transport) and an expansion of ancillary services (Engineers, Medical, Education, etc.) Each was anxious to accept the benefits of demobilisation but not to share the costs involved.

The problem of costs, i.e. redundancies, proved the most intractable. Several delicate operations were involved: choosing those to be demobilised, agreeing a time-table and a system of priorities, and making arrangements for their reintegration in civilian life. There was always the risk that the exercise would be seen as a "witch-hunt" by those most affected. The army that emerged from the civil war was not only incomparably larger but also infinitely more varied and complex than that which had seized power in 1966. One can distinguish three main groups, each of which had reason to fear demobilisation.

There were the 70,000 Yoruba, recently recruited and with no long tradition of military service. A significant proportion of them had received some previous education and many had originally transferred from jobs in government or the public service. It could be argued, therefore, that there were fewer obstacles in the way of their reintegration in civilian life, and that they would suffer least from large-scale and rapid demobilisation.

There were also the veterans who had re-enlisted at the start of the civil war and contributed greatly to the success of the federal campaign. The First Division, in which they were particularly well represented, was also the most effective. Their continued presence in the army, long after the end of the war, held up the resumption of normal recruitment, blocked avenues of promotion and reduced the efficiency of the army, for many of them were indeed veterans. However, the fact that they had volunteered in large numbers, in a time of national crisis, and had fought well and bravely throughout the war was to some, an effective and even compelling argument for retaining them on payroll, or for ensuring that they were adequately compensated upon retirement. Redeployment would in their case prove particularly difficult.

In a somewhat similar predicament were the soldiers from the Middle Belt, who now comprised the great majority of the army at almost every level. Drawn from an area that had long furnished recruits for the military profession, they were mostly farmers—unskilled, with few educational qualifications and, consequently, without prospects of suitable civilian employment. They were regarded as useful soldiers and had, on the whole, a good record in the civil war. In favour of their retention was also the fact that, while some might be integrated in the public services, most would stand little chance, without extensive retraining, of earning a livelihood outside the army.

The problem, for the senior officers and the government, was to agree categories, determine priorities, apportion cuts and distribute whatever relief was available—without provoking accusations of ethnic bias, professional jealousy, or discrimination on any other grounds. Gowon, who at first had inclined towards reductions, provided they did not disturb the delicate equilibrium within the army, now decided against any compulsory retirement. The army was to be slimmed to 150,000—the combat units being reduced by one-third with smaller reductions in the specialist services—but this would be achieved mainly by encouraging voluntary retirement.

The army was by no means unanimous about the need for retrenchment. Many soldiers, of all ranks, were alarmed or hostile. There already existed some resentment at the treatment accorded the army by their military colleagues in office and relations between the two groups of officers—those in government and the great majority who were not—had gradually deteriorated. The officers in barracks had mixed feelings about the country's apparent post-war prosperity, based on expanding oil revenues. They viewed with some concern the increasing disparities of wealth, the spectacular emergence of new centres of economic growth and political power following the creation of the twelve states and, and most striking of all, the unprecedented expansion of the middle classes. In these circumstances it was perhaps inevitable that the officers should compare their lot unfavourably with that of the senior civil servants and businessmen. Whereas the civil servants enjoyed security of tenure, good working conditions and apparently boundless prospects of job diversification and accelerated promotion, the military operated in a climate of job uncertainty, under conditions that were far from ideal and with the knowledge that promotions above the rank of major had become as exceptional and as difficult after the war, as they had been rapid and assured while it lasted. Whereas the civil servants, businessmen and professional classes benefited handsomely from the government's programme for increasing Nigerian participation in foreign-owned companies, the first phase of which was completed in 1974, only a very small percentage of army officers was able to profit therefrom.

Given the steady deterioration in accommodation and living standards and the consequent malaise among the army cadres, the reluctance of the government to clarify its position, in regard to demobilisation and other important areas of the reorganisation programme, helped weaken morale within the army and drew an increasingly critical response from its commanders.

Back to barracks?

While the debate on reorganisation was confined largely to the army and to senior officers, discussion of civil rule and the return of the army to barracks was conducted in a much wider context and attracted, initially at least, little comment from army leaders. During the discussion there emerged several more or less distinct options: (1) elections and the formation of a government composed entirely of civilians; (2) dyarchy, which entailed both military and civilian representation in government; (3) a presidential system in which Gowon (or his successor?) would continue as Head of State, but with a civilian rather than a military coalition; and (4) continuation, for a more or less indefinite period, of the existing military regime.

The options were themselves ill-defined and there was considerable overlap in some cases, notably between options three and four. Depending on the form of military representation adopted, e.g. joint participation with civilians on a National Security Council, dyarchy might even be defined so as to be compatible with civilian rule. The proposal for a presidential-type system was perfectly compatible with either civil rule or dyarchy. Without a clear and coherent lead from the government, and in the absence of organised parties the discussion tended to be both abstract and fluid. None the less, certain tentative alignments did begin to emerge during the debate, reminiscent of those which had crystallised during the life of the First Republic. Although less obvious under military rule, and certainly much modified as a result of developments after 1966, notably the proliferation of new states, affinities from this earlier period persisted and could again become an important factor in Nigerian politics after 1979.

The alignments are themselves a product of the continuing tension in Nigerian society between so-called "majority" and "minority" peoples. The former have, on the whole, been more enthusiastic about the prospect of civil rule. Whereas once they had dominated the public life of the three regions, their access to key positions in the military hierarchy was now limited. Indeed the Ibo were practically excluded from the upper and middle echelons of the army as a result of the civil war. Among the politicians, therefore, it was the Hausa, Yoruba and, more cautiously, the Ibo, who registered their fairly unanimous support for a return to electoral politics and unqualified civil rule. Their former party leaders now in opposition or semi-retirement, notably Obafemi Awolowo and Inuwa Wada, had least to lose and were among the first to enter the debate. Like most other politicians who chose to intervene, they had little patience with Azikiwe's proposal to give the military special representation in government after 1976. And it is probable that the views of Azikiwe's fellow Ibos were more accurately interpreted by the late Sir Louis Mbanefo, who warned that "the military will have to hand over power to civilians in 1976 if they are to retain their credibility with the public and ensure that a fair situation prevails in the country after the promised target date".[9]

Federal and state commissioners, enjoying some of the privileges and responsibilities of civilian ministers, had necessarily to be more guarded in their comments. Rather than criticise the military directly several of them, including Aminu Kano (Hausa, Kano), Femi Okunnu (Yoruba, Lagos) and Ali Monguno (Kanuri, Borno), waxed indignant at Azikiwe's proposed coalition of civilians and the military. As the debate progressed, however, their demands for military withdrawal became more insistent and even strident—as if to compensate for their earlier flirtation with the military.[10]

The military governors closest to the "majority" peoples in background and sentiment, Brigadiers Oluwole Rotimi (Western State), Abba Kyari (North-Central) and Musa Usman (North-East), also identified cautiously but unmistakably with civil rule.[11] But, as soldiers and prominent members of the Gowon administration, they had no wish to be confused with the politicians, whose activities they found increasingly irksome and distasteful. They were thus compelled to maintain a low profile throughout the debate.

As the debate progressed even the military in barracks must have been affected by the expression of political (and partisan) sentiments. Yoruba and Hausa officers came to view civilian rule as an opportunity to improve their position within the army command and compensate for any weakness in their representation at other levels. Some may have been directly influenced by the views of individual politicians. Murtala Muhammed, who made no public pronouncement on the subject of civil rule, no doubt noted the opinions of his uncle, Inuwa Wada, former Minister of Defence in the First Republic and a leader of the banned Northern Peoples' Congress who, in July, 1973, had called for immediate military withdrawal and a sharp reduction in expenditure on defence.[12] Likewise, senior Yoruba officers may have been receptive to the attitude of Awolowo, former Premier of the Western Region and leader of the old Action Group party, who had resigned from the Federal Executive Council at the end of the civil war rather than give continued support to a military regime.

In a somewhat different situation were the "minority" peoples, located mainly in the Mid-West, the South-East and the Middle Belt of Nigeria. They were better represented in the military than they had been in the councils of the old political parties, and, although their political future was brighter now that they had their own states, their present influence in the army and with the administration was more certain. Given their geographical dispersion and numerical weakness, it could be argued that they had most to lose by a return to civil rule and electoral politics. Not all would lose equally, however, and some (e.g. the Tiv and the Idoma) hoped to gain, locally, from the use of the ballot box. Thus there was no strict correlation between "minority" status, however defined, and opposition to civil rule. Nevertheless, as the "minorities" provided most of the military and much of the civilian support for the Gowon administration they tended to be identified with options other than an unqualified return to civil rule.

The proposal that General Gowon should continue after 1976 in the role of a "civilian" president did not feature prominently in the debate and was never publicly canvassed by Gowon himself. It had the merit, however, of being compatible not only with complete military withdrawal but also with some form of civil-military coalition. It was thus reassuring to many of those in office, including Gowon's military and civilian advisers, some of whom entertained serious misgivings about their place in a government dominated by politicians, while other wanted guarantees for the future conduct of a civilian administration. In May, 1974, there was an attempt to draft Gowon for election as president in a successor regime. It had the backing of Major-General Emmanuel Ekpo, a member of the Supreme Military Council who belonged to a minority group in the South-East. It was seconded by Colonel Olu Bajowa, a senior Yoruba officer then acting as military governor of South-East State.[13] Gowon himself had proposed an executive presidency as a desirable feature of any future regime but the suggestion had been strongly criticised by leading northern officers and, in particular, by Murtala Muhammed. Ekpo's initiative was condemned by Muhammed's uncle, Inuwa Wada, who indicated that, after 1976, he was prepared to accept Gowon only as a ceremonial and not as an executive president.[14] The proposal was also attacked by another senior northern Officer, Major-General Hassan Katsina, deputy Chief of Staff and, like Ekpo, a member of the Supreme Military Council. He insisted that the Head of State would, from all indications, remain a professional soldier and would not take any political office in the next civilian government.[15]

An alternative suggestion that had the approval of a number of the military governors, including two of those closest to Gowon, Brigadier Samuel Ogbemudia (Mid-West State) and Police Commissioner Joseph Gomwalk (Benue-Plateau), was to prolong indefinitely the life of the existing military government. Indeed civilian rule, with or without military representation, had little attraction for many of the military governors. Power-sharing seldom appeals to those in office and, by the very nature of their task and the conduct of their administration, most of the governors had not only forfeited their base in the armed services but were also unlikely to win future electoral support. Some, such as Ogbumedia, openly maintained that the military alone could guarantee stability in the country; that military rule worked; and that military participation was an aspect of African government almost everywhere, even under so-called civilian regimes like that of Kenneth Kaunda in Zambia.[16] Others such as Mobolaji Johnson (Lagos) took refuge behind the argument that the target date was conditional; a return to barracks was 'subject to the full completion of the government's time-table of reconstruction.'[17] It was the most convenient and attractive argument for other governors, sympathetic to a continuation of the existing regime but, like Johnson, administering states where it was politically inadvisable openly to oppose civilian rule. They included the former academic, Ukpabi Asika, (in East-Central State with its overwhelmingly Ibo population) and Police Commissioners Usman Faruk (North-West) and Audu Bako (Kano) in the far North.

The army commanders carried, perhaps, most weight in the debate. To them it must have seemed that there were obvious advantages to be gained from at least a partial withdrawal. As the authority and prestige of the military government continued to decline, a return to barracks offered probably the best and perhaps the only opportunity to restore the reputation of the army and protect the interest with which they were closely identified, even if some had political considerations in mind. Thus it was that, early in 1974, Brigadier Yakubu Danjuma looked forward to civilian rule as a means of insulating the army from the divisive effects of the continuing debate.[18]

Nevertheless the commanders, particularly those from the Middle Belt, home of many of Nigeria's minorities wanted firm guarantees about the conduct of the civilian administration after 1976. Although Danjuma insisted that the military must in no way become involved in political activities, he nevertheless welcomed the participation, *ex officio,* of military officers in a future civilian government. Brigadier Illiya Bissalla seems to have favoured a similar solution. 'If the country's constitution allowed an army *cum* civilian regime, the members of the armed forces would participate in the future government', but it was to be left to Nigerians to decide how they should be ruled and what sort of constitution they wanted for the country.' Brigadier Ibrahim Haruna likewise stressed that a military presence in government, even after the return to civilian rule, would be prudent provided it was acceptable to the new leaders.'[19]

The strategy of the army commanders, as it was being formulated at the beginning of 1974, was apparently based on two suppositions. Either Gowon would remain as a civilian president, which would reassure "minority" opinion within the military but would in no way compromise the reputation of the army itself. Or, there would be a civilian government whose leaders, however unsympathetic, would have to come to terms with the army and with its principal constituencies. In either case, the army would be able after 1976, to return to barracks, repair its unity and retrieve its reputation.

The prospect of repeated military intervention in the country's political life appealed to no one in or out of the army. Dyarchy was attractive, therefore, both as an alternative to praetorianism and as a means of giving the army a veto over certain aspects of governmental policy—and would preserve intact the army's prestige and its capacity to intervene should circumstances require it. As Haruna warned: 'Although it is often said that history repeats itself, it is our duty to ensure that certain incidents of our history do not repeat themselves.'[20]

The pressures on Gowon

Dissatisfaction with the government and its conduct of the administration, particularly at the state level, gave a new edge and added significance to the continuing debate over civil rule and army reorganisation. Gowan's government was generally seen as a military one, notwithstanding his reliance on the civil service and civilian commissioners. Only a very small percentage of officers participated in that government—considerably less than a hundred at best—but the army as a whole had to bear much of the responsibility for activities which lay outside the confines of military discipline.

It was the conduct of government at the state level which threatened to bring most discredit on the military. The authorities in Lagos depended to a considerable extent on the twelve state administrations created at the beginning of the civil war. With one or two exceptions, the military governors in charge of the states were fairly junior and inexperienced officers chosen, in 1967, from the heavily depleted ranks of the federal armed services and the police. Few remained popular for long and all but two have since been found guilty of corrupt or improper conduct and dismissed from the forces—by the military administration which, in 1975, replaced Gowon. Nevertheless, partly from a sense of loyalty to his war-time colleagues, partly because he was uneasy about the prospect of collaborating with their successors, but mainly because it would inevitably bring demands for changes elsewhere, Gowon was unable to implement his often repeated promise to replace the military governors.

The issue of corruption and the publicity that it required finally pushed the army commanders in the direction of complete and early withdrawal. In August 1974, the national press published several affidavits containing detailed allegations of corruption involving the governor of Benue-Plateau State, Joseph Gomwalk, and Joseph Tarka, the state's representative on the Federal Executive Council. It was no accident that of those suspected of corruption, Gomwalk and Tarka were singled out in this manner.

Benue-Plateau State provided a considerable and very senior part of the armed forces and was in a very real sense the heartland of the regime. The state was also a microcosm of the various pressures that were building up within the country, which the government was scarcely able to contain and which tended now to converge on the question of civilian rule. As rivalry developed between the constituent provinces of the state, relations between its leaders, Gomwalk and

Tarka, deteriorated until there were demands not only for the removal of the governor, but also for the creation of a separate Benue State, and for an adjustment of boundaries that would make possible the transfer to Benue of the Igala people from Kwara State.

To expose Gomwalk and Tarka openly in this way was to challenge the legitimacy of the administration as a whole. Moreover, at least three other affidavits were at this time being prepared against various governors and the morale of the government as a whole was severely shaken by the prospect of further revelations. Nevertheless Gowon found it as difficult to act here as in the matter of army reorganisation. Whereas Tarka felt compelled to resign, Gomwalk was exonerated following Gowon's personal intervention.

Maintaining Gomwalk as governor of Benue-Plateau State had the effect of confirming all the other governors in office. Given the publicity that the issue had received Gowon now had little alternative but to abandon the attempt to return to barracks in 1976. Hitherto the key man in the military hierarchy had kept his own counsel. By leaving all his options open for as long as possible Gowon had avoided an early confrontation with his opponents. The creation of a civilian regime with a strong president had offered him the most convenient escape from the contradictory pressures building up around 1976 but that alternative had been effectively blocked by opposition within the army. Now, with the pressures mounting from many quarters for a definite disengagement by the military, Gowon made his announcement of October 1, 1974.

He had decided to continue in office, giving as his reason that there had emerged 'such a high degree of sectional politicking, intemperate utterances and writings', designed 'to whip up ill-feelings within the country for the benefit of a few', that 'there is no doubt it would not take them long to return to the old cut-throat politics that once before led the nation into serious crisis.'[21]

The October 1st, 1974 broadcast necessitated a change in the tactics of everyone involved. Gowon's critics could no longer think in terms of forcing him to act but had instead to plan his removal. Gowon, for his part, had to conduct a finely balanced holding operation. Thus the next ten months were passed in an elaborate series of manoeuvres until, in the end, Gowon and his state governors were largely isolated. Gowon sought to retain the initiative by having recourse to various expedients. He reconstituted the Federal Executive Council so as to allow his military colleagues better representation in government; the civil service and the army, the two pillars of the regime, were each given a generous increase in pay; and an attempt was made to provide the army with decent living conditions by hastening the construction of barracks. All these moves worked however, to Gowon's disadvantage, making the task of his critics and potential successors all the easier. For they, too, had their difficulties and had to move with circumspection.

Gowon's first priority was to reach a new accommodation with the forces which maintained his administration in office. To this end he sought to disembarrass himself, as far as practicable, of those politicians whose presence in the government was a provocation to the military and a source of vexation to the bureaucrats. It had been proposed that the civil commissioners should retire at the end of September 1974, to be replaced by a predominantly military team; in this way the administration had hoped to avoid the charge of favouring any one group of politicians during the terminal phase of military rule. In the new circumstances Gowon chose instead to retain the commissioners until the end of the year, after which a new Federal Executive Council would be installed. Even so, the composition of the new executive council was not announced until late January. So intense was the competition for political appointment among senior army officers that Gowon experienced serious difficulty in reconciling their conflicting expectations. Civilians were retained on the Council partly to avoid the nomination of soldiers to posts which were thought to be outside their technical competence—finance, economic development, mines and power, justice—or within sensitive policy areas such as external affairs. But their representation was substantially reduced—from thirteen commissioners to eight—while that of the military and police was increased from four to twelve, nine of whom were army officers. If the specialists were better represented than their numbers in the army would seem to warrant it was a tribute to their professional skills and administrative competence and a recognition of their influence outside the military.

Gowon sought to balance military preponderance on the council not only by retaining some civilian commissioners, but also by directing that permanent secretaries participate more fully in its work. Other civil servants were invited to attend as and when required. To his critics in the army the result appeared to be greater military responsibility for policies that were being decided increasingly by the civil service. By reducing the number of politicians on the council Gowon had removed a useful and effective barrier between army officers and civil servants—

the principal components of the regime. The groups were now in direct and continuous contact and the opportunities for conflict were multiplied accordingly.[22] This had the advantage of confirming Gowon in his familiar role of arbiter and was probably the only alternative to a more collective form of decision-making, but it could not be the basis of a stable and enduring system of government.

The Supreme Military Council was retained intact, including all twelve military governors and and continuing to exclude the divisional army commanders. This, in turn, focussed attention on what was probably the major grievance of the military out of office: the failure of the Head of State to re-assign his governors, despite the promise contained in his speech of October, 1974, and renewed in May and July of the following year but never implemented.[23]

The creation, in April, 1975, of six new federal ministries foreshadowed the appointment of additional commissioners, offering alternative employment for some of the governors. But a new and more serious obstacle seems to have arisen. The threat of court action, arising from the affidavits, prompted the governors to demand legal immunity from any subsequent judicial pursuit. Aware of their impending retirement, some of the governors had engaged in extravagant and even flagrant acts of corruption, particularly after September, 1974.[24] While this increased the concern of senior officers for the reputation of the army and revived demands for the prompt removal of the governors, it made the latter even more determined to protect themselves, their dependants and their newly-acquired assets.

Many of the contradictions in the new administration were apparent well before the middle of 1975. To remain in office the government needed to extend and consolidate its power base. Instead, that base continued to contract while the administration remained pre-occupied with problems of internal balance. The removal from the executive council of so many politicians added to the external pressures on the government for an early return to electoral politics. Their replacement with military commissioners only aggravated relations within the government between army and civil service, between different branches of the army, and between Gowon and his commanders.

Far from extending the range of effective participation, the administrative procedures of the government became increasingly ill-defined until at last it was difficult to identify any coherent power structure. 'We had almost reached a stage where nobody seemed to be in charge.'[25] The proposal for the creation of additional states, which would have considerably widened the scope for participation and relieved some of the pressure on the centre, was repeatedly deferred as it would involve gubernatorial changes that were likely to reduce still further the cohesion of the regime. Even the advisory councils which Gowon had promised in October, 1974, and which were intended to provide for civilian representation at all levels of government, failed to materialise. Their creation would have offended those in the armed forces who already considered the regime too civilian while the politicians were bound to regard them as an attempt to perpetuate the existing administration or as a step towards presidential rule.

The second initiative, an increase in civil service salaries, followed on the report of the Public Service Review (Udoji) Commission, submitted in September, 1974. After a two year inquiry into the organisation and operation of the public services, the Udoji Commission had recommended comprehensive administrative reforms and appropriate changes in scales and levels of remuneration. Salaries in most of the public sector had been frozen for the duration of the investigation and the government hoped to be able to use the proposed pay increases to ensure the loyalty of the administration.

Pressure to announce the salary increases before Christmas prevented more detailed study of the Commission's proposals for civil service reform. The government was, in any case, reluctant to implement recommendations that seemed to challenge the existing hierarchy. Nor was it disposed to heed the commission's warnings about the inflationary impact of large and retrospective salary increases in the public sector. Many salaries were doubled and the increases were generously backdated to April 1, 1974, with provision for the arrears to be paid in a lump sum—half the arrears to be exempt from taxation. In the new year there was also a generous review of allowances and a decision to revise upwards the minimum rate of increase payable to all civil servants.

In its haste to implement Udoji the government encountered unexpected opposition from many quarters. There were protests from public servants with professional qualifications who, despite Udoji, continued to be excluded from the top administrative posts and, in some cases, now found lower limits placed on their maximum earnings; from others in the intermediate grades, with technical, scientific and other specialist training, whose new scales compared unfavourably with those of their administrative colleagues; and from many in the junior grades, who were adversely affected by the erosion of existing differentials.

There was unrest, too, among workers in the public corporations and the private sector, who were excluded from the Udoji review and were now invited by the government to negotiate separate wage agreements with their employers. The White Paper emphasised that such workers should not expect increases of the same order as those awarded the civil servants as they had not previously been subject to the same wage restraint. However, as the prices of essential commodities had already begun to rise steeply in anticipation of Udoji, this decision was an invitation to widespread labour unrest.

The new year saw a major outbreak of industrial disputes as various categories of public employees sought to maintain salary differentials, while workers and unions in the private sector bargained for wage rises similar to those enjoyed by civil servants and academics. Agitation began with the doctors and other medical staff in government service, who complained of discriminatory treatment. They were soon joined by dockers and railwaymen, then by the electrical power workers and, finally, the airline pilots. In the private sector, the lead was given by the militant National Union of Nigerian Bank Employees, whose members struck three times in as many months. Confronted by the worst labour troubles since 1964 the government tried conciliation, then coercion, before admitting defeat. It then conceded wage settlements based on Udoji and allowed professionals in public service a greater measure of parity with administrators. Unrest had spread even to the countryside with farmers in the Western State organising a food 'hold-up' until the relevant bodies agreed to more satisfactory prices for their produce. The great majority of the population, however, had little or no protection against the inflationary consequences of Udoji.

The administration itself had no very effective means of regulating retail prices or controlling distribution. Notwithstanding the efforts of the Price Control Board and the National Supply Corporation, the cost of many basic commodities soared while others disappeared altogether from shops and markets. The constant labour disputes disrupted the economy during the first three months of the year and severed normal distribution networks, beginning with Lagos docks. This, in turn, aggravated the usual shortages of essential items such as petrol, kerosene and tinned milk. The result was to discredit the new administration almost from its inception.

Before announcing its version of the Udoji recommendations, the government had hastened to assure its other important constituency, the military, that a body had been appointed to review their salaries and wages. Officers and other ranks were advised that they could expect comparable treatment with the civil service, with increases payable from April, 1975, and backdated a full twelve months. While this may have secured for General Gowon and the government the continued support of most of the army—although there were complaints of discrimination against those in some of the specialist services—it did not appease the commanders who continued to insist on immediate implementation of the reorganisation programme. The increased rates of pay merely swallowed up an even higher proportion of the defence budget and reinforced their contention that the army could not remain at its present size without forfeiting all pretention to being a credible fighting force.

To avoid the risk of discontent spreading in the army, and in a bid to placate his commanders, Gowon sought to expedite the construction of barracks. Five years after the end of the civil war the great majority of soldiers were still without suitable accommodation. It was only in July, 1972, after the completion of the necessary plans and surveys, that contracts began to be awarded. As late as 1976 the Chief of Army Staff could still complain that 'as at this moment not one army barracks has been fully completed'—although five or six would soon be ready for occupation.[26]

In order to expedite construction the Ministry of Defence authorised a special purchase of cement from abroad, but it arrived in quantites that far outstripped port capacity.[27] Delays at the docks affected a wide variety of commodities other than cement, creating shortages in shops and markets which then helped boost inflation. To help remedy the situation, import duties were waived or substantially reduced, temporary berths were improvised, new equipment was ordered from America, and Gowon's successors tried to re-negotiate the cement contracts. Despite these measures there were four hundred ships waiting to unload at Lagos in the latter part of 1975.

Notwithstanding Udoji, neither the military nor the civil service was well placed—or even pre-disposed—to sustain the government during the first six months of 1975. The civil service, already under critical scrutiny following the report of the Udoji Commission, and now invited to assume additional responsibilities in the new government, found itself in an increasingly isolated and therefore vulnerable position. For the first time, too, suspicions were being voiced openly about the probity of some of those at the top. The federal administration was, moreover, the subject of a major reorganisation exercise following the creation of additional ministries and the appointment of a new service head, Allison Ayida, in late April. There had been intense lobbying by departmental heads throughout the exercise and the undignified scramble for posts continued until the final appointments were announced at the end of June.

The thirteen new permanent secretaries included a former commissioner and others recruited from the state administrations. This and the attempt to strengthen the cabinet office seemed to denote a break with some of the practices and priorities, and even with the personnel of the previous nine years. Whilst there were misgivings about this new style administration, dissatisfaction was also expressed in some quarters at the redistribution of jobs and the allocation of departmental responsibilities. Senior northern personnel seem particularly to have resented their continued exclusion from the inner circle of administrators grouped around the new service head. Nor was bureaucratic unrest confined to the federal capital. During the first half of the year administration throughout much of Nigeria was seriously impaired, and in some cases paralysed, by agitation for the creation of new states—a campaign in which civil servants were especially prominent.[28]

Within the army, the tensions that had accompanied the reconstruction of the Federal Executive Council in January revived in anticipation of the replacement of the military governors and their reintegration in the command structure. It was feared that, while the proposal to enlarge the executive council once again might provide 'plenty of jobs at the top', it would undermine still further cohesion within the government and in the army.[29] Meanwhile, the military commissioners who had accepted office at the beginning of the year soon found themselves shouldering much of the responsibility for a chaotic labour situation which was not of their making and which the government seemed unable to resolve on its own terms. Aware of their somewhat tenuous base in the army as a whole, and possibly frustrated by their exclusion from a number of key ministries, these commissioners were under constant pressure not only from their military colleagues, concerned about the declining prestige of the army, but also from important sections of the civilian population impatient for a return to electoral politics.

Gowon had failed to achieve his objective. He was unable to satisfy the army commanders; the country was beset by a wave of inflationary pressures and, at a time of unprecedented revenues there was the paradox of chronic shortages. Gowon's various attempts to consolidate his position had served only to unite his opponents.

Gowon's removal

The loss of support was all too apparent from the peaceful manner in which the change of leadership took place. The acquiescence of the public was assured, the key figures in the army no longer stood in the way and the moment was carefully chosen—Gowon was out of the country attending an O.A.U. summit conference.

The press played an important part in preparing the ground, not only by reporting the views of the government's critics but also by showing its own disaffection. This was particularly true of the *New Nigerian*—despite the fact that it was owned jointly by the governments of the six northern states. The paper both reflected and helped shape opinion in the far North, and its adverse comments evoked frequent outbursts from senior members of the government. Already on the eve of Gowon's broadcast of 1 October 1974, and in anticipation of a revival of political activity, the newspaper had begun serialisation of Chinua Achebe's novel, *A Man of the People*. A study of moral corruption and political venality under the First Republic, it was presented to readers with the comment that 'the situation has barely changed; only the characters are different'—had the novel been written now 'the main characters would not be men in agbada but men in khaki'.[30]

During June and July 1975 there were reports of statements in favour of a military withdrawal by Aminu Kano, Shehu Shagari, Tanko Yakasi and Ishaya Audu. The first three were closely associated with the Gowon administration as civilian commissioners and Audu, Vice-Chancellor of Ahmadu Bello University, stood close to Gowon personally. In an editorial at the end of May, the *New Nigerian* described the Gowon administration as 'a system of drift' and maintained that 'even the unrepentent sycophants in the corridors of power have conceded the fact that in the long run this country must return to a representative and responsible system of government'.[31] Several days before the July *coup,* the same newspaper gave considerable prominence to an attack on the regime by the Grand Khadi of the northern states, Abubakar Gumi, who in a televised debate had complained of tyranny and oppression, and of an elite that was degenerate and corrupt. There could be no question of divine intervention and the remedy was in the hands of the leadership as a whole. 'But I do not think there is anybody who is trying to put the house in order'.[32] The day of the *coup* the *New Nigerian* carried an editorial insisting that 'military system of government is an aberration which should be endorsed only in an emergency'. Although there was no reference to impending events, there did appear on the front page and in a very different context a photograph of Colonel Joseph Garba, commander of the Brigade of Guards, whose intervention in Lagos later that morning helped precipitate Gowon's removal.[33]

The key actors in the *coup* were clearly the divisional commanders, the director of military intelligence, the commander of the Brigade of Guards stationed at Lagos, and a small but cohesive group of middle-ranking and fairly young officers. Brigadiers Danjuma, Haruna and Bissalla all made public statements indicating their alignment with those pressing for a military withdrawal.[34] Of particular significance was Danjuma's press conference on the eve of the *coup*, in which he said 'there is nothing wrong with people agitating for a return to civil rule since the army had already made up its mind eventually to return power to civilians', adding that 'the public agitations for a return to civil rule are merely a reminder to the military regime that it was overstaying its tenure of office'.[35]

Confirmation that the *malaise* had penetrated to the very centre of the regime was provided by the defection of those primarily responsible for security and for Gowon's personal safety. The director of military intelligence Col. Abdullahi Mohammed could scarcely have been unaware of the impending *coup* and presumably did nothing to warn Gowon before his departure for the Kampala meeting. The cooperation of the commander of the Brigade of Guards, Col. Joseph Garba, was equally vital, for although his duties were largely ceremonial he was one of Gowon's closest colleagues. He came from a neighbouring part of Plateau province, had been sent at a comparatively early age on a senior officer's course at Camberley and was ear-marked for one of the new posts in the Federal Executive Council. He had easy access to Dodan Barracks, the seat of government, and had troops ready at his disposal. His defection and that of Abdullahi Mohammed helped reduce the threat of counter-measures, of possible armed confrontation and civil disorder. It was Garba who broadcast immediately after the *coup* and both men entered the new administration, Garba as Commissioner of External Affairs, and Abdullahi Mohammed as governor of Benue Plateau state.

Acting with Garba were several other middle ranking and fairly young officers who had not the means to impose themselves on the army as a whole but were prepared to take the initiative for others to follow. Efficient, and in many cases outstanding soldiers, they had distinguished records of service in the civil war; and drawn largely from the North, they were influenced by and shared the views of several of their contemporaries in Ahmadu Bello University and on the *New Nigerian*. Their main objective seems to have been to reform the character of the army and retrieve its reputation. This, they maintained, had . been compromised by long participation in a government where civilians were nearly as prominent as soldiers, and whose leaders had yet to honour their undertaking to restore civil rule. A leading member of this group was Lieutenant-Colonel Shehu Yar'Adua, Garba's deputy in the Brigade of Guards and the present Chief of Staff, Supreme Headquarters. An able soldier with an excellent war record, he won early and rapid promotion. Commissioned in the Nigerian army in 1964, at the age of twenty-one, after initial training at Sandhurst, he was a company commander by 1967, later Assistant Adjutant-General in the Second Division, and already a brigade commander and Lieutenant-Colonel in 1968. Like Murtala Muhammed, he was also well connected politically. He came from Katsina where his father, Alhaji Musa, was a member of the Native Authority Council, having been prominent in the Northern Peoples' Congress and Federal Minister for Lagos Affairs under the First Republic.[36]

The success of the *coup* was assured only after it had received the support of officers in command of the main combat troops. It seems that their support was not at first unanimous and was the subject of some hard bargaining. The result was a new military coalition and an important shift in alignments—completing the process already begun earlier in the year—with the promotion of Danjuma to the post of Chief of Army Staff. This title, which soon replaced the narrower designation, Chief of Staff (Army), reflected not only Danjuma's professional status and the ascendancy he enjoyed within the military, but the fact that, as 'swing man', his support, with that of other commanders, was essential to the successful conclusion of the *coup*.

The composition of the new ruling elite appears to have been the product of further negotiation. Murtala Muhammed was chosen to lead the government because, although often impetuous, he seemed, particularly to the young officers, to possess the requisite qualities of drive and determination. With his appointment as Head of State and that of the more cautious Olusegun Obasanjo as Chief of Staff, or *de facto* prime minister, the task of conducting the new administration was thereby entrusted to the most senior of the service officers. Neither seems to have played any prominent part in the execution of the *coup*— Muhammed only returned to Nigeria the morning of Garba's announcement—but their nomination, the retention of five other military commissioners from the previous government, and early confirmation of the appointment of Allison Ayida as civil service head, helped ensure a large measure of administrative continuity.[37] Those who now entered the Supreme Military Council, Danjuma, Yar'Adua and the new divisional commanders (two Yoruba and one from the Middle Belt) occupied a special place in the new administration with a right of veto over a wide range of government decisions.[38] The military were thus well placed not only to direct the new administration but also to scrutinise its policies and evaluate its performance. Of the former members of the Council, only Bissalla retained his place—a tribute to his innate caution and the respect he continued to command within the army. But his nomination as Commissioner of Defence, where he succeeded Gowon, served to confine him within a largely administrative role.

Officers above the rank of brigadier were immediately retired. The new executive council included a quota of civilian commissioners but, in keeping with the military profile of the government, these were academics and technical experts rather than politicians. Civil servants were no longer permitted to attend and participate at meetings of the council unless specifically invited to do so.

A fresh start

After some weeks of further debate, Gowon's successors won for themselves widespread support and a measure of legitimacy by proclaiming their commitment to civil rule and presenting a detailed programme for its implementation, with 1979 as the new target date. While there was no abrupt break with the other policies of the Gowon administration, there was a marked contrast in style as objectives were, on the whole, more clearly defined and the government seemed determined to execute them promptly. There was an almost unprecedented degree of administrative activity in the first months of Muhammed's rule as various commissions were created to investigate and report on issues outstanding from the previous regime.

The new administration acted boldly to reject the results of the 1973 census, to approve the creation of additional states, and to endorse the removal of the federal capital from Lagos.[39] These decisions, and the not wholly successful attempt to determine the ownership of properties 'abandoned' during the civil war, were intended to remove some of the more contentious issues that might otherwise have delayed the transfer of power to civilians. There remained only the intractable problem of corruption, most apparent in the public services but by no means confined thereto, the vexed question of the role and size of a peace-time army and the much debated constitutional issue of an acceptable framework for the conduct of government after 1979.

A thorough-going re-appraisal of the civil service was long overdue and was the more urgent with the prospect of civil rule in 1979. Obasanjo, himself, warned that 'the service must prepare itself for civilian rule when civil servants will execute policies rather than make them'. This would entail a reduction in 'the dominant role which civil servants had played in policy-making and the direction of government policy'.[40] To this end the military leaders embarked, in the second half of 1975, on a comprehensive purge of those in public employment. The exercise, starting with the police and the federal and state civil service soon extended to the various public corporations, boards and companies, the universities and, finally, the army and resulted in the removal of some ten thousand government employees. More drastic in its early than in its later phases, the exercise was by no means uniformly applied in every state, department or corporation, as the opportunities for corruption varied widely while suitable replacements were not always at hand. Nevertheless many were removed who were corrupt, elderly or inefficient, and the campaign had a salutary effect, at least temporarily.

The government soon recognised the inadequacy of the methods used in the purge and became increasingly concerned not only about the many cases of wrongful dismissal but also about the unsettling effects of the operation on the administration and on the country as a whole. The social and economic consequences were by no means confined to the public officials involved—or even to their immediate families. Given the pervasive nature of kinship ties in Africa, the compulsory retirement of a civil servant, however junior, could adversely affect the economies of several households. Already in September, 1975, the authorities acknowledged that the exercise had naturally caused 'concern, panic and uncertainty in the ranks of

serving officers'.[41] The following month the Head of State, himself
insisted that 'the aim has been to strengthen the services and there is no
intention whatsoever of allowing the exercise to degenerate into witch
hunting.'[42] As civil servants became increasingly reluctant to offer
advice or assume responsibility—'people are applying excessive
caution in their work to point of paralysis'—the Chief of Staff found it
necessary to assure the administrators that 'it is not our intention to
over-scrutinise every decision and single out every small infringement
or departure from regulations'. The exercise was concluded at the end
of November 'because it had an unsettling effect on the services';
'everybody can now settle down to a calmer life'.[43] A year later,
however, Obasanjo was still complaining of low morale in the federal
civil service and of the persistence of old and discredited patterns of
behaviour.

The most pressing problem was still reorganisation of the army
particularly as the new administration had committed itself to
withdrawal by 1979. Moreover, as a government which claimed to
have rid itself of civilian encumbrances, it was under a clear obligation
to act decisively. Yet the problem was no less intractable. On the
question of numbers, the criteria for selection, the manner of
redeployment and the problem of securing a balanced army, there were
still divisions of opinion. Bissalla, now Commissioner for Defence, let
it be known, in August, 1975, that the government was considering a
fairly extensive programme of demobilisation.[44] His remarks were
echoed in October by Colonel Isa Bukar, brigade commander in Benin
City.[45] At the end of the month however, the GOC, First Division,
Julius Akinrinade, explictly denied 'the wild rumour that a general
demobilisation exercise was imminent in the army': only those above
fifty-five years of age would be involved and they would receive their
full gratuity and pension entitlement 'without the usual difficulties'.[46]
Despite this disclaimer, the Chief of Army Staff, Yakubu Danjuma,
announced in December that it was the firm intention of the
government to proceed with a demobilisation exercise aimed at
reducing the strength of the army to some 100,000 soldiers.[47]

Bissalla appears, in retrospect, to have been definitely at variance
with Danjuma and with some at least of the other commanders. This
may have been due to contrasting experiences during the war. As
military secretary, Bissalla had remained at Lagos for much of the
campaign, concerned primarily with administration and co-ordination
until the final months of the war when he moved to Enugu to assume

command of the First Division. Less experienced, perhaps, in the
actual conduct of military operations and naturally cautious in
outlook, he may nevertheless have acquired some insight into the
complexity of the administrative process and the nature and variety of
the interests that have to be accommodated both in government and
within the Army. Danjuma and the other commanders whose
experience was more in the field may have given less weight to political
and administrative considerations. There was no doubt also an element
of personal rivalry. Bissalla, along with some other senior officers,
probably resented the elevation of Danjuma as Chief of Army Staff
and the appointment of so many middle ranking officers to such key
posts; and he chafed, perhaps, at his new administrative
responsibilities as Commissioner of Defence which, although broad in
scope, effectively separated him from his military base. Thus, the
question of demobilisation became entangled, to some extent, in a
dispute about control of the army which would return to barracks in
1979. Perhaps because of such disagreements, there emerged no clear
and coherent rationale for demobilisation. Linked at first to the purge
in the public services, it remained restricted in scope and under the
broad supervision of the government.[48] By October, however,
Danjuma was emphasising other, more ambitious goals, thereby
assuming responsibility for an operation to be conducted according to
military criteria.[49] These criteria, which were incorporated in the four
year programme of army reorganisation, themselves reflected the
varied and often conflicting interests of the military constituencies. At
his press conference of October, 1975, Obasanjo, presumably with
Muhammed's approval, was at some pains to emphasise the need to
maintain a certain organisational balance within the army. 'What
makes a credible striking force is not the bodies you have alone. You
must have the bodies, you must have the communications, you must
have the transport. All these go together . . . .'[50] Himself a 'specialist',
like the Head of State, Obasanjo wanted adequate provision in the
reorganisation programme for the development of the service sector
and its various branches. 'Our concept of a credible force is to have the
right type of forces blended with the right type of weapons and
adequate communications and transport'.

By the end of the year Danjuma was attempting a similar synthesis
between the requirements of the combatant and specialist units
admitting the need for greater mobility but insisting also on additional
armaments. Within the confines of the existing budget this could only

be achieved by substituting fire-power and mobility for excess manpower. Thus he maintained that 'Nigeria could not afford to keep her army at its present size', because to arm and equip the existing divisions with sophisticated weapons would absorb sixty percent of the country's national income. Meanwhile the army did not and could not constitute an effective fighting force. It had grown more by accident than by design, was 'completely immobile, without the right equipment and without shelter'; it was 'almost the only army in the world where serving soldiers died of old age'.[51]

Finally, there seems to have been little or no agreement about the timing and implementation of demobilisation. By giving advance warning of the exercise without carefully defining either its scope or the specific measures to be taken to protect the welfare of the soldiers involved, the army commanders compromised the success of their programme. Initially, at least, they may have seriously underestimated the strength of opposition among the officers and other ranks and the ability of their critics to exploit that dissatisfaction. Here General Gowon had perhaps been closer to the sentiments of the rank and file. As the *Nigerian Tribune* commented: 'Every public statement made without a clear-cut programme of action can only create panic among the rank and file of the armed forces and provide ammunition for evilly-disposed persons.'[52]

As opposition mounted in the army, the future of the reorganisation programme became increasingly problematical. Danjuma appears nevertheless, to have retained the initiative for most of the time, demanding prompt action by the government not only to halve the size of the army but also, as a matter of urgency, to create jobs for those to be discharged. As the economic situation deteriorated in the latter part of 1975, the exercise became increasingly unrealistic as the government was no longer in a position to finance a costly and extensive resettlement programme. If it was to proceed, the necessary finance would have to come from cuts in the defence budget, a course of action which Danjuma had rejected from the outset, probably because it was unacceptable to his military constituency.

Those who led the government tried to avoid a public debate on the issue, allowing Danjuma and the army commanders to accept full responsibility for the conduct of the exercise. Murtala Muhammed refrained from any statement on the question, while Obasanjo's approach was both prudent and circumspect, with its emphasis on preliminary planning and realistic targets. The problem was to devise a suitable set of priorities and then to consider the most appropriate and satisfactory way of implementing them within the agreed time. In his press conference of October, 1975, Obasanjo maintained that, provided 'demobilisation was planned and phased', the social and human problems could be minimised or avoided altogether. The government had no wish to create additional unemployment, least of all among those 'who have served their country in the time of crisis', which was why 'the operation must be planned—with adequate provision for the future of those affected.'[53]

Finding his programme threatened and opposition growing not only in the army but also within the government, Danjuma warned the administration in January, 1976, of the serious political consequences it would face unless it could offer alternative employment to the large number of soldiers soon to be made redundant. Where there had been considerable social unrest after 1945, with the demobilisation of ten thousand servicemen, there would now be ten times that number. 'There is no question at all that we can simply close our eyes to these problems'.[54] On the eve of their congress, at the end of January, the Nigerian Federation of Ex-Servicemen cautioned the government that if it were not vigilant 'it would confront a lot of problems during the exercise.' The Commissioner of Defence advised delegates that, while the operation would begin soon, all those awaiting discharge would receive gainful employment: the government and the military 'were only too well aware of the catastrophe that would befall the nation if soldiers were to be demobilised indiscriminately.'

Dissatisfaction was not confirmed to junior officers and the other ranks. Reorganisation of the army also involved the more senior members of the officer corps, not least those who had been commissioned during the civil war but lacked appropriate training. As Danjuma admitted to the first intake at the new Army Command and Staff College: 'We made a lot of command and staff mistakes in the course of fighting the war.'[56] To improve the quality of the leadership, the Chief of Army Staff had, towards the end of 1975, improvised a conversion exercise, which entailed a re-assessment of each officer's intellectual and military potential on the basis of a series of examinations and practical tests. The exercise aroused considerable misgivings, particularly among middle ranking officers, veterans of the civil war, whose performance was now to be judged by criteria which were unfamiliar and therefore suspect. Moreover, the exercise was only one of several concurrent efforts to 'clean up' the army, beginning with the purge of some 216 officers at the end of November.[57]

Despite the growing unrest within the army and rumours of several abortive *coup* attempts at the end of 1975, the decision was taken, early in 1976, to proceed with the promotion to the rank of General of fourteen senior officers, including most of those prominent in the government. The promotions created discontent close to the top, where officers, including Major-General (previously Brigadier) Bissalla, found themselves being overtaken by former subordinates like Lieutenant-General Danjuma. There was dissatisfaction, too, among the middle ranks which had not been included in the exercise. And, at a time of increasing insecurity, the promotions tended to isolate the commanders from the troops they had to lead. Moreover, following as they did the extensive purge in the civil service, the promotions were also criticised as being inconsistent with the aims and ideals of the July *coup*. The Students' Union at the University of Ibadan, which had enthusiastically endorsed the new government and its energetic measures to curb corruption, now expressed 'utter disgust and disappointment' at promotions which were 'completely out of tune' with the 'low profile' hitherto adopted by the regime.[58]

Danjuma was quick to defend the government's decision, arguing that the army was grossly under-officered and that there was no reason why officers discharging important responsibilities should not enjoy commensurate rank. There were vacancies for twice as many generals and the government was now considering a further series of promotions for officers in other grades.[59] The Commissioner of Information, Major-General Haruna, revealed that the promotions had been planned as early as 1973 but that Gowon had been reluctant to proceed with them. Since then the officers concerned had been paid at the higher rates despite the fact that they had not been given the appropriate military rank. The commissioner recognised, however, that 'the political climate might militate against the promotions' and excused the failure to advance middle ranking and junior officers on the grounds that 'promotions are easily done for the highest grades in the officer corps but the middle and lower ranks always consitute a major exercise.'[60]

The Dimka coup

The Dimka *coup* of February 13, which saw the assassination of both the Head of State, Murtala Muhammed, and the military governor of Kwara State, Colonel Ibrahim Taiwo, and the detention, for a time, of the military governor of Bendel State, was poorly planned, badly coordinated, and scarcely coherent in execution. Despite the large number of subsequent arrests and condemnations, it seems to have had little organised support in the army and the government furnished no evidence of widespread backing elsewhere. In the event the *coup* was easily put down, but only after a delay of several hours—a fact which later occasioned some adverse comment.

The participants themselves offered various reasons for their action but the precise motivation for the *coup* remains obscure. Those entrusted with its execution, for the most part junior and middle ranking officers, seem to have been prompted mainly by fears regarding individual career prospects, inspired by the 'conversion' exercise; and the threat of demobilisation; by antipathy to the aggressively 'professional' approach of the new army commanders, which was translated into hostility to the so-called promotions exercise; and, in the case of Lt. Co. B. S. Dimka the officer most prominently associated with the *coup,* apparently by a combination of ambition, frustration and a (misguided) sense of public duty.

Lt. Col. Dimka, the inarticulate and somewhat unstable director of the Army Physical Training Corps, later maintained, when under arrest and awaiting a probable death sentence, that he had acted throughout at the instigation of Major-General Bissalla, with the connivance of the former governor of Benue-Plateau State, Joseph Gomwalk, and that his first meeting with Bissalla was prompted by a conversation he had had with General Gowon, in London, towards the end of 1975. Gowon, himself, has denied any complicity and Dimka's published testimony at the official inquiry leaves many important questions unanswered.

The *coup* apparently began as two quite distinct movements. The first was a conspiracy hatched in Kaduna in the course of the conversion exercise by three majors who had complained of the difficulty of the various tests conducted during the exercise. They were later joined by a somewhat larger body of junior officers. The second was a plot conceived in Lagos, and involving officers of the rank of Colonel and Lieutenant-Colonel who were stationed, for the most part, in the South. It was later alleged that Bissalla was the driving force behind this group to which Dimka became attached shortly after his return from London. As a 'link' man, Dimka was apparently expected to try and coordinate both movements. It is, however, possible that he attempted, on his own initiative and evidently with no great success, to extend their narrow base by hinting at support in higher quarters. There was also considerable, if often indirect, evidence of the ethnic character of the *coup*. Most of those subsequently sentenced for their part in the affair, notably Bissalla and Gomwalk, and others accused of complicity were drawn from the same or adjacent areas of the Middle Belt, notably Plateau State and Southern Zaria.

Although otherwise unsuccessful, the *coup* did revive—and in an acute form—tensions that had long been dormant in the country and would persist long after the event itself. Muhammed's death came close to precipitating riots in his home town of Kano, while there was widespread unrest throughout the far North, contained only by the strenuous efforts of local rulers, assisted by the military governors and politicians like Aminu Kano. Relations between the different communities were so strained that Yoruba students attending the university at Jos, in the Middle Belt, left the campus in a body and returned home. Prominent southern officers seem to have feared retaliatory action by northern soldiers on the pattern of July, 1966, and took similar evasive action. The *New Nigerian* expressed concern and alarm at 'the political instability of our society and the lowering of the *coup* threshold': the 're-emergence of violence in the political process' suggested that there was 'something wrong with us as a nation'.[61]

The unanimous acceptance of Obasanjo as Murtala Muhammed's successor and the appointment of Brigadier Shehu Yar'Adua, one of the principal instigators of the July *coup,* as Chief of Staff, guaranteed a certain continuity in administration. But the ethnic balance had been seriously disturbed. For the first time since independence there is now a Yoruba Head of State. Yar'Adua, although drawn from the far North, is a relatively junior officer first commissioned in 1964. Despite his recent promotion he is still—in that sense—junior to many of the officers now subordinate to him. Moreover, he does not enjoy anything like the status or the following which Muhammed commanded in the far northern area. After February, 1976, the Kaduna-based press continued to speak of a Muhammed-Obasanjo government, but it was Murtala's portrait that remained in administrative offices throughout much of the old North.[62]

Meanwhile Danjuma's control of the army was severely, if only temporarily shaken. Among the officers and soldiers held responsible for the abortive *coup,* and subsequently executed, was the Commissioner of Defence, Bissalla. He was so out of sympathy with the recent policies of the government, notably demobilisation and the promotions exercise, that he had offered to resign from the Supreme Military Council earlier in the year—when he had also complained of being effectively excluded from its deliberations. Bukar was likewise sentenced to death and the executions, when completed, marked the end of the Dimka affair—although there was always the possibility that they, too, might become a future source of unrest.

Having restored order in the country, the new government proceeded quickly to try to reconstitute its military base and, most important, to review existing security arrangements. The Inspector-General of Police, Muhammed Yusufu, who was blamed by some for inadequate security at the time of the Dimka *coup,* lost responsibility for the Special Branch.[63] Meanwhile, Abdullahi Mohammed was recalled to Military Headquarters, Lagos, and appointed to the Supreme Military Council as director of Military Intelligence with additional responsibility for police security. The strategically-located Lagos Garrison Organisation, re-constituted as the Fourth Infantry Division under the reorganisation programme, was completely reformed and given a new commander—as was the Brigade of Guards, responsible for security at Dodan Barracks.[64] Both appointments were made from a small, but increasingly important core of officers, graduates of Bida Middle School and for the most part Moslem. Already entrusted with important responsibilities by General Gowon in his last year of office, they were now promoted to some of the more sensitive positions in the army where they replaced other officers from the Middle Belt.[65]

The commanders of the three main divisions were unchanged while the composition of the Supreme Military Council was modified somewhat to accommodate alterations in the government. Of the other senior personnel, Brigadier Olu Bajowa, a Yoruba advanced by Gowon, remained as Quartermaster-General, and a far northern officer, Brigadier Abbas Wali, was recalled from London to become the new Adjutant-General. This last was a relatively junior appointment to an important post, indicating on the one hand a serious shortage of officers following the July *coup,* the subsequent purge, and the recent executions and retirements that concluded the Dimka affair, and on the other the willingness of the present regime, wherever possible, to promote able, middle ranking officers.[66]

Meanwhile commanders multiplied their appeals for order and discipline, and special tribunals were created to try those accused of disloyal conduct.[67] The Chief of Army Staff warned that, in such cases, the courts would no longer accept a plea that the defendant was 'obeying the orders of a superior officer'.[68] To* avoid further controversy over promotions, the Army Council was re-constituted, while comparable bodies were established for the other services. By this means the government was able, in May, 1976, to confirm the promotion of 691 officers, mainly in the middle and junior ranks.[69]

Reorganisation of the army proceeded apace with a determined effort to accelerate the construction of barracks—even when it meant substituting foreign for Nigerian contractors.[70] Twenty new barracks were promised for the end of August, 1976, with another seven to be completed before the new year.[71] The administration was evidently aware that, as the *New Nigerian* had previously warned, the joker in the pack is still the barracks programme. All soldiers must be accommodated in barracks by 1979 when the government hands over power to civilians.[72] The re-training programme was also stepped up, particularly for those commissioned from the ranks during the civil war but without the necessary formal qualifications. Even more senior officers, who had not received training abroad, were now eligible for the Army Command and Staff College, whose first distinguished, if somewhat reluctant intake included two military governors.[73] Established at Jaji, near Kaduna, with assistance from the British government, the creation of the college had been approved by General Gowon before the 1975 *coup*.

But the importance of demobilisation as a factor in the Dimka *coup* was suggested in the brief statement, made at the end of July, 1976, by the new Chief of Staff, Yar'Adua, who finally announced that 'there would be no outright demobilisation in the popular sense.'[74] Such were the sentiments aroused by the abortive scheme that, on several occasions later in the year, troops had to be assured by their commanding officers that their deployment in the *Operation Feed the Nation* was in no way connected with demobilisation.[75] The same promise was given to a brigade of infantry at Enugu, before they were replaced by a detachment of the armoured corps as part of the reorganisation programme which includes the establishment of a ring of mobile brigades stationed at Enugu, Bauchi, Gusau and Ilorin, under the tight control and close supervision of the divisional commanders.

It was a much more modest operation that Danjuma outlined at Benin in April, 1977, following the discharge, the previous month, of five thousand ex-servicemen, who had re-enlisted during the civil war.

They would be followed, shortly, by ten thousand disabled veterans. The exercise would be supplemented by a scheme for voluntary retirement, similar to the one Gowon had proposed, with generous financial incentives, and the entire exercise would be completed by the middle of 1978.[76] The government now seemed resigned to keeping the army at a reduced but none the less substantial level until the hand-over to civilians in 1979. There is more recent evidence, however, that the commanders are themselves anxious for further large reductions before returning to barracks. There is the statement to that effect by the GOC, Third Infantry Division, Emmanuel Abisoye, together with the documentation exercise (military census) carried out within the army, and the implied criticism of certain aspects of the re-habilitation programme by the Chief of Army Staff.[77] Some army commanders may even be considering postponing the date for civilian rule so as to be able to complete the demobilisation exercise on their own responsibility. If it is not completed there would be the disturbing prospect of very limited recruitment for the foreseeable future and greatly restricted opportunities for promotion, particularly in the junior grades.

Conclusion

In office General Gowon had maintained a complex balance of interests which enabled him to achieve a broad measure of political agreement among his supporters, both during and after the civil war. By similar means he was able to revive morale and discipline in an army almost broken by the events of 1966 and completely re-cast during the subsequent military campaign. By recalling his commanders to a sense of national duty, by upholding the principle of seniority and by insisting on respect for existing military structures, Gowon did much to alleviate the crippling ethnic tensions, regional animosities, sectional rivalries and personal jealousies so much in evidence at the outset of his rule.

Furthermore, by emphasising the professional aspects of military service, by rewarding efficiency and achievement and by remaining sensitive to the views and aspirations of the junior officers and other ranks, Gowon was able, for a time, successfully to insulate the army from the divisive pressures and the often de-moralising routine of day-to-day administration. Only a tiny percentage of the officers were entrusted with political responsibilities in what was nevertheless considered a military regime. Initially this was a source of considerable stability but, as dissatisfaction with the government grew, following the civil war, so, too, did contradictory demands from within the army itself. There were demands for greater military participation on the one hand, complete military withdrawal on the other, and support, notably among the Middle Belt commanders, for a form of dyarchy.

In these circumstances, Gowon's decision, announced in October, 1974, to postpone civil rule indefinitely and to prolong the life of the existing regime, had the unexpected effect of uniting most of his military critics and facilitating his removal the following year. In January, 1975, the army abandoned its low-profile to participate more fully in government in the hope of recovering its former popularity or, at least, preventing any further decline in its prestige.

Its representatives in the administration found themselves exposed, almost at once, to mounting political and social pressures that could no longer easily be contained—particularly in the context of an ailing economy, beset by inflation and widespread labour unrest. These pressures, the rapid deterioration in the public image of the army, and the growing divisions within the military, itself, were all momentarily resolved by the *coup* of July, 1975, and the decision of the new military administration to return to barracks in 1979. The military character and the energetic and efficient approach of the new rulers was widely appreciated. The large-scale purge of public employees undertaken by the new regime was immediately popular with most sections of the army and in the country as a whole. But there was a price to be paid for the sweeping and unexpected changes that followed the July *coup*.

The enforced removal of Gowon, the compulsory retirement of the most senior officers, the rapid elevation of the new Chief of Army Staff, and the appointment of many young and middle ranking officers to senior posts in government and the armed forces, all tended to erode the corporate unity of the army. The promotions exercise, overlapping as it did an ill-timed and badly-presented programme of army retrenchment, found the commanders and the leaders of the new administration occupying an extremely exposed and delicate position. Ethnic tensions, service rivalries and personal animosities began once more to surface at every level of the army hierarchy.

The Dimka *coup,* which superficially resembled the Lieutenant Arthur *coup* in Ghana, opened up a far more serious situation, for it upset the long-standing but delicate balance within the military leadership that had persisted even after Gowon's removal. There was no officer from the far North of sufficient stature and seniority to replace Murtala Muhammed and counter-balance the succession of a Yoruba as Head of State. The situation in the country after the *coup* at once recalled the critical events of 1966, as tension quickly mounted in the North and elsewhere, particularly between the Hausa and Yoruba communities. However, once it was clear to the northern elites that the attempted *coup* was not, as they initially suspected, engineered in the South, and that they would continue to be represented in the government at the highest level, then no effort was spared by them in an endeavour to contain the unrest in the North and to avoid incidents that would almost certainly have ended in violence.

It was in these circumstances that blame began to be attached to Gowon. The former Head of State has denied any knowledge of the affair while the military government has formally requested his return to Nigeria to expedite its own inquiries. From the vehemence of his critics and the nature of the subsequent campaign for his 'extradition' it is possible, however, to see Gowon as a scapegoat, providing a convenient (because absent) target for the pent-up fears and frustrations of the Nigerian elites in a renewed period of crisis— aggravated by the more general sense of insecurity in the country as a whole. The condemnation of Gowon and the elevation of Muhammed to the status of a national hero served in various ways to legitimise the new administration and helped counter the initial tendency to see Muhammed's removal as the outcome of ethnic forces. Earlier suspicions of Yoruba complicity in the Dimka *coup* were thereby removed. The Middle Belt leaders, closest to Gowon in the past, were able not only to dissociate themselves entirely from Dimka but also to repudiate their old attachment to Gowon. Moreover, the northern elites, embarrassed by their abrupt changes of attitude shortly after the abortive *coup,* could now direct their resentment elsewhere and were the more easily reconciled to an administration in which they no longer supplied the leading figure but wanted to strengthen their position in the critical period before the return to civilian rule. Meanwhile the attack on the British High Commissioner in Lagos, because of alleged delay on his part in advising the authorities of Dimka's visit on the morning of the *coup,* was intended, perhaps, to answer criticisms that the military leaders might themselves have acted more promptly in suppressing the *coup.*

In one sense the Dimka *coup* probably facilitated a quick return to civilian rule. The new and openly reluctant leadership was eager to quit the political arena as soon as practicable. With the assassination of Murtala Muhammed, however, regional and ethnic rivalries that had remained latent re-appeared in an acute form and, although subsequently allayed, have since persisted. In this respect Gowon, as a member of the tiny Angas community, was better insulated than either of his successors both from ethnic pressures and the conflicts of loyalty that they engender, and from the more corrosive effects of the regional stereotypes that abound in Nigerian debate. The present administration is certainly more exposed to accusations of the kind that have long bedevilled Nigerian politics, especially those that arise from the long-standing rivalry between North and South. Conversely, the present leadership is also under much greater pressure than was Gowon to relinquish office in accordance with their timetable.

Within the military other pressures, not necessarily ethnic or regional in character, have been building up around the now apparently inseparable questions of civil rule and army reorganisation. The commanders themselves appear increasingly reluctant to concede the first without securing a definite commitment regarding the second. There is even discussion of delaying civilian rule to permit the completion of the reorganisation programme. Despite the retirement, promotion or secondment of many senior and middle ranking officers, there are growing demands from below for more rapid promotions and for greater participation by the junior officers in the key military and administrative posts.

Having relieved much of the pressure that had accumulated in the middle echelons of the army during the long tenure of the Gowon administration, the present military leaders are now compelled to look again at the sensitive issue of demobilisation as a means of reviving an increasingly senile army, of restoring mobility to its ranks, and of introducing greater flexibility into the fairly rigid career patterns, notably in the junior ranks.

It has been argued, among others by the present Chief of Army Staff, that civil rule without army reorganisation is unlikely to be stable or enduring. Thus the *New Nigerian,* which had welcomed the unequivocal commitment of the new regime to civil rule, later reminded its readers that the army had been in power for a considerable time during which it had 'to a very large extent shaped the nation's destiny and wielded a lot of influence.'

> To assume, therefore, as some are apt to do, that the influence of the military will simply peter out immediately they quit the stage for a popularly-elected government, is simply to live in a cloudcuckoo land. The implication of a prolonged military rule is that demilitarisation becomes highly problematic.[78]

To forestall a return to power by the military the newspaper preferred the creation of formal channels of communication between military leaders and the civilian executive, rather than an experiment in dyarchy. The establishment of a National Security Council and of a Defence Council would do much to help 'prevent the suspicion that may otherwise characterise relations between the military and the civilians.' Even more important, 'the Ministry of Defence should keep senior military officers fully in touch with the thinking in government circles and seek their views.' The object was, hopefully, to create a climate of mutual trust and confidence.

Since then the same newspaper has expressed doubts about the competence of the politicians to conduct or even supervise the reorganisation of the Armed Forces. Accordingly, the *New Nigerian* insists that

> a condition of political stability in the post-1979 era is an arrangement under which the duly elected civilian government retains the present service chiefs for the express purpose of carrying through the on-going programme of reorganisation in the Armed Forces. [79]

Obansanjo's government has yet to admit that the programme of reorganisation, which remains a very contentious issue within the army, cannot be completed in the time originally allowed. But if this were to prove the case, a cruel dilemma might arise: whether it would be better to postpone civilian rule once again until the task had been completed or to acknowledge that it had become, almost by default, a responsibility of the incoming civilian government, with all the risks that this might then entail for future civil-military relations.

NOTES

The author is indebted to Professor James O'Connell for his invaluable comments on earlier drafts of this chapter.

1. For an interesting discussion of some of the problems of military withdrawal in a West African context see D. Austin and R. Luckham, *Politicians and Soldiers in Ghana, 1966–1972* (London, Cass, 1975).
2. *New Nigerian* (Kaduna), 14 Mar. 1973.
3. *Daily Times* (Lagos), 5 Dec. 1973 (Aminu Kano's request); *Daily Times,* 18 Dec. 1973 (Gowon's reply).
4. *Daily Times,* 18 Dec. 1973. Whatever regime emerged after 1976, Ayida was particularly concerned to defend the concept of an independent, non-partisan civil service.
5. *Sunday Times* (Lagos), 29 Oct. 1972. For a critique of Azikiwe's proposals see *New Nigerian,* 24 Oct. 1970 and 1 Nov. 1972.
6. T. Y. Danjuma succeeded two Yoruba commanders at the head of the Third Division, Benjamin Adekunle and Olusegun Obasanjo, while I. D. Bissalla and G. S. Jallo assumed command of the First and Second Divisions which had earlier been led by two officers from the far North, Mohammed Shuwa and Murtala Muhammed. Of the three divisions the second experienced most changes of command—Murtala Muhammed, Ibrahim Haruna, G. S. Jallo, and finally a Yoruba, James Oluleye. After the war Muhammed and Obasanjo returned to their specialist posting as Inspectors of Army Signals and Engineers, respectively while Adekunle and Shuwa were given assignments at Army Headquarters.
7. Murtala Muhammed was invited by Gowon to draw up new establishment levels for the army while Danjuma was apparently asked to submit recommendations on structure and staffing.
8. Olusegun Obansanjo, 'The Military as an Instrument of Modernisation,' Zaria, July 1972.
9. *New Nigerian,* 14 Feb. 1974.
10. At the end of the civil war Aminu Kano had urged the Federal Military Government not to be in too much haste to return power to civilians: 'let them first complete their plans which might take more or less than three years.' *Daily Times,* 2 Feb. 1970. Later he would maintain that 'the military is like a fire brigade' having extinguished the blaze 'they go back to their fire station'. *New Nigerian,* 26 Feb. 1974.
11. *New Nigerian,* 26 Apr. 1974 (Rotimi); *Daily Times,* 3 July 1967 (Kyari); *New Nigerian,* 31 May 1974 (Usman).
12. *New Nigerian,* 28 July 1973.
13. *New Nigerian,* 4 May 1974 (Ekpo); 15 June 1974 (Bajowa).
14 *New Nigerian,* 28 June 1974. At the end of the previous year Gowon had indicated: 'We must re-examine the Westminster model because of its shortcomings in the Nigerian situation.' *Nigerian Observer* (Benin), 4 Dec. 1973.
15. *New Nigerian,* 1 July 1974. No further attempt was made to involve Gowon in the debate and shortly afterwards General Ekpo resigned as Commandant of the Nigerian Defence Academy, to re-emerge in January, 1975, as Federal Commissioner of Agriculture.
16. *New Nigerian,* 22 Mar. 1974. The leaders of the Zambian army and air force are Ministers of State for Defence.

17. That, at least, was the account given in one newspaper. *New Nigerian,* 6 July 1973. According to another source Johnson also explained that the military were 'gentlemen who attached much importance to the dates they gave'. *Daily Times* 6 July 1973.
18. *New Nigerian,* 24 Jan. 1974.
19. *New Nigerian,* 24 Jan. 1974 (Danjuma); *Daily Times,* 4 Dec. 1973 (Bissalla); *New Nigerian,* 25 Dec. 1973 (Haruna).
20. *New Nigerian,* 25 Dec. 1973.
21. *Daily Times,* 2 Oct. 1974.
22. Three months after Murtala Muhammed had been appointed Commissioner of Communications he had been involved in a dispute with the Director-General of Posts and Telecommunications, T. O. Akindele. At first the Federal Public Service Commission supported the Director-General but later he was invited to proceed on leave. Akindele claimed that Muhammed deliberately flouted civil service procedures in trying to deal directly with subordinate officers in his department. *Daily Times,* 12 Nov. 1974; *New Nigerian,* 13 Nov. 1974.
23. By May, 1975, Gowon was again assuring journalists that the governors would be changed 'very soon', while defending them against their critics and recalling their services to the country during the civil war. In July he told a conference of RSMs that the governors would be removed before the end of the year; meanwhile they would remain at their posts until after the projected Royal Visit in October.
24. According to S. R. Bathish, the former Director of Works in North-West State, who was himself closely associated with the military governor, Usman Faruk, more contracts had been concluded in the past twelve months than in the whole of the previous six years. Believing they were to be replaced in January, 1975, the various governors had indulged in 'a free for all affair'; the period since September, 1974, had been 'a rush hour for awarding contracts.' *New Nigerian,* 23 Sept. 1975.
25. *New Nigerian,* 1 Jan. 1976.
26. *New Nigerian,* 2 Jan. 1976.
27. A total of 20 million metric tons was ordered in early 1975, 16m tons by the Ministry of Defence alone. The Third Development Plan had envisaged imports at around 2m per annum. Consumption of cement in Africa as a whole in 1974 was under 30m tons.
28. 'It is necessary to sound these notes of caution because the atmosphere has become perfectly foul in certain capitals since civil servants talk of new states and very little else.' *New Nigerian,* 26 Nov. 1974. The agitation was particularly acute in North-East, North-Central and North-West States, Benue-Plateau and South-East; it was also important in East-Central and Western States. See also Ch. 7.
29. *New Nigerian,* 5 Apr. 1975.
30. *New Nigerian,* 25 Sept. 1974.
31. *New Nigerian,* 24 May 1975. In April, 1975, the newspaper had been strongly attacked by the military governor, Abba Kyari, for publishing a composite photograph of officers attending a conference of Chiefs of Staff, GOCs and heads of departments and services, to discuss the training programme for the following year: the photograph showed mainly subordinate officers and was considered to be 'mischievous'.

32. *New Nigerian*, 26 July 1975. The newspaper headline read: '"Our Society is Sick", says Grand Khadi'. Murtala Muhammed later appointed Gumi chairman of the National Pilgrims' Board. One of the Khadi's complaints against Gowon had been the participation of non-Moslems in the organisation of the annual pilgrimage to Mecca. Towards the end of 1976 Gumi was to criticise strongly the federal government's proposals to allow women in the North to vote at the local government elections. *New Nigerian*, 11 Sept. 1976.
33. *New Nigerian*, 29 July 1975.
34. *Daily Times*, 29 July 1975, *New Nigerian*, 30 July 1975 (Danjuma); *Daily Times*, 9 June 1975 (Haruna); *New Nigerian*, 14 July 1975 (Bissalla). There is an unconfirmed story which suggests that the coup was originally timed for April 1975, following the announcement of details of the federal budget, but that Bissalla warned those involved that he was opposed to any such action while Gowon remained in Nigeria. It is claimed that the coup was then postponed until the Head of State was due to attend the Kampala conference of the O.A.U.
35. *Daily Times*, 29 July 1975; also reported later in *Nigerian Herald* (Ilorin), 15 Feb 1976.
36. *Nigeria Today*, No. 70, July 1976; Daily Times, 1 June 1970.
37. Ayida retired as secretary to the Federal Military Government in April, 1977, when he was replaced by Liman Ciroma, a northerner from Fika emirate, which has recently provided several distinguished federal administrators.
38. Besides Garba and Abdullahi Mohammed, whose promotions have already been noted, Lieutenant-Colonel Ibrahim Babangida became director of the new armoured corps division comprising the former Recce squadrons; Lieutenant-Colonel Paul Tarfa became Provost Marshal-General and was responsible, under Danjuma, for the 'clean up' campaign in the four divisions of the army—after which he was entrusted with an exercise, *Operation Ease the Traffic*, designed to reduce congestion in Lagos City; as Federal Commissioner for Transport, Yar'Adua was himself responsible for dealing with the problem of port congestion in Lagos harbour, until his appointment as Chief of Staff, Supreme Headquarters. Others whose participation in the planning and execution of the coup is not certain include Lieutenant-Colonel Muhammadu Buhari, a Katsinawa, like Yar'Adua. Previously director of Supply and Transport, he was appointed military governor of North-East State to supervise its division into three separate states, and was then recalled to Lagos where he was co-opted on to the Supreme Military Council and appointed Federal Commissioner for Petroleum and Energy.
39. In the creation of new states it is interesting to note that Danjuma's own division of Wukari—where the Jukun and Tiv were old enemies—was removed from Benue State and attached to Gongola State in the far North. There had been a similar situation in 1967 when Muhammadu Yusuf was instrumental in securing the creation of North-Central State by insisting that his native province of Katsina be attached to the much smaller province of Zaria, in preference to either Kano or Sokoto.
40. *New Nigerian*, 22 Nov. 1975.
41. *Daily Times*, 20 Sept. 1975.
42. *New Nigerian*, 2 Oct. 1975.
43. *Daily Times*, 22 Nov. 1975.
44. *Daily Times*, 20 Aug. 1975 (Bissalla).
45. *Daily Times*, 18 Oct. 1975.

46. *New Nigerian,* 30 Oct. 1975.
47. *New Nigerian,* 12 Dec. 1975. In the future army 'we may be thinking of about 100,000 soldiers.'
48. *New Nigerian,* 25 Aug. 1975 (Obasanjo); 2 Oct. 1975 (Muhammed).
49. *Daily Times,* 9 Oct. 1975.
50. *New Nigerian,* 27 Oct. 1975.
51. *Daily Times,* 13 Jan. 1976; *New Nigerian,* 13 Jan. 1976; also *Sunday Times,* 18 Jan. 1976.
52. *Nigerian Tribune* (Ilorin), 17 Mar. 1976.
53. *New Nigerian,* 29 Oct. 1975.
54. *New Nigerian,* 2 Jan. 1976.
55. *New Nigerian,* 26 Jan. 1976 (ex-servicemen), 31 Jan. 1976 (Bissalla).
56. *New Nigerian,* 9 June 1976.
57. *Daily Times,* 28 Nov. 1975.
58. *New Nigerian,* 13 Jan. 1976.
59. *New Nigerian,* 19 Jan. 1976.
60. *New Nigerian,* 26 Jan. 1976.
61. *New Nigerian,* 25 Feb. 1976.
62. The federal government has since issued legal tender bearing Muhammed's portraits: with this token of the country's recognition the government indicated that photographs of the late Head of State could now be removed from public offices.
63. *New Nigerian,* 18 May 1976.
64. Colonel M. I. Wushishi, GOC, Fourth Infantry Division; Colonel M. J. Vatsa, Commander, Brigade of Guards. *New Nigerian,* 16 Mar. 1976. It was announced in June, 1976, that the members of the Second Guards Battalion had staged a mass desertion (some 172 soldiers!) while on posting from Lagos to Gombe, in the North. They were at once dismissed by Danjuma with orders that they were not to be re-admitted. *Nigeria Today,* No. 69, June 1976.
65. Graduates of Bida Middle School formed an Old Boys' Association in January, 1974. They included Colonel Ibrahim Taiwo, Colonel M. I. Wushishi, Lieutenant-Colonel Mamman J. Vatsa, Lieutenant-Colonel G. A. Dada, Lieutenant-Colonel M. Magoro, Lieutenant-Colonel M. Ndakotsu and Captain S. Gamba.
66. *New Nigerian,* 16 Mar. 1976 (changes in Federal Executive Council and Council of States); 3 May 1976 (changes in Supreme Military Council); 23 Nov. 1976 (new Adjutant-General).
67. For appeals from senior officers for order and discipline see *New Nigerian,* 10 May 1976, 22 May 1976, 28 June 1976.
68. *New Nigerian,* 3 May 1976.
69. *New Nigerian,* 3 May 1976 (Army Council re-constituted); 10 May 1976 (promotions).
70. *New Nigerian,* 14 Aug. 1976.
71. *New Nigerian,* 31 July 1976.
72. *New Nigerian,* 8 May 1976.
73. 'We feel that the two military governors who were chosen to attend this course should, in fact, be grateful for being given the chance to do so.' (Danjuma) *New Nigerian,* 20 Nov. 1976. Three military governors were included in the subsequent course together with Ibrahim Babangida, a member of the Supreme Military Council and director of the Armoured Corps. It was later revealed that, following this second course, two Lieutenant-Colonels had been reduced in rank and

dismissed from the service for cheating in the examinations. In future the college will revert to its intended role: to provide a professional formation for middle ranking officers only.

74. *New Nigerian*, 31 July 1976.
75. *New Nigerian*, 21 July 1976, 9 Aug. 1976.
76. *New Nigerian*, 23 Mar. 1977; *West Africa* (London), 4 Apr. 1977.
77. According to Abisoye, 'in view of the current size of the Army it was imperative for the Federal Military Government to reduce it to a more manageable size.' He added that 'the Army of today is not like yesterday's when we had to beg people to join'. His division alone would lose some eight battalions. Nevertheless 'no single able-bodied soldier with fine qualities would be thrown out. Demobilisation is not a witch-hunting exercise and no soldier will be discharged forcibly.' This apparent contradiction is an indication of the dilemma confronting the army commanders. *New Nigerian*, 2 June 1977.
78. *New Nigerian*, 15 Oct. 1976.
79. *New Nigerian*, 28 May 1977.

4

Corrective Government: Military Rule in Perspective

M. J. Dent

In the study of military regimes much comment has been directed to the conscious or unconscious bias of the military, to their class and ethnic composition and other social or economic influences. It is also assumed that their declared goals in government are likely to be rationalisations of their power objectives. Furthermore it is assumed that in the case of third world countries most military structures are made up of so many selfish and warring factions that it is meaningless to talk of a conscious policy in government or a trusteeship relation to the civilian body politic.[1] Clearly there is some truth in this kind of analysis. Those with guns may impose themselves and act for purely selfish aims and there is always a danger that even a well-intentioned military will relapse into *usurpation or tyranny* (in the Aristotelian sense of the word), set up a Praetorian state directed solely to the interests of those in power, outstay its welcome and nullify all the healthy processes of the body politic.[2]

Military government in Nigeria can, however, only be properly understood if analysed from quite a different perspective. At least the officers had a clear view of their role as trustees of the body politic and when their leaders and military governors departed from that role they felt acute unease. Furthermore there was a general civilian expectation that the military would fulfil an ameliorative role of a limited duration for the sake of an improved civilian polity. The phrase most frequently and most aptly used to describe this particular role of military trusteeship is Corrective Military Government.

The Nigerian military failed to achieve any substantial measure of success in their goal of corrective government until the emergence of the regime headed by Murtala Mohammed after the overthrow of Gowon. The enormous respect, verging on adulation, for the memory of Mohammed thoughout Nigeria is a sure sign that, at least for the six months of his rule, Nigeria was set on the path of corrective government. Through the combination of skills and policies and of popular response which that delicate operation requires, Nigeria achieved a sense of national purpose and wellbeing. Even when one has discounted all those elements which spring from martyrdom, there still remains a large element of 'securus judicat orbis' (so universal an opinion must have a sound foundation). A year after the death of Mohammed his memory remains as strong as ever and is inseparably linked with the idea of Nigerian unity and a resurgence of national life. The standard which he set is used as a criterion to judge current performance. For example, students of Bayero College and the press recently criticised military governors who were said to have ignored the Mohammed mould of simplicity and accessibility and to have dug themselves in like the military princes of the Gowon era. The instinct which regards the Mohammed period as peculiarly creative and as the successful exercise of corrective military government is a sound one. It provides new insights into the typologies of military government in general.

Corrective Military Government is a distinct category. It comes under the genus of Military Trusteeship which contrasts with the corruptions of military power—Military Usurpation or Tyranny. All forms of military trusteeship assume a genuine role for military government vis-à-vis the civilian body politic. They differ however on a wide spectrum according to the degree of change which they seek to effect before restoring civilian control. Corrective Government occupies a middle position between Military Caretaker Government and Military Revolution.

The caretaker model takes as its purpose the mere maintenance of Government itself. It keeps the peace and carries out certain simple but essential processes for a return to civilian rule. The first military government in Ghana, the National Liberation Council (N.L.C.) was of this kind: Its self-appointed task was to wind up the remaining vestiges of the Nkrumah government which it had overthrown, to enquire publicly into the corrupt practices of that regime, to invite civilians to draw up a new constitution and to vest power once again in civilian hands, excluding however Nkrumah and his principal supporters. The N.L.C. did not seek to remedy any profound imbalances or structural defects in Ghanaian society, nor in any way to discipline the Ghanaian elite. Only in the field of finance did it seek to make profound changes by reimposing strict economy and classical profit considerations. The return of the military only two and half years after the restoration of civilian rule indicates that perhaps the N.C.L. should have adopted a more corrective approach rather than that of a mere military caretaker.

Oliver Cromwell, who from 1649 to 1658 had sought repeatedly but unsuccessfully to set up a new and stable equilibrium in English Government, concluded at the end of his life that he had been 'like the good constable of the parish', i.e. the classic caretaker of law and order.

A caretaker regime may, of course, be far shorter. The National Interim Council of Sierra Leone, which deposed Col. Juxon-Smith in 1968, handed over power within a matter of days to Siaka Stevens, the leader of the party deemed to have won the last election. The soldiers of the National Interim Council considered that it was not their business to seek to mould the body politic as Col. Juxon-Smith had tried to do. It was not that they were conservative but they regarded government as a matter for civilian politicians. Their action was a measure of military diffidence in civilian government. Indeed Juxon-Smith had been advised by several members of his National Reformation Council to hand over power to a civilian national government with all speed but 'Beberebe Power' (too much power), as he was mockingly nicknamed in Creole dialect, chose to embark on a regime of corrective government without, however, possessing the political skills or the popular support needed for such an exercise and so suffered ignominious arrest by his own private soldiers. [3]

An exaggerated belief on the part of the military in their unique qualifications to put right fundamental defects in the body politic may lead to a regime of the opposite kind, one of military revolution. Whereas the caretaker regime's mandate is to change little or nothing, the regime of military revolution seeks to alter the very fundamentals of political and social culture and to put new groups into permanent power. Essential to the success of this revolution is a profound change in national psychology, a new type of revolutionary man, who will be motivated by unselfishness and tireless dedication to the common cause. It is assumed that almost everything in the society is capable of

change and one lives in that heady euphoric spirit common to
revolutionaries in power in every age. Such a regime is prepared to use
a large measure of coercion and to invade the private sphere of life
whenever it considers it necessary in the interests of the revolution. It
considers itself to be at war with the 'enemies of the revolution' who
seek to perpetuate the old order and overthrow the new.

Often this kind of regime develops a civilian corps to match the
discipline of the military. The classic case is the People's Party set up by
Mustapha Kemal to carry forward side by side with the military the
coercive modernisation of Turkey but there are many other examples
of regimes which start with a military coup and then develop a
revolutionary party organisation.

Regimes of military revolution may run into profound difficulties,
through attempting to change too many things too rapidly and from
ignoring the attitudes of the broad masses of the people who are
divorced from the ideas of this radical elite. Furthermore, these regimes
may well become extremely fissiparous and unstable as we have seen in
Ethiopia, in Dahomey and in the early history of Portugal under the
armed forces movement.[4]

Midway between the two extremes of military caretakership and
military revolution is the type of military corrective government. This
has always been the broad aim of the vast majority of the Nigerian
military rulers and it found its most practical application during the six
month period of military rule under Murtala Mohammed. This sort of
regime does not assume that the whole of the political order has to be
changed and social and business relations turned upside down. It does,
however, take as its starting point the conviction, usually painfully
obvious to all at the time of the military coming to power, that the old
civilian order will not work because of certain profound deficiencies. In
the Nigerian case these deficiencies related to several distinct spheres:
malfunctioning of the Federal system owing to lack of national unity,
lack of national dynamism owing to inert administration, corruption
throughout national life, over-dependency on outsiders in foreign
affairs and lack of indigenisation in business, failings in the political
process through deficiencies in the Federal Constitution and in the
political class who operated it and excess elitism in many spheres.
These errors did not constitute the whole of Nigerian life. It was
assumed that at root its close-grained and traditional structure was still
sound and that despite the failures of the political process, Nigeria had
made real advances in modernisation up to 1966.

Only a small minority sought to change the existing system of private business interlocked with a considerable state sphere of economic activity, or to overthrow the traditional system of free individual access to land through membership of clan, tribal or local groups. The myth of the Nigerian revolution as part of the general African Revolution had been a leading train of thought among the intelligentsia ever since Azikwe's book *Renascent Africa* in which he had tried to rally 'young Africa' and 'new Africa' against 'imperialism and old Africa' in the early days of the nationalist movement. Peter Enahoro in his superbly humorous sketches on 'How to be a Nigerian' neatly captured the ethos of this 'fifth estate'. 'There is', he wrote, 'something colourful about the progressives which has delighted adoring Nigerians for a long time. For example, no other section of the community has had so many conflicts with the authorities as have the progressives, who clearly have no ambitions for power and only would like to take office away from successive authorities'.[5] Nigerian society was open and ebullient, sophisticated and urbane. Highest among the inheritances of colonial rule it cherished the 'sacred right to grumble', but few really wanted to change the fabric of social life which on the whole suited people well. When the Sardauna wrote in his autobiography of the 'need to preserve the old decencies' he spoke for many who did not share his conservative political views.[6] It is indeed a paradox of Nigerian political culture that a general desire for change coexists with a profoundly conservative local culture. James O'Connell has related a most interesting story of a distinguished Ibo Professor, who went back from Ibadan in early 1967 and tried to speak to his clansmen at Nimmo of the desperate plight of the Eastern Region. He found them, however, concerned with the task of building a village hall worthy of their community. When he at length managed to interrupt their lengthy discussions, he was told to be silent, for the affairs of Nimmo were more important. It had been there from the beginning and would last throughout the ages whereas no one knew what would happen to the Eastern Region. In the long run the conservatism of the villagers proved more realistic than the modern perspectives of the Professor.

It was the object of the military, therefore, to develop Nigeria economically, socially and politically but to develop without destroying its previous identity. Their task was in their own eyes partly one of restoration of the Nigerian polity to the proper path of development from which it had begun to stray since 1960.

In one sense this was a task of reform and civilian regimes have often produced reforms without losing the representative principle. They do this by one of two ways. Either by representing the desires of a large emergent body of opinion, that itself desires these reforms and expects to benefit from them, or by using its overall popularity from other issues to balance the temporary unpopularity from the necessary but harsh reforms which it has to introduce. The military regime is, however, corrective rather than reformist. That is to say, its style is one of military order rather than persuasion; although it seeks in general to retain the trust of the people, it insists that in particulars it is not responsible to public opinion and must act as an army commander acts in his unit, by orders issued firmly at his own discretion, according to military principles and coercively enforced if necessary. There was also a body of civilian opinion willing to welcome this headmasterly attitude. Tai Solarin, for instance, himself a disciplinarian headmaster, welcomed the original coup of January 1966 as a chance for national discipline, declaring that Nigeria was a nation of fifty-six million people on parade, awaiting the word of command from the General Officer Commanding.

There are, of course, dangers in the use of this sort of non-responsible government. It may seek to retain and exercise power for its own sake and become a regime of military usurpation as opposed to one of military trusteeship, the category to which caretaker, corrective or revolutionary government must belong. This element was continually to intrude in Nigerian military government (for instance in the attitude of the State governors towards the end of the Gowon regime) for no system is entirely pure. It was indeed only after the overthrow of Gowon that the purpose of corrective government became effectively dominant.

The difficulties experienced in the preceding nine years had been partly the result of a basic contradiction in the military ethos itself. It is based on obedience from inferior to superior. To prevent this from becoming mere exploitation and oppression, it demands a corresponding ethic on the part of the officers, that this power is to be exercised for the purpose of their country and for the benefit of those under them in preference to their own benefit. I well remember the emotion with which as a cadet in the Indian Army at Military Academy, Dehra Dun, I used to read the words cut in stone on the Chetwood Hall.

'The honour, safety and welfare of your country comes first always and every time.

The safety, welfare and comfort of your men comes next always and every time.

Your own welfare and safety comes last always and every time.' This is the ideal yet in practice armies often do not operate like this; the standards of the officers' mess take priority, the well-being of those at the top is thought to be the main purpose of the unit, the whole system becomes oriented towards the men at the top, and the conditions of military rule make this tendency doubly dangerous. The response to this kind of commanding is likewise a sharp departure from the ideal type of the obedient soldier, loyal to his unit and to his officers. An extreme example of this was provided by an old corporal arrested at the Niger bridge during the civil war for alleged desertion. The corporal was furious, not only because he claimed to have been on medical leave after a period of active service to go back to Kano, but because of the way he had been treated by his officers. 'Our British officers' he said were 'Yaron Iska (hooligans) but the present lot are even worse; just wait till I find the officer alone on a dark night'.[7] In the Nigerian army there were always examples of the opposite attitude to this, pockets of fine discipline and excellent command, but its morale and structure of loyalty had to be established and fought for, day by day, against the twin evils of insubordination from below and arrogant self regard from above. Often it reached that state condemned by General Dan Jumaa in his broadcast in 1976 when he stated that the army was corrupt, permeated by secret societies and protection rackets.[8] This meant that for the purposes of corrective government the correcting instrument itself was often gravely deficient. The whole army could not be the kind of educational institution for purpose of national development that it is in Israel, Switzerland and China.

The period prior to July 1975

For much of this period the army was overwhelmed by the very same forces that it had come in to remedy. It had intervened to secure unity, yet within a year of coming to power it had experienced a countercoup far more bloody than that by which it had originally come to power, and the country was divided into hostile camps unable to resist the descent into seccession and civil war. It had claimed to bring law and order and yet in the massacres of May and of September 1966 had failed to prevent violence at least as great as any occurring under civilian rule. It had intervened to clean Nigeria of corruption and yet the civil war into which it had led Nigeria resulted in a spate of corrupt practice, sweeping from arms procurement into all aspects of governmental activity, and for six years after the end of the war virtually no attempt was made to check it. In the 'Biafran' move to secession, there had been a suggestion that the revolt was not just against Nigeria as a political unit but against 'Nigerianism', the mixture of corruption and inefficiency at the top with which all Nigerians had become only too familiar. Among the lower levels on the secessionist side, the stresses of war and the cause to which the Biafrans were devoted did indeed produce discipline and dedication, but at the higher levels many behaved in exactly the same way as their counterparts on the Federal side, making large sums of money out of the contributions of their sacrificing fellow Biafrans. On the Federal side also the discipline and gallantry of officers and men in some units contrasted with incompetence or corruption in other parts of the war effort.[9]

After the war the military achieved a reconciliation, unequalled for its generosity in the annals of civil conflict. In this they were largely helped by the absence of a legislature. After the American Civil War it had been Congress under the implacable leadership of Thaddeus Stevens which had continued to wave the bloody shirt and hinder the process of 'binding up the nation's wounds'. Gowon had no such barrier in his successful attempts to impose his own generosity of spirit upon Federal thinking, in the task of reconciling those defeated in the civil war. This demonstrated the peculiar advantage of the military in moulding opinion. In contrast to their enormous hostility to each other before the war, the military now behaved as an institution more national in character than any other. During the civil war I remarked to Colonel Shuwa on the absence of any medals for the campaigns, only to be met with the admirable reply that in a war of brothers one could not give medals, since this would embarrass their present adversaries when they were reunited again into the brotherhood of fellow officers.[10]

The 'doctor's mandate' which the military had assumed to cure the ills of the body politic remained unfulfilled. The only treatment prescribed for the patient seemed to have been a prolonged period of compulsory abstention from self government, while the necessary decisions were taken by the bureaucracy and by the military. The tumultuous energies of the people were directed to the economic and social rather than political fields. They expressed themselves especially in business, but even in this field the dimension of irresponsible bureaucratic government was considerable. Neither in the field of local elective government, nor in that of corporate interest group representation in a responsible system, could Nigerians attain political fulfilment.

Authority both at the central and at the state level was essentially administrative, and was in many ways of the colonial type. Yet this system, tolerable if certain profound changes were being effected, was in fact almost fully devoted to maintaining the administration itself in being. At the central level the Government had lost the idea of its own limited time span and concentrated on self-perpetuation. At the state level, Governors like military princes ruled with more pomp and less responsibility than even British Governors in colonial days and seemed to prove irremovable. They had indeed almost entirely lost connection with the military or police bodies from which they had sprung, but to which they had apparently no intention of returning.

There seems to be a law of incompatibility between the imperatives of reform and those of the establishment of a permanent government. Those who are in power for a short time, and who have no immediate constituency, are ideally placed to effect change that is temporarily unpopular though beneficial in the long run. Even in a liberal democratic system this element is used for certain limited purposes to produce this kind of corrective change. When a British Government, for instance, wants to close down uneconomic but socially popular railway branch lines, it commissions a non-representative figure such as Beeching to produce a report. Many an unpopular but necessary reform will be preceded by a Royal Commission report, not merely because the Commission is thought to be expert, but because being non-political, temporary and without a constituency, it can afford to be ruthless in a way which is more difficult for the Minister. The secret of this kind of action is that the unpopular authority is outside the system and, having no permanent position to maintain, does not have to worry about making friends and avoiding enemies. But once let him have a permanent position in the system to maintain and he will normally become far less ruthless in corrective action. In military regimes this becomes even more the case. If the military authority reckons to be in power for only a short time, it can afford to act with decision; if it is seeking to perpetuate itself, it acts in a far more circumspect manner and loses those very qualities of military promptness and precision that are its real justification in military corrective government. Furthermore, the authority, whose mandate for continuance in office rests on the inability of the political actors to function in a civilian system on their own, has a vested interest in keeping the body politic sick as long as possible in order to perpetuate its own stay in office.

During the Gowon regime the record was, in general, one of a doctor of the body politic that would neither proceed with the cure of the patient nor let him out of the enforced stay in the hospital of military government. It was small wonder that, at the end of the period of Gowon government, a general mood of revolt had spread, taking occasion from individual cases and grievances to challenge implicitly the government itself.

The divisions of the political leaders were one of the main reasons for military government. Yet under Gowon, several of them were co-opted to the cabinet but given no tutelage in unity, no responsibility for working out the conditions for a more unified return to civilian rule. Indeed the momentum for such a return had been totally lost and the civilian figures, progressively bereft of political power, became courtiers to the military or else secret encouragers of opposition to government. It is almost a truism that those without responsibility behave irresponsibly. Certainly this was the case of the Nigerian political figures when faced with the clear administrative muddle of the 1973 census. Their quarrels were taken as a reason not for firm military tuition in the politics of unity, but rather for the indefinite abandonment of the idea of the return to civilian rule.[11] The dangerous evocations of the old antagonisms between North and South, which began to appear in the crisis over the census, were themselves a reflection on the failure of the military to attain an organic as opposed to a purely administrative unity. In this sense the military were in a position analogous to that of a colonial power preparing a country for self government. The true justification of its policy (as Mill declared to a committee on the government of India in the 1850's), would be found if it rendered itself superfluous in the shortest possible time. Unfortunately, a policy of preparing the body politic for self-government becomes all too easily a policy of 'divide et impera' should those in power feel in any way threatened.

In some matters the Gowon government did take steps for national unity. After a level of administrative mismanagement and failure to consult that caused a student strike, it did eventually succeed in launching the youth service corps and in making it work. In finance it was able to change the system of revenue allocation so that the revenue from oil was more equitably distributed among all the states, a reform facilitated by the fact that the two main oil producing states, Midwest and Rivers, had been manifestly dependent upon federal soldiers for the expulsion of the Biafran army during the civil war.[12] Beyond the sphere of conscious government action, a process of nation building was indeed taking place during the Gowon period. The common participation in rapid economic development of infrastructure made possible by oil revenue, and the thriving and thrusting business life in which the private sector operated, often with government assistance or dependent upon government contracts, created a sense of common community. The 'Pax Nigeriana' that was re-established so quickly after the civil war was itself to some extent a unifying factor. But all this was without the conscious corrective action of Government.

At the end of his period of rule, Gowon seemed to reach almost total paralysis. There is a curious sense in which at the end of the periods of rule of Abubakar, of Ironsi and of Gowon the outer limbs of the body politic seemed to be beyond the power of the centre to control. The nerves and motor power proved too weak. There was no lack of ideas and of good counsel, but actually to decide upon and implement a course of action with resolution seemed beyond the power of Government. Issue after issue was just swept under the carpet.[13] The census, clearly unacceptable because of its extraordinary differentials in growth rates, was neither abandoned nor fully affirmed. The contentious issue of the creation of states was raised and discussed but no formal machinery was set up to consult and prepare the way for a decisive military decree. The location of the capital came increasingly in question, but no group of experts was commissioned to produce definitive reports on which to base a firm decision.[14] The Udoji report did result in much needed pay increases for the lower levels and also for those with high-level responsibility. But those in the middle ranks were curiously neglected, and as experience was to show they were a potent influence of political discontent. Moreover, the inflation released by the Udoji awards and by the removal of import restrictions on a whole host of goods reached fifty per cent in a few months. Government had taken no effective measure to insure an increased supply of goods to meet the increased demand.

Government at state level moved from the sphere of corrective trusteeship to what one can only describe as personal usurpation. There was a principle of instability in the uncontrolled and personal rule of State Governors, since all the representational aspects of government were absent and they were responsible only to their superiors. Government was by lobby and edict. The only remedy would have been the rapid transfer of Governors. In the military style of operation the absence of control from below must be compensated for by firm and effective control from above. This was conspicuously absent under Gowon. It is curious that an officer, who had consistently attained the grade of 'outstanding' in his confidential reports under British Army officers should have proved so poor a disciplinarian.[15] It seems likely that when Gowon found himself unable to halt the enormous tide of corruption that flowed into central and state government during the civil war, he lost heart and eventually allowed himself, somewhat unwillingly, to be drawn into some doubtful practices.[16] On the Supreme Military Council the Governors commanded a majority and were not slow to gang up if their collective interests were threatened.

The extent of general disaffection with many aspects of the Gowon government is illustrated by the case of Mr. Aper Aku who denounced the corruptions of Gomwalk, Governor of Benue-Plateau State. The bulk of his information was clearly supplied by civil servants discontented with their master; when Gomwalk finally decided to arrest Aku and detain him, the police contrived to fail to find him for several weeks thus giving Aku a vital opportunity to reach the Magistrate's Court in Jos and swear an affidavit as to Gomwalk's corruption. Clearly there must have been considerable sympathy in high places with his cause in that the *New Nigerian* and *Daily Times* both of which were in fact subject to fairly effective informal censorship of items to which government objected, gave great prominence to Aku's denunciation which they quoted in full. The *Daily Times* had given similar prominence to Dabo's denunciation of Tarka, a Federal Commissioner.

There is a saying of Burke that 'tyranny is a weed that grows in every soil'. Its presence needs no special explanation, once the inhibiting factors are removed. We must not suppose that the twelve individuals chosen as State Governors were anything other than a good cross section of the military, police and academic elite when appointed; indeed Mohammed Abdullahi, the new Governor of Benue-Plateau State, once described how when he was first appointed Governor in 1967 Gomwalk was the hero of younger officers like himself, and many civil servants in Benue-Plateau have told how simple, straightforward and enthusiastic Gomwalk was in the first year or so of his administration.[17] The fault was surely in the system rather than in the individuals. The Governors were allowed to become military princes rather than being 'men under authority', obeying military orders for the good of the community. The behaviour of the Governors conformed as one might have expected to the truth of the Tiv proverb of political wisdom: 'Uwar Tsen Swem Hure (Left to itself the river of power flows crooked).' In extreme cases of irresponsible Government there is a kind of mould of rottenness that has great similarities even in very different political systems. The actions of the extraordinary fraud 'Doctor' O and his role in Jos correspond with uncanny similarity to those of Rasputin in Tsarist Russia. Introduced to Jos by a local businessman-cum-politician, O started by claiming to be able to treat Governor Gomwalk's physical ailments by electric shock treatment. He went on to amass a strange collection of electronic gadgetry which he used to make forecasts and assessments for the Governor. Not surprisingly these corresponded to Gomwalk's own prejudices. He eventually seems to have had a great influence and patronage in state affairs. One of his more lucrative creations was the company known as 'VOTENINSKI' (vote for us the sky is the limit with modern technology) which had on its board many people close to the Governor and which received numerous state Government contracts and advances, but appeared to be totally incapable of completing any work at all. The main purpose of the company seems to have been to syphen off state funds into private pockets; and after the overthrow of Gowon it was wound up and its assets were seized.

The existence of this level of corruption, in a state controlled by a member of Gowon's own Angas tribe, and Gowon's failure to take any action to investigate or to correct it, even when Aku's denunciations had made some of the corruptions of the Governor public knowledge, greatly weakened the respect in which Gowon was held as a man of unquestioned integrity.[18] Eventually the middle and upper ranks of the officer corps could no longer stand this situation. They sent two highly respected members of the Supreme Military Council to warn Gowon to mend his ways but without effect.

The Murtala Mohammed Government

The coup that removed Gowon commanded general support, in the army and in the civilian population. Only one army commander mobilised his unit in Gowon's favour, but his action came too late.[19]

After some discussion, lasting for almost twelve hours after the coup, Brigadier Murtala Mohammed, an old opponent of Gowon, was asked to become Head of State. He was associated in an informal triumvirate with Brigadier Obasanjo as Chief of Staff Supreme Headquarters and Brigadier Dan Jumaa as Chief of Staff Army. Dan Jumaa, an extremely effective though sometimes ruthless officer from Takum in Benue, ensured the necessary military support. He had in the early years been very close to Gowon but had finally become disillusioned.[20] The intellectual background to the regime was supplied by Obasanjo, a graduate in engineering, and also by sympathetic civil servants, especially the late Yusufu Gobir, a most able civil servant, who had been passed over by Gowon for the headship of the civil service, and who seems to have had a considerable hand in the genesis of the coup and in the formation of its corrective policies.[21]

Mohammed provided much of the driving force and also contrived to keep contact with the people, through an extremely simple and informal style of official life. He had the rare quality of being a man of action, and in earlier years had tended to act in a headlong way without discretion.[22] The Mohammed who came to power in 1975 was very different from the precipitate young turk of ten years earlier who, chafing at Gowon's peacemaking initiatives, had wanted immediately to attack and settle scores with Ojukwu. The importance of the ability to ensure action cannot be overstressed in the Nigerian context. So often those in authority start with good ideas but find that objections, sheer inertia and multiple preoccupations inhibit action. 'There are many men' Cromwell once said 'wiser than we, but not many who know how to act, therefore we must do what is needed to save the commonwealth'.

For the first time Nigeria experienced genuine corrective government. Issue after issue which had been pending for the last six years was taken up, enquired into systematically, and dealt with effectively by decree or administrative action. The old Governors were removed and enquiries began into their corrupt practices. In due course it was discovered that ten of the twelve had misappropriated a total of ten million Naira, which they were ordered to repay. The new Governors were acting in a very different role. They were all military figures on a military posting, clearly responsible to Obasanjo as Chief of Staff Headquarters and removable if they failed in their duties. Indeed within two weeks of appointment; one of them was replaced for insufficient determination in his governorship. The Governors no

longer discussed their collective affairs with the Head of State in the
Supreme Military Council but in a more subordinate body, the Council
of States. In the course of interviews with two of the Governors, Col.
Mohammed Abdullahi of Benue-Plateau State and Col. Atom Kpera
of East-Central State, I was able to observe their crisp and fresh
approach. They lacked that pomposity in·office so common among
those who regard themselves as irremovable and irresponsible officials.
Like a good military commander in a battle, both Governors kept
themselves relatively uncluttered with detail. They operated from
separate command headquarters removed from the state civil service
and had material pre-processed so that they could concentrate on the
essentials of corrective government. Both faced the potential danger
that fellow tribesmen from their states of origin would attempt to take
advantage of their new powers of patronage and both effectively
resisted this pressure. Both built up genuine reputations for honesty in
the States which they ruled.

The new administration announced its intention to purge corrupt
officers from every branch of government activity and gave an example
by proceeding to purge the army itself. The purge then spread to the
police, the civil service at Federal and State levels, the statutory
corporations, the universities, and all other governmental institutions.
It had hitherto been almost unknown for people in high positions to be
dismissed for corruption; the worst to be feared was a posting
elsewhere. No Federal Commissioners or Permanent Secretaries had
ever been dismissed for corruption. The only Commissioner ever to
have resigned from office after an allegation of corruption was Tarka
but there was no official enquiry and his guilt was neither established
nor disproved. A fair number of State Commissioners had been
replaced from time to time but it was impossible to distinguish cases of
corruption from the much more common instances of disagreement
with dictatorial governors or simple changes in personnel. At the lower
levels some disciplinary action had of course been taken but the process
was desultory and gravely impeded by the fact that those responsible
for taking action were themselves in need of discipline.

Once the new regime had declared its intention of instituting a purge
of corrupt officers and had itself named those removed from the top
echelon, authorities at lower levels caught the spirit of the purge.
Indeed in many cases they produced far more names for dismissal than
the State Governors and others wished. In Benue-Plateau State for
instance, the Executive Council produced a very long list and the

Governor had to remind them that he did not wish to cause unnecessary suffering but only to remove the comparatively few officers who were either notoriously corrupt or unproductive. The former were dismissed; the latter, the so-called 'deadwoods', were retired with benefits.

This kind of corrective government was a most delicate operation depending on careful balance. The extent of executive power used for the purge and for structural reform was carefully balanced against the firm promise of its short duration and of a return thereafter to representative government. Likewise the power exercised by Mohammed personally was balanced by a collegiate style of government. The new Supreme Military Council had in it an element of a 'council of the army' (through the presence of twelve designated officers of middle rank) to represent the desire for reform of the officer corps as well as its commanders. The formidable powers vested in Mohammed were rendered tolerable by his populist style of power without pomposity. He dispensed with the vast escorts and security precautions that had cluttered the style of both Gowon and Ironsi Governments. He was easily accessible in the Dodon barracks and drove almost unescorted in his own Mercedes. Ultimately he was to pay with his life for this trust of the people but it was a visible token of identification with ordinary people and won him great support. One may contrast it with the pomposity of the style of Juxon-Smith and see in it part of the reason for the acceptance of Mohammed's corrective rule and the humiliating rejection of that of the Sierra Leone leader

The changes which the Government sought to effect were of the utmost importance and it had chosen its priorities correctly but they were balanced by a sensible conservatism in other matters. For instance the honoured traditional role of chiefs was again emphasised in contrast to the uncultured and hectoring attitude to these father figures of many young Governors of the Gowon regime. As one close to the Wali family in one of the greatest of Northern emirates this respect came naturally to Mohammed and he strictly enjoined it upon his Governors.

In the enforcement of reform emphasis was laid where it was most needed, upon honest and energetic administration, upon structural reform and on building national unity. In the developing world the most important contrast is often not between left and right but between institutions and arms of government that work and those that do not The innovation of the new government was not so much to create new institutions (although some innovations such as the ombudsman were made) but to infuse the existing ones with the necessary energy.

The reforms and the purge were in contrast to purges carried out in the past in that they did not represent the triumph of one party or faction over its opponent. The Muffet commission which in 1962 had probed the corruption of Kano Native Authority was not appointed solely in the cause of honest administration but was also a manifestation of the Sardauna's rivalry with the Emir of Kano, itself a continuation of the long historical conflict between Sokoto and Kano. Likewise the Coker Commission which had enquired in 1962 into the corruption of Statutory Corporations in the Western Region was a means used by the new UPP (later NNDP) administration to highlight offences on the part of its opponents in the Action Group. After the military coup of 1966 the misdeeds of the NNDP leaders were in turn the subject of enquiry by Col. Fajuyi who had been appointed Governor of the Region and whose sympathies lay with the AG. Mohammed's purge was different. It partook of that essential quality for effective military action in a corrective or 'suprapolitical' role, and as such the purges met with an all-Nigerian acceptance.[23] Mohammed did not allow himself to be influenced by his own close family connections with Inuwa Wada, former Minister of Defence in the Federal Government and a representative of the N.P.C. old guard. Indeed it might at first sight seem paradoxical that Mohammed who was the most aristocratic in background of Nigeria's heads of government should have been the man to take the most radical reforming action and to be identified with the progressive cause. In fact there is a simple explanation. Mohammed's social background allowed him to take firm decisions and avoid compromise unlike his predecessor who had to rule by cautious consensus.[24]

The Mohammed government kept the rules of good government. It did not make change for change's sake but concentrated on those that were necessary and could be made to stick; it sought to unite and not to divide the nation and it did not use any total blue print for society. In an open society such as Nigeria this kind of piecemeal social engineering, directed to an agreed national purpose, was more relevant than a rigid or utopian blueprint. The regime was free from the rhetoric of right or left and valued above all its capacity to act rather than to talk. It did however during the course of its corrective actions generate an energy that won the support of 'progressives' and created some of the excitement and sense of purpose often associated with revolutions.

Perhaps 'the left' in Nigeria regarded the Mohammed government as a military preliminary to a more consciously socialist civilian successor regime, and after Mohammed's death Ikoku and other Marxists paid especial reverence to his memory in the 'national mourners association'.[25] But during his period of government the Mohammed Government 'froze' as it were the issues of left and right and paid no attention to the rival claims of private enterprise and of socialism, for in this sphere its policy was pragmatic. Furthermore if one examines the class basis of the beneficiaries and victims of the Mohammed purges one can find no correlation. The Government was to acquire a favourable reputation as a 'poor man's government' but this was because the abuse of office is, in a rural society with reasonably free and equal access to land, the chief source of inequality.

The regime conducted a purge that was wholesale in volume but much less than revolutionary in severity, and a detailed examination shows the nice balance that was maintained, always on the edge of the corrective and never quite going over into the revolutionary.

A few close associates of Gowon were retired, for instance Edwin Ogbu, the able Nigerian representative at U.N. and Suke Kolo the High Commissioner in Great Britain. Ayida, a most competent civil servant promoted by Gowon as head of the civil service but unpopular for having designated himself as a 'Super Permsec', continued as head of the civil service without, however, the same access as of right to the Supreme Military Council meetings. The senior army officers above Mohammed's own rank were retired, as were those of the navy and air force, but they received their full benefits and all honour. Indeed so upset were the new regime at reports that Gowon had been protested against by students at Warwick, and at the pictures of him lining up with a student's lunch tray at the refectory, that they sent Dan Jumaa, who had always been closest to Gowon, to see him and ask him to come back with all honour to Nigeria (though of course without governmental power). When Gowon refused, and insisted on continuing his academic course, the military government decided to pay him not only his full pension but also a substantial monthly sum through the High Commission. These payments only ceased when the Obasanjo Government became convinced of prima facie evidence linking him to the February 1976 abortive coup, in which Mohammed was murdered. Hassan was particularly respected by the officers who had made the coup and was offered the Chairmanship of the N.N.O.C. but refused it, preferring to remain in contented retirement.

Lower down in the ranks of the army many officers were dismissed or retired. The exercise of sifting through the list to distinguish the efficient from the inefficient and corrupt was done with speed but also with care. Many of those dismissed had been extremely lax in their duties in the past, some had been involved in large scale financial corruption and others had been absent from their units without reason, for long periods.

The Inspector Generalship of the police was conferred upon Alhaji M. D. Yusufu on the retirement of Kem Salem. As head of the special branch under Ironsi and Gowon, M. D. Yusufu had always been an influence for honest government and for the preservation of the conditions of freedom to which Nigeria was accustomed. A purge of corrupt and inefficient police officers now followed. One hundred and fifteen were dismissed or retired.[26]

The senior Federal Civil service were also purged. Five Permanent Secretaries and one Deputy Permanent Secretary were retired, as was the Chairman of the Federal Public Service Commission, Alhaji Sule Katagum, who had held the post for over a decade and came from the same sort of Muslim Northern background as Mohammed himself. His replacement by an Ibo was a significant move not only because the post itself is perhaps the most influential of all in terms of potential patronage but also because there were no suitable senior Ibo officers available for appointment as State Governor (one was appointed when the seven additional states were created in February 1976). By making an Ibo, Prof Ogan, Chairman of the P.S.C. and another, Dan Ibekwe, Attorney General, Mohammed did a great deal to convince the Ibo people, who during the civil war had regarded him with some fear as a young turk, that he was indeed acting with fairness in the interests of all Nigeria.

At the State level the new Governors replaced nearly all the Commissioners. Many of the top officials were purged presumably on the advice of the remaining senior civil servants in Lagos, who had a shrewd idea as to who were honest and who were not. Below that level, the purging seems to have been left to individual State Governors and their Executive Councils. In some exceptional cases elements of personal vendetta occurred and in others there was an element of arbitrariness.

The purge extended right down to the lower ranks of the civil service and resulted in some 10,000 being dismissed or retired. It affected also all the public corporations and the universities. Several Vice-

Chancellors were replaced, including one dismissed because of 'conduct unbecoming in an academic'—an allusion to his considerable connections with business interests. At Ibadan University, out of some 300 people affected, only six were academics but the number was higher in other Universities where the Students' Unions had supplied the Military Government with lists of staff considered to be slack in their teaching duties.

In carrying out the purge, the authorities could in many cases make use of reports in personal files and in audit reports, many of the audit queries having been left unanswered for years. In other cases they were assisted by the numerous committees which Federal and State Governments set up to investigate particular scandals. They could also draw on police files. If none of these sources of information was available then the Government relied on the general knowledge which is readily available in a small community of face to face relationships with a habit of prolonged discussion of public personalities and issues. The procedure was certainly rough and ready, a little reminiscent of the original idea of the jury, where the 'twelve good men and true' were chosen, not because of their ability to hear and assess evidence but because of their knowledge of the character of the accused. The results were not always perfect, but on the whole the Mohammed purge seems to have been accepted as reasonably well directed.

The whole operation took some four months and at the end the Military Government had to assure the people that the purge was over. Although there was to be a continuing strictness in standards, and disciplinary action taken against any who fall below these standards, the wholesale exercise of clearing away the accumulated corruption of the last fifteen years was over. Indeed, so fearful were the military that it might have gone too far in some areas, that they appointed the senior and respected Chaplain of the army, Colonel Martins, to see if any army officers had been unfairly treated. He eventually recommended that it would be fairer to allow those dismissed to be retired on pension.[27]

The exercise caused a level of deprivation to a number of people and to their dependants but it had none of the vicious overtones of revolutionary liquidations or wholesale expropriations in a revolutionary context. So many people were involved that in the typical Nigerian manner, it became something of a joke, as well as a tragedy. For instance, in the Ibadan University children's pantomime put on by the University staff, when the two 'doctors', who had unsuccessfully tried to cure the sleeping princess, were 'Dismissed Without Benefit' the whole audience broke into laughter. In view of the fact that those convicted of armed robbery had been shot in public, and some 400 had been shot in the six years since the end of the civil war, those who had enriched themselves by official corruption rather than by threat of violence were escaping with relatively minor punishment: it was a corrective rather than a revolutionary measure.

Some Nigerians, including a number of State Governors and a number of left wing commentators, made this comparison and demanded that the former Governors and others guilty of large scale corruption should be shot. Fortunately, the Military Government ignored this advice; indeed they probably erred on the side of leniency by declining to place any restrictions on the movement of the former Governors. In Nigeria, once a person has been a 'big man', he is always to some extent a 'big man' in popular esteem. The former Governors were all men with a grievance and potential centres of effective discontent; one of them, Gomwalk, was to prove a most important conspirator in the attempted coup of February, 1976, after which he was tried and shot.

In putting emphasis on the eradication of corruption in official business as the most important of all their corrective measures, the Military Government were clearly reflecting the opinion of Nigerians in general. To the rural masses of Nigeria the word for oppression and the word for official abuse of office are almost the same; for instance, in Hausa both would be translated by 'Zalunci'. The system has for a long time been one in which a man became rich because he had political or official power, rather than vice versa. The word in Hausa for poor man, 'talaka', is exactly the same as the word for a man without office. A basic equality was assured by equal access to the soil in one's area of origin, by the state marketing of cash crops at fixed prices and by the growing of food crops for subsistence or sale in local markets; any inequalities of an excessive sort sprang from the corruption of those in power. There was no sense of the whole system being oppressive. However corrupt the actual official, the Governor, Chief or District Head might be, there was still the strong image of the 'good ruler', who would operate within the existing system, but operate honestly. In terms of cash income the farmers had enjoyed an almost 100% increase through a change in marketing board policy in the last two years of the Gowon regime. For the first time the farmers were actually paid at a level equal to world market price, less essential expenses of buying and marketing, instead of being forced to finance 'development' and corruption through marketing board surpluses.[28]

Only in the West had farmers risen in revolt, in the Agbekoya movement they had protested against the high level of taxation and possibly also against the more commercially stratified agricultural sector in the West, with its great inequality of land holdings.[29] Curiously enough the movement seems to have arisen partly in revolt against the official farmers' union, which Bola Ige, an elite Ibadan lawyer of ideological left wing views, had tried to set up when Commissioner for Agriculture in the Western Government under Adebayo. The protest in the West was also essentially populist rather than revolutionary, and by the time of the end of the Gowon regime had totally subsided.

At the end of the Gowon period there did seem to be some danger that the new elite might be getting their hands on the people's farms, as well as on their tax and oil money. For instance, Audu Bako, Governor of Kano, had acquired two very large farms as private property; Ogbemudia in the Mid West had acquired ten or twelve small estates. The corrective measures resulted in Government taking most of these farms away from the two former Governors.

In the urban sector there is clearly the potential for great class conflict, and revolutionary potential. The growing number of wage labourers are almost all without property, living accommodation is extremely short and controlled by landlords who evade the rent control of the military government. The variation in income between rich and poor is greater than in more developed countries. But the existing system is safeguarded by two important factors. Ties of kinship and extended family usually provide a rich or influential protector and helper for the poorer workers. The numerous class of 'applicants' are only enabled to live by the socially compulsory assistance of their richer tribesmen, who will often even keep them as non-paying guests in their houses for long periods. Second, the business world is still fairly fluid and everyone has the expectation of trading and making a profit Nigerians have a reputation as a nation of businessmen; from the cook to the Governor, from the farmer to the General, from the messenger to the professor or lawyer, almost every Nigerian seems to be longing to launch out on his own on the seas of commerce. Even in Moscow Nigerian students are those who offend most frequently against Soviet laws prohibiting profit making trade.[30] If the world of business were to become dominated by a few large operators, limiting entry for others, the system itself would indeed come under challenge. This danger had begun to arise with the establishment of businesses by those making important Government decisions on contracts and licences or by those with privileged access to such persons. Under the Asika administration, for instance, regular contractors and businessmen had publicly complained that they could not compete against businesses run by the Permanent Secretaries. Commissioners at Federal and State level were also often associated with businesses of their own, as were the former State Governors and many senior officers, including some who were themselves members of Mohammed's Government. The new reforms did something to reduce this connection, but have failed to make a complete severance.

In assessing the effectiveness of the clean up, one must distinguish between short and long term results. In the short term the shock to existing practices of corruption was great and salutary. Whereas contracts had almost invariably in the past involved substantial kick backs and had often depended chiefly on the connections of the contractor, a real element of objectivity now entered the process.[31] The personal performance of public officials improved enormously, people arrived on time, worked harder and spent less time on private business. In the long term one must be more doubtful whether the mere fear of being purged will be a sufficient motive to effect a permanent change. Perhaps the most that any Government can do is to prohibit the grosser forms of corruption, and to produce a jolt from time to time. The achievement of more total honesty requires the growth of a new ethic, or a change in the whole style of society. The exhortations appearing in the Nigerian newspapers 'Be proud, be patriotic, don't give or take bribes,' may not be enough to change fundamental attitudes and Nigerian society is too involved in the period of 'unbridled capitalism', the frantic pursuit of wealth in business for conspicuous consumption, to be deterred from corruption by anything other than an equally powerful force. In this, the most central field of corrective government, the military had achieved a real but partial success.

There is indeed a danger of these measures proving counterproductive, unless joined to a more powerful deterrent. The military have rarely taken away the assets of corrupt figures. The strong Federal intervention in the Lakumi case in 1967, in which the Federal Military Government passed a decree which retrospectively validated a Western Region edict, under which a former politician's assets had been seized, and which prohibited all further litigation on the subject despite the contrary ruling of the Western Supreme Court, opened a path to the seizing of the assets of the corrupt. But the process required Federal as opposed to State action. The Attorney General of Benue Plateau State explained to me how in the seizing of the assets of Voteninski they had to be very careful to get the Federal Government to act for the State otherwise the State Government was in danger of being overruled in the courts. Assets have been seized from the former State Governors and in the Voteninski case, but for the most part the prizes of office have been left with the corrupt beneficiaries. The danger now arises that in future those with an inclination to corruption when in office will make a real killing while the going is good, so that like the corrupt steward in the Bible, they can provide adequately for their future after their dismissal. The experience of former administrative officers (like the author), when carrying out purges on corruption at the local level, tended to be like that of a zealous gardener removing the weeds from his little plot. After a great deal of hard work, the weeds seemed to have been rooted out one by one and the land was clean, but a few months later the weeds of corruption had come in again, and grown almost as tall, either from seed from outside, or from new growth from roots in the plot itself.

The attack on corruption was part of a general emphasis on the ordinary man as against the big officials. It was much less than a full social revolution but was a real change in emphasis towards populism. One instance of this was the creation of the Public Complaints Commissions at Federal and State levels to hear complaints and deal with them in a simple and effective manner. Maitama Sule, appointed the Chief Federal Commissioner, clearly took his task extremely seriously. He assured me that he had a higher law even than the Constitution to which to work and that this law lay in his Koran, as in my Bible; it is the law of hearing the complaints of the poor and doing equal justice to all. Maitama Sule has a legitimate political interest in success, since he has a great potential political future after the return to civilian rule, and a genuine reputation as a tribune of the people is a great asset in such a career. He has reported difficulties in obtaining answers to his enquiries and has been unable to deal with complaints made against members of the Armed Forces and Police, as these are outside his jurisdiction.[32] He and his fellow ombudsmen at State level have however achieved real success in bringing justice to underprivileged complaints.

The Government lost no time in dealing with two outstanding questions concerning the political structure of Nigeria; the creation of additional States and the resiting of the capital. Both were handled with an admirable mixture of the three elements of popular consultation, expert opinion, and decisive military action. The creation of twelve States under Gowon had been carried out on the eve of the secession of the East and in the knowledge that that secession was imminent. It was an essential measure in the context of the approaching confrontation so that the secession could be seen not as that of the whole Eastern Region against the North but as that of a majority in one State trying to secede from a federation of twelve. Gowon's state creation was necessary surgery, but it was rough surgery. There had been no consultation, the units were dramatically unequal in size, and in at least two cases proved to involve forced marriages of incompatible partners. The creation had been announced as being a temporary measure to be refined later by boundary adjustments and the creation of new states. But despite the destabilizing effects of uncertainty nothing was actually done until the Mohammed Government appointed a five-man advisory committee to hear evidence all over Nigeria and make recommendations to the Supreme Military Council which took the decision in early February to increase the number of States to nineteen. The States were made more equal in size and in some cases entities hitherto regarded as sacrosanct were divided.[33]

Simultaneously the Government dealt with the second issue, the question of resiting the capital. Many were in favour of moving it nearer the centre of Nigeria but inertia and vested interests prevented action, while more and more money was poured into the overcrowded and constricted city of Lagos in a vain attempt to cope with the twin functions of being both administrative and commercial capital of Nigeria. Again acting on the advice of a committee, which visited potential sites and new capitals abroad such as Islamabad and Brazilia, the Government designated a virgin site near Abuja. The completion of a capital city could take many years and the Government will have to begin the work of construction in the near future if they are to avoid loss of credibility. The Tanzanian case of Dodoma shows that it is possible for a Government to decide on the site of a new capital but, by doing nothing to implement the decision, to lose credibility.

The contentious census issue was put temporarily into abeyance by a firm decision to reject the 1973 census and to work for the time being

on the 1963 figures. This decision was a demonstration of political
strength since it rejected figures favourable to the North. Only
Mohammed had sufficient status as a Northerner to persuade
Northern notables that this was a necessity.

In the field of local government, after a decade of unsettling and
largely ineffective changes, it was decided to undertake a systematic
but conservative reform.[34] The kind of situation that had been allowed
to develop may be illustrated by reference to the Tiv. Police, prisons
and courts had been removed from the control of the Native
Authorities in the North (redesignated as 'local authorities' to denote
their change in role and status). The new courts worked only
moderately well and in Tiv areas they acquired a reputation for
considerable corruption. The transfer of jurisdiction over land cases to
them from traditional authorities resulted in a rash of land disputes
and in minor clashes, which in former times had usually been settled
satisfactorily at the level of clan and kindred heads without the
intervention of formal government authorities. The divorce of the
police from local control and the posting of policemen to areas other
than their local area had advantages for the building up of national
sentiment and the avoidance of local discrimination; for the more
prosaic task of catching thieves, however, it proved a distinct
disadvantage.

Moreover, under the Gowon Government, State Governors had
often behaved with uncultured rudeness towards the Chiefs in their
Provinces. This was resented and often resulted in tacit resistance. The
Tor Tiv, for instance, became convinced, as did most other Tiv people,
that the Governor's prime purpose was to divide the Tiv people the
more easily to dominate them. On one celebrated occasion, addressing
Gomwalk in Tiv through an interpreter, he told the Governor that he
was trying to divide the Tiv people and was behaving like a politician.
Tor Tiv acquired considerable popularity as a champion of his people.
When Col Mohammed Abdullahi was appointed by Mohammed to
succeed Gomwalk as Governor he saluted Tor Tiv smartly, introduced
himself as the new Governor and soon established a quite different
kind of relationship, one of mutual trust.

The conservative reaction of the majority of the Tiv people to a
period of ceaseless administrative change was to ask for the 'Jir Tamen'
the 'Great Judgment' to be restored. This great institution of Tiv
government had been introduced by the British in the 1940's and
involved a two-week meeting of all the seven hundred clan and kindred

heads of Tiv and of the 'five fathers' of the intermediate areas. It sat as both the supreme council and the supreme court of the whole land of Tiv. It had been a dignified as well as an effective part of the political system, each chief arriving with his dancers and his band. It had provided a great spectacle and talking point to all Tiv, where the art of Tiv oratory was practised and where the District Officer, the Tor Tiv and the Resident had spoken in dialogue to the Tiv people. This institution had been suspended by Gomwalk in 1971 when he divided the former Tiv division into three. The Mohammed Government very sensibly extended the process to create six divisions in Tiv land, but at the same time returned to some of the old Tiv institutions, the old clan areas, as a basis for the Jir Tamen. This was a welcome relief to the Tiv who looked for a principle of stability, having suffered from too many changes and counterchanges. 'We are continually making changes in administration, to persuade ourselves that we are thereby making progress' wrote Petronius of the Roman Empire of the second century AD and the same fallacy had been all too common in Nigeria. Mohammed's Government had the sense to realise that some reforms are non-functional and are made just for the sake of change, while others are of real use, and it was on these that Government concentrated, while allowing stability in other fields.

In December 1975 a conference in Kaduna considered a Federal Government proposal for a uniform system of local government throughout Nigeria. Several State Permanent Secretaries for Local Government insisted on the right of local areas to preserve their own peculiar local institutions and the result was a sensible compromise, providing for elected local government authorities controlling areas of a size between 150,000 and 800,000 people but allowing traditional authorities to participate in the councils. In the Tiv areas elections to these councils were marred by a number of procedural irregularities but viable and prestigious authorities with full-time Chairmen have been established in each of the six Divisions.

The most important step in a return to civilian rule was taken by the creation of a constitutional commission and a firm promise to return power to civilians in 1979. Unlike the Gowon promise of civilian rule in 1976, this seems to carry credence. There are no stated preconditions, other than the creation of the necessary institutions for ensuring representative and accountable government. Correction by constitutional provision may not, however, be as effective as correction by military decree.

In foreign affairs the Mohammed Government was at its most socialist. It is of course a commonplace of political analysis that there need be no exact fit between the level of ideology in internal policy and the attitude to ideological conflicts abroad. In the Angolan civil war the corrective regime of Mohammed gave full support to the revolutionary regime of the MPLA. This corresponded to the general expectation of the Nigerian elite that in so doing Nigeria was supporting the 'progressive' side against the reactionary. I remember the ardent interest and pleasure with which a very senior official, himself far from being a communist, was listening in his house to the news of MPLA victories, an enthusiasm clearly shared by those present. The stinging rebuke with which Mohammed replied to the rather patronising letter circulated by the United States to African Heads of State in this issue earned the Mohammed Government greatly increased support as a spiritual defender of Africa against South African and American intervention. There was no corresponding feeling against the Cuban initiative.

In trade union affairs the Nigerian Government took even-handed corrective action to deal with the warring factions of left and right. The trade union movement was chronically divided on grounds of personality and ambition and this was further aggravated by a relationship of clientage to rival international trade union organisations and the receipt of considerable sums of money from these external patrons. The Military Government decreed that there should be a single overall labour organisation. This insistence that Nigerian trade unionists should stand on their own feet was reinforced by a commission of enquiry into trade union finances and a strict prohibition on receipt of any money from outside the country. Its report resulted, a year after Mohammed's death, in the banning from all trade union activity of the three established leaders, Immoudu, Bassey and Wahab Goodluck, the protégé of Moscow. The Government no doubt hopes that, with the old guard removed, a new and more responsible leadership will emerge but the authoritarian code of conduct produced by Abiodun, the Government supervisor of trade union affairs, has provoked great criticism.

The combination of a firm decision to give up power in a period of three years with an equally firm decision to act with vigour to make the necessary reforms during the three years' period has been the strength of the Military Government, both before and after the death of Mohammed. For the first time under Mohammed and his successors

Nigeria has had a decisive Government commanding real popular support. It was considered to have done more in six months than previous Governments in ten years.

The assassination of Mohammed

The degree of support for the Government was demonstrated by the wave of popular anger that greeted the abortive coup of February 1976, in which Mohammed lost his life.

Any reform, however acceptable to society at large, will create powerful enemies if it affects the interests of established groups. In the civilian sphere there were numbers of dismissed officials, formerly men of great influence, who had reason to hate the Mohammed Government. Just as the dispossessed politicians were a threat to the Ironsi Government in 1966 so were the victims of the Mohammed purge in 1976.

This source of discontent coincided with that of sections of the army. There were three dissatisfied groups. The overthrow of every Head of Government in the history of Nigeria has left a feeling among those from his home area that they also have been dispossessed of a privilege. In the case of the overthrow of Gowon there was a nucleus of discontent from the Plateau-Southern Zaria area, although some officers from this area were ardent supporters of the change, eg Garba, commander of the Federal guard at the time of the coup, who became Commissioner for Foreign Affairs under Mohammed. Secondly there were those who had expected to benefit from the coup by personal promotion but had been disappointed. Most notable among these was Major-General Bissalla, the fourth most senior man in the Military Government, whose role seems to have been that of planning, supporting and blessing the coup without actually taking part in its operation.

Finally there were those who feared for their posts because of the Government's commendable decision to cut down the swollen numbers of the unproductive army. Nigeria, almost alone among the countries of the world, had twice as many soldiers as teachers, as Professor Dudley had complained in his inaugural lecture at Ibadan. Moreover, its relations with the civilian population were, at times, marred by acts of lawless violence.[35] On coming to power the new Government had bravely decided that it would reduce the size of the army by planned stages; this involved a 'conversion course' to weed out officers who were not of high quality. The resentment it aroused seems to have been the original factor leading to plans for a coup. Discontent among some majors against the colonels had already led to abortive plans for a coup on Christmas eve but this had been nipped in the bud and those concerned had been dealt with without any publicity. The coup of 13th February seems to have been unconnected with this; it apparently involved a number of disparate groups (including those affected by the conversion course) who, on learning of one another's existence, came together in a loose coalition under the leadership of Bissalla. According to the allegations of Dimka, (who was captured and interrogated after the coup) the plotters also obtained the blessing of Gowon in exile, who had put them in touch with Bissalla. If Gowon knew of the murderous intentions of the plotters he could not honourably have acquiesced, since the coup against himself had been deliberately bloodless. The murder of all three leading members of the Government seems to have been intended, in particular that of Dan Jumaa. Murtala Mohammed was killed when his unescorted car was intercepted in heavy traffic. After a brief occupation of the National Broadcasting Corporation in Lagos and an extemporised visit to the British High Commissioner by Dimka in an attempt to get a message to Gowon (a request which the High Commissioner refused) the coup makers were quickly overthrown by forces loyal to the Government. The overwhelming majority came from Plateau and Southern Zaria though some high ranking and distinguished soldiers such as Colonel Isa Bukar came from other areas of the North. Bissalla's wife was the sister of Helen Gomwalk, former Director of Voteninski, who appear to have been the courier for the coup, according to the evidence released in the subsequent trials. Thus it appears that the coup, while it had specific army roots, was not unconnected with the clean up policies of the Mohammed Government. Bissalla also claimed that 'the Government had become Communist.' This was patently an excuse for a reaction against the Government's policy of support for the MPLA.

With the murder of Mohammed the cause of corrective government acquired a martyr to set the seal upon its reforms; from this time onward Nigerian history had undergone an irreversible change. Succeeding Governments, whether military or civilian, might reneg on the new principles, administration might temporarily slip back into the old ways, but a new factor had been introduced into the political equation, that of a determined nationwide public opinion aware that higher standards are possible, as under Mohammed, and determined to consolidate the gains of this period. A new pattern of thought had been created and the enormous veneration of Mohammed's memory indicated that it had wide and continuing national support.

We must not think of the period of corrective government as one in which the natural 'goodies' take over from the 'baddies'. Rather it is a general change of attitude to the task of government. Mohammed and his coadjutors had themselves all been field commanders in the civil war and the attitude of field commanders to spoils of war had often been robust rather than meticulous. Mohammed himself is said to have quietly made restitution of certain properties. If this is so, he may well have been acting as a devoted Muslim from a family with a long religious tradition as much as from political motives, purging himself before releasing 'reformation in a flood' upon the public services of Nigeria.

After Mohammed's death, Obasanjo succeeded to the headship of the Federal Military Government, while his place as Chief of Defence Staff was taken by Yar' Adua from Katsina. Dan Jumaa continued as Army Chief of Staff. The new Head of State was at pains to assure Nigerians that there would be no change in policy, that the Government was still Mohammed's team and that much of the inspiration for the achievements of the Mohammed period had come from their collective enterprise. The coup makers were nearly all captured and tried; some fifty people were executed, mostly army officers, including Major-General Bissalla and many colonels and majors. In this drastic action, which probably in the heat of the moment erred on the side of severity, the Government was showing its abhorrence of the murder of Mohammed and trying to put an end once and for all to the fissiparous and conspiratorial tendency which had logged the military. The Nigerian officer corps had indeed paid a high price for the dangerous burden of office. Of the 300 or so officers with regular commissions in January 1966, something like 60 have been killed by their brother officers in the course of carrying out coups or executed following unsuccessful coups.

In the interests of the integrity of their own corporation and in the fulfilment of their corrective duty to the nation, the Obasanjo Government has carried on with the task of handing power back to an elected civilian authority. Local government elections were duly held in December 1976, the draft constitution published for general discussion and preparations begun for the election of the constituent assembly. The draft constitution contains no provision whatever for military participation in government except for the presence of the heads of the

Armed Services on the National Defence Council, a normal feature o
any civil constitution. The President could possibly be a military ma
who has resigned to contest the elections and some military men coul
be appointed to sensitive ministerial posts such as Minister fo
Defence. But this is not incompatible with accepted constitutiona
practice. Dan Jumaa in a recent after dinner address to the Britis
Chiefs of Staff spoke of the army 'giving up its self-imposed task' an
handing back power to civilians. All the signs are that by the end o
1979 it will have done this.

It remains to be seen how the gains of the period of correctiv
government will be maintained. Some feared a lapse under Obasanjo
He is a more intellectual and more cautious leader than Mohamme
but appears to have stuck to the same policy. The purge was alread
over before the death of Mohammed and it was necessary that it shoul
be succeeded by a period of consolidation. To continue to purge at tha
wholesale level would have decimated the civil service and destroye
morale. That humorous but penetrating work *Parkinson's Law* has
chapter on 'Injelititis' which admirably fits the Nigerian dilemma. Thi
disease of administrative structures based on a mixture o
incompetence and jealousy, reinforced by smugness and acceptance o
the second best as the norm, can produce totally moribund an
unproductive organisations. Lacking all power to cure themselves
they can only be reformed from outside and by injecting two attitude:
one that 'the best is scarcely good enough' and the other that excuse
for corruption and inefficiency cannot be tolerated. Parkinson suggest
that the latter attitude is 'drawn from the bloodstream of regiment
sergeant majors' (one might add colonels and others who have traine
at Sandhurst under RSMs). However this injection cannot be applie
repeatedly. After the initial shock a more permanent cure is needed, th
introduction of new and healthy blood drawn from a similar organism

In the Nigerian case the maintenance of higher standards depend
partly on an alert public opinion able to detect and to criticis
corruption and incompetence, without being so over-vehement as t
interfere with all administration. Aper Aku, now recognised as a ma
of great courage and integrity for his role in the denunciation c
Gomwalk, holds that ·those like himself must still be alert i
denouncing corruption wherever it occurs, since the present leadershi
is no more immune from the danger of temptations than any othe
government.[36] The spirit of the reform has to be consciously kept aliv
The element of fear released by the impact of the purge naturall

subsided as the purge came to an end; it needs urgently to be replaced by an inner socialisation to honest and efficient behaviour springing from high morale.

Government on its part maintained the momentum by exhortation, by warnings of continued disciplinary action and (in March 1977) by replacing several Federal Commissioners.

The question remains as to how far the civilians will maintain the gains of this period. The experience of the Turkish democratic party under Menderes shows the dangers that a civilian regime may forget the duty of maintaining the gains made under military rule and thus in due course themselves fall victim to a further coup by the enraged military. The free expression and representation of opinion under civilian rule will unfreeze the class antagonisms and polarities of left and right. Indeed this has begun to happen already. The vociferous debate on the constitution has unleashed ideological and sectional forces which had previously been concealed by the national consensus under Mohammed and held in check by the disciplined debate and compromise of the draft constitution. The degree of class formation in the urban and business sectors is such that one may expect a major theme of politics to be in the future the conflict between left and right. The present conflict between landlords and tenants is an indication of this potential hostility. Such a possibility is an inevitable concomitant of the open party competition on which Nigeria has embarked as part of her quest for freedom. But the politicians may too easily assume a false optimism and fail to realise that conscious effort and specific conventions will be necessary if the political system is not to slip back into the old ways of corruption, muddle and division. If they should begin to lose the gains of corrective government they will meet two forces, on the one hand a hostile public opinion and on the other an army which might feel tempted to repeat the dose of corrective government. As Dan Jumaa warned in 1974, 'If we (soldiers) continue to say that we are not politically inclined, we will be deceiving ourselves. That the soldier is no longer ruling does not mean that he is blind to whatsoever is happening about him.'

NOTES

1. See for instance the argument in Decalo, S. *Coups and army rule in Africa: Studies in military style.* New Haven 1976.
2. The theme of the praetorian state has been admirably developed by David Rappoport in his chapter 'A comparative theory of Military and Political types' in *Changing Patterns of Military Politics.* (ed. S. P. Huntington) New York 1962.

3. See Cox T. *Civil Military relations in Sierra Leone* (London 1976) I am indebted for this account to a Sierra Leone informant who was in Freetown at the time. The nickname Beberebe derives from the Fanti word for 'very much' or 'too much.'

4. Regimes of communist party rule have also been established by the action of the army as in China and Cuba, but in such cases, although the leaders of the civilian regime are often the same as those who commanded the armies in the struggle for power, it is the firm dictum of Communist policy that 'The party controls the gun and not the gun the party.' Army leaders are but the armed wing of the political movement and are subject to its control. Where specifically military regimes have been established they are jealous of any independent civilian mass party even though both their own ideology and that of the mass party may be equally left wing. This has been admirably shown in S. E. Finer's article 'The Mind of the Military', (*New Society* 7 August 1975 pp 297–99). Where the military and not the party command the revolution, its progress is fraught with difficulties.

5. Peter Enahoro 'How to be a Nigerian' Daily Times Publication (Caxton Press).

6. Alhaji Sir Ahmadu Bello *My Life* Cambridge 1962 p 227.

7. Incident observed personally, December 1975.

8. Daily Times February 1976.

9. For instance in the middle of the civil war, Alhaji Yusufu Gobir, Permanent Secretary Ministry of Defence, complained that the war would have been over already but for corruption in the ordering of army supplies. This was hotly denied in an equally public statement by Atta, Permanent Secretary Ministry of Finance, but Yusufu Gobir's assertion was not without foundation.

10. Interview with Col. Shuwa, Enugu 1968. In an interview with Gowon I commented on this admirable attitude, and was told that a suggestion, made to the Officers Association that medals should be given for gallantry in the civil war, had very wisely been rejected for the reasons which Col. Shuwa gave.

11. These events are admirably dealt with in Ian Campbell, *Nigeria: Prologue to a Coup* (Warwick University).

12. I am indebted to John Smith, formerly Permanent Secretary Ministry of Finance, Benue Plateau State (now Governor of the Gilbert and Ellis Islands) for this information. Apparently at the conference of Permanent Secretaries of Finance, where this matter was discussed, there was considerable debate and when the Midwest pressed its case for the retention of a larger share of the royalty on oil produced in the State, it was met with a firm statement from other States that, since soldiers from all over Nigeria had been dying to liberate the Midwest, the oil revenue should be shared among all of them.

13. I am indebted to a former British High Commissioner in Nigeria who also served in Pakistan at the time of the rule of Ayub Khan for the observation that Ayub also found it extremely difficult to make up his mind and that his civil administration suffered in consequence. In his military capacity Ayub constantly stressed the value of decisiveness. He told the army cadets in the Pakistan Military Academy 'A saying that I frequently like to remember is "I may be wrong, but I have no doubts." When in a difficult situation let boldness and daring be your counsel.' Quoted by Khalid B. Sayeed in J. Van Doorn *Armed Forces and Society* (The Hague 1968 p 281–2). It is apparently the transition from the relatively straightforward field of military decision making to the more complex and unfamiliar field of decisions in the governing of the body politic that causes so many army heads of government to lose their nerve and their military decisiveness.

14. It has been suggested that Gowon was deterred from his inclination to take action on this issue by his close connections with Alhaji Fajemirokun and other great Lagos businessmen, who stood to lose a good deal if the capital were moved.

15. I am indebted to Colonel Lewis, one of Gowon's former Commanding Officers, for this information. His admiration for Gowon's military abilities was very high, as was that of the last British General Officer commanding the Nigerian army, Major General Sir Christopher Welby-Everard.

16. On the question as to how far, if at all, Gowon was personally involved in the corruptions of his regime there is not sufficient evidence for a conclusive answer. There is evidence that a lot of people tried to involve him in actions which were not in keeping with a strict code of conduct, as when they gave vastly overgenerous presents to his son or even to himself on his wedding. The Rayfield lodge affair related in the Belgore report shows how Gomwalk attempted to sell to Gowon in his personal capacity a lodge taken from the A.T.M.N. on which government expenditure far in excess of the purchase price had just been made. However, since the keys of the lodge were only handed to Gowon's brother at the very time of the coup that overthrew Gowon, it may be that Gowon was unaware of the details of what Gomwalk was doing. Since the coup the Federal Government has mentioned Gowon as being one of the people involved in dealings with Lockheed but has released no evidence. There is no doubt in my mind at all that Gowon was totally honest when he came to power and remained so at least for the first three years. When he was eventually overthrown he does not seem to have had excessively large means and therefore the Federal Government gave him a most generous allowance to help him 'live in a state fitting to a former Nigerian Head of State' while at Warwick.

17. Interview with Col. Abdulahi Mohammed, Jan 1975. Gomwalk and Asika were the only two graduates among the Governors. Their performance in office did little to enhance the reputation of academically trained people in power.

18. The Belgore Commission of Enquiry set up by the Mohammed Government was given many details of this and other acts of corruption in Benue-Plateau State, most of them emanating from the Governor or his entourage.

19. The commander in question was not so much worried by the principle of the coup, but that he had not been given any foreknowledge of it. He suffered a severe reprimand but in due course he was given high office under Mohammed.

20. Gowan's failure to ensure proper rights for his Ibo citizens in Port Harcourt was partly to blame. Dan Jumaa had been local army commander and an ex-officio member of the Rivers State Executive Council. He had disagreed fundamentally with Diette Spiff, the Governor, on this issue.

21. The death of Alhaji Yusufu Gobir in a tragic motor car accident in Spain in August 1975 robbed Nigeria of a most perspicacious civil servant, whose advice on policy making would have been invaluable to the new military government.

22. See M. J. Dent 'The third (and last?) military coup in Nigeria' in *World Today* (Chatham House) September 1975 (p. 356).

23. See S. E. Finer *The man on horseback* 'Their politics is the politics of the "suprapolitical"' for an analysis of this essential quality of military government. See also M. Janowitz in J. Van Doorn, Ed., *Armed Forces and Society,* p. 28.

24. Explanation given by a senior civil servant from Bornu. Mohammed was close to the family of the Wali, expert adviser to the Emir on Muslim law, and was related not only to Alhaji Inuwa Wada, but to all the distinguished Wali family, most notable of whom was the late Alhaji Isa Wali, at one time Nigeria's High

Commissioner in Ghana and perhaps the most able member of the foreign service.

25. Samuel Ikoku is perhaps the ablest Marxist theoretician in Nigeria. After serving as Secretary of the Action Group, he fled to Ghana at the time of the treason trials and became a leading adviser to Nkrumah. After the fall of Nkrumah he was returned under arrest to Nigeria but passed rapidly from detention to VIP status for, with the coming of the civil war, he became a federal emissary to communist states and did much to win the support of the left for the federal cause. After the civil war he first served as a commissioner under Asika, in East-Central State, then resumed as lecturer in economics at Lagos University. He has since come sufficiently to terms with the realities of life in a 'capitalist' system as to resign from the University and make far more than his University salary as a successful businessman. He was a member of the Constitutional Draft Commission and clearly knows how to marry Marxism and constitutional practice.

26. See lists of retirements and dismissals from the police in Federal Gazettes for September to December 1975. The detailed breakdown of ranks is as follows: Assistant Superintendent 46; Deputy Superintendent 20; Superintendent 18; Chief Superintendent 13; Assistant Commissioner 10; Deputy Commissioner 3; Commissioner 3; Deputy Inspector General 1; Inspector General 1.

27. Individual cases were still being reviewed in April 1977.

28. See *West Africa,* 22nd Jan 1973. Also S. E. Oyovbaire, Ch. 7.

29. The levels of concentration of land holding leading to the discontent in the West and the other roots of the Agbekoya movement are dealt with in more careful detail in C. E. F. Beer: *The Politics of Peasant Groups in Western Nigeria* (Ibadan 1976). See also H. Bienen, Ch. 2.

30. Information from a Russian teacher at Lumumba University.

31. Evidence from a consulting engineer doing contract work in Lagos. This vital parameter of the efficiency of the contract giving process is very hard to measure empirically.

32. *West Africa,* 26 March 1977, p. 634.

33. The flag-bearing emirate of Bauchi for instance lost its non-Muslim district of Jarawa to Plateau State, but this was balanced by the creation of Bauchi itself as a State capital. The Government ignored Tor Tiv's firm demand that if Plateau rejected Benue and demanded a separate state, then that state should on no account take away any of the former Benue province. Lafia and Nassarawa divisions were attached to Plateau, and Wukari division, whose population is roughly fifty percent Tiv, was attached to the new Gongola State. In compensation, however, the Igala parts of Kwara were excised and joined to the new Benue State whose capital was situated in Makurdi on Tiv land. The Tor Tiv was delighted as were the men of Bauchi; both celebrated the creation of new states with their towns as capitals, and forgot about the loss of areas formerly attached to them. The Wukari issue may however cause trouble at a future date, if the Wukari authorities were to follow the mad advice suggested in evidence to the Commission, in the evidence of the former chairman of the P.S.C. of Benue-Plateau, that with the creation of a Benue State for the Tiv, all Tiv should be asked to leave Wukari! The danger of the state issue is that it can arouse primordial sentiments of the 'sons of the soil' against strangers resident in their area. For further discussion of the reform see Ali Yahaya, Ch. 7.

34. See A. E. Gboyega and Oyeleye Oyediran, Ch. 10.

35. The worst of these occurred at Ugep on Christmas Eve 1975 when almost the whole of the population of this medium sized town was driven into the bush by

infuriated soldiers after the body of a soldier had been found in the town. The official casualty figures were eighteen and the damage was great. If the private soldiers, who were of course acting against orders in a mood of anomic violence, had had access to arms and ammunition instead of to cutlasses, the damage would have been far higher. The incident was fully reported in the press and the Government set up an 'Ugep disaster fund.'

36. Interview with the Aper Aku. Ibadan, Dec. 1975.

Part Two

POLITICAL ECONOMY

5

Elements of the political economy

Douglas Rimmer

On political economy

The term 'political economist' is enjoying a revival. It has become a
label self-consciously worn by scholars who hold that the ways in
which livelihoods are earned cannot be adequately studied unless
regard is had for the legal and institutional framework of economic
activity, and hence for facts and relationships additional to those
usually called economic.[1] On the surface, this argument is
unexceptionable and makes no denial of more conventional economic
studies; it merely expresses preference for a different level of
abstraction. The findings of the political economists tend nonetheless
to offend economic reasoning. For instance, a statement that a farmer
in the savanna grows groundnuts because this role has been chosen for
him by the international capitalist order[2] is in principle compatible
with a statement that he grows groundnuts because it pays him best.
But the former statement is relatively so difficult to formulate
theoretically and establish (or refute) empirically that more
conventional economists may well think its effect is not so much to
deepen as to distract attention from economic understanding. Helped
by such insight, we know less than before.

It would appear that the difficulty lies not in the initial premise of the
political economists but in the applications of their method—
applications not unrelated to political objectives they hold dear. Their
treatment of class conflict provides the major illustration. It must be
agreed that the interests of 'classes' or other social groups are apt to

conflict in the course of economic activity and that the legal and institutional framework, and changes made in it from time to time, reflect resolution of these conflicts. But what constitutes a 'class' in this context? The political economists' analyses of conflicts of economic interest identify rich and poor, workers and capitalists, nationals and foreigners. These categories are imposed by ideology, not discovered from observation. For a class interest to emerge in practice, it must possess firmer cement than perception of differences in incomes, economic roles or nationality. Its members must be aware of sufficient community of interest to act in unison to promote or defend it. The categories mentioned do not generally attain such cohesion.

Conflicts of economic interest nevertheless exist and they may have an economic basis. This basis commonly consists in payment of prices lower or higher than would obtain in an alternative market order. Thus objective conditions of conflict will be present where sellers (or buyers) of a particular good or service, acting as individuals, are confronted by a monopolistic buyer (or seller); or, conversely, where sellers or buyers acting together are able to assert a group interest in conflict with the interests of others.[3] Producers of a crop who can sell only to a statutory marketing organisation may be an example of the first case; suppliers of a service who limit production by restriction of entry to their industry illustrate the second. These objective conditions are neither necessary nor sufficient cause of conflict. On the one hand, illusory conflicts may arise; a group may believe itself disadvantaged even when no practicable change in selling or buying opportunities would benefit it. The common West African perception that middlemen exploit producers and consumers may be a case in point. On the other hand, there must be perception of and more or less organised reaction to objective conditions before conflicts can result from them. For example, the fixing of minimum wage-rates in public employment by Nigerian governments restricts the amount of employment in the formal or enumerated sector where wages and working conditions are relatively favourable to employees; but this result is not sufficient reason for conflict between those thus denied such employment and those who have found it.

Conflicts of economic interest can also have a political basis. Raising tax revenues is not inherent in market processes. If taxpayers resist tax-collectors, the conflict has political origins. Similarly, disputes over the allocation or uses made of tax revenue—where sectional interests in a national population may be sharply revealed—are politically rather than economically based.

In practice, the division between economically and politically based conflicts is indistinct. For, first, the economic conditions of conflict would often be transient but for political intervention. There are strong economic inducements to by-pass, undermine or default from monopolistic buying or selling organisations. Where such organisations survive and are effective over long periods, the reason most commonly is that they have been given statutory recognition and powers. Hence public (or publicly supported) monopolies are a more potent source of conflict than private. Secondly, a government in taxing and spending and using other coercive powers in economic life frequently influences market opportunities to the advantage of some groups and disadvantage of others. Discriminatory taxation can reduce profitability of an industry and discourage supply of its products, as seems to have happened in Nigerian agricultural exports in most of the period since 1945. Tax revenues can be used to subsidise an industry which buyers' demand alone would not support. Through such devices as tariffs, licensing of production, control of credit and public patronage, a government may intentionally or inadvertently create or strengthen group interests, supplying cohesion they could not find themselves.

In these circumstances there is a natural tendency for groups conscious of effective or nascent community of interest to appeal for governmental support or preferment. A government may resist such claims by emphasising its role as referee of economic life. It may insist that law must rule; that all interests remain subject to blind impersonal rules that (however they may have been arrived at) cannot be varied to advantage or penalise particular groups. But in Nigeria as elsewhere in the last thirty or forty years governments have not been content to serve as economic referees. They have claimed an active—indeed, the leading—role in the game. They have seen themselves as regulators of economic fortunes and prime movers in economic change. The rule of law in economic life has consequently been surrendered in favour of government more or less arbitrary: the conscious selection of interests to be promoted, cossetted and defended at the expense of others and the devising of appropriate policy measures. General resistance to sectional interests has been abandoned. In consequence economic life has become extensively politicised. Economic opportunities are recognised to be commonly dependent on political decisions and political influence to be therefore a condition of economic success. The political decisions tend to countenance the interests best organised to influence them. As the more conventional economists have long remarked, particularist interests (as in the profits and employment derived from making a product) tend in these circumstances to be favoured at the expense of more general interests (as in the cost of the product to consumers).

Political economy in Nigeria (and elsewhere) therefore deserves to be taken seriously. The economic history of the country, certainly in the last thirty years, cannot be adequately understood from economic data alone. Nor can the present economy and economic prospects of Nigerians. The interaction of economic behaviour with law and institutions does merit analysis. But in saying so we are not obliged to accept categories and relationships derived from ideological needs and unsupported by evidence. Workers, for example, are not evidently a class in conflict with others if they supply highly diverse services in many markets and are unconscious of community of interest and unorganised to defend it. Foreigners whose trades are also heterogeneous and who compete with one another as well as with nationals are not evidently a distinct interest group, except so far as discriminatory legislation gives them a common grievance. In contrast, we can observe conflicts of interest that satisfy nobody's ideological needs but have been profoundly important in practice. It may be doubted that any groups in Nigeria have been more conscious of their distinct interests and better organised to advance them than the regional governments of 1954-67 whose rivalry eventually tore the federation apart.

In what follows the political economy of Nigeria will be examined in three periods. First, outlines of the colonial regime up to the second world war will be briefly sketched. Secondly, changes in the style of political administration of economic life in the later colonial period and the early years of independence will be described. Thirdly, features of the period since the civil war will be considered at greater length.

The colonial period up to the second world war

The earlier colonial period is often regarded as the time of political economy *par excellence,* when economic life in the dependency was adapted to the convenience of the imperial power; what came later is no more than 'neo-colonialism'. It is difficult to find in Nigeria convincing evidence for this view. Compared with later times, the interaction of economics and politics before 1939 appears slight. An alien governing class, relatively uninterested in the ambitions and rivalries of those over whom it ruled, helped produce this result. No doubt a degree of primacy attached, as always, to the comfort of the governing class itself, but, relatively to other governments, colonial administration was poorly found, thinly spread and cheap. Its pretensions were restrained by shortage of revenue, especially in the nineteen-thirties, and an expectation that the dependency would be financially self-supporting. But what of other British interests? They were held in check by the doctrine of the dual mandate. On the one hand, trusteeship for the native peoples was interpreted to mean that land might not be acquired freehold by outside investors;[4] agricultural production consequently remained almost entirely in African control. On the other hand, trusteeship for the commerce of the world meant an open door for imports from non-British sources and rights of establishment for non-British enterprises.[5] Competition among the expatriate businesses in the import and export trades was muted since the markets were sufficient to support few of them at a feasible scale of operation, but the trading pools created during the forty years from 1899 never enjoyed the approval of the colonial government and seem to have been of modest effectiveness.[6] It was for want of competitive power, not because of legal discrimination, that African merchants (mainly before 1900) lost ground to these expatriate trading companies. The limited interventions of the colonial government—mainly in enforcing law, creating public order, and building and operating railways, ports, roads and other public works—were remarkably productive of economic change, though not always of the changes intended.[7] By widening trade outlets and lowering transport costs, they powerfully affected relative prices (notably the relative prices of leisure and material income) and unlocked latent productive capacity. A volume index of exports (very largely the crops of independent African farmers) shows an increase more than fivefold between 1900-02 and 1936-38.[8] The economic structure of the country diversified in response to this growth, but not as much as later critics of the colonial order held to have been desirable; large-scale manufacturing plants were still extremely few in 1939. Though the colonial market might sometimes be represented as a preserve for imported manufactures, measures to make it so are hard to find in the historical record.[9] For suppliers of imported manufactures the bulwark against local competition was the inadequate local resources, not the colonial administration. Apart from the important political restraint on transactions in land, economics rather than political economy explain the structure of the colonial economy. For the most part that structure resulted from individual producers and traders and consumers, African and expatriate, responding to economic inducements and deterrents in a relatively unpoliticised economic order.

The later colonial period and early years of independence

The political innocence of the colonial economy was largely dispelled in its last fifteen years. Growth in export earnings underlay the change. By the mid-fifties the commodity terms of trade (ratio of export and import price indices) had shifted some 60 per cent in Nigeria's favour compared with immediate prewar years; even when the trend was broken at the beginning of the 'sixties, these terms remained 'better than at any time in the 35-year period between 1915 and 1950'.[10] At the same time the volume of exports was rising—by over 4 per cent p.a. on average. Even before petroleum exports became significant in the early 'sixties, the export volume index had roughly doubled by comparison with either immediate prewar or postwar years.[11] Consequently the income terms of trade (commodity terms multiplied by export volume index) improved more than the commodity terms and continued to improve when the favourable trend in the commodity terms was checked; by the early 'sixties Nigerian purchasing power over imports was about three times what it had been both immediately before and after the second world war.[12]

Relative prosperity coincided with major political and constitutional innovations. First, by a 'constructive interpretation' of trusteeship the developmental ethos made its appearance in British colonial territories. Colonial government, whose responsibilities had been conceived primarily as maintaining justice and equal rights and preventing abuses, came in the 'forties to be regarded also as an instrument for raising living standards and promoting social welfare.[13] The Colonial Development and Welfare Act of 1940 was the legislative landmark of this new philosophy. One of its results was the first official development plan for Nigeria, produced in 1946. From that date government in Nigeria explicitly accepted the charge of economic development and generation of welfare. But the rising export proceeds, rather than metropolitan funds, were to finance pursuit of the new ambitions.[14]

Secondly, concessions to nationalist opinion led in 1951 to establishment of Federal and Regional authorities responsible to mass electorates. Party politics appeared, African politicians obtained ministerial offices, Africanisation of the civil service was accelerated. In 1954 the federal character of the constitution was accented, and the regional governments acquired rights to revenues that together accounted in later years for 40 to 50 per cent of total budgetary revenue in Nigeria. The main principle governing distribution of these revenues was 'derivation', i.e. each region's share was to depend on proceeds derived from taxed transactions within its borders.[15]

As a natural result of coincidence of rapid growth in Nigerian export earnings with emergence of new conceptions of the purpose of government, making it protagonist in an economic struggle, the additional earnings became the financial foundation of development policies. Government command over resources increased faster than private command. Government and other corporate spending on fixed and allegedly productive assets increased relatively to the so-called consumption expenditure of households. According to official GDP estimates for 1950/51 to 1960/61 both government current spending and gross investment in fixed assets increased at an annual average rate of about 12 per cent, but consumers' spending at only 3 per cent.[16] Government appropriated an increasing proportion of available resources through a fiscal regime based largely on taxation of external trade. In addition the Marketing Board system, retained after the Second World War supposedly for the purpose of stabilising the incomes of export-crop producers by disconnecting their prices from world market prices, became an instrument for collectivising savings for use by public authorities. By 1954 the Boards had accumulated £120 millions, of which trading surpluses in the seven years since 1947 amounted to £100 millions, or two-thirds as much as the aggregate yield of import and export duties in the same period. A further £30 millions were accumulated in the seven years from 1954 to 1961.[17]

At the same time constitutional changes were under way that introduced electoral politics, replaced alien by native norms in public administration and the conduct of public enterprises, and devolved resources and power on the constituent units of the federation where the political parties had their bases. Again by a natural progression in the circumstances of the time, additional resources entering the public domain in the name of development were used to serve political ends— party, communal and personal—of less abstract kinds. Not entirely but to a substantial extent, they were used primarily to secure political loyalties, repay political debts, and build personal fortunes. Adaptation of the 'development effort' to such political exigencies was most pronounced in the regional governments. Their 'welfare and public works powers . . . . offered huge opportunities for patronage and went far to consolidate the power of each governing party'.[18] Reconstitution of the Marketing Boards and their associated Development Boards as regional institutions in 1954 gave the regional governments access to the vast accumulated funds of those bodies and command over policy instruments lying outside the civil service and its procedural rules.

Patronage could merge with delivery of social welfare, as most notably in the schemes of universal and fee-free primary schooling on which the Western and Eastern governments resolved even before 1954. Similarly, wage-fixing became from 1951 'the battlefield of the political parties'; increases by regional governments in effective minimum rates in formalised employment in 1954-55, 1960, and to a limited extent in 1964 following the Okotie-Eboh settlement, were swayed by electoral considerations.[19] Patronage with narrower purposes—serving the pecuniary interest of a ruling party, its leaders, or influential supporters—was frequently associated with lending and investing by the regional Development Corporations and spending under the capital budgets of the regional governments. Marketing Board reserves were the major source of funds for these operations. In the early days of the peacetime Boards P. T. Bauer had warned of the political temptation offered by their accumulation of surpluses,[20] but 'it is doubtful . . . . whether even he foresaw the convoluted collaboration of government, Party, public corporation and private business that was disclosed in the Western Region as a result of the split in the ruling faction in 1962, or the similar intrigues that were revealed in other parts of the Federation after the military coup.'[21]

In contrast to the relative isolation of economic activity from politics in the early colonial period, by the nineteen-sixties the fortunes of businesses, communities and households in Nigeria hinged on governmental favour and political influence. Farmers were subjected to marketing monopolies because governments required control of surpluses extractable from their labour. Wage-earners were raised up from time to time because their votes were believed marketable and their hostility dangerous. One community received amenities because its political support was needed; another was denied them because it had voted wrong. Through public patronage, credit, contributions to equity, and protection from competition, those businesses prospered whose owners possessed or were willing to buy official goodwill. 'By the 1960s nearly all businessmen were necessarily in politics, because the state had become the main source of both finance and contracts; and nearly all politicians were in business.'[22] Government no longer acted (or even pretended to act) as impartial referee of economic life. The adamantine rectitude of early colonial trusteeship had been replaced by an urge to get things done. Government had become open to suggestion. In place of impersonal rules it substituted discretion and flexibility, waivers and concessions, planning and bargaining. To understand such a 'national economy' the perspectives of political economy are needed. While, for example, the virtual absence of large-scale manufactures from Nigeria before the nineteen-fifties is explicable by economic considerations alone, the subsequent appearance of these enterprises is not.[23] One needs also to interpret as political economy such conflicts of economic interest as became manifest in smuggling of crops outward and manufactures inward, the 'general strike' of June 1964, the 'tax riots' in the West at the end of 1968, and perhaps even the break-down of the federation in 1967—even though none of these conflicts was of poor with rich, workers with capitalists,[24] or Nigerians with foreigners.

Thus economic life in Nigeria became politicised: less through imposition of colonial rule than its withdrawal: the result of a process inspired by the cause of development, financed by improving terms of trade, mediated by decolonisation and a federal constitution.

The period since the civil war

The years since the civil war, like those that followed the Second World War, have been a period of rapid growth in export earnings. The expansion this time has resulted from emergence of a new export commodity, crude petroleum. Agricultural exports have contributed nothing to it; their official production index, based on 1960, records a decline in volume of nearly 40 per cent between 1964-66 and 1972-74 and, while rising prices for these exports since 1973 have allowed proceeds at current prices to be maintained about the level of the mid-sixties, in real terms there has been a substantial contraction.[25] In contrast, as is shown in Table 1, the volume of petroleum production increased more than five-fold between 1966 and 1974 and the current-price value of petroleum exports nearly thirty-fold. Beginning in 1958, petroleum exports rose as a proportion of total exports from 10 per cent in 1962 to over 90 per cent by 1974. Between 1969 and 1975 (the latter a year when petroleum exports temporarily fell in volume and value) total exports at current prices increased from N.636 millions to nearly N.5000 millions. Even assuming import prices to have doubled in the same period, which is probably an overestimation, purchasing power of Nigerian exports quadrupled in the six years following the civil war.

TABLE 1

PRODUCTION AND EXPORT OF CRUDE PETROLEUM,
1962, 1966, 1969-75

	Production index (1965 = 100)	Value of petroleum exports (N.m)	Petroleum exports as % of total exports	Av posted price (US $ per barrel)
1962	25.9	33.5	9.9	
1966	152.3	184.0	32.4	
1969	197.1	262.0	41.2	2.17
1970	389.1	510.0	57.6	2.25
1971	568.5	953.0	73.7	3.05
1972	662.5	1176.2	82.0	3.39
1973	750.0	1893.5	83.1	4.80
1974	822.8	5365.7	92.6	14.69
1975	650.9 (prov.)	4629.6 (prov.)	92.9	12.95

Sources: Central Bank of Nigeria, *Annual reports* and *Economic & Financial Review*, various issues; posted prices (of API 34 crude) from UN, *Monthly Bulletin of Statistics,* Nov 1976. Note: Production in 1965 was 100,065,294 barrels; the index numbers are therefore nearly equivalent to production in millions of barrels.

In the nineteen-sixties outlays of foreign exchange by the petroleum extracting companies (mainly on importing goods and services) were large relatively to the gross value of their output and hence to the value of petroleum exports. In 1969 the oil companies' contribution to the Nigerian balance of current payments, or net external earnings, was only some 40 per cent of the value of their exports. After 1969 this ratio rose rapidly, as is shown in Table 2, reaching nearly 97 per cent in 1974. In consequence the net value of total Nigerian exports (net of foreign-exchange costs and payments on foreign-owned capital of the exporting industries) must have increased even faster after 1969 than the gross value. Again making the generous assumption that import prices doubled between 1969 and 1975, the increase in this period in the real value of Nigerian exports net of foreign-exchange outlays involved in their production was probably five or six-fold.

The difference between gross and net external earnings from

petroleum has narrowed mainly because of increasing taxation of the industry. As the industry's proceeds grew through expansion of output and increases in unit-values, a rising proportion was appropriated by government.

TABLE 2

CONTRIBUTION OF PETROLEUM COMPANIES TO BALANCE OF CURRENT EXTERNAL PAYMENTS, 1966, 1969-74

	N.m.	As % of value of petroleum exports
1966	86.0	46.7
1969	106.6	40.7
1970	253.2	49.6
1971	604.8	63.5
1972	808.1	68.7
1973	1403.3	74.1
1974	5192.9	96.8

Source: Central Bank of Nigeria, *Annual reports*. Note: The totals are the sum of the companies' payments to government, other local expenditures and additions to cash holdings, *less* local receipts (mainly from sales of crude for local refining).

By the Petroleum Profits Tax Ordinance of 1959, 50 per cent of companies' net profits were payable to government as royalties, rentals, and a residual profits tax. Revenues from petroleum had reached nearly 10 per cent of total government revenue by 1966. From that year a series of changes in fiscal arrangements for the industry was made. It included reductions in 1966 and 1971 in the rate of allowable depreciation of investments, definition in 1967 of royalties as costs of production instead of offsets against profits tax, and increase in 1971 of the tax rate from 50 to 55 per cent. The most important change was the introduction in November 1967 of the OPEC device of a posted price.[27] Taxable profits had previously been computed on the basis of 'realised prices' which, because of the integrated character of the companies' operations, were internal transfer prices determined at their discretion. The posted price substituted for realised prices was a price negotiated between government and the companies. By early in 1972 increases in the posted price and changes to the disadvantage of the companies in the method of deriving the tax reference price from it had roughly doubled the tax-take per barrel as compared with November 1967.[28] These changes were modest compared with what followed. By virtue of the bargaining power of the oil cartel, the Nigerian posted price was raised to $8.31 in November 1973 and

$14.691 (almost seven times the price of November 1967) in January 1974. Average annual posted prices from 1969 to 1975 are shown in Table 1.

Table 3 shows the increase in current revenue of the federal government between 1970 and 1975 and the associated rise in the proportion of the revenue derived from petroleum. At current prices total revenue nearly trebled between 1970 and 1973 and more than trebled between 1973 and 1975. In 1975 over three-quarters of the total came from petroleum, even though revenue from some other sources (import duties and company tax) had also risen fast.

TABLE 3
RE CURRENT REVENUE OF FEDERAL GOVERNMENT AND
PROPORTION DERIVED FROM PETROLEUM, 1970-1975

	Total current. revenue (₦.m.)	Petroleum revenue ₦.m.	As % of total
1970	633.2	166.4	26.3
1971	1169.0	510.2	43.6
1972	1404.8	764.3	54.4
1973	1695.3	1016.0	59.9
1974	4537.0	3726.7	82.1
1975	5514.7	4271.5	77.5

Source: Central Bank of Nigeria, *Economic & Financial Review,* December 1975. Note: Figures shown as petroleum revenue are the sum of proceeds of petroleum profits tax and mining royalties, rents, fees, etc; all but a few per cent of the latter item are obtained from petroleum extraction.

The enormous growth in revenue provided means for both a fast-growing recurrent budget and the ambitious second and third plans of national development. Public investment spending in 1970-74 totalled over ₦.2200 millions; under the Third Plan it was originally projected at ₦.20,000 millions between 1975 and 1980. By 1975/76 the Federal Government's recurrent spending had been allowed to reach ₦.3430 millions and its capital spending stood at ₦.4129 millions.[29] As in the nineteen-fifties, additional external earnings have been used to raise government spending and investment at faster rates than households' expenditure. Between 1970/71 and 1973/74 government current spending grew at twice, and gross fixed capital formation at three times, the rate of increase in private consumption;[30] after 1973/74 these divergences almost certainly widened.

So for the second time since 1945, but now on a scale both absolutely and relatively larger, additional export earnings have provided means for pursuit of great ambitions in Nigeria. As the three national plans bear witness, independence in 1960 and the turmoil of subsequent years did nothing to weaken official acceptance of the developmental ethos. The latest plan continues to embody 'the government's determination to translate the country's vast potential into a permanent improvement in the living standard of all Nigerians' and looks forward to arrival within the income-bracket of developed countries in two decades.[31]

While these aims of government remain intact,[32] the political system of Nigeria in the 'seventies has been different, reverting in some of its features to the earlier period of colonial rule. Electoral politics have been eliminated and scope for organised political activity greatly curtailed. Whatever influences have shaped policies, they have not included the need to bring out the vote.

Financial resources and political power have shifted to the centre.[33] Like the provincial administrations of colonial times, the States have been instruments of the centre rather than its constitutional peers. Power has lain with officials, military and civilian, whose authority has depended on their appointments, not on organised popular support. Like the colonial government, military government serves the people not because they are its masters but because it has their interests in trust and knows its duty.

Does it follow that economics have again been substantially detached from politics in Nigeria? There might appear ground for such an interpretation. Reduction in the autonomy of the State governments accords with a federal ideology that the centre has always been high-principled and only the lesser administrations venal. The importance in the economic life of the country of those great regional institutions, the Marketing Boards, has lessened and they have been placed under federal control. Attempts have been made to diminish the bargaining strength of trade unions against government. Partial nationalisation of several industries and majority public shareholdings in some new foreign enterprises have been represented as curtailment of the political influence of foreign businessmen. Even the indigenisation programme, while clearly discriminatory, might be held to do more for industry and commerce than the old colonial order did for agriculture, viz. to impose general restraints on foreign incursion in order to protect the weak. There follows some account of and comment on these measures.

The Marketing Boards attracted much criticism, even in official circles, during and immediately after the civil war but less on account of the abuse and waste of their funds that had occurred than of the effects on agricultural exports attributed to their price policies.[34] Early in 1973 the power to fix producer prices was transferred from the Boards (effectively from the State governments) to the federal government. Export duties and the States' produce sales taxes on crops handled by the Boards were replaced by a single federal tax of 10 per cent *ad valorem* (itself removed in the following year). One purpose was to maintain higher producer prices. Indeed these prices would be fixed with no trading surpluses in view. If they turned out excessive in relation to realised export prices, the difference would be a charge on the federal budget. In the next two years most producer prices were doubled (trebled for palm oil), though much of these increases must merely have offset the rise in producers' living costs since the civil war.[35] The Marketing Board reform was an item in the shifting of power from the States, to be followed in 1977 by the replacement of the State Boards by a national board for each commodity. It had another important implication. Stabilisation of local prices among seasons was the purpose for which the peacetime Boards had been established, raising of public revenue for development the purpose subsequently discovered for them. The latter purpose had now been disavowed while the crucial aspect of the former—the subsidising of a local price in time of low export prices—was to be undertaken by the federal treasury. Judged by these purposes, the Marketing Boards had therefore become redundant. Each statutory export monopoly could be replaced by an official residual buyer offering the guaranteed minimum price. It seems that this is effectively what has happened for those crops for which home markets now overshadow export. But the breaking of the monopolies here has owed less to a reforming initiative by government than to the growth of markets to which the Boards could not control access. And for cocoa, the one crop that survives as a major export,[36] the buying monopoly is illogically retained and the opportunity to free trade has not been taken.

The economics of determination of wages in formalised employment in Nigeria have always been highly political, though for long not by conscious design. Until the civil war, the apparent intention was to build a replica of what was then the British system of industrial relations, with wages and other terms of employment determined by collective bargaining and the government acting only to make good deficiencies in voluntary organisation—as by provision of conciliation or arbitration with the consent of both parties to a dispute, and establishment of wages boards in a very few instances. But the legal and institutional framework thus created 'can be seen as encapsulating the form, rather than the substance, of industrial relations'.[37] In practice wages and other terms of employment changed mainly as outcomes of government commissions of inquiry set up from time to time in response to labour agitation or other political stimulants. Wage awards based on recommendations of these commissions—the latest of which have been Morgan (1964), Adebo (1970-71), and Udoji (1974)—have had immediate reference only to the public services but have been emulated by, or subsequently forced on, the larger private employers.[38] Major changes in the forms of industrial relations were made during the civil war. In 1969 strikes were prohibited and resort to arbitration became compulsory when negotiating procedures were exhausted. National emergency could be used in justification. But new procedures for settlement of disputes laid down in 1976 and replacing these temporary restraints still left small opportunity for lawful strikes. As compared with the period before 1969, the voluntary principle has thus been much curtailed, but changes have been greater in form than substance. Strikes continue to occur. Wages changed mainly by government decision before 1969 as they have done since. Where changes of substance have occurred is in the disappearance (along with party politics) of competitive wage-fixing for political advantage among the governments of the federation, and possibly in recent attempts by the federal government to obtain political control over the central organisations of trade unions.[39] These changes affect the bargaining power of labour organisations within procedures of wage determination that remain politicised and cannot help but so remain, given the price leadership of government in the formalised labour market.

Striking changes have occurred since the civil war in official attitudes toward private economic enterprise, especially foreign enterprise.

In 1958 foreign capital 'and the skilled overseas personnel which may be necessary to make it successful' had been officially welcomed and 'encouraged in every form of industrial enterprise' except public utilities. There was 'no rigid insistence on local participation', though partnership between overseas and local capital was favoured and governments of the federation might wish 'to share in the financing of certain large enterprises which have a special significance to the public'. The governments had 'no plans for nationalising industry beyond the extent to which public utilities are already nationalised' and foresaw no such proposals arising.[40]

Independence produced no immediate change in these attitudes. A motion proposed in 1961 by Chief Awolowo, as Leader of the Opposition in the federal House of Representatives, approving the principle of 'nationalisation of basic industries and commercial undertakings of vital importance to the economy of Nigeria', was heavily defeated.[41] The value of foreign economic interests in Nigeria continued to be emphasised officially even though criticism of these interests was highly popular. Thus inconsistently with official policy the Federal Minister for Economic Development told the House of Representatives in 1964 that 'most of Nigeria's economic difficulties can only be solved when foreign business concerns operating in Nigeria are in the hands of Nigerians'; until then, all talk about economic progress would be useless.[42] Demands for substitution of public for private ownership and control (nationalisation), private Nigerian for foreign ownership and control (indigenisation) and Nigerian for expatriate senior personnel (Nigerianisation) were not as a rule clearly separated.

By 1970 the shift had been made and official attitudes were blatantly populist. The second national development plan quoted the old saw, 'political independence without economic independence is but an empty shell', and declared: 'A truly independent nation cannot allow its objectives and priorities to be distorted or frustrated by the manipulations of powerful foreign investors.'[43] Were indigenous investors assumed to be more careful of national objectives and priorities? According to the Plan, 'indigenous ownership and control in strategic industrial areas' were essential 'to maximise local retention of profit, increase the net industrial contribution to the national economy, and avoid explosive socio-political consequences.'[44] But more emphasis was put on the arresting inference that it was 'vital . . . . for Government to acquire and control on behalf of the Nigerian society, the greater proportion of the productive assets of the country.' Towards this end government would acquire equity participation in 'strategic industries' to be specified from time to time. Exploitation of 'strategic natural resources' would be undertaken by government alone or with private concerns as technical partners, 'provided that in all cases the Government remains the dominant partner'. And because industry and mining were likely to be important generators of resources for future development, 'Government must play a leading ole in these two sectors in order to harness the fruits of economic growth for the overall development of the Nigerian society.'[45]

Before the civil war, public participation in the capital of foreign enterprises had been undertaken partly as means of securing in them local stakes that would eventually be released to private Nigerian ownership. The Second Plan declared this aim to flow 'from the narrow conception of the role of Government in national development which is not tenable in Nigerian circumstances.' Private investors, foreign and indigenous, would continue to have a place in Nigerian economic development, but 'as partners in progress led by the public sector.'[46]

Government participation in industries regarded as strategic proceeded from 1971. By 1975 the Nigerian National Oil Corporation had become majority shareholder in all the companies extracting petroleum, as also in the refining and internal distribution of petroleum products. Since its establishment in 1971 this parastatal body has been sole beneficiary of new licences for petroleum exploration and mining. Substantial public shareholdings have also been acquired in the foreign-owned commercial banks and insurance companies and in several newly established manufacturing firms. Majority public stakes were prescribed in the Second and Third Plans for major projected industries including iron and steel making, petrochemicals, fertilisers and liquefaction of natural gas. Substantial indigenous stakes (government or private) were prescribed for other industries including food processing, forest products and building materials, construction and plantations.

Meanwhile the interests of junior Nigerian partners in progress were advanced by the Nigerian Enterprises Promotion Decree of 1972. A schedule to the decree listed twenty-two activities which were to become reserved to Nigerian nationals.[47] They included retail trade (other than in department stores and supermarkets), many urban services, and some small-scale manufactures. In thirty-three further activities, listed in a second schedule, foreign enterprises were to be excluded unless above a stipulated size and having at least 40 per cent of their equity in Nigerian ownership. This second schedule included wholesale trade, department stores and supermarkets, construction, and a number of manufacturing industries. To facilitate Nigerian acquisitions, a Nigerian Enterprises Promotion Board and a publicly-funded Bank for Commerce and Industry were set up and commercial banks were directed to allocate at least 40 per cent of their loans and advances to Nigerian businesses. A second phase in the programme of indigenisation was decreed early in 1977 for completion by the end of 1978. New first and second schedules appeared, specifying forty and fifty-seven activities respectively, and under the second, minimum Nigerian participation was raised from 40 to 60 per cent. In all activities not appearing in either schedule minimum Nigerian shareholding of 40 per cent was to be required; indigenisation had thus become a comprehensive programme. Inclusion in the second schedule of mining, banking, insurance, iron and steel making and fertiliser manufacture suggests that partial nationalisation or public contributions to equity capital are regarded as satisfying the requirements of indigenisation.[48]

Nigerianisation of the more responsible and better-paid jobs had been largely accomplished in public administration by 1962. It proceeded much more slowly in industries, including those partly in public ownership. In 1958 there had been no more than official 'expectation' that posts would not be occupied by expatriates if they could be efficiently filled by Nigerians.[49] From 1967 an Expatriate Quota Allocation Board attempted to restrict both the number and duration of expatriate appointments. In 1970 the Second Plan complained: 'One of the reasons for encouraging private investment . . . is the expectation that investment activities will generate employment opportunities for Nigerian nationals. The Government therefore cannot continue to tolerate a situation in which high-level Nigerian personnel educated and trained at great cost to the nation, are denied employment in their own country by foreign business establishments.'[50] The Third Plan promised an effective enforcement agency for decisions of the Quota Board and announced new stratagems for displacing foreigners from employment.[51]

Conclusion

On balance it seems implausible to interpret the tenor of official policy since the civil war as separation of business from politics. Suspension of parties and elections admittedly removed a major medium for interpenetration of economic and political life. But much else remained, above all the responsibility for development officially accepted in 1946. Populist policies of the nineteen-seventies drew government further into economic life. Even crediting officials with a disinterested intention to remove abuses of power, the outcome of their measures was to heighten the economic significance of political decisions. Perhaps this was another natural progression in the circumstances of the time; for precisely because officials know best and distrust spontaneous pursuit of self interests, their inclination is not to stand aloof but to intervene. Such an inclination is observable in a previous bureaucracy, that of the earlier colonial period, but the economic interventions of colonial administrations were constrained by shortage of funds and inhibitions laid on them from the metropole. The developmental ethos removed the inhibitions; government could become in good conscience star player in the economic game, no longer merely referee. For the military government of the 'seventies financial constraints were removed by the petroleum boom, as they had been for the party administrations of the 'fifties by the boom in export crops. Indeed, the alternative which, in principle at least, had existed in the 'fifties of allowing additional export receipts to accrue to those who had earned them did not exist in the 'seventies. The production function, ownership and markets of the petroleum extraction industry were such that the easy pickings, if they were to be taken at all in Nigeria, could be taken only by government. The sour fruits of independence had made administrators still more persuaded of a need to define and promote collective interests, still more attached to the conception of development of a national economy. The rapidly growing resources at public disposal were used to extend the area of economic life under official control.

It is unlikely that official partiality and political influence became any the less important to individuals, businesses, social groups and communities seeking to advance their interests in Nigeria. The politics of the pork barrel were not extinguished along with elections. Economic success did not cease to depend on political approval because parties were disbanded. Corruption was not ended, and perhaps not even reduced, because power devolved on soldiers and civil servants; not even the old Western Region government produced anything to match the cement scandals in which the Ministry of Defence was involved in 1975. For Nigerians further growth of the public sector and discrimination against foreigners did not mean that doors were locked against them but that more could be (or had to be) knocked on. For foreign businesses the obligation to take Nigerian partners made influential local friends the more necessary.

Tasting the sour fruits of independence, patriotic Nigerian administrators might well have concluded they must do more in future. It could as well be deduced they must do less. Reflecting during the civil war on the problems Nigerians would face in 'growing together again',

Wolfgang Stolper wrote: 'It is essential to realize that the future will require governments to restrict their activities; to use policy rather than administrative discretion; to use indirection; to make it therefore easier for local initiative to emerge. All factors come together to argue limitations on the power of the state and decentralization.' These conclusions were held to flow from the 'recalcitrant nature of the economy', plurality of Nigerian society and shortage of administrative capacity. To ignore the practical limitations on the power of government to exert its will would lead to economic inefficiency and retrogression, continuing corruption and intolerable strain on the cohesion of the national society; it 'must lead to a gradual, and eventually accelerating dissolution of society'.[52]

There appears to have been no disposition in the military government to heed such advice. The ambitions of the central authorities are larger now than they were in the 'sixties when Stolper already thought them excessive. It has been suggested above that this progression was assisted by substitution of officials for elected politicians. Certainly it was helped by discovery that Nigerian economy was not as recalcitrant as it had appeared. Petroleum unexpectedly spilled a cornucopia on Nigeria and encouraged belief that further easy riches could be won by combination of governmental control over natural resources and foreign expertise in high-technology industries producing for export. Stolper had in mind reactions of Nigerians to the possibly disappointing results of investments for which they had had to make sacrifices, but in the period of the Third Plan sacrifices were not required, at least in design (the sacrifices inadvertently imposed by inflation resulting from execution of the plan are another matter).

While petroleum has removed, at least for a time, financial constraints on the power of government, others remain. Nigerian society, like most societies contained in national boundaries, is fissured ethnically and in other ways; if we do not observe great social classes in dramatic conflict, one reason is that the society is too heterogeneous to allow their formation. Public administrative capacity, as in most countries nowadays, is inadequate to sustain the burdens placed on it. Attempts to execute the Third Plan have made apparent another constraint consisting in limited physical capacities to import and distribute goods. The Nigerian peoples and their environment are still unyielding clay in the hands of planners of development.

A commitment has been made to hold elections and restore civilian government by 1979. Attempts will be made in a new constitution to prevent the abuses of power associated with the parties of the 'fifties and 'sixties. They are unlikely to be successful. It is not primarily because of their moral infirmity that governments are bought but on account of what they have to sell, and there appears no reason to believe that the governments of 1979 will be selling less than their predecessors. The tendency to centralise power, even if it survives the ending of military rule, will not necessarily make for probity. The more power is centralised, the less can be done without its support and the greater will be the demands for its goodwill. Only reversal of the trend toward politicisation of economic life can reduce the importance of political favour to players in the economy, and there is nothing in the projected evolution of the Nigerian polity to suggest such a reversal.

One need not believe that the colonial government was much liked by Nigerians in order to suggest that its successors have been more execrated. Of course more was expected of them, and their shortcomings accordingly more keenly felt. But more was expected because more was promised. At all levels of human affairs, the result of undertaking responsibilities one cannot hope to discharge efficiently and equitably is to be distrusted and eventually despised. The civilian governments of the federation knew this truth by 1965; the military government discovered it in 1975. The same reward seems likely to await a government constituted in 1979. However that may be, it can be predicted with some confidence that the perspectives of political economy will be as necessary for the understanding of Nigerian affairs in the nineteen-eighties as they have been in the last thirty years.

NOTES

1. For a recent statement of this view see Ann Siedman, 'Changing theories of political economy in Africa', in C. Fyfe (ed.), *African studies since 1945: a tribute to Basil Davidson* (Longman, London, 1976).
2. Such as might be distilled from Samir Amin, *Neo-colonialism in West Africa* (Penguin Books, Harmondsworth, 1973), c. 1.
3. The analysis here follows Lionel Robbins, *The economic basis of class conflict and other essays in political economy* (Macmillan, London, 1939), pp. 3–28.
4. William Lever is the best-known casualty of this policy. In the early years of the century he was unable to acquire land freehold for the establishment of oil palm plantations in Nigeria. (Charles Wilson, *The history of Unilever* (Cassell & Co., London, 1954), Vol. 1, pp. 165–7).
5 Additionally in Nigeria non-discrimination depended on an agreement of Great Britain and France in 1898 not to discriminate against each other in most parts of West Africa and extension of the immunity to other countries through most-

favoured-nation clauses. It was partially breached in 1934 by British termination of the Anglo-Japanese commercial treaty of 1911 so far as it applied to the West African territories. The Anglo-French agreement was terminated in 1936, by which date all of French West Africa had been brought within the preferential tariff regime of the French Empire, but the opportunity was not taken to introduce British preferences in Nigeria.

6. Discussions of this topic are included in J. Mars, 'Extra-territorial enterprises', in Margery Perham (ed.), *Mining, commerce and finance in Nigeria* (Faber & Faber, London, 1948), pp. 43–136, and P. T. Bauer, *West African trade: a study of competition, oligopoly and monopoly in a changing economy* (Cambridge University Press, London, 1954). Bauer's summary conclusion was that: 'It would seem that in general neither the high degree of concentration nor the market-sharing agreements have secured substantial monopoly profits, or exceptionally wide gross margins to the firms for any prolonged period, except when government controls have restricted entry or stifled competition' ('Some aspects and problems of trade in Africa', in E. F. Jackson (ed.), *Economic development in Africa* (Basil Blackwell, Oxford, 1965), p. 109).

7. Thus groundnuts, rather than the cotton that had been expected, flowed down the Kano-Lagos railway on its completion in 1912; see J. S. Hogendorn, 'The origins of the groundnut trade in Northern Nigeria', in Carl K. Eicher & Carl Liedholm (eds.), *Growth and development of the Nigerian economy* (Michigan State University Press, East Lansing, 1970), pp. 30–51. The promotion of the Kano railway by the British Cotton Growing Association appears one of the clearest instances of collaboration between the colonial government and a distinct British commercial interest. It is also an instance of the failure of such collaboration from the point of view of the promoters.

8. From 12 to 68 on the annual average (1953 =100): Gerald K. Helleiner, *Peasant agriculture, government, and economic growth in Nigeria* (Richard D. Irwin, Homewood, 1966), Appx., Table IV–A–2, pp. 494–6.

9. Thus the only instances produced by Carl Liedholm in his paper on 'The influence of colonial policy on the growth and development of Nigeria's industrial sector' (in Eicher & Liedholm, *op. cit.*, pp. 52–61) are (1) the United Africa Company's being 'dissuaded by the government', according to J. Mars (*op. cit.*, p. 74), from establishing a textile mill in northern Nigeria and a garment factory near Lagos at dates unspecified; (2) the opinion of the World Bank Mission of 1954 that the authorities had given a 'cool and overcautious reception' to proposals for the establishment of textile mills; and (3) maintenance in the 'thirties of a rate of export duty on palm kernel oil which was higher, both absolutely and as a ratio of the price of the product, than the rate of export duty on palm kernels. In connexion with the last point, it may be noted that processing of palm kernels had been abandoned in Nigeria before the first world war.

10. Helleiner, *op. cit.*, p. 31 and Appx., Table IV–A–6, p. 500. Helleiner's index of the commodity terms of trade (1953 =100) moves from 63 to 108 on the annual average between 1936–38 and 1954–56.

11. *Ibid.*, Appx., Table IV–A–2, pp. 494–6. The export volume index averages 68 in 1936–38, 72 in 1946–48, and 138 in 1959–61.

12. *Ibid.*, Appx., Table IV–A–6, p. 500. Helleiner's index of the income terms of trade (1953 =100) averages 44 in 1936–38, 45 in 1946–48, and 147 in 1961–63.

13. Lord Hailey, 'A new philosophy of colonial rule', *United Empire*, XXXII, 8, 1941, pp. 163–9.

4. Nigerian governments received £35·6 millions in UK grants for colonial development and welfare in the period 1946/47–1960/61, or less than £2   millions p.a. Helleiner, *op. cit.,* Table 54, p. 227.

5. Derivation was tempered from 1959 by the creation of the Distributable Pool, following the Raisman-Tress Report. It still remained the basis for distribution of about two-thirds of the revenues collected centrally for distribution among the regions.

6. These estimates, which are at constant (1957/58) prices, are reproduced in W. F. Stolper, *Planning without facts: lessons in resource allocation from Nigeria's development* (Harvard University Press, Cambridge, Mass., 1966), Table 2, pp. 96–7. During the same period, total available resources (i.e., GDP *minus* exports *plus* imports) increased at an annual average rate of just over 6 per cent.

7. Helleiner, *op. cit.,* pp. 160–6.

8. James O'Connell, 'Political integration: the Nigerian case', in A. Hazlewood (ed.), *African integration and disintegration* (Oxford University Press, London, 1967), p. 153.

9. T. M. Yesufu, *An introduction to industrial relations in Nigeria* (Oxford University Press, London, 1962), pp. 141–6; Peter Kilby, *Industrialisation in an open economy: Nigeria 1946–66* (Cambridge University Press, London, 1969) pp. 288–9.

0. Thus in 'The reduction of fluctuations in the incomes of primary producers' (*Economic Journal,* LXII, 1952, p. 778) Bauer and F. W. Paish wrote that the surpluses 'provide a strong temptation to local political parties, and will serve to give immense power to those parties which best appreciate their political possibilities.'

1. C. C. Wrigley, *The development of state capitalism in late colonial and post-colonial Nigeria* (Paper presented to a conference of the African Studies Association of the UK, Liverpool, 1974).

2. *Ibid.*

3. Growth of the Nigerian market and eventual arrival at what Peter Kilby termed 'competitive thresholds' remain the principal explanation of establishment of manufactures in which private (usually foreign) interests had a stake, but government inducements (more particularly, contributions to capital and offers of tariff protection) were important initiating factors (Kilby, *op. cit.,* Part II). Establishment of manufactures wholly in public ownership proceeded with less (and sometimes no) regard for profitability.

4. As many as 750,000 workers may have been involved in the general strike of 1964, and they received some support from persons outside the organised labour market. It was nevertheless a strike to secure higher pay for a narrow segment (perhaps 5 per cent) of the working population. It happened because the governments acted as price leader in the formalised labour market so that wage bargains of general application could be struck, and there was an effective but temporary combination of trade union centrals which resulted from the federal government's political insensitivity and dilatoriness in handling their claims. Robin Cohen (*Labour and politics in Nigeria,* Heinemann, London 1974, pp. 159–168) points to parallels with the earlier general strike of June–July 1945.

5. The production index (which is of Marketing Board purchases of scheduled crops and exports of other agricultural commodities) fell from 121 to 72 on annual average between 1964–66 and 1972–74. Both the production index and an index of London Market prices of Nigerian agricultural exports appear in the *Annual Reports* of the Central Bank of Nigeria.

26. A Nigerian import price index is not available for recent years. The export pric
    indices of important Nigerian trading partners, the UK, the USA, Japan and Wes
    Germany, rose by 111, 86, 57 and 36 per cent respectively between 1969 and 197
    (UN, *Monthly Bulletin of Statistics*).
27. Though the Nigerian government did not join the Organisation of Petroleu■
    Exporting Countries until July 1971.
28. Details of these fiscal changes up to 1972 are given in Ronald K. Meyer & Scott R
    Pearson, 'Contributions of petroleum to Nigerian economic development', i■
    Pearson & J. Cownie (eds.), *Commodity exports and African Econom■
    development* (D. C. Heath, London 1974), pp. 160–61.
29. Lawrence Ripley, 'Budgetary trends in Nigeria', *West Africa* (London) 29 No■
    1976, pp. 1810–11, and 'Rebalancing the budget', *ibid.*, 14 Feb 1977, p. 327. Th■
    1976/77 Estimates are ₦.3591 millions recurrent and N.4618 millions capit■
    expenditure.
30. The average annual rates of increase are 17·9, 27·4 and 9·2 per cent according t
    the estimates of GDP at current prices in Federal Republic of Nigeria, *Thir■
    national development plan 1975–80* (Lagos, 1975), vol. 1, Table 2.9, p. 22. In th■
    same period total available resources are estimated to have increased at 13·1 pe■
    cent p.a.
31 *Ibid.*, vol. 1, pp. 5, 27.
32. In the international community reservations have been made in recent years abou
    objectives of development and some of the methods used to pursue it. Greate
    GDP has been discredited as a goal unless accompanied by sufficient regard fc
    distribution of income and dispersion of employment opportunitie■
    Industrialisation under cover of protection and making use of advance■
    technology has been held to produce uncertain economic results and untowar
    side-effects. In Nigeria even such reservations have obtained only mute■
    expression (as in *ibid.*, vol. 1, pp. 27–33).
33. The effects of growth in public revenue and changes in its allocation among th■
    governments during the period of military rule have been (a) to reduce th■
    importance of derivation as a basis for dividing statutory States' revenues amon■
    the States and to increase the importance of the Distributable Pool, half of whic■
    is allocated equally among the States and half in proportion of their estimate■
    populations; (b) to increase revenue retained by the federal government relative■
    to revenue statutorily allocated to the States; and (c) to increase the importance c
    non-statutory federal grants to the States (especially from 1975): see chapter ■
34. Thus the *Second national development plan 1970–74 first progress report* (Lagos
    n.d.) stated: 'The indications show that the (marketing board) system as present■
    operated discourages increased efforts and production by the farmers. Th■
    stagnation in the output and export of some cash crops is attributed to th■
    marketing board system. The time has come for a serious review of the situation■
    (p. 66).
35. The increase in producer prices between 1972/73 and 1974/75 is shown in *Thir■
    national development plan 1975–80*, vol. 1, Table 2.2, p. 15. There was littl■
    change in producer prices between 1969 and 1972. No cost-of-living index fo■
    rural areas is available but the official index for the lower income group in urba■
    areas more than doubled on monthly average between 1969 and 1975.
36. There is relatively little local use of cocoa beans. As a proportion of total export
    excluding petroleum, cocoa beans have risen from 21·3 per cent in 1965 to 51·1 pe■
    cent in 1975.

37. Robin Cohen, *op. cit.,* p. 185.
38. Outside formalised employment in the public sector and large-scale private enterprises, wages have depended on economic rather than institutional forces and 'sub-minimum' rates and working conditions have persisted.
39. In 1973 the number of central organisations of trade unionism was reduced to two by legislation and at the end of 1975 the Nigerian Labour Congress emerged as a single central organisation. A decree of September 1976 appears to have disowned the Congress and put the common affairs of the trade unions in the hands of an administrator appointed by the federal Commissioner of Labour. Recent policies of the federal government toward industrial relations and trade unions are discussed by Peter Waterman, 'Industrial relations and labour unrest in Nigeria', *Business Times* (Lagos) 14, 21 and 28 December 1976.
40. Joint statement of the Governments of the Federation of Nigeria on 'Opportunities for overseas investment', reprinted as an appendix to the official *Economic survey of Nigeria 1959* (Lagos, 1959), pp. 119–21.
41. An account of this episode is given in David R. Mummery, *The protection of international private investment: Nigeria and the world community* (New York, 1968), pp. 22–29.
42. Waziri Ibrahim, quoted in Paul O. Proehl, *Foreign enterprise in Nigeria, laws and policies* (Chapel Hill, N.C., 1965), p. 172.
43. Federal Government of Nigeria, *Second national development plan 1970–1974* (Lagos, 1970), p. 289.
44. *Ibid.,* p. 144.
45. *Ibid.,* p. 289.
46. *Ibid.*
47. And to other Africans whose governments gave reciprocal treatment to Nigerians.
48. Even under the 1972 decree, the line between indigenisation and nationalisation appears to have been blurred; thus of nineteen million shares offered by the United African Company in 1974 in compliance with the decree, twelve million were allocated to State governments.
49. *Economic survey of Nigeria 1959,* p. 119.
50. *Second national development plan,* pp. 288–9.
51. *Third national development plan,* vol. 1, p. 382.
52. Wolfgang F. Stolper, 'Economic growth and political instability in Nigeria: on growing together again,' in C. K. Eicher and C. Liedholm (eds.), *op. cit.,* pp. 328–351. Stolper had served as Head of the Economic Planning Unit of the Federal Ministry of Economic Development from 1960 to 1962.

6

Commercial Capitalism and the 1975 Coup

Terisa Turner

'An effective oil policy is one which . . . . above
all ensures political stability.'

Abdul Atta
March 1971

This study is concerned with the relationship between profit making
and the Nigerian state. The overwhelming proportion of relations
between countries are economic relations. Nigeria has an import-
export economy and an indigenous business community engaged
largely in commerce. By describing how this commercial system
operates, I hope to go some way towards explaining the instability of
the Nigerian state. Part I outlines the pattern of competition which
characterizes a commercial political economy such as that of Nigeria
and shows how a policy of state intervention to promote economic
development intensifies competition and introduces a new set of actors.
Part II, a case study of the 1975 coup, is an attempt to illustrate how
these relationships contribute to instability.

Part I: The Pattern of Competition

PROFIT-MAKING
Contemporary political economies characterized by commercial
capitalism are those which depend on foreign industrial production for
virtually all locally-consumed manufactured goods. Although trade

flourishes, there is little indigenous capitalist production of final consumer goods. In such an import-export economy, most business takes the form of commercial activity: importing, distribution and transport, wholesale, retail and petty trading. Agricultural primary products may be exported or foreign-based extractive industries may export minerals from an enclave. But for most local businessmen, profits are made predominantly through commerce: even in the local import-substitution sector, to the extent that it exists, profits stem more from market control than from value added through assembly and processing of largely imported inputs. The particular sub-group of commercial political economies of interest here is that comprised by oil-rich countries with a low level of industrialization.

Much commercial activity takes the form of middlemanship. The local businessman organizes the foreign seller's access to local markets. Final consumers constitute a market, but the state itself is becoming an important market especially if it can command vast incomes from oil. Now, more than during the colonial or pre-second world war period, access to national markets is restricted by the state. State control stems mainly from its role as a major buyer, but also from its regulatory powers over other commercial activities. Because the state controls opportunities to profit through commerce, politics becomes dominated by struggles for positions in the state or for access to those who have influence over government decisions.

THE TRIANGULAR RELATIONSHIP

The relationship between foreign businessmen and local actors from the national private and public sectors is called a 'commercial triangle' in this study, because it involves three parties to a buying or selling transaction. These parties are first, the businessman who represents the multinational corporation; second, the local middleman from the national private sector; and third, the state official who assists the foreign businessman in gaining access to the local market.

How does the triangular relationship work? A foreign businessman comes to the country to sell his firm's products. He hires a local citizen as a go-between with the state. If a contract materialises, the state official is usually rewarded with a payment arranged by the go-between or middleman. While its manifestations in real life take a great many forms (since the state not only awards contracts, but it sets terms for the sale of oil, crops or for the establishment of a business), the description which follows is meant to capture the commercial triad's essential features. Each member of the triangle can be described in turn.

The multinational corporation

In seeking business foreign firms are in competition for access to a country's economy. Competition is usually for markets, but it is also for opportunities to extract primary commodities or to use labour. The businessmen compete for access to state officials with the power and the inclination to give them government business on profitable terms. The greater the country's foreign reserves, the larger the number of businessmen and the more intense is the competition for government custom. Foreign businessmen sometimes deal directly with the state. But usually they approach government officials through middlemen who have privileged access to decision makers. The kickback or bribe, it is argued below, is an important means of securing competitive advantage in today's global marketplace.

The local middleman

The second member of the triangle is the local middleman who puts the businessman in touch with the market.[1] Those falling into the middleman group are sometimes expatriates themselves. For example, Levantines organize imports in some countries; the Indian or Chinese community does so in others. In the more formalized part of this 'intermediate' sector, businessmen act as importers, exporters, representatives for foreign salesmen and marketing firms, representatives for foreign firms seeking a particular contract, job-finders, advisers, facilitators, intermediaries, brokers, agents, contact men and assistants of all varieties. For this intermediary service the middleman gets a retaining fee and usually a bonus when the contract or deal comes through. Some of this income is normally paid to officials in government who made the transaction possible. The middleman may conceptualize the state official's cut as part of his own 'expenses.' The relationship between the middleman and the state is emphasized by Adamu who writes of the Nigerian case that invariably the middleman is[2]

> .... either a front for a public servant, or an employee of a private company which would like to remain faceless and who has the opportunity to offer contracts to himself to be executed by himself. Or he receives contracts or

import and export licences, only to present them to a waiting expatriate with the capital for a small fee called a commission. And more likely than not he serves as a collector of commission for a civil servant who surcharged individuals for duties rendered . . . .

Middlemen are dependent upon connections with the state and with foreign firms. Their dependent and intermediary role creates intensely competitive pressures within the local private sector and—because of the close interaction of the two—within the state. Since there are fewer state officials than there are aspiring middlemen, the bottleneck arises in getting access to the state. The middleman's usefulness to the foreign businessman is his special contacts and relationships with influential officials of state. Thus, the premium on establishing such contacts is high. Local businessmen compete intensely with each other for access to powerful government officials. Many aspiring intermediaries have little chance of succeeding and are bitter at patronage going to someone else.

In a commercial capitalist political economy, the dominant business class is not composed of capitalists who organize labour, capital, raw materials and energy to produce a product for the market. Among the reasons for the near absence of productive entrepreneurship are capital shortage, pre-emptive concentration of foreign firms[3] and more profitable alternatives. The absence of industrialization is commonly explained by reference to a 'Lack of appropriate technical skills and managerial know-how . . . .'[4] This explanation fails to take into account the fact that many nationals with these technical and managerial qualities become middlemen, not capitalists. Many middlemen have professional qualifications as accountants, business administrators, lawyers, etc., and have been diverted from the practice of their professions by more promising opportunities in commerce. They find little incentive to produce when middlemanship requires little capital, when it complements and facilitates—but does not compete with—foreign capital, and most important, when it offers easy profits. It may be that the reasons for the perpetuation of commerce in certain political economies include its unparalleled success in enriching indigenees and foreign businessmen alike.[5]

The state comprador

The third actor in the commercial triangle is the state official whose position allows him to influence state spending and government policy,

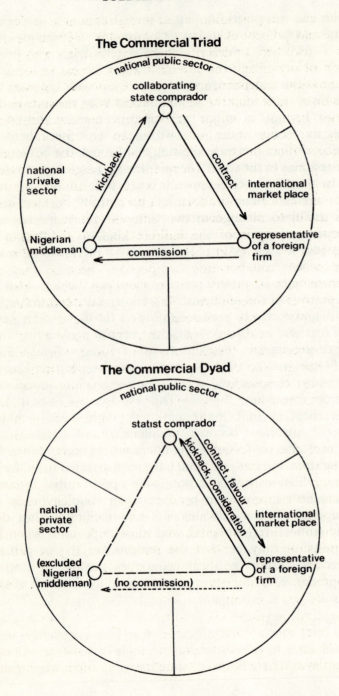

The Commercial Triad

national public sector

collaborating
state comprador

national
private
sector

kickback

contract

international
market place

Nigerian
middleman

commission

representative
of a foreign
firm

The Commercial Dyad

national public sector

statist comprador

national
private
sector

contract, favour
kickback, consideration

international
market place

(excluded
Nigerian
middleman)

(no commission)

representative
of a foreign
firm

and who uses this position to assist foreign capital in its dealings with the state and indigenous society. 'Comprador', a Portuguese word for 'buyer' is used here to describe those state officials who perform the function of organizing the foreign traders' access to local markets. With political independence of the European colonies and the expansion of trade after the Second World War, the state in these new countries became a major market and market regulator. With sovereignty, some state officials began to perform a kind of 'gatekeeper' function: they allow the entry and exit of goods and in the process may exact a 'toll' for performing the service of 'opening the gate'. In the following discussion, state officials who perform this function are called compradors, or alternatively, 'gatekeepers'.

It is useful to distinguish two different gatekeeper roles: where gatekeeper activity is of the indirect kind, a middleman is used. Gatekeepers who work in partnership with private local middlemen can be called 'collaborating compradors' because they and the middlemen join to carry out transactions which also include representatives of foreign firms. This triangular relationship is shown in the diagram of the commercial triad. However, the gatekeeper activity can also be direçt, that is, the official deals directly with the foreign businessman. Instead of being triadic, the relationship is dyadic. Officials who deal directly with foreign businessmen can be called 'statist compradors' since they exclude the private national sector from transactions between the state and foreign multinationals. This direct relationship is shown in the diagram of the commercial dyad.

The exclusion of middlemen from taking part in transactions involving state officials and foreign businessmen is resisted by aspiring middlemen. This resistance is articulated in terms of opposition to state encroachment on the private sector's spheres of activity. Opposition to an enlargement of the state's role in the economy is at least partly a campaign to retain triads and the associated roles of middlemen in the face of pressures from foreign firms or state officials, in certain fields, to close out middlemen and set up exclusive dyads.

Comprador state officials are competitive. In countries in which the civil service has a prominant role in actually making, as well as in implementing decisions (as is often the case, for example, under military rule), much of the competition among compradors is struggle within the civil service to secure and retain positions with decision-making power. There is also a tendency to rationalize competition by

reducing the number of officials involved and removing decisions from
open forums. Since this tendency towards the concentration of power
is a significant source of instability, it bears a little more discussion.

Competition among international firms is reproduced in the local
context through the proliferation of triangular relationships. The
triads increase in number depending both on the number of foreign
suppliers interested, say, in winning a contract, and on the number of
decision-makers within the state. For example, if a contract award is to
be decided in the country's top decision-making forum, theoretically
each of its members could form triangles with their respective
middlemen and foreign firms and compete for the award. Such a
situation may be insoluble. The work of arriving at a compromise is
considerable, time goes by, foreign firms get impatient, market
conditions change as do prices and the stakes are diluted by the larger
numbers involved. This experience leads to the formation of cliques
which can operate in particular spheres of interest. It also produces a
strong impetus to limit the number of government officials who have
access to and knowledge of these decisions—which as a result come to
be made not in open forums but behind closed doors. The tendency
towards monopoly of power and advantage within the state leads to
suspicion and hostility from the out-groups not privy to decisions.

The political economy of a commercial capitalist society is defined
largely by efforts to establish these triangular relationships and to
operate them profitably. Instability is endemic in the struggle among
middlemen for state patronage, and in the competition among officials
of state for control of decisions. In these circumstances, politics is a
form of business through which actors seek influence in the state, not in
order to make and apply general rules, but in order to secure
advantages.

THE INTERNATIONAL MARKET

The basic source of competition among commercial triangles, and
therefore of instability, is foreign business rivalry. The intense nature
of this competition and its ultimate 'dog-eat-dog' character follow
from the urgent need on the part of individual corporations to secure
markets and raw materials, especially when jobs and balance of
payments conditions in their home countries depend on making
foreign sales. An efficient method of competing is through the purchase
of favour with bribes. In 1916 Lenin argued that 'considerations' were

an integral feature of a world market dominated by oligopoly or monopoly:[6]

> Finance capital has created the epoch of monopolies and monopolies introduce everywhere monopolist principles; the utilization of 'connections' for profitable transactions takes the place of competition on the open market.

The efficiency of bribes as a means of competition and the prevalence of oligopolies are interconnected. Bribe competition has none of the drawbacks of price competition which in an oligopolistic market can easily mean price war. Bribes are inexpensive and relatively easy to administer. Once a system of kickbacks and commissions is established, small firms and newcomers are subjected to pressure to conform if they are to do business. The commercial nexus between oligopolistic international firms and the state, now such a large economic concern in all countries, provides opportunity for the exercise of favour by compradors and the purchase of profitable terms by the corporate representative. Large firms among which there exists a high degree of oligopolistic world market control, obtain advantages through means other than price competition. One of the more prevalent and simplest methods of securing competitive advantage especially when dealing with the state, is the kickback.

While the means by which multinational firms seek profits can be identified as a fundamental source of political instability, the question of 'blame' is hardly relevant. The notion of moral business behaviour is vague; an act of bribery involves a giver and a receiver and international firms cannot be held responsible for adapting to a given business environment. A United States Conference Board study in February 1976 showed that even those businessmen who favoured a code of business ethics acknowledged that if 'faced with a problem of losing a major sale or not they would pay up and keep quiet about it.'[7]

It is useful to examine some of the determinants of buying decisions which predominate over what C. G. Tether calls 'normal considerations in international trade.'[8] A foreign businessman is a successful salesman not because he offers a competitive price, high quality produce, efficient service, or the commodity which best suits local needs. Oligopoly is a major factor which can make consideration of these sources of competitive advantage almost irrelevant. In most instances a businessman is successful because he has made contact with the right middleman and gets access to the right government official who finds the foreign firm's proposal attractive.[9] The main focus of competition, then, is for access to officials of state. Foreign salesmen of defence equipment, for example, make claims for their products which the buying government, and much less the local middlemen, usually have little ability or inclination to test. But clearcut competition can occur through inducements or bribes.

Bribe-bidding is a logical means of seeking competitive advantage. Furthermore, this pattern does coincide with what, impressionistically, would seem to be prevalent practice in several countries. As Tether observed, 'normal commercial considerations are clearly going to play a subsidiary role—if, indeed, they exercise any influence at all . . . . if orders are to go to producers [most effective in] greasing the palms of those who are well-placed to determine the final choice on the buying side . . . .'[10] The descriptions of bribes suggest that they are forms of competition: they are 'pay-offs' to 'promote the company's substantial sales' or 'gifts made to potential customers.'[11]

The foreign businessman is faced with the situation in which a major source of competitive advantage is the kickback. The choice to patronize one aircraft salesman over another appears to turn largely on the calculation of which deal is more profitable personally for the decision-maker. A report of the U.S. Senate Subcommittee on Multinationals, published in February 1976, indicates that Lockheed, the U.S. Government's largest aero-space and defence contractor, admitted to bribing foreign officials over the last fifteen years and spending $22 million in kickbacks in the last five years in at least eight countries. Among these eight countries is Nigeria where, U.S. Senate sources confirmed, Lockheed paid about $3·6 million on a $45 million deal.[12] The corporation's sales have been substantial and were projected to reach $4 billion between 1975 and 1980. Not only Lockheed (which received $195 million in U.S. Government loans between 1971 and 1976) but the total U.S. defence industry has demonstrated its international competitiveness: Senator Proxmire reported that U.S. arms manufacturers sold nine times as many arms as the French and fifteen times as many as the British in 1974. U.S. military sales in 1976 were expected to reach $10 billion, triple the level of 1972. The point of importance here is that the world predominance of Lockheed, or other corporations, depends on foreign sales. Therefore the methods by which sales are secured, in the face of competition from corporations based in other countries, are integrally a part of Lockheed's growth and survival. Given the importance of the defence contractor's products in the U.S. military programme, the well-being of Lockheed can also be appreciated as a condition for United States military predominance on an international scale.[13]

Far from being an anomaly, the business bribe or commission is an essential element of the modern world system. Its centrality has to do with the profit-orientation of the corporate operation: it does not stem primarily from personal greed and lack of knowledge or planning on the part of the buyer. Corporations which are successful at profit-making have grown, squeezing out smaller firms and making the entry of new competitors increasingly difficult. Large multinational firms currently have oligopolistic control over certain industries. For example, the oil industry is dominated by seven major corporations and there are a similar number of major producers of cement for the international market. Aircraft and defence producers are even fewer in number. Firms in an oligopoly are reluctant to enter into price competition since a single price cutter can expect retaliation from other members of the oligopoly in other markets. A price war will only drive all members of the oligopoly into the red. Thus a premium is placed on securing contracts by offering inducements which may be large to the recipient, but which account for a small proportion of the firm's turnover, while keeping prices at a level agreeable to members of the oligopoly. For example, the $68 million which Northrop, a defence equipment manufacturer, allegedly paid to Saudi Arabia's middleman Adnan Kashoggi, is only 2·83% of the $2·4 billion contract the U.S. firm secured. Again, it is alleged that Grumman paid a commission of $28 million or 1·27% of an Iranian deal worth $2·2 billion.[14]

Mention should also be made of small firms for which a single contract or concession could mean the difference between profit or collapse. These firms have a special incentive to offer kickbacks to secure a niche in a market dominated by large corporations. Finally, inducements are used not only to swing decision-makers over to a particular firm, but also to encourage the state to make purchases which would not otherwise have been made. U.S. Senator Church emphasized how this method of expanding markets distorts the development programmes of poor countries by discouraging the optimum allocation of scarce (and often borrowed) resources.[15]

Since governments are responsible for a great deal of expenditure in poor countries, the full pressure of an oligopolistic market is brought to bear on state officials. Local intermediaries and foreign businessmen who are unable to gain access to the decision-makers of the moment look forward to their replacement. State officials who cannot obtain positions which allow them to influence decision-making similarly seek to unseat those in power. In this conflict-ridden context the power of guns and money plays an everyday role.

TECHNOCRATS AND ECONOMIC NATIONALISM

Mention has been made of three sets of actors who participate in commercial triangles: foreign businessmen, local middlemen from the indigenous private sector, and state officials who carry out a gatekeeper or comprador function. In addition to these three groups, the political economies of commercial capitalist countries are influenced by another group of actors within the state—technocrats. Technocrats are those with professional training in some area of production who are employed in public corporations. Since they have professional education and jobs in production-oriented corporations, technocrats may also aspire to be state capitalists. That, is, they may be personally oriented towards engaging in capitalist production locally despite the predominance of commercial capitalist relations. But whether technocrats actually do perform the tasks of state capitalists depends on the relationship between the state corporation in which they are employed and the ministry or state institution which supervises the corporation. If a state corporation is controlled by a ministry headed by commercially-oriented gatekeepers, it is unlikely that the technocrats in the state corporation will be allowed to fulfil their potential of becoming state capitalists. This could give rise to frustration among technocrats, since they have been trained and hired by the state to engage in production. A public corporation which is under the direction of compradors in a ministry might be diverted from its potentiality for capitalist production, and become defunct or inefficient.

The key defining feature of technocratic state officials is their ability to produce commodities. This ability stems not only from training, but also from membership on a team of production-oriented professionals who are organized in a corporation in such a way as to make complex productive activities possible. Technocrats are often trained by foreign manufacturing and extractive firms and in institutions of education which service these industries. They have the potential of being state capitalists, but this potential can be realized only if the state corporation employing the technocrats is allowed to function as a profitable unit of capitalist production. Technocrats' jobs in the various public corporations involve combining technology, finance and managerial skills in a profit-making organization to produce a tangible result (a steel plant, an irrigation system). The division of labour in such an economic agency requires an interdependence among specialists, the success of which is measured firstly in terms of actual production and secondly in terms of profits. Individual technocrats, by virtue of their technical training and (for some) experience in foreign-based industry, are accustomed to rational, impersonal and universal criteria for making decisions and for assessing their own accomplishments. Professional standing, the grounds for job mobility, depends on getting results which in turn depends on co-operation with others in the production organization.

Technocrats are capable of operating industrial concerns; gatekeeper state officials are not. Gatekeepers are committed to and engaged in facilitating commerce. The interests of these two strata of the local section of the world bourgeoisie are at variance, although both fundamentally support the option of private ownership of capital. Technocrats are relatively uncorrupt, not because they possess special moral qualities, but because they tend to see their function in terms of reducing dependence on imported products. In contrast, the gatekeeper role of mediating the entry and exit of goods tends to stand as an obstacle to industrialization and to the realization of technocratic plans. Although the tensions between technocrats and compradors stem mainly from the conflicting strategies of productive capitalism on the one hand and commercial capitalism on the other, in practice it is likely that the form which production takes in hitherto unin-dustrialized countries (for example, the assembly and processing of imported components) would maintain national dependence on industrialized countries.

The policy of state-led capitalist development of production usually entails exclusive state control over certain sectors (the 'commanding heights') of the economy. Control is normally established through a state corporation which functions, ideally, as a profitable business operation. But it has been noted that if state corporations are under the control of ministries (the existence of which in most cases predates that of the corporations) then there is a tendency for those in charge of the Ministry to establish their own direct relationship with foreign firms. The more state corporations there are, the more opportunities exist for direct communication between compradors and representatives of foreign firms. In these direct relationships, 'statist' compradors are able to exclude middlemen from the local private sector, and in effect, replace some triangular relationships with bilateral ones.

Policies of economic nationalism and state-led development were manifest in the programmes of many non-industrialized countries by the 1970s. The new types of gatekeeper—the statist compradors—were appearing in the oil exporting commercial political economies just as oil incomes became significant in magnitude. Statist compradors are much more powerful than the earlier collaborators, given the former group's command of the revenues from oil and the associated projects for industrialization which technocrats are hired to realize.

The policy of state intervention gives rise not only to a stratum of technocrats and to statist compradors but also to disaffected middlemen who are excluded from triangular relationships by the direct deals established in what are usually the most lucrative areas of the economy. In addition, aspirant compradors whose middle-rank positions mean that they are precluded from entering major bilateral deals also resist the policy of state monopoly in certain economic areas and align with middlemen in demanding private sector involvement in all economic activities.

Reference has been made to another type of tension which develops around issues of policy between technocrats and statist compradors—the two groups of civil servants in charge of implementing state-led capitalist production plans. Both oppose the involvement of middlemen in strategic areas and are therefore divided from local businessmen. Technocrats are hired to make functional ventures in state capitalism. But these are under the ultimate control of traditional comprador administrators who have the opportunity, with the new policy, to form bilateral relationships with foreign firms. In so doing, they threaten to divert the policy of economic nationalism from increasing local capabilities to intensifying links with foreign capital. Such a diversion leaves technocrats with little role to play and this in turn leads to frustration and opposition.

In sum, a commercial capitalist political economy in the 1970s is inherently unstable due to the triangular dynamic and to the policy divisions between comprador and technocratic factions within the state. To the competitive tensions generated by the drive to establish successful triangular relationships is added, in connection with state intervention in the economy, still more tensions. In this unstable situation a coup is possible any time and is more likely if some minimal level of cohesion is struck among members of the 'out group.'

To what extent is the general framework outlined in Part I useful in aiding our understanding of the instability of the Nigerian state as manifest in the 1975 coup? The following case study of some of the events surrounding the overthrow of General Gowon illustrates the tension between public officials charged with the technical implementation of state capitalism and those who were at the political helm. The tension between these two strata of state officials took on an added dimension when a loose alliance of would-be compradors, middlemen and 'outs' joined forces with frustrated technocrats in making allegations of comprador-type behaviour on the part of military leaders and their political advisers. Analysis is restricted to relations in the oil sector since these may have actually triggered the coup and because they illustrate clearly the instability of the Nigerian state.

Part II: The 1975 Coup

OIL ADMINISTRATORS

During the five years of civilian government (1960-65) politicians took little interest in oil and civil servants remained on the margins of the industry; no policy was initiated. But after January 1966 Shell-BP, responsible for most of the oil production, offered the new military regime improved financial terms. Since these oil-related matters had to do with funds, they were handled by the Ministry of Finance which established a Petroleum Section and began to initiate the making of oil policy. The oil ministry (Mines and Power) remained in the background and had even less of a role with the decrease in production during part of the civil war. Its traditional function was that of regulating foreign oil companies and this it continued to do with a small and ill-equipped staff.

Abdul Atta, Permanent Secretary of the Ministry of Finance and later Secretary of the Federal Military Government, advocated a strong state role in the oil industry and formed cadres of professional oil technicians to realize his policies. Atta, whose influence with General Gowon was considerable, in 1971 successfully sold the idea of joining OPEC to a reluctant leadership which knew little about oil and feared loss of sovereignty. Before his death in June 1972, Atta worked on setting up two institutions—the Petroleum Advisory Board as an open forum to promote informed oil policy making and the Nigerian National Oil Corporation (NNOC) to implement policy in a co-ordinated and efficient way.

Administrators in the Ministry of Mines and Power viewed with alarm the expansion of the Ministry of Finance into their sphere of

interest.[16] Oil companies had reason to oppose the interventionis
policies of Atta and the oil experts who were then concentrated large!
in the Ministŕy of Finance's Petroleum Section. The foreign firms ha
entered Nigeria under a favourable set of regulations inherited fror
the colonial period and stood to gain from a continuation of the o
ministry's role of regulation and non-intervention. Nevertheles:
Nigeria, in line with OPEC, adopted a programme of '*direc*
participation in the mining sector' (my emphasis) as part of·the 1970-7
Second Development Plan.[17]

With this plan, Nigeria initiated a policy of mild economi
nationalism. The state undertook to promote indigenous privat
capitalism and to establish public control over the 'commandin
heights' of the economy.[18] Dozens of parastatals were established b
1975. Some were to provide local would-be capitalist producers witl
funds and guidance. Others were state corporations which wer
designed to operate as public enterprises. Each of these state extension
had a budget, a purpose, an interest to defend and a complement c
staff who, because of their technical training and productive functior
tended to behave differently from gatekeeper state officials wh
nevertheless were their superiors in the bureaucratic hierarchy. Th
attempts which were made to implement the policy of fosterin
capitalist development had the effect of increasing competition an
divisive tension in the Nigerian political economy. Whether it had th
effect of promoting productive capitalism, public or private, is an ope
question which needs to be investigated.

In April 1971 Phillip Asiodu took up his post as Permanen
Secretary of the oil ministry, while his associate A. Ayida replaced Att
in Finance. In that year the Nigerian National Oil Corporation—th
institutional means for securing state participation in the oil industry–
was established as a parastatal under the oil ministry's control. Th
corporation's decree[19] included three provisions which limite
NNOC's freedom to exercise power:

—spending overN100,000 had to be approved by the Federal Executiv
  Council after recommendation from the NNOC Board (the norma
  spending limits for parastatals);
—while the corporation was in charge of all stages of oil activity fron
  production to marketing, it did not have *exclusive* power in these areas
  and
—the Chairman of NNOC's Board was the Permanent Secretary of th
  Ministry of Mines and Power.

A chief executive was to be appointed by the Federal Executive
'ouncil on the advice of the Commissioner for Mines and Power, but
s long as none was appointed, Asiodu, as Permanent Secretary, was in
large of NNOC. The corporation gradually built up its staff of
rofessionally qualified persons so as to be able to administer the
ate's participation interest in the oil companies and sell the
overnment's share of the oil. Whereas prior to 1971, oil experts in the
Iinistry of Finance's Petroleum Division had provided much of the
pposition to the oil ministry's regulatory policies, after 1971 and
pecially since 1973, most opposition stemmed from a technocratic
iction made up of NNOC staff. This shift in the source of opposition
) oil ministry initiatives reflects the evolution of policy from an
mphasis on oil income to concern with state control of the industry.

From mid-1973 until the July 1975 coup, tensions accumulated
etween technicians and professionals in the oil corporation and
eneralist administrators in the oil ministry. However, this
haracterization of the division is too sharp since there were
rofessionals in the Ministry of Mines and Power who, on occasion,
orked with NNOC officials. The tendency was for oil specialists in
INOC to pursue significant revisions in oil policy while more powerful
dministrators in the Ministry adhered to regulatory practices. While
iere has been published no official evidence of impropriety lying
ehind either conception of the national interest, the belief that
ersonal gain motivated certain actions was widespread.
'onsequently, suspicions about corruption play a significant role in
ie development of tension between NNOC and the Ministry and
etween personalities in each institution.

HE OIL AUCTION

'he first major difference arose in connection with a crude oil auction
1 1973. At the time oil was scarce on the international market. Prices,
vhich had been rising since 1970, skyrocketed. The Nigerian
overnment had opted to lift its royalty oil and was entitled to crude by
irtue of participation in producing companies. Some 300,000 barrels a
ay (bd) were available for sale.[20] But in the wake of the Arab-Israeli
var which involved oil production cut backs and selective embargoes
on Portugal, U.S.A., The Netherlands and South Africa), the price of
 barrel was difficult to determine. Following the example of other
)PEC countries, NNOC's Marketing Division advertised an auction
nd called for bids. The Ministry of Mines and Power had not officially

authorised the oil corporation to undertake an auction of crude oil, n
had it ordered a halt to the exercise. The pressure from hopeful buye
was so intense that a refusal by Nigeria to sell its oil to the highe
bidder would have aroused outcry in some quarters. However, at tl
same time there was some support for measures which stabilized rath
than further disrupted oil prices and crude offtake patterns in a time
uncertainty and crisis. During October and early November 1973 whe
the auction was getting under way, Asiodu was in London on extende
medical leave. Consequently, the oil corporation did not have tl
benefit of his direction.

Before leaving Lagos the Permanent Secretary had differe
publically with Alhaji Monguno, Commissioner for Mines and Powe
on the issue of who could buy government oil. Monguno, like oth
Commissioners, usually took a back seat to his permanent secretar
But in late September 1973 he announced to the Nigerian Chamber
Commerce that private Nigerians could submit bids in the cruc
auction. The following week in the same forum Asiodu stated that n
crude would be allocated to Nigerians since they had no means of usin
it and were only acting as intermediaries for refiners abroad. The issu
of the role of middlemen remained unresolved. A NNOC statemen
asserted that only final users of crude could be considered fc
allotments,[21] but the Nigerian private sector and foreign buyers we
aware that two earlier crude sales by the Ministry of Mines and Pow
had involved a local middleman, who had made a great deal of mone

Originally bids were to be closed on 19 October, but by then Liby
and the Arab states had established higher posted prices. The closin
date for bids was put forward to 15 November to allow buyers to refi
on the basis of new Nigerian posted prices of $8.40. When NNOC an
Ministry of Finance officials opened over one hundred bids o
November 19 they found that the highest price offered was $16.50
barrel. The task was then to select bidders willing to pay $16.50 an
sign contracts immediately. Exports were expected to start on Januar
1, 1974 and normally 45 days notice is required to obtain tank
services. NNOC made a great effort to have buyers chosen an
contracts signed. However, Asiodu, who had returned to Nigeria i
mid-November after a six-week medical leave, took no steps t
conclude contracts, despite reported urgings from NNOC.

At the time of the crude auction the oil corporation was without
General Manager since the Federal Executive Council had nc
appointed one. In the absence of a chief executive, Asiodu, as NNO

'hairman, supervised second-rung managers who would normally
port to a General Manager. Yet the Permanent Secretary could not
adily direct NNOC to call off the auction since it was getting
emendous international attention. Local interest was also at a high
tch as hundreds of crude buyers descended on Lagos. If the long-
tablished patterns of crude marketing were changed by selling the
ate oil to bidding companies rather than to Shell-BP and other
naller producers, Nigeria would be venturing into unknown areas at a
me of international oil crisis. The reasoning which favoured the
aintenance of stable offtake relations was somewhat weakened by
e Ministry's sales of at least two allotments of crude to Tenneco (a
J.S. minor firm) and Gelsenberg (German state-private company) in
iid-1973. Neither firm produced oil on its own account in Nigeria.
Iowever, the oil market was much more unsettled at the end of 1973
ian six months earlier when these third party sales of government
rude were arranged. Whatever the reasons for the oil ministry's
pposition to auction sales, it was unable or unwilling to officially
ancel the exercise after it was under way.

A month passed since the November 19 auction, and contracts
emained unsigned. Meanwhile NNOC was urging the Permanent
ecretary to choose buyers from the bidders primarily on the basis of
ighest price since 'a random allocation of crude [was] tantamount to
atronage and could damage future Government efforts to secure high
rices for its oil.'[22] Asiodu reported that[23]

> After various discussions with the Commissioner, Alhaji Ali Monguno, it
> was agreed to hold an auction amongst 14 selected substantial bidders from
> USA, Japan, E.E.C. and Brazil as in *Nigerian circumstances no one could
> take the responsibility for accepting a price only to be accused later of
> rejecting a higher price* . . . .

Finally, on December 18 and 19 NNOC sent invitations to
ompanies to state whether they were interested in purchasing
Iigerian state oil at the price offered by the highest bidder in the
uction exercise. Seven companies responded on December 21, 1973,
vith mandates to bid. Four companies (Mitsubishi, Texas Chemical
nd Plastics, Coastal States, and Phillips Petroleum) agreed on
December 22 to pay $22.60 per barrel for about 40,000 bd each over a
vo year period, with contract revisions possible each three months in
ccord with market conditions.

When the four companies, including one large U.S. firm, arrived to
onclude oil deals which would make pricing history, the foreign crude

buyers were advised only to *initial* the agreements, and sign after th
holiday period. This direction came from Asiodu acting on behalf o
the Head of State. World prices for 'spot' purchases of crud
plummeted on the embargoed Rotterdam market between 7-1
January 1974. The four never signed. According to Asiodu the
'declined to execute and perform pleading U.S. and Japanes
Government pressure against performance.'[24] The crude remaine
unsold except for 50,000 bd to the Ghana Supply Corporation whic
was not among the final high bidders but which had been promised o
by General Gowon. Shell-BP, the principals of which were badly i
need of the oil,[25] and the smaller producers took the unsold royalt
crude at prices which were low compared to those offered in th
auction.

Why did prices fall? The open market prices which had been offere
for direct sales by the Nigerian state rose from $5.21 in July 1973 t
$22.60 and even $23.00 by the end of 1973. By January 30, 1974 price
on offer had plummeted to around $14.00. What triggered thi
international price collapse despite the continuation of the Ara
embargo? The reduction in price followed from the U.S. Government'
Mandatory Allocation Program which limited all U.S. refiners' crud
supplies to three-quarters of their 1972 throughput. This ensured tha
American companies without their own producing fields were nc
driven out of business by the shortage, but it also meant that thes
companies could not import extremely expensive oil even if they wer
in a position to do so. Some firms were seeking oil at prices higher tha
those at which they could resell it mainly in order to expand their shar
of the consumer market. U.S. companies with excess oil were requirec
under the U.S. law, to sell it to a pool from which it could be purchase
by those in short supply for around ten dollars a barrel. Much of th
incentive to import high-cost OPEC oil was thereby eliminated. I
expensive oil was brought in, it could only be sold to the pool at a lowe
price. The Rotterdam market, which is a sensitive indicator of price
for freely-traded crude, was flooded with oil originally destined for th
U.S. Prices fell by a third overnight.[26]

Shell-BP got the crude during the 1973-74 crisis months.[27] Give
that the auction had created tremendous excitement both in
ternationally and among Nigerian middlemen, its failure raisec
questions among businessmen and officials of state. Not only wa
Nigeria in the international limelight to suffer humiliation when the
auction failed, but thirty-five Nigerian businessmen had, on their ow

account, participated in the bid to no avail. Suspicions were voiced about the conduct of the sale and the final disposition of the oil. While there may have been sound reasons for declining to move quickly to auction state oil, these reasons were not stated or made public at the time. The first attempt to clarify the auction events came in February 1977 with Asiodu's paper on 'Aspects of Nigerian oil policy 1971-1975.' Consequently, in 1974 the officials of NNOC and private Nigerians who sought allotments of oil to pass on to foreign buyers were ready to harbour suspicions of impropriety on the part of state officials. More generally, private Nigerian businessmen viewed the auction as one more manifestation of state monopoly in a lucrative area which, at least as regards crude sales, should be open to nationals. Those middlemen who were frustrated in their attempts to secure oil compared their failure with the conspicuous success of one Nigerian who mediated in the earlier Gelsenberg and Tenneco Ministry sales.

DIVISIVE ISSUES

As time went by, officials in the oil corporation became increasingly frustrated by the removal of projects to process crude oil from NNOC's control, by the closing of forums for relatively broad-based decision-making and by the distribution of agencies responsible for handling oil matters so widely that a co-ordinated policy was impossible. Participation in foreign oil companies was acquired on terms more favourable to the companies than those set by some other OPEC members.[28] Price calculations were worked out by specialists in NNOC to conform with OPEC's single pricing system only to be revised downward by the Ministry. Since the price was falling over much of 1974 and 1975 the oil ministry's practice of calling negotiations long after the beginning of the quarter, reduced the state's bargaining strength. Under the Permanent Secretary's chairmanship, the Petroleum Advisory Board atrophied. Meetings were simply not called and many oil issues were settled outside of the Federal Executive Council. Five projects for processing and transporting hydrocarbons which by NNOC's decree were within the corporation's scope were set up as independent firms having little relationship to the oil corporation, except that most were under Asiodu's chairmanship.

Professionals and technicians in NNOC witnessed the inexorable reduction of the corporation's scope. The concern was not with the fact that the oil ministry, through its permanent secretary, had the decision-making power. Rather, NNOC staff were concerned that policy did not allow them to develop oil-related activities within the corporation, which was becoming a shell without function. Matters worsened in January 1975 when a commission, which had been set up under Chief Udoji to examine wages and conditions in the civil service, issued its report. The report was unfortunately inconsistent in its recommendations with regard to NNOC. The Government's White Paper denied NNOC personnel the higher salaries they had hoped for and removed from the corporation Board its autonomous powers in such matters.[29] Following the Udoji Commission report and White Paper which increased civil servants' salaries, but which favoured administrators over professionals, industrial unrest broke out in all sectors including state corporations.[30] The National Electric Power Authority (NEPA) staff had grievances against their management and offered government an ultimatum: make reforms and remove the Chairman or the flow of electricity to the capital would be cut. The deadline came and went but after some 24 hours of blackout the chairman was removed. NEPA's chairman had been Asiodu. This event fed NNOC's resistance to the oil Permanent Secretary's style of administration.

Shortly thereafter NNOC prepared price proposals for the first half of 1975. When the Ministry expressed reluctance to adopt the proposals in negotiations with Shell-BP, NNOC technocrats went to Gowon who backed their price regime. The example of NEPA workers in dislodging Asiodu and Gowon's support on the price issue encouraged NNOC management to take a stand on the way it and oil policy were being administered. In so doing, technocrats supplied state officials with a record of Ministry activities in oil. NNOC's submissions, commonly known as the First and Second Memoranda, apparently triggered actions which contributed to the overthrow of the Gowon regime.[31]

This account of a series of events is tentative, given the limited information available, the nature of the issues, the death or exile of key actors, and the confidentiality of much documentary evidence. For example, two contradictory accounts exist of some events. Ex-Permanent Secretary Asiodu has stated of the reported investigating committee that 'No such committee was set up.'[32] Yet he corroborates much of the following account, while leaving many questions unanswered, as of necessity does this assessment.

In February 1975 NNOC management drafted the First Memorandum and forwarded it to all members of the Federal

Executive Council. This was in itself a step which was contrary to normal civil service procedure since any Council memorandum usually proceeds from the appropriate ministry via its commissioner to Cabinet Office and then to all Council members prior to its scheduled discussion at a meeting.[33] The memorandum from NNOC management included the resignation offer of the corporation's top executives who stated that they were drawing their salaries but performing no services. In the memorandum NNOC requested that Council

(a) define the oil corporation's functions,
(b) establish clear lines of authority between the Ministry of Mines and Power and the Nigerian National Oil Corporation,
(c) remove the Chairman of the Board, Phillip Asiodu, and
(d) appoint a General Manager.

The release of this document was followed by several specific actions. Since it had gone to all members of the Federal Executive Council, some steps had to be taken towards investigating NNOC's complaints. Furthermore, the corporation's request for a definition of its function required a response. According to interview data, Gowon set up a committee to investigate the situation. On it sat permanent secretaries, a commissioner, and as chairman, Alhaji Y. A. Gobir, Permanent Secretary of the Federal Ministry of Transport. This appointment was an indication which supported widespread assumptions that Gobir was earmarked to replace Mr. C. O. Lawson who was retiring as Secretary to the Federal Military Government on March 31, 1975.

Asiodu's response to NNOC's First Memorandum was to advocate that NNOC be restricted to undertaking new exploration and production in defined areas of its own and to acting as a holding company for downstream operations.[34] Asiodu's reply included personal attacks on individuals in the corporation whom he cited and accused of generalised wrong-doing. NNOC immediately prepared a response on behalf of the corporation. Each officer named in Asiodu's statement prepared his reply and attached documents from the files as evidence. The Second Memorandum consisted of four volumes of detailed history of Nigerian oil administration. It included

(a) a report on the corporation's activities,
(b) a list of the disagreements between Asiodu and NNOC,
(c) illustrations of the Chairman's style of administration and handling of financial matters, and

(d) calculations of the amounts of money which NNOC alleged were foregone through accepting terms favourable to the oil companies. According to these calculations, quantifiable losses amounted to over one billion dollars since 1973.

NNOC management was divided over what to do with the Second Memorandum. The document was explosive mainly because the steps which it alleged that Asiodu had taken could not have been executed without the knowledge and implicit sanction of the Head of State. Some members of NNOC management wanted copies of the Second Memorandum circulated to all who had received the First Memorandum and Asiodu's reply—which meant in effect all members of the Federal Executive Council. But the other members of NNOC management wanted a limited circulation of the damning document. The issue was settled when Gobir, the chairman of the investigating committee, read the memorandum. He strongly advised that distribution be limited to members of his committee. He reminded NNOC technocrats of their duty to avoid destabilisation and to preserve national unity. Gobir assured them that he was running a bonafide investigation which could well find in their favour. 'Why kill a mosquito with an atom bomb?' he asked. But Gobir had miscalculated. When the other members of the investigating committee received copies of the Second Memorandum, the group ceased to exist. Gobir was unable to convene any further meetings.

Ayida, not Gobir, was made Secretary to the Federal Military Government. NNOC's managers had made a mistake in limiting distribution of their defence. The Second Memorandum gave Asiodu powerful leverage over the Head of State who had announced to the press in March 1975 that 'Nobody could sell oil without my authority.'[35] It appears that the Second Memorandum was now reason for actions which covered up rather than aired the charges. Ayida was placed in charge of the civil service. Both C. O. Lawson and Alhaji Gobir had demonstrated their desire for an examination of NNOC complaints. Lawson, about to retire, had declined to remove two officers from NNOC on the grounds that he had no evidence of their wrongdoing. The double reponse to the Second Memorandum was to appoint a General Manager and to isolate the two NNOC officials who were closely associated with the memoranda. According to interview data, Asiodu's choice for General Manager was Mr. I. G. T. Ordor, then head of the country's only refinery at Port Harcourt. Two managers were removed or 'deseconded' from NNOC without investigation or hearing and contrary to civil service procedure. Attempts to have them detained did not succeed because Alhaji M. D. Yusufu, then Deputy Inspector General of Police, would not take steps in the absence of evidence against NNOC officers. Asiodu's 1977 account of the events brings out some of these points:[36]

> On February 24, 1975 Asiodu again urged on S.F.M.G. (Mr. Lawson) the need to have the issues properly investigated and decisions taken. In reply Mr. Lawson (SFMG) copied to Mr. Asiodu the Head-of-State's minute to Mr. Lawson agreeing that something must be done but adding 'I still await the Commissioner's comments.' The Commissioner circulated no comments. Instead, the Commissioner, Monguno and the Permanent Secretary, Asiodu, met with the Head-of-State towards the end of March. Both the Head-of-State and the Commissioner considered that the position of G. M., NNOC must be held by an indigene. The Permanent Secretary was instructed to make suggestions which were subsequently submitted to the Commissioner on 1st April, 1975 . . . . On April 8, 1975 after a further meeting with the Commissioner and the Permanent Secretary, the Head-of-State directed that the two NNOC petitioners should be deseconded from NNOC and Mr. Ordor appointed G.M., NNOC. A draft memorandum on Ordor's appointment was submitted to the Commissioner on April 22, 1975.

During late June 1975 Mr. Ordor's name was widely discussed but the straw vote indicated no support for the Port Harcourt refiner. Monguno, Commissioner of the newly-named Ministry of Petroleum and Energy, in particular refused to nominate or support this candidate, apparently in part because of strong resistance from Northern Federal Executive Council members to Mr. Ordor who had been prominent in supervising Biafran oil production during the civil war. The view was widely held that Ordor was subject to Asiodu's influence. Certain Council members were new Commissioners, having been appointed six months previously in January 1975. One of these, Murtala Muhammed, backed a candidate with only four years' work experience in a job with Agip since graduation: but he was from the North. Asiodu records that a two-month delay separated his submission of a draft memorandum on Ordor's appointment to Monguno and the Commissioner's circulating a 'draft memorandum to Council [which listed] two names instead of the one candidate only (Mr. Ordor) selected for presentation to F.E.C.'[37] Despite clear resistance to Ordor, his name appeared on the Federal Executive Council's July 4, 1975 agenda along with the names of three others who had little or no experience in oil.

Since Monguno was unwilling to recommend Ordor he absented himself from the meeting and his Permanent Secretary, Asiodu put the refinery chief's name forward. Council overwhelmingly rejected Ordor. The other candidates lacked an oil background and therefore were no serious contenders. In summing up the Council conclusions Gowon began by announcing a Federal Executive Council decision to appoint Ordor. Brigadier Murtala Muhammed, then Commissioner for Communications, interrupted the General. How could the Head of State conclude that Council had chosen Ordor when it had spent hours rejecting him? It would have been more honourable for Gowon to announce that he had appointed the man himself by Executive Order. The explosive Council meeting ended on that note.

Ordor's appointment was made by Gowon, not by the Federal Executive Council as Decree 18 required. On July 14 the press carried news of the appointment with effect from July 4th. The way the decision was forced through Council added substance to suspicions that the choice for General Manager was part of a cover-up.

THE COUP

Twenty-five days after the fateful Council meeting on Tuesday July 29th, 1975 Colonel Garba, then head of the Brigade of the Guards announced that General Gowon, then in Uganda at an OAU meeting, was no longer Head of State due 'to the events of the last few months.'[38] Muhammed, the new Head of State, explained that the affairs of state had become 'characterised by lack of consultation indecision, indiscipline and even neglect.' Governors had been running their fiefs like 'private estates.'[39]

Mr. Ordor's appointment to NNOC was annulled on August 6 by a letter from Brigadier Obasanjo, then Chief of Staff, Supreme Headquarters, which said 'In view of the fact that your appointment was not regular, it has been decided that the appointment be terminated.'[40] On August 13, 1975 Muhammed banned permanent secretaries from Council unless specifically invited. On September 12 Asiodu, who had been demoted from the oil to the housing ministry on August 8, was among those removed from the civil service. According to the *Tribune* the permanent secretaries 'were partners in crime with their political heads and quite often the master minds of business deals.'[41]

In sum, tensions between administrators in the oil ministry and professionals in the oil corporation resulted in the release of allegations of impropriety on the part of state officials in their relations with oil companies. NNOC's memoranda provided a rallying point for opposition while simultaneously forcing certain steps which for some had the appearance of cover-up actions. One of these—the appointment of Ordor as General Manager of NNOC—was clearly irregular. These divisions within the public service oil administration only contributed to the downfall of the Gowon regime. The appointment of Ordor, according to Muhammed, was 'the straw that broke the camel's back.'[42]

While the struggle over different conceptions of oil policy did not 'cause' the coup, it was an important constituent in a vast network of conflict and competition. We have seen how middlemen resisted their exclusion from the oil sector, especially when it came to the sale of state oil. In the same way they opposed their exclusion from other sectors which were being absorbed by the state. Just as the number of decision-makers decreased in the oil arena, there was a tendency towards monopoly and 'closed doors' elsewhere. To this web of interaction among middlemen and state officials was added a split between generalist administrators and the increasingly frustrated group of professional specialists in state corporations. The oil technocrats' challenge gave 'ammunition' to compradors and middlemen for whom a prerequisite to establishing successful triangular relationships was the replacement of the Gowon clique.

This case study of instability provides some indications of the utility of the general framework outlined in Part I. In particular, the behaviour of indigenous businessmen in attempting to arrange transactions and resist state monopoly, and the behaviour of public servants in the oil ministry and oil corporation are to some extent elucidated by the concepts of commercial triangles, compradors and technocrats. Whether or not impropriety actually characterized the relations which Ministry officials had with oil companies has not been demonstrated. Rather, the operative fact is that within a wider context of triadic and dyadic relationships, the belief that impropriety prevailed was readily adopted and disseminated. For actors who were unsuccessful in seeking a role in commercial or professional activities, disappointment and restriction to the margins of power may have reinforced suspicions of corruption. The account given of the part played by oil administrators and the petroleum industry in the 1975 coup is necessarily incomplete. Informed as it is by the general theory, it is nevertheless a plausible account but one which deals with only a few of the straws which broke the camel's back.

POST-COUP DEVELOPMENTS

It is important to note that oil technocrats did not win a victory fo
their conception of oil policy. The new administration showed littl
sign of questioning existing arrangements, apart from an adjustment i
oil prices. These were at first lowered by five cents a barrel, a decisio
which seems to have been a carry over from the previou
administration and one which went against the trend of the market a
companies stocked up in anticipation of OPEC's expected pric
increase in September 1975.[43] While the Algerians protested that the
were being undersold, the oil ministry described the action as a gestur
of 'goodwill' towards the oil companies.[44] This cut in price retroactiv
to July 1, was moreover accompanied by at least two sales to thir
parties of state oil through Nigerian middlemen at even lower prices

However in January 1976 this pattern of price moderation wa
revised, the market price of all state participation oil being increased
full 14 cents above the level OPEC would have found consistent with it
single pricing system. Despite a 'storm of protest' which was reporte
to be building up. among oil companies[45] and oil press reports tha
'Nigeria may decide to permit margins to remain somewhat abov
those in the Middle East . . .',[46] the strict terms were eventuall
implemented, bringing Nigerian oil prices more in line with the pric
regime devised by OPEC.

On 13 February 1976 a coup attempt resulted in the death of Genera
Muhammed. Under the new Head of State, General Obasanjc
progress has been made with several outstanding downstream project
For example, significant steps have been taken towards completing
second refinery at Warri, initiating a liquefied natural gas project wit
Shell-BP, and arranging for Nigerian tanker services. Relation
between the government and the oil companies appear to be good. I
may be that General Obasanjo, who was trained as an engineer, has
stronger commitment to building national capabilities in oil than di
his predecessors.

But can a technocratic orientation be created within the stat
through the efforts of committed military leadership? In the past th
military has shown itself to be part and parcel of the stratum formed b
triangular and bilateral relationships. A pro-technocratic militar
leadership would have to separate itself from the business communit
which resists exclusion from middlemanship. Military rulers in favou
of technocracy and state capitalism would have the task of obtainin
compliance and co-operation from generalist administrators who ar

currently vital to the day-to-day functioning of the government. This group is composed largely of people who have the know-how to run the administration—the very people who have in the past been prominent in organizing triangular and bilateral deals.

One positive step was taken by General Obasanjo towards establishing a technocratic state. In May 1976 the Ministry of Petroleum forwarded a memorandum to the Commissioners of the Federal Executive Council for their consideration. Entitled 'A memorandum on the restructuring of the public sector oil industry,' the document makes the case for a merger of the oil ministry with NNOC and gives the new entity, the Nigerian National Petroleum Corporation (NNPC), widespread freedom to become a commercial or profit-making company. However, a prerequisite for the operation of such an agency is the employment of qualified personnel who, in the Nigerian context, have to be paid at a level competitive with the private oil companies. If salaries within a state organ were indeed that high (two and three times the civil servants' incomes) it is likely that professionals and technicians in other state corporations would strike for comparable salaries, and thus precipitate a situation not unlike that which followed the 1975 announcement of Udoji payments.

One year after the memorandum was placed before Council, a decision to establish a single oil agency, NNPC, was published.[47] Whether the creation of the NNPC will lead to major changes in Nigerian oil policy remains to be seen. However, the creation of a single oil agency is, in itself, a major step forward and is a prerequisite for stable, efficient state regulation of an involvement in the Nigerian oil industry.

NOTES
1. On the powers of the independent Nigerian state to allocate profitable opportunities, see Gavin Williams, 'Nigeria: a Political Economy,' p. 11-54, in Gavin Williams (ed.), *Nigeria: Economy and Society*, (London: Rex Collings) 1976.
2. Haroun Adamu, 'A Nation of Commissioners,' *Sunday Times* (Lagos) November 9, 1975.
3. In the case of Nigeria, E. O. Akeredolu-Ale shows that the concentration of foreign firms in various economic activities leads Nigerians to either avoid those areas or to associate with the foreign operations. See his *Underdevelopment of Indigenous Entrepreneurship in Nigeria*, (Ibadan: Ibadan University Press) 1973. On the obstacles to capitalist development see also Peter Kilby, *Industrialisation in an open economy: Nigeria 1945-66*, (London: Cambridge University Press) 1969, and Akeredolu-Ale's review of Kilby, 'The competitive threshold hypothesis and Nigeria's industrialisation process,' *Nigerian Journal of Economic and Social Studies*, No. 14, 1972.

4. S. A. Madujibeya, 'Economic enclaves, technology transfer and foreign investment in Nigeria,' (London: duplicated) November 1975, p. 2. Paper presented to a University of London, School of Oriental and African Studies Seminar on Urban Culture, November 1975.

5. The *Third National Development Plan (1975-80)* states that 'In a country growing as rapidly as Nigeria, trading activities normally represent the quickest means of increasing income whereas manufacturing projects usually have long gestation periods.' (Lagos: Ministry of Economic Development and Reconstruction), 1975 Vol. I, p. 152.

6. V. I. Lenin, *Imperialism, the highest stage of capitalism: a popular account* (Moscow, Foreign Language Publishing House) n.d., p. 108.

7. The Conference Board, *Unusual foreign payments: a survey of the policies and practices of U.S. companies,* (New York: United States Conference Board) 1976 No. 682. Reviewed in the *Financial Times,* (London) February 16, 1976.

8. C. Gordon Tether, 'The disregard of moral standards,' Lombard Column *Financial Times* (London), February 11, 1976.

9. S. Cronjé, M. Ling, G. Cronjé, *Lonrho: portrait of a multinational,* (London Penguin and Julian Friedmann) 1976, shows how the skills of Tiny Rowland in making contacts enabled his firm to grow rapidly into one of the more important multinationals operating in Africa.

10. C. Gordon Tether, 'The disregard of moral standards,' Lombard Column *Financial Times* (London), February 11, *op. cit.* Jim Hougan stated that 'Northrop's corruption, for example, was a direct, *defensive* response to Lockheed's. Thus, as if by a variation of Gresham's law, bad business drove out the good.' 'The business of buying friends,' *Harper's* (New York), December 1975, p. 45.

11. *Financial Times* (London), February 1976, various issues.

12. *Financial Times* (London) February 16 and 17, 1976. In November 1976, Brig Garba, Commissioner for External Affairs, said of an investigation into the purchase of C-130 military transport aircraft by the Nigerian Airforce that the information made available to the Federal Government by the US Government was 'insufficient to warrant or justify the apprehension of any of the Nigerians who are known to be linked with Lockheed in this international scandal particularly as the exact nature and extent of benefits, if any, derived cannot be ascertained or determined.' Arrests were continuing with the aid of Interpol according to the *West Africa* report of 29 November 1976, p. 1827. For comment on the difficulties of obtaining evidence, see Jim Hougan, *op. cit.,* p. 44, 47.

13. *Financial Times,* (London), February 16 and 17, 1976.

14. *Ibid.,* February 16, 1976. Theoretically, firms could use their oligopolistic power to eliminate kickbacks. By dividing international markets amongst themselves the need for competitive advantage would be reduced. In practice this level of agreement is too difficult to establish and maintain. Only the oil industry has been relatively successful. See John M. Blair, *The Control of Oil,* (New York: Pantheon Books) 1976.

15. *Multinational corporations and U.S. foreign policy,* Part 12, (The Lockheed hearings), U.S. Government Printing Office, Washington D.C. See also Jim Hougan, 'The business of buying friends,' *op. cit.,* p. 45.

16. For instance, the Ministry of Mines and Power reacted sharply to Finance involvement in the award of concessions offshore in 1971. This was a matter for the oil ministry to decide, but Chief Awolowo and A. Atta—Commissioner and

Permanent Secretary, respectively, in Finance—intervened to regularize the process of making awards with the justification that the exercise involved funds and therefore the Ministry of Finance. Lagos, interview, 1975.

17. *Second National Development Plan 1970-74,* (Lagos: Ministry of Information), p. 134.

18. Nigerian policy on private capitalist development shifted from a general commitment in 1962 to 'enable businessmen to control an increasing portion of the Nigerian economy,' (1962-8 Development Plan, p. 24) to *requiring,* through the 1972 indigenisation decree, that foreign firms sell shares to Nigerians. Policy on state ownership has been completely reversed. In 1961 the government 'did not believe that [it was] desirable for the state itself to own and operate every important organ of economic activity.' (P. A. Prechl, *Foreign Enterprise in Nigeria: laws and policies,* Chapel Hill, 1965, p. 163, quoting a Ministry of Finance statement). By 1970 the government announced that it would 'seek to acquire, by law of necessity [sic], equity participation in a number of strategic industries' which by 1975 included 'heavy industry, power, communications, mining and transport . . . .' *Second National Development Plan,* p. 289 and *Third National Development Plan,* Vol. 1, p. 341.

19. *Decree 18 of 1971,* establishing the Nigerian National Oil Corporation, April 1971.

20. Estimates of the exact amount of royalty oil available vary. Moreover, no participation oil was strictly speaking yet available from the companies which were negotiating participation terms in late 1973. Estimates of total volumes of oil under state control vary from 300,000 bd (interviews with NNOC officials) to 425,000 bd (*The Times,* London, 24 September 1973.)

21. NNOC standard reply to potential crude oil buyers, *Petroleum Intelligence Weekly,* October 8, 1973, p. 8 stated that 'Nigerian National Oil Corp. will not deal with middlemen or agents of whatever description be they Nigerians or any nationality whatsoever in negotiating or contracting for the purchase of crude oil.'

22. Document seen by the author, Lagos, 1975.

23. P. C. Asiodu, 'Some aspects of Nigerian oil policy, 1971-1975,' (Lagos: duplicated) 1977, p. 2.

24. *Ibid.* Asiodu states further that 'On January 2, 1974 after the Christmas and New Year Holidays the Commissioner minuted that the Head-of-State had approved signing the contracts and the instruction was promptly relayed to the Head of the Auction Panel. . . . . [That the companies did not perform] was according to them due to the irresistible pressures of U.S. and Japanese Governments which had nothing whatsoever to do with NNOC or F.M.G.'

25. See Anthony Sampson's account of the pressure exerted on Shell and British Petroleum by the Heath Conservative Government in the last months of 1973 to supply oil sufficient to take some of the sting out of the British coal miners' strike and prevent the imposition of a three-day week on 5 December 1973. His source is the Chairman of BP, Sir Eric Drake who along with Frank McFadzean of Shell, met Heath at Chequers on October 21, 1973. Heath insisted that the companies could not cut their supplies to Britain, but retreated from his demands rather than put in writing which other countries should suffer. *The Seven Sisters,* (London: Hodder and Stoughton) 1975, p. 263.

26. If the buying companies had signed the Nigerian oil contracts at $22.60, they would have re-negotiated the price downward or forfeited their deposits, whichever was most advantageous. The larger significance of the auction failure is

that it meant no extremely high pricing precedent was set at the time, when the international crude market had only a few thousand barrels under 'free market' direct sales and OPEC was in the process of determining 1974 prices. As David Ottaway noted in *The Guardian* (London), December 6, 1973: 'If Nigeria decides to sell its highly valued oil at $15 or $16 as most oilmen here [in Lagos] expect it to do, another round of enormous price hikes throughout the Arab world is almost certain to occur. Nigeria is thus for the first time in a position of being able to lead the oil producers in determining oil prices.'

27. In the midst of the crisis, the Board of Shell (Dutch and British) decided that Holland should suffer no more than other countries which were not embargoed by AOPEC. 'By trebling deliveries from Nigeria and doubling them from Iran, Holland experienced no more than the average supply cutbacks.' Paper issued by Shell Nederland BV to the Dutch Parliament, March 18-20, quoted by Anthony Sampson, *The Seven Sisters,* (London: Hodder and Stoughton) 1975, p. 262-3.

28. Terisa Turner, *Oil and Government:* The Making and Implementation of Petroleum Policy in Nigeria, (University of London, London School of Economics and Political Science: unpublished Ph.D. thesis, Department of Political Science) 1977, Chapter 3. In 1977 operating agreements had yet to be signed, although informal arrangements were in practice for state operational involvement.

29. The Udoji Commission recommended that 'The ranking and compensation of employees in commercial public agencies should be comparable to those of the private sector enterprise with which they compete.' Public Service Review Commission, *Report on Grading and Pay,* Vol. II, 'Proposed Ranking System for Parastatals,' p. 12. (Lagos: Ministry of Information) 1975. Incongruously, the White Paper put NNOC under category 'B' thus putting it within the structure of the Civil Service as established by the Statutory Corporations Service Commission for utilities corporations.

30. Peter Waterman, 'Third World Strikes, an invitation to discussion,' *Development and Change,* Vol. 7, No. 3, 1976. Also see his 'The Lot of the Lagos Dock Worker,' *Management in Nigeria,* No. 12, 1976, p. 8-19. The Udoji White Paper denied the existence of notable tension between administrators and professionals, saying it had been exaggerated.

31. The account of the coup is based on documents seen by the author, published accounts and media reports, interview information, Lagos, 1975 and Asiodu's 'Aspects of Nigerian Oil Policy 1971-1975,' *op. cit.* See also Terisa Turner, *Oil and Government:* The Making and Implementation of Petroleum Policy in Nigeria, *op cit.,* for a fuller treatment.

32. Asiodu, *op. cit.,* p. 6.

33. Asiodu refers to the memorandum 'dated February 11, 1975, which had been improperly copied to all members of F.E.C. and some officials.' *Ibid.,* p. 6.

34. *Ibid.,* p. 7.

35. *Daily Times* (Lagos), March 6, 1975.

36. P. C. Asiodu, *op. cit.,* p. 7.

37. *Ibid.,* p. 7.

38. *Daily Times* (Lagos). July 30, 1975.

39. *Daily Times* (Lagos) July 31, 1975. For an account of the coup see 'Nigeria Capitalism and the Coup,' P. Collins, T. Turner and G. Williams, in G. William (ed.), *Nigeria: Economy and Society,* (London: Rex Collings) p. 159-84.

40. *Sunday Punch* (Lagos) August 26, 1975.

1. *Nigerian Tribune,* August 13, 1975.
2. After swearing in the new Commissioners on August 6, 1975, Muhammed is reported to have given an account of the reasons for the coup, during which he used this expression in connection with Mr. Ordor's appointment. Interview, Lagos, August 1975.
3. *Petroleum Intelligence Weekly,* August 4, 1975, p. 2; *Petroleum Economist,* November 1975, p. 417; *Petroleum Intelligence Weekly,* August 11, 1975, and P. C. Asiodu, *op. cit.,* p. 10.
4. *Petroleum Economist,* November 1975, p. 417 and *Petroleum Intelligence Weekly,* August 4, and August 11, 1975.
5. A 'storm of protest' was reported by the *Petroleum Intelligence Weekly,* January 12, 1976. See also the *Financial Times* (London) January 13, 1976.
6. *Petroleum Intelligence Weekly,* February 2, 1976, p. 3.
7. *West Africa,* 9 May 1977. NNPC appears to be organized along the lines suggested by the memorandum of May 1966, Col. M. M. Buhari, formerly the Commissioner, Ministry of Petroleum Resources (the oil ministry under a new name), was made Federal Commissioner for Petroleum in charge of the NNPC Board of Directors. Other members of the Board are the Permanent Secretaries of the Ministry of Finance and the Ministry of Economic Development, the NNPC Managing Director and three others to be appointed by the Federal Executive Council.

The research for this chapter was funded by the Canada Council.

Part Three

FEDERAL REFORM

7

The Creation of States

Ali D. Yahaya

The speed with which the Murtala Mohammed government acted in creating additional states was in stark contrast to Gowon's dilatoriness in this matter. Only two weeks after taking office an advisory panel was appointed and given less than five months in which to report.

In acting so promptly the new leadership was as much concerned with the restoration of the military's own good name as it was with resolving a contentious issue. It was one of a series of measures taken by the new Government to recover faith in the military as a disciplined dedicated profession, led by gentlemen and men of honour. This image had been tarnished by widespread allegations of corruption especially against the State Governors and by Gowon's failure to live up to his promise of a return to civilian rule in 1976.[1] A restoration of the specifically military virtue of probity and efficiency required not just a change of personnel but also a change in the whole style of Gowon's administration. The most effective demonstration of this lay in a speedy implementation of the nine-point programme of 1970 of which the creation of States was an essential ingredient.

The Background

The re-drawing of administrative areas is not new to Nigeria. Between 1900 and 1945, in periodic adjustments, new administrative units were created either by sub-dividing existing units (as in the case of Ibadan, Oyo, Rivers, Owerri, Zaria and Katsina Provinces) or by merging parts of several neighbouring units (eg Plateau Province which was constituted from parts of old Bauchi, Muri and Nassarawa Provinces.)

Any such reorganisation raises a problem of the criteria to be used for determining the new boundaries. In Nigeria these criteria have been much debated not only in recent years but also in colonial days. At the time of the amalgamation of Northern and Southern Nigeria, in 1914, alternative proposals were put forward by E. D. Morel, the Editor of the African *Daily Mail* and C. L. Temple, the Acting Governor of Northern Nigeria. Morel suggested units 'which corresponded as far as possible to natural geographical boundaries' and recommended the division of the country into four Provinces.[2] Temple on the other hand stressed administrative criteria and recommended seven Provinces.[3] These two proposals were rejected by Lugard who preferred the North-South division of the country, sub-divided into provinces, twelve in the North and nine in the South.

The subsequent regrouping of the Southern Provinces in 1939—the river Niger being roughly the line of separation between East and West—instituted the tri-partite division of Nigeria which was to last until independence and beyond. It was a division which came to be bitterly contested. In the first place the Northern region was larger than the other two regions combined, which put it in a dominant position. Secondly, each of the three Regions was based on one of the three dominant ethnic groups. Other ethnic groups found themselves treated as minorities under this arrangement and, during the decolonisation process of the 1950s, began to demand creation of additional Regions or States. The Willink Commission was appointed in September 1957 to consider this possibility, although only as a last resort. A total of nine proposals for the creation of states was put forward to this Commission. From the Western region came demands for a Yoruba Central, an Ondo Central, a Midwest and a Lagos State. From the Eastern region came the demands for a Calabar-Ogoja-Rivers State and alternative demands for separate Ogoja, Rivers and Cross River States. Only one demand was made in the North and this was for the creation of a Middle Belt State. The Willink Commission rejected every one of these demands giving preference to constitutional guarantees of individual rights and to provision of ad hoc development Boards or Councils for areas needing special attention.[4]

These proved ineffective and the campaign for the creation of states remained a prominent issue in party politics through to 1966. The only satisfaction obtained was the creation of a Mid-West Region in 1963. The minorities of the Northern and Eastern regions were able to press their claims afresh during the upheavals of July-October 1966 and they found in Gowon a firm supporter of their cause. In his speech of November 30th he committed himself to the creation of states on the basis of the following principles:

(a) no one state should be in a position to dominate or control the central government;
(b) each state should form one compact geographical area;
(c) administrative convenience, the facts of history and the wishes of the people concerned must be taken into account;
(d) each state should be in a position to discharge effectively the functions allocated to regional Governments;
(e) it is also essential that the new states should be created simultaneously.[5]

On the eve of the civil war, Gowon announced the creation of twelve states. Only the Mid-West survived intact. Lagos absorbed a small part of the West. The Northern Region was divided into six states and the Eastern Region into three. Even so, this did not satisfy all demands, notably those for a break up of the West and for a further subdivision of the North.[6]

After the civil war new and far more numerous demands came to be made. Gowon's own indecision was largely to blame for this. He claimed in October 1970 that 'the twelve states structure had in fact produced a basis for political stability in that the structural imbalance of the First Republic has been decisively corrected.' Yet in the same speech Gowon promised to review the matter at the end of four years, Nigeria being 'a dynamic society', and in the event of the Government becoming convinced that it was in the national interest, to create more states 'before handing over power to an elected government'.[7]

Before the end of the four year period many prominent Nigerians had come out openly in favour of the creation of more states, e.g. Dr. Azikiwe, Chief Enahoro, Shettima Ali Monguno and Chief Awolowo.[8] All believed that more states would strengthen the Federation. Yet all that Gowon had to announce on October 1st, 1974 was a commitment in principle to the creation of more states, the implementation being left in suspense. This was, in the opinion of the *New Nigerian,* the worst possible way of handling the issue. To announce that the Government was committed to the creation of more states without simultaneously creating these new states was merely to undermine the existing state administrations. The agitation for the creation of states would simply be intensified in an attempt to convince the Government that demands were genuine.[9] Gowon's empty announcement did indeed act like Pandora's box. It produced a spate of newspaper advertisements—the main method used to publicise demands. Between October and December 1974 no less than 19 such advertisements appeared in the daily newspaper the *New Nigerian*.[10] No decision had been taken by Gowon before he was removed from office on 29th July, 1976.

The Panel for the Creation of States

The Panel appointed on August 7th, 1976 had five members. Its Chairman was a Justice of the Supreme Court, Justice Ayo Irikefe. The other members were an Army Brigadier, a university lecturer in political science, a retired civil servant and a lawyer in private practice. None was associated with any movement for the creation of states.

The panel was given up to the 31st of December 1976 to submit its report. The setting of a deadline was an innovation which served to emphasise the new Government's intentions not to delay and it became the general pattern. The brief time allowed—less than five months— may be compared with the ten months which the Willink Commission required to complete a simpler task.

The Panel was given the following terms of reference:

(i) To examine the question of the creation of more States in the Federation and, should the Committee find the creation of more States necessary and desirable to:

(a) advise on the delimitation of such states;
(b) advise on the economic viability of the proposed States;
(c) advise on the location of the administrative capitals of the proposed States, and
(d) examine and advise on all other factors that may appear to the Committee to be relevant, so as to enable the Government to take a decision which will ensure a balanced Federation.

(ii) To receive and examine written representations from individuals, groups, organisations or associations who may have views on the desirability or otherwise of creating States in particular areas.[11]

The Panel began by inviting individuals or groups who might have views 'on the desirability or otherwise for the creation of states' to make written submissions to it. The response was overwhelming. Over 1,000 memoranda were received before the deadline for their submission (Sept. 12th). Most came from groups of people, usually a community, professional association or friendly society, supporting the cause of a particular state movement. The individual memoranda were, on the other hand, from men who had outgrown their localities such as university teachers, or prominent public figures and their views tended to be of a general nature.

The greatest number of memoranda were received from the South East, Midwest, West and East Central States where popular movements for change had been sustained over many years. The large number of submissions from these areas also reflected the relatively high level of social mobilisation. Their inhabitants were convinced that more scholarships, more employment and more social and welfare amenities would be available for distribution if more States were created.

In order to ascertain popular demand the Panel decided to undertake a one month tour of the whole country. Public sittings were held at which individuals were allowed to come forward to make verbal representations. These meetings generated widespread interest and the response was startling. Most of the arguments put forward indicated quite clearly that ethnic loyalty was still strong among highly placed Nigerians.[12] The tour also enabled the Panel to learn from extensive consultations with civil servants the nature of the administrative problems involved as well as the extent to which their work was being undermined by movements for the creation of States.

The Proponents of the Creation of States

The main proponents of more states can be classified into four groups. In the first category were leading personalities such as Dr. Azikiwe, Chief Obafemi Awolowo, Sir Louis Mbanefo, Alhaji Sule Katagum, Shettima Ali Monguno and Chief S. Adebo, men whose long record of public service had won them a national reputation. They either spoke as individuals or represented the views of some Association of which they were leading members. For instance Chief S. O. Adebo and Chief J. O. Udoji submitted proposals in the name of the Nigeria Society. The Abeokuta Improvement Association and a Committee of Nigerian Citizens were similarly represented. These national figures did not all remain aloof from specific demands. Dr. Azikiwe endorsed the movement for the creation of a Niger State to comprise Onitsha and the Ibo communities of the Midwest State, but was opposed by Sir Louis Mbanefo, who advocated that two States be formed out of the old Owerri and Onitsha Provinces. Shettima Ali Monguno supported the creation of a Borno State corresponding to the old Borno Province. The second group was composed of those former politicans whose involvement in the States movement was seen as a continuation or extension of their former political activities. Their role in politics was to secure an ample share of national resources for the furtherance of local interests. This would win them a body of localised support and enable them to speak for and on behalf of 'their people'. Several of the State movements were organised by persons in this category. For example, prominent in the Enugu State movement were Chief J. U. Nwodo, formerly a Minister in the Regional Government, and Chief Aja Nwachuku, a one-time Federal Minister. The Ondo State movement owed much to the long-standing efforts of Chief G. B. A. Akinyede, an ex-MP, supported by the ex-Federal Minister, Chief Obu Akinfosile. The Bauchi State movement was led by Alhaji A. D. Rufar and Alhaji Ahmed Kari, well known local politicians.

In the third category were people best designated as communal leaders. They were by and large people of local reputation with a record of political struggle for the cause of a local community. They tended to be leaders of merger movements, that is, they sought the incorporation of their local community either with an existing neighbouring state, in which case it was no more than a request for a boundary adjustment of relatively minor importance, or with a state still to be created, and in this case the local community was joined with others in a wider movement for the creation of that state. A good example was the Lere district, located in the Bauchi Emirate. Its inhabitants are ethnically different from the Bauchi political class and even in colonial days they had sought recognition as a separate division. To them and to their long-standing leader, Peter Gonto, the proposed State of Bauchi had no attraction; they preferred instead to join those advocating a Plateau State.

Finally, young civil servants and students actively participated in State movements often in the hope that they would thereby find official employment. This was especially true of areas where there was apparent manpower shortage. Both the Plateau and Niger State movements were spearheaded by this group of people. The Plateau Students Association had been opposed to the decision in 1967 to create a Benue-Plateau State and it continued thereafter to campaign vigorously for a separation.

Chiefs and other traditional leaders—a possible fifth category—tended to support local demands. The Oyo State Movement was openly supported by the Alafin of Oyo, the Olubaden of Ibadan and other chiefs in the area. The Ondo State Movement also had the full support of the local Obas and Chiefs. Even in the emirates where Emirs tended to avoid expressing openly their political preferences, one witnessed Emirs who on this occasion came out openly in support of the creation of States. The Bauchi State Movement had the full backing of the Emirs in the Province.

Proposals submitted

The Panel received memoranda of two kinds: those which proposed some general criterion for the creation of States and those which urged the creation of particular States. The latter were by far the most numerous. Two general criteria were suggested: first that States should be created on the lines of the old Provinces and, secondly, that States should reflect Nigeria's ethnic and linguistic diversity.

A reversion to the boundaries of the old Provinces was recommended in the belief that the Provinces had proved to be the most cohesive political unit in Nigeria's administrative history. There is, however, little historical basis for such a belief.[14] The Provinces had been simply an administrative umbrella covering a number of communities each recognised as separate Native or Local Authorities. There was little integration at provincial level. The Provinces merely served to enhance the regulatory capacity of the colonial state. Moreover the boundaries of the provinces were never completely stable: they shifted and changed over the years as indicated in Table I below. In 1927 there were 22 provinces, in 1944 the number was increased to 23, in 1965 to 25 and by 1963 it had risen to 32: it is true however that at least nineteen could claim a continuity of over forty years both in name and area.

The demand for the creation of states based on Provinces was rejected by the Panel because it was not obvious that it would be generally acceptable. Where the demand was made, it became the Panel's recommendation, as in the cases of Ondo, Niger, Sokoto, Bauchi and Borno. There were, however, other cases where what was demanded cut across old provincial boundaries.

The creation of states on linguistic lines is most prominently associated with Chief Obafemi Awolowo. He listed ten major linguistic groups in Nigeria each large enough to constitute a state: Hausa, Yoruba, Ibo, Efik or Ibibio, Kanuri, Tiv, Ijaw, Edo, Urhobo and Nupe. He suggested seven additional states to be formed out of the smaller linguistic groups. These were to be merged on the basis of common history, geographical contiguity, and economic viability.[15]

TABLE I
PROVINCIAL UNITS IN NIGERIA

1927	1944	1956	1963
Colony	Colony	Colony	Colony
Ijebu	Ijebu	Ijebu	Ijebu
Abeokuta	Abeokuta	Abeokuta	Abeokuta
Oyo	Oyo	Oyo	Oyo
		Ibadan	Ibadan
Ondo	Ondo	Ondo	Ondo
Ilorin	Ilorin	Ilorin	Ilorin
Kabba	Kabba	Kabba	Kabba
Benue	Benue	Benue	Benue
Plateau	Plateau	Plateau	Plateau
Adamawa	Adamawa	Adamawa	Adamawa
Zaria	Zaria	Zaria	Zaria
Niger	Niger	Niger	Niger
Sokoto	Sokoto	Sokoto	Sokoto
	Katsina	Katsina	Katsina
Kano	Kano	Kano	Kano
Bauchi	Bauchi	Bauchi	Bauchi
Borno	Borno	Borno	Borno
Benin	Benin	Benin	Benin
Warri	Warri	Delta	Delta
Onitsha	Onitsha	Onitsha	Onitsha
			Enugu
Owerri	Owerri	Owerri	Owerri
		Rivers	Umuahia
			Yenagoa
			Degema
			Port Harcourt
Ogoja	Ogoja	Ogoja	Ogoja
Calabar	Calabar	Calabar	Calabar
			Abakaliki
			Annang
			Uyo

The Panel found this criterion and the associated concept of ethnicit⸱
no more suitable than that of the Provinces and the Governmen
rejected it out of hand as a 'disruptive force'[16] (discussed more full⸱
below.)

In the second type of memoranda as many as thirty States wer⸱
proposed. With only two exceptions, referred to later, they were sub
divisions of existing States. There are listed in Table II. This als⸱
indicates the supporters of each proposal and whether or not ther⸱
were advocates of the status quo.

TABLE II

PATTERN OF DEMAND FOR THE CREATION OF STATES

State in question	Demand made	Main proponents
Benue/Plateau	Benue State	Idoma and Igala intelligentsia, Tiv neutral.
	Plateau State	Students, civil servants businessmen and chiefs.
	Status quo	Lafia and Nasarawa leaders of thought and Tiv intelligentsia.
East Central	Enugu State	Former politicians, leaders of thought and chiefs.
	Imo State	Former politicians, lawyers and chiefs.
	Abakaliki State	Abakaliki Movement
	Status quo	People of Njikoka Division
Kwara	Kabba State	Bassange Community Igbirra and Kogi Division intelligentsia and the Attah of Igala
	Status quo	People of Ilorin, Kabba, Oyun, Igbomina-Ekiti, Lafiagi, the Emir of Ilorin and the Obaro of Kabba.
Lagos	Status quo	Chiefs and people of Lagos State—old politicians, women's associations and professionals.
Midwest	Delta state	Urhobo & Isoko communities
	Warri State	Itsekiri community of the Midwest.
	Status quo	Obisa traditional rulers, chiefs and people of Aniocha, Ika Divisional Union, Ukwuani communities in Aboh Division.
North Central	Katsina State	Young civil servants
	Zaria State	Chiefs of southern Zaria and advocates of states on provincial basis.
North East	Adamawa/Sardauna State	Civil servants and Chiefs.
	Sardauna	Young civil servants and Chiefs.
	Bauchi State	Emirs, former politicians, and civil servants.
	Borno State	Emirs, former politicians and civil servants.

State in question	Demand made	Main proponents
North West	Sokoto State	Civil servants and former politicians.
	Niger State	Emirs, old politicians and civil servants
	Gurara State	Young civil servants
	Kainji State	People of Kontagora.
Rivers	Port Harcourt State	Chiefs and the intelligentsia of the 'nationalities who live on the low coastal plane impinging on the Delta of the Niger' or the non-Ijaw elements.
South East	Cross River State	Chiefs and people of all the communities in the following divisions: Oron Calabar, Akamkpa, Obubra, Ikom, Ogoja, Obudu.
West	Oyo or Yoruba Central State	The Alafin of Oyo, Obas, Chiefs, politicians and people of old Oyo Province.
	Ondo State	Obas, Chiefs, politicians, retired civil servants and the people of old Ondo Province.
	Ogun-Yewa State	The Alake of Abeokuta, Chiefs and people of Egba Egbados and Ibarapa.
	Ijebu State	The Ijebu steering committee on behalf of Chiefs and people of old Ijebu Province.
	South Western State	The Ijebus Steering Committee (an alternative to an Ijebu State)

Not included in this list are the two exceptional proposals which cut across existing State boundaries. These were

(i) the merger of the Ibo-speaking Divisions of Midwest with the Onitsha Division of East Central to form a Niger State (not to be confused with the demand for a Niger State in North West). The Niger State Committee supporting this proposal comprised the Onitsha elite, notables and chiefs.

ii) the merger of minority groups in Benue-Plateau, North Central and North-West to form a Nassarawa State. The proponents were intellectuals and young civil servants, especially from Southern Zaria.

That only two of the proposals were not simply subdivisions of existing states suggests that old boundaries had acquired a certain prescriptive status. Indeed the Nassarawa proposal harks back to the old Nassarawa Province, which was dismembered in 1919, and perhaps merely confirms the strength of historical links forged by a common administrative experience. The view that new States should be modelled on the old Provinces was further testimony of this, as was the composition of the Cross River State movement in which people of Ogoja, Ikom and Obudu associated themselves with the people of Calabar Division, despite their greater cultural affinity with the Idomas and Tivs of Benue-Plateau.

The only State not listed in Table II is Kano, for the simple reason that there were no proposals for its sub-division. Why this was so, whereas no fewer than six separate proposals came from East Central and five from West, is a question best answered after consideration of the types of argument used in justification of particular demands.

Arguments Advanced

The demand for the creation of States was justified by each movement based on four main arguments. These had as their themes balance, domination, linguistic affinity or cultural incompatibility, and development.

BALANCE

It is widely believed that Nigeria's political crises of the independence decade can be attributed very largely to an imbalance in the structure of its federal arrangement. One Region contained more than half the total population of the country and easily translated its numerical strength into electoral support and hence political dominance. The creation of the twelve States in 1967 went far towards rectifying this anomaly and it was contended that a further sub-division was advisable in the interests of greater stability. This was the view expressed, for instance, by Chief Anthony Enahoro at the National Union of Students Convention held in Zaria on September 26th, 1974. He voiced his apprehension 'that the relatively large states may demand special

treatment or consideration and thereby be a source of unrest in th
country.' More revealing was his remark 'that the smaller the units th
stronger the federation, and the whole country has come to accept tha
our common ambition must be to build a strong Nigerian Federation
This clearly links the two issues, although it does so in a way that i
misleading. If it is suggested that the strength of a Federation lies in th
dominance of the Federal Government this is to ignore th
requirement that a federation should be composed of units wit
sufficient political, economic and financial standing of their own t
allow them to exercise their constitutional powers with a certain degre
of autonomy. The Federal and State Governments should be co
ordinate and interdependent powers. In considering how far to go i
creating additional States in Nigeria, some weight also needs to b
given to the fact that the status and powers of the Federal Governmen
have increased since 1967 due to the nature of a military government
to the drift in skilled manpower from the States to the Feder
Government, to the massive organisation effort which the civil wa
necessitated and to the enormous financial resources accruing to th
Federal Government from oil. There are strict limits to the optimur
number of states, even if, as the Government White Papers stated
'there is no scientific formula'.

The Federal Government attached the greatest weight to th
argument that the creation of States would enhance stability. Th
Government paid relatively little attention to the question of th
States' autonomy and viability: the existing twelve States were alread
heavily dependent on central revenues. It also favoured a large
number of States which necessarily subdivided the large ethnic group
and so made quite clear that ethnicity was not at all a relevant factor i
the creation of States. For the Federal Government, state creation wa
regarded as a political issue, designed to lower tension and to create
conducive environment for nation building.

DOMINATION

Domination refers to official discrimination in employment, in th
distribution of amenities, and in the provision of basic infrastructur
facilities. It was a complaint voiced by many and indeed it was difficu
to resist the conclusion that demands for the subdivision of a State wer
tantamount to an indictment of its administration.

The Enugu, Cross River, Niger (of Northwestern State), Ond
Delta, Abakaliki and Bauchi State movements all argued their cas

partly on the basis of neglect. Their arguments may be illustrated by outlining the allegations made by the proponents of Enugu and Niger States.[17] Spokesmen for an Enugu State claimed that between 1951 and 1953 when Eyo Ita was the Leader of Government Business in the Eastern Provinces, no Minister or Parliamentary Secretary was appointed from their area. His successor, Dr. Azikiwe, appointed three junior ministers, but only after very strong protests had been made, and this still left the area under-represented in proportion to its population. There was no improvement when Dr. Okpala became Premier: out of sixteen Ibo ministers only four were from the Enugu area. During the civil war it was totally unrepresented in Ojukwu's government (a strange ground for complaint!). After the war, when as part of East Central State it constituted half the population, it provided only three, later four, of the twelve commissioners. Their area fared no better in appointments to the Boards of statutory corporations, being accorded only two posts of Chairman. Its share of posts in the entire civil service of East Central State, numbering over 28,000, was said to be no more than 2.5% and it could boast only two Permanent Secretaries or positions with the rank of Permanent Secretary, out of a total of forty-one. Even in religious institutions there was discrimination; most of the Bishops were from the southern Ibo areas.

It was alleged that the Enugu area also suffered from a lack of education facilities, and in the award of scholarships. In 1960 it had only nine post-primary institutions as against 95 in southern Ibo areas and the same disproportion obtained in 1975: 35 out of a total of 360. Of the 3,522 primary schools in the East Central State only 1,039 were located in the Enugu area. The attention of the Panel was also drawn to the 1975/80 Development Plan for evidence of discrimination in the provision of health facilities, roads and piped water. Twelve of the urban towns selected for development during the 1975/80 plan at a cost of N34 million were in the 'southern' Ibo areas, whereas only four were in the Enugu area and they would receive only N12 million. All this was attributed to domination.

The spokesman for a Niger State did not complain that it was an area discriminated against in terms of appointments. Most of the key positions in the North West State were in fact controlled by people from that area. They complained, however, about the discriminatory manner in which the 1970/74 Development Plan had been implemented, particularly with respect to the location of industry, electrification, water supply and education. The only three industries

to be established, a tannery, a furniture factory and an oil mill, had al
been located in Sokoto Division, although Minna or Abuja would have
been a better choice for the furniture factory because of the local supply
of wood. Other projects listed in the Plan for which Niger Province
could supply the raw material, such as starch processing, fibre
production and rice milling, were simply not started.

The only places to have been supplied with electricity by the end of
the 1970/74 plan period were Talata Mafara, Gumi, Jega, Gwadabawa
and Birnin-Kebbi, all located in Sokoto. None of the towns listed from
Niger Province, such as Baro, Abuja and Kontagora had benefitted.
The improvements in water supply were concentrated in Sokoto
Province; it was allocated two thirds of the town projects and 70% of
the new wells. In the matter of schools, Sokoto and Niger Province
each had in 1967 six secondary schools and five teacher training
colleges. By 1974 Sokoto had a total of eighteen secondary schools and
fourteen teacher training colleges while Niger had to be content with
thirteen and eleven respectively.

A catalogue of such grievances was typical of many other
submissions. The frequency of the allegations highlights a problem
which is not necessarily resolved by creating additional States. If new
majorities and new minorities emerge, as was indeed the case after the
creation of States in 1967, the problem is merely transferred to a lower
level. A well designed and faithfully executed policy of 'even
development' may prove just as elusive within the new boundaries as
within the old ones. One cannot indulge in an infinite regress
periodically creating new States in response to each new set of
grievances. Allegations of domination of this kind were no guide to the
Panel when making its recommendations nor to the Government when
making its decisions, except in acute cases where feelings of frustration
were so strong that some adjustment of the boundary seemed necessary
in the interests of political stability.

LINGUISTIC AFFINITY OR CULTURAL INCOMPATIBILITY

Mention was made earlier of the general proposition that state
boundaries should correspond to linguistic divisions. There were
several specific instances in which those seeking a change of boundaries
wished to group themselves with others on the grounds of linguistic
affinity or to disassociate themselves from others (albeit perhaps of the
same language group) on grounds of cultural incompatibility. Appeal

was made to arguments of this type by advocates of Yoruba Central, Plateau, Niger (East Central) Cross River and Imo States.

The proposed Yoruba Central State encompassed the old Oyo Empire whose inhabitants have long claimed to be the 'proper Yorubas' of different descent, customs, political organisation and dialect from other Yoruba. In submission to the Panel works on the history and sociology of the Yoruba peoples were cited in support of this claim.

Advocates of a Plateau state stressed both the cultural identity of its inhabitants and the cultural differences separating them from the inhabitants of Benue Province, especially the Tivs and Idomas. The argument that the Plateau inhabitants are culturally united could not be sustained by reference to a common ethnic origin for nearly 100 ethnic groups have been identified, but it was claimed that there is a similarity of political institutions, social organisations and customs. An important influence in promoting a sense of solidarity was perhaps the experience of having been administered for a period of nearly forty years as a single Province. The assertion that they were culturally distinct from the major ethnic groups of Benue Province took the form of contrasting the 'domineering inclinations and attitudes' of these peoples with their own 'simple, less assuming, sincere, honest, hardworking and God-fearing' qualities.

The proposed merger of the people of Anamba, Ogbaru, Onitsha and Oquta Divisions of East Central State with those of Ancocha, Ika and Abo Divisions of Midwest State, to form a Niger State was argued on the basis of a long historical association and certain cultural characteristics, especially the tradition of kinship, which distinguish them from other Ibo Divisions.[18]

As has already been stated, neither linguistic nor ethnic differentiations were found acceptable as general criteria for determining state boundaries and this tended to rule them out of consideration even in particular cases.

ACCELERATED DEVELOPMENT

It was commonly believed that the creation of States entails social and economic development.[19] After 1967 all the new State capitals began to enjoy the paraphernalia associated with government headquarters. Hospitals were expanded, water supply, urban roads and drainage were improved, various governmental institutions were established. They became centres of intense economic and political activities. Other

infrastructural facilities such as trunk roads, neglected by the forme
regional Governments, were reconstructed. More scholarships wer
awarded for higher education, many rural areas obtained electricit
and local entrepreneurs were helped to industrialise. The notion o
bringing government closer to the people, which had wide currency i
offical circles, was seen to have a positive value for the lives of th
people.

If the oil revenues had not proved so buoyant it might have been a
different story. But the Federal Government was the great provider
especially through the Distributable Pool Account. The States share
half of that Account on an equal basis, the other half according t
population.[20] The sub-division of a state was likely to result in ar
overall increase in revenue. It was in the areas of greatest socia
mobilisation that the existing resources were stretched the most, an
that the pressure was greatest for multiplication of States. It is thi
factor which no doubt explains the acquiescence of Kano State in th
status quo and the large number of proposed States from East Centra
and Western States.

Table III shows the statutory allocation of Federal revenue to th
old 1967 States in their last financial year 1975/76 and the amoun
received by the new 1976 States in their first year.

Recommendations and decisions

There was no lack of criteria to be taken into consideration. Th
difficulty was to know what weight should be given to each. In additio
to the five criteria laid down by Gowon in 1966 (see p.203), two mor
were added in October 1974:
—the need to bring the government nearer to the people, and
—the need to ensure even development.
The Panel formulated three additional criteria of its own:
—the need to preserve the Federal structure of Government;
—the need to maintain peace and harmony within the Federation;
—the need to minimise minority problems.[21]
Most weight was in fact given to political factors: to the creation o
states which would be acceptable and so, have legitimacy in the eyes o
their inhabitants. Considerations such as the economic an
administrative viability of the States were not entirely disregarded bu
were certainly subordinate to the need to redress deep-seated
grievances. In many ways the decision to increase the number of State
in 1976 to nineteen is a follow-up to the decision in 1967 to creat

TABLE III

STATUTORY ALLOCATION OF FEDERAL REVENUE TO STATES

States		Total in million of naira			Percentage		
Old	New	1975/6	1976/7	1977/8	1975/6	1976/7	1977/8
	Ogun		48.6	62.4		3.57	3.48
	Ondo		61.3	81.4		4.50	4.54
	Oyo		87.5	117.0		6.43	6.53
West		113.8	197.4	160.8	10.80	14.50	14.55
	Borno		64.0	84.6		4.70	4.71
	Bauchi		55.6	77.1		4.08	4.30
	Gongola		64.2	80.2		4.71	4.47
North East		100.4	183.8	241.9	9.53	13.49	13.48
	Niger		45.6	59.3		3.35	3.30
	Sokoto		80.8	107.4		5.93	5.99
North West		83.7	126.4	166.7	7.94	9.28	9.29
	Benue		64.7	77.0		4.75	4.30
	Plateau		54.5	71.9		4.00	4.01
Benue Plateau		70.6	119.2	148.9	6.70	8.75	8.31
	Imo		81.0	112.4		5.95	6.26
	Anambra		63.7	93.5		4.68	5.20
East Central		108.7	144.7	205.9	10.32	10.63	11.46
Kano		84.0	94.2	125.1	7.97	6.92	7.00
Kwara		57.3	56.8	66.8	5.44	4.17	3.73
Lagos		49.1	47.5	62.9	4.66	3.49	3.50
North Central	Kaduna	70.5	76.1	101.1	6.69	5.59	5.65
South East	Cross River	66.9	70.9	94.4	6.33	5.21	5.26
Mid West	Bendel	135.9	121.1	159.3	12.90	8.89	8.89
Rivers		113.0	123.6	160.2	10.72	9.08	8.94
		1,053.6	1,361.7	1,793.0	100	100	100

twelve states in lieu of four Regions. This had been a last minute attempt to reintegrate the Federation by acceding to the long-standing demand for the creation of states and, although it came too late to prevent the secession of the Eastern Region, it undoubtedly contributed to the success of the struggle to maintain Nigerian unity. The creation of additional States in 1976 was likewise a belated correction of the grievances which the 1967 boundaries had engendered. Some of these had been voiced immediately but the Boundary Delimitation Commission which should have dealt with them was never appointed.

By 1976 there had developed a much greater swell of discontent, based largely on alleged discrimination on the part of the State Governments. In the interests of stability these could not be ignored.[22] The adjustments of 1976 were in this sense a completion of those undertaken in 1967.

The Panel and the Government were nonetheless opposed to a 'proliferation' of States and, to be able to distinguish deserving cases from less deserving ones, some criteria had to be used. The paragraph in the Government's White Paper expresses these in the vaguest of terms—

> The Government's decisions were guided by considerations of what factors were likely to stabilise, enhance and improve the Federation both in the short and long run. Dramatic boundary adjustments or departure from established norms of political acceptance would create a long period of adjustments and possible instability. States are to be created only where demand has been long, strong and widely articulated and where the population and the area justify such an action and where administrative convenience and security, are assured.

What this meant in practice was a number of ad hoc decisions which conformed to demand in so far as this was consistent with the need for a balanced federation (i.e. not too great a disparity in the size and population of the states) and consistent with geographical/adminis-trative realities (e.g. a Sardauna State, which would have consisted of two parts geographically separated one from the other, was declared inadmissable). This statement of criteria is notable for one deliberate omission. There is no reference to linguistic/ethnic considerations. As we have seen, these were in many cases a factor in making particular demands. It was not however officially acknowledged as a relevant one.

Some break up of the West and East-Central States was considered necessary, if only to make less intractable the problem of resource-allocation among two large, highly educated and very demanding sets of people. The precise division had to be a little arbitrary, especially in East-Central, but there was no questioning the demand and the need to satisfy it. In the case of the North-West and the North-East their very size made a subdivision inevitable and in the case of Benue-Plateau the demand for separation was too strong to ignore.

Two of the Panel's recommendations were rejected. One was the proposed division of South East State whereby the Ejik, Ogoja and Obuda areas would have been separated from the Ibidio-Annang areas. The Government held that such a split 'would not be in the best interest of all concerned in the long run' and believed that 'the charges of maladministration and neglect by the previous administration will be met through a conscious attempt to spread even development throughout the state'.[25] The only concession was in the name, Cross River, the name of the movement that had sought separation. The Government also rejected that Lagos be merged with the former Abeokuta and Ijebu Provinces, to form an Ogun State. It was unacceptable because the people of Lagos 'would be going into the State as a minority after enjoying Statehood for a period of nine years'.[26] Consequently, Ogun and Lagos form two separate states.

The Government was reluctant to accept some of the boundary adjustments recommended by the Panel—only six out of twelve were approved. The Government's attitude was consistent with its view that ethnic consideration should carry very little weight. Only where geographical factors suggested that a boundary adjustment was administratively necessary was it accepted. For instance, in the case of the three Igala Divisions of Kwara State, now merged with the new Benue State, the River Niger had constituted a physical barrier creating enormous problems in the administration of these three Divisions. Indeed members of these divisions jokingly refer to themselves as 'Kwara Overseas'. The merger of Borgu Division with the proposed Niger State, recommended by the Panel, was held for administrative reasons not to be in Borgu's own interest. It was to remain with Sokoto.[27] To deal with the many minor boundary disputes, on which the Panel received a good deal of evidence, a Boundary Adjustment Committee was established. It was given three months in which to report and the adjustments allowed by the Government have already been implemented.

Conclusion

One may be left wondering whether the 1976 structure will not in due course produce its quota of discontents, just as in the case of 1967. It is easy to see in the present structure potential minorities. The Government believes however that there are two ways of making the 1976 settlement a lasting one.

The first is to declare it to be permanent and thus different from the 1967 structure which was never more than a temporary one. 'The atmosphere in which the 12 States were created gave the impression that the boundaries were temporary.[28] The 1976 structure, on the other hand, was to be the last word without hope of revision or only under very strict conditions. The Panel considered the question of what constitutional procedures there should be for dealing with future demands. Its proposal was rejected by the Government as an 'open door provision', 'far too liberal' which would 'not make for continued stability'. The matter was however left to the Constitutional Drafting Committee where it proved equally controversial. Pressure for further changes is bound to continue, especially in Cross River (formerly South-East) where there is strong disappointment at the Government's reversal of the Panel's recommendation. The problem is to provide a 'safety valve' without it becoming an 'open-door'.

Secondly, a policy of 'even development' is seen as an antidote. Invariably the demand for a change of boundary was fired by accusations of neglect. The Government, in its White Paper, laid very great emphasis on even development as a means both of remedying existing grievances and of forestalling any accusations of this kind in the future. Unfortunately the notion implies comparisons and one has to be clear as to what is the unit of comparison. It could be an administrative district, it could be an 'ethnic group', or a combination of geographical and sociological boundaries. Administrative districts vary in size and population and although there have been recent attempts at equalisation, this has not put an end to argument about inequitable distribution.

A surer way of undermining inter-area tensions would be to expose the artificiality of the cleavage. The movements for a realignment of State boundaries are primarily movements by elites seeking to consolidate their influence in their own localities. Leaders of State movements, especially those which emerged between 1967 and 1975, saw the Government's commitment to create States as an opportunity to share booty. This was particularly true of those complaining that their 'people' were under-represented in Government at the highest level. There is however a growing awareness—and it needs to be encouraged—that the basic contradiction in Nigerian society is between town and countryside, between elite and masses. When the rural population and the urban poor become better organised agitation for the creation of States could lose ground.

Two suggestions are made in this connection: a decentralisation of power to village communities and the designation of special development areas. The basic administrative unit must be a community in which there is a strong sense of common identity, a desire for social and political cohesiveness and a strong sense of solidarity. Such units cannot be meaningfully created beyond the village level. The villages therefore should be constituted into units of administration with a basic developmental role and should have the political organisation which will allow them to make decisions with respect to the provision of infrastructural facilities, social and welfare amenities as well as to organise programmes of political education, community development, and agricultural extension. The villages should be integrated into the higher levels of the planning system by being required to submit proposals to the local government authority council for a definite plan period. There is no need for an intermediary institution between the local government councils and these villages. Such intermediary bodies would create additional political problems of control and frustrate the felt and real needs of the villages.

The special needs of certain areas should be entrusted to the Federal Government. A Ministry for Regional Development should have authority to participate directly in the development of areas designated as 'depressed', be responsible for the distribution of relief in disaster areas, and be directly responsible for water-based populations, nomadic communities and communities which are not easily accessible because of a harsh terrain.

A proposal of this kind was made by the Panel but the Government took the view that it would 'cut across and undermine the authority of the State Governments affected'. It preferred to put its faith in a distribution of resources by State Governments on 'an equitable divisional basis' and in ad hoc bodies such as a Delta Basin Authority.[29]

NOTES

1. See for instance *Daily Times* August 31st, 1974.
2. A. H. M. Kirk-Greene, *Lugard and the Amalgamation of Nigeria: a documentary record* (London, Frank Cass 1968) p.10.
3. Ibid. p.214-223
4. ·*Report of the Commission appointed to enquire into the fears of Minorities and the means of allaying them,* London 1958, p.1.
   Also J. P. Mackintosh: *Nigerian Government and Politics* (London, G. Allen & Unwin 1966) p.31-35
5. S. K. Panter-Brick ed. *Nigerian Politics and Military Rule: Prelude to the Civil War,* London: The Athlone Press 1970 p.194
6. Ibid. p.267-276
7. *New Nigerian,* October 2, 1970
8. Dr. Nnamdi Azikiwe in a lecture at the University of Nigeria, Nsukka, *Sunday Times,* May 19, 1974; Chief Anthony Enahoro in a lecture at NUNS convention held in Zaria. *New Nigerian* September 28, 1974.
9. *New Nigerian,* Oct 4th, 1974
10. They were:
    The Case for Bauchi State: October 24, 1974; Our Stand for a Plateau State, November 4, 1974; Appeal for the Creation of the Adamawa State, November 6, 1974; The Case for the Separation of Igala land from Kwara, November 7, 1974; Lafia and Nasarawa Divisions want BP to remain, November 13, 1974; Adamawa State—Count Gwoza Out, November 16, 1974; Separation of Igala from Kwara—the Stand of Bassa-Nges, November 19, 1974; Demand for Benue State, November 21, 1974; Creation of Kabba State, November 23, 1974; The Case for a State Based on the Old Kabba Province, November 25, 1974; Creation of More States and the Stand of Nasarawa Emirate December 2, 1974; The Stand of Tiv People, December 3, 1974; Proposed Cross River: Case No. 6, December 3, 1974; Separation of Igala land from Kwara State—the stand of Igalas at home, December 14, 1974; Ogoja Province Supports Cross River State, December 16, 1974; The Stand of the People of Wukari and the Stand of Igbiras at Home on the Creation of Kabba State, December 16, 1974; Warri Reject Delta State Idea, December 28, 1974.
11. *Federal Military Government Views on the Report of the Panel on Creation of States* (Federal Ministry of Information, Lagos 1976) p.5 (cited herafter as Government Views). The Report of the Panel was not published but is summarised in the White Paper.
12. 'The Panel observed from its tours the strength of ethnic loyalty, mutual suspicion and even hatred among the diverse peoples which make up Nigeria'. Government Views p.9.
13. *Sunday Times,* May 19, 1974.
14. Government Views p.11.
15. Obafemi Awolowo. *Thoughts on the Nigerian Constitution* (Oxford University Press, Ibadan 1966) (Appendix 3).
16. Government Views. p.11.
17. Taken from memoranda presented to the Panel eg by 'the Wawa speaking people of the East Central State.'
    Reference was made to Samuel Johnson *History of the Yorubas* edited by Dr O. Johnson (London 1921) and to N. A. Fadipe *The Sociology of the Yoruba* (1939).

18. Memorandum submitted by the Niger State Committee.
19. 'The Panel's firm belief is that the basic motivation in the demand for more states is rapid economic development. All other reasons adduced by State agitators are in the view of the Panel to a large extent mere rationalisations to achieve the basic purpose of development.' Government Views. p.10.
20. See Ch.8, The Politics of Revenue Allocation, p.258.
21. Government Views, paragraph 44 p.14-15.
22. 'The Panel . . . came to the conclusion that . . . the political stability of Nigeria cannot be guaranteed if new States are not created.' Government Views. paragraph 22 p.10.
23. Ibid, paragraph 49, p.15.
24. Ibid, paragraph 38, p.13.
25. Ibid, paragraph 123. p.30.
26. Ibid, paragraph 84, p.22.
27. Ibid, paragraph 97, p.24.
28. Government Views, paragraph 17, p.8.
29. Ibid, paragraph 23, p.10 and paragraph 92, p.23.

8

The Politics of Revenue Allocation

S. Egite Oyovbaire

It is not possible in a Federation to assign some sources of revenue to the Federal Government and other sources of revenue to the State Governments in such a way that the resources available to each unit of government will always match its obligations. Revenue yields and expenditure needs are never constant over the years and therefore do not lend themselves to any long-term fixed apportionment. While some sources of revenue may be assigned exclusively either to the Federal Government or to the State Governments, revenue from other sources must be shared and the precise allocation varied from time to time in accordance with circumstances. All federations have some such system of revenue allocation and it is a central feature of 'fiscal federalism'.

Circumstances in Nigeria changed greatly in the decade up to 1976 and consequently also the system of revenue allocation.[1] The most important factors making for change were: the removal of open competitive politics by military rule; the multiplication and reduction in size of the component parts of the Federation (from four Regions to twelve States in 1967, and to nineteen States in 1976); the emergence of a national consciousness on the part of the country's rulers; and the overwhelming importance of the oil industry as a source of revenue. These were the main factors which made necessary, and at the same time facilitated, quite radical changes in the rules for the allocation of revenues to the Federal Government and to each State Government.[2]

The following analysis of the changes in the period since 1967 is divided into four parts:

. An outline of the structure of fiscal authority. This sets out the statutory allocation of revenues to both the Federal and State Governments.

. A short comparative analysis of the actual revenue accruing to each unit of government from various sources. This shows the magnitude of the oil revenues and of the changes in the fiscal relationship.

. An examination of the political issues raised by a reform of the revenue allocation system, with particular reference to the reforms proposed in 1969 by the Interim Revenue Allocation Review Committee.

. An analysis of the circumstances in which the post-1970 reforms were carried out and a view of future relationships.

Section 1: Structure of Fiscal Authority

Although the States retained their budgetary autonomy *vis-à-vis* the Federal Government, the statutory allocation of revenue underwent considerable revision. Table 1 shows the structure in force when the twelve states were created in May 1967. It illustrates the distribution of tax revenues. (It leaves out of account other sources of revenue such as loans, trading surpluses, grants, etc.) Lines 2 and 3 indicate the principal means used to allocate to the States revenues collected by the Federal Government. One was the principle of derivation, that is, the right of each State to the taxes that its inhabitants are assumed to have contributed, and the other was the DPA. The taxes in question were among the most buoyant, certainly more buoyant than those allocated exclusively to the States (Line 4). Consequently the States were particularly dependent on the taxes which were allocated on the basis of derivation and through the DPA. The major changes in Nigeria's system of revenue allocation have been essentially alterations in the relative weight given to these two modes of allocation. It is true that Federal grants and loans are also of crucial importance but these were until recently of modest proportions. The key to an understanding of the reforms effected in the period 1967-75 lies in the diminishing weight given to the principle of derivation and in the adjustments made to the DPA.

The system which prevailed in 1967 raised four main problems. In the first place many of the States found themselves with insufficient revenue with which to meet their reponsibilities. The revenue-

TABLE I
THE STATUTORY ALLOCATION OF REVENUES
STRUCTURE OF GOVERNMENT REVENUE, MAY 1967

1. Revenues raised, collected and retained by the Federal Government:

Company taxes	Import and excise duties on beer, wines and liquor	Mining rents and royalties — 15%
	Import duties (except on motor spirit, diesel oil and tobacco) — 65%	

2. Revenues raised and collected by the Federal Government and transferred to State Governments on the principle of derivation:

Export duties on primary produce	Import and excise duties on motor spirit, diesel oil and tobacco	Mining rents and royalties — 50%

3. Revenues raised and collected by the Federal Government, credited into the Distributable Pool Account and shared among the States on a fixed percentag basis:

	Import duties (except on beer, wines, liquor, motor spirit, diesel oil and tobacco) — 35%	Mining rents and royalties — 35%

4. Revenues raised, collected and retained by State Governments:
   Personal Income and Poll Tax
   Sales tax on produce (except tobacco, motor fuel, hides and skins)
   Licence and Government Service fees
   Fines, rents on Government property
   Revenue from lotteries, etc.

Source: Sections 136 to 145 of the 1963 Constitution of the Federal Republic of Nigeria as amended by the Allocation of Revenue (Constitutional Amendment) Act, 1965.

yielding base of the new States was naturally much smaller than that c the old Regions; it also differed widely and in some cases wa manifestly inadequate. The Mid-West (now Bendel), a pioneer small size unit of Government, had experienced this problem of inadequat revenues in the first years of its existence (1963-67).[3] With the creatio of twelve States in 1967 the problem became much more general an progressively more acute. The growth in the economy led to increase revenues but the principal beneficiaries were the Federal Governmen (and the two oil-producing States) whereas the burden of increase expenditures fell most heavily on the States and especially the large more heavily populated States.[4] This imbalance could only be resolve ither by the Federal Government taking over some of the States' esponsibilities (eg parts of the educational system, of the road network ind broadcasting) or by a change in the distribution of revenue which he Federal Government collected on behalf of the States. There was in act a recourse to both remedies.

Secondly, the allocation of revenues on the principle of derivation nade the finances of each State very dependent on the level of its own imited productive activities (eg of export crops and mining) and on its evel of consumption (eg of petrol and tobacco). State revenues were hus liable to considerable fluctuation, more so than would be the case f each State had a share in the country's economic performance as a vhole.

Thirdly, and deriving from the second, the system gave rise to inacceptable disparities between States. Since the financial receipts of vell-placed States were not necessarily related to their share of the iational population, size of territory, capacity to foster development or existing commitments on social overheads, the principle of lerivation tended to accentuate still further the existing imbalances of he national economy. Its effect in inhibiting the growth of a political onsensus and a healthy development of the Federal polity in the veriod before 1970 was closely observed by Adedeji:

> . . . . the derivation principle bedevilled the development of a rational and equitable system of revenue allocation. It poisoned inter-governmental relationships and . . . . exacerbated inter-regional rivalry and conflict. Perhaps more than any other single factor it hampered the development of a sense of national unity and common citizenship in Nigeria.[5]

finally the formula for sharing the funds of the Distributable Pool Account became quite arbitrary. Before the creation of states in 1967, he Account was divided among the Regions in the ratio of 42% for the North, 30% for the East, 20% for the West and 8% for the Midwest. This distribution was said to be based on a combination of four factors: iamely, population, financial need, contribution to revenue and valanced development. There was no more precise formulation of hese criteria. It was therefore difficult to alter these percentages on any objective basis to meet the needs of the new twelve-state system. As the iew State boundaries did not cut across those of the Regions, the Regional allocations were simply sub-divided.[6]

That of the former Northern Region was divided equally among the ix new states, each receiving 7%. That of the old Eastern Region was livided among the three new states in the ratio of 17·5% for East

Central, 7·5% for South East and 5% for Rivers. The old Wester
Region's share was re-allocated in the ratio of 18% to the new Wester
State and 2% to Lagos State.[7]

Whereas relative population would appear to have been the basis o
re-allocation among the five new southern states, as it was when th
Midwest was established in 1963, this was obviously not the criterio
used in the case of the six northern states. This aroused considerabl
resentment in the three more populous and larger states, Kano, North
Central and North Western. They argued that insufficient account ha
been taken of their inherited constitutional responsibilities, thei
declining revenue-yielding capacity (ie export duties), and the need fo
a balanced development throughout the Federation.[8]

This structure of revenue allocation was so manifestly defective an
such a source of conflict that a Revenue Allocation Review Committe
was appointed in 1969. Although its report (discussed below in sectio
III) was rejected by the Federal Government, the defects of the existin
system could not be totally ignored. Early in 1970 the Federal Militar
Government made substantial alterations in revenue allocation. Thes
were embodied in *Decree No. 13 of 1970* with retrospective effect from
April 1969.[9]

The Decree introduced five major changes to the existin
arrangements. Firstly, excise duties on sales of tobacco and petroleum
products, previously paid to the States on the basis of their relativ
consumption, were now shared equally between the Federa
Government and the DPA. The State Governments were thus partiall
deprived of the 'ownership' of such revenue. Secondly, export dutie
previously transferred wholly to the State of derivation, were shared i
the proportion of 3:2 by the State of origin and the DPA. Thirdly,
mining rents and royalties, previously allocated in the ratio of 50% t
the State of derivation, 15% to the Federal Government and 35% to th
DPA, were now shared 45%, 5% and 50% respectively. Fourthly, th
import duty on motor fuel, previously paid wholly to the States on th
basis of relative consumption, was divided 50% to the Federa
Government and 50% to the State Governments. Finally, the basis o
sharing the DPA was altered; one half was divided equally among th
States and the other half shared on the basis of relative population

These changes had three cumulative effects. They increased th
financial strength of the Federal Government vis-a-vis the States; th
amount of revenue accruing to the Distributable Pool Account wa
increased; and they introduced some measure of fiscal equalizatio

TABLE II

SHARE OF THE DISTRIBUTABLE POOL ACCOUNT AS A RESULT OF DECREE.NO. 13 OF
1970

State	May 1967–April 1969 (% share)	Since April 1969 (Approximate % share)	Percentage share of National Population (Total: 55·6 million)
Benue-Plateau	7·0	7·8	7·2
Kwara	7·0	6·3	4·3
Kano	7·0	9·3	10·4
North-Central	7·0	7·8	7·3
North-Eastern	7·0	11·3	14·0
North-Western	7·0	9·3	10·3
East-Central	17·5	10·6	11·2
South-Eastern	7·5	7·4	8·2
Rivers	5·0	5·6	2·8
Western	18·0	12·7	17·0
Lagos	2·0	5·5	2·6
Midwestern	8·0	6·4	4·5
Criteria	Not stated; appears arbitrary	50% on equality basis, 50% on population	——

Source: Federal Ministry of Finance, Lagos.

among the States. In all, such changes toned down considerably the
earlier emphasis on the principle of derivation. Table II illustrates the
degree of equalization in the new formula for allocating the DPA. By
reducing the weight which the previous structure of fiscal federalism
assigned to the principle of derivation, the new arrangements have, in
effect, emphasized the principles of need, of equality among the States
and of balanced development. These changes were strengthened in
1971 by the Federal Government's distinction between revenue from
on-shore and off-shore production of oil, and its decision to take over
all royalties, rents and other revenues' from off-shore oil
production.[10] Revenue which, on the principle of derivation, had
accrued to those States off whose shores oil was produced now went to
the Federal Government.

The Federal Military Government went on to make several other
changes in the fiscal structure. A reform of the Marketing Board
system in 1973 had the effect of depriving the States of one of their
independent sources of revenue. Between 1954 and 1973, the

Marketing Boards were Regional corporations, exploited by the governments of the Regions (and the States after 1967) for revenue purposes. The difference between the price paid to export crop producers and the price at which the produce was sold in the world market was 'lent' to the Regional (State) governments and ploughed into a variety of activities. Although there was a substantial decline in such surpluses from the early 1960s onwards, nevertheless the Boards remained a definite source of State revenue until April 1973.[11] With effect from that date the Federal Government took over the former national agent of the Marketing Boards, the Nigerian Produce Marketing Company (NPMC). As a consequence, 'the Marketing Boards inversely became the agents of the NPMC for the purpose of purchasing produce from the farmers.'[12] The Boards' earlier function of generating surpluses from their operations and converting these into Government revenue ceased. The Federal Government became the price fixing authority for export crops with the aim not of accumulating a surplus over and above 'producer prices' but of encouraging production by a redistribution of incomes among primary export producers. The prices paid to producers were 'equalised' by using the receipts from one crop to 'subsidize' the price of another.[13] At the same time the export taxes previously paid to the States were abolished and, in the following year, so were the sales tax and export duty on rubber ('the only remaining dutiable export commodity'). The State Governments were compensated for their loss of revenue by means of Federal Government grants but it was another blow to the principle of derivation.[14]

The 1974/5 and 1975/6 Budgets were the occasions for three further adjustments. One concerned income tax; it remained a State revenue but the power to fix the rates of tax and allowances was centralised by the Uniform Tax Decree No. 7 of 1975 (with retrospective effect from April 1974). This was to 'facilitate the mobility of high level manpower' and was regarded as 'another step towards social and economic integration.'[15] Secondly, one traditional source of revenue, not unimportant to the States in the Northern part of the country, disappeared. With the prolonged drought the 'age-old cattle tax' ('jangali') was abolished, so as to 'bring some relief to the cattle owner on his capital and to encourage him to keep his cattle within the country.'[16] Thirdly, and most important, a fundamental change was made in the composition of the DPA, although the formula for its distribution remained the same. Arguing the need 'to give credibility o the development programmes of the State Governments' and to take advantage of the 'recurrent budget surpluses of the Federal Government', it was announced that:

> as from the 1st April 1975, all portions of Customs and Excise duties formerly payable to the State Governments on the basis of derivation would be payable to the Distributable Pool Account; the percentage of royalties payable to State Governments on the basis of derivation would be reduced from 45 to 20 and the Federal Government will surrender its entire share of both on-shore and off-shore royalties into the Distributable Pool Account.[17]

Table III sets out the changes that were made under Decree No.6 of 975.

The key casualty of the 1975 changes was obviously the principle of derivation, to many the 'devil' of Nigerian fiscal federalism.[19] It would no longer be possible to contend that Federal payments to the State Governments were, in essence, part of the latter's 'independent revenue', being derived from State production and consumption.[19] Only in the case of mining rents and royalties was an element of the derivation principle retained, and at 20% it is now relatively small. The dependence of the State Governments upon federally collected taxes, more apparent than real so long as they were allocated on the principle of derivation, became very much a reality once these taxes came to be paid into the DPA and redistributed on the alternative principles of need', 'equity' and 'balanced development.' Notwithstanding the lack of any agreed means of measuring such criteria and the rough and ready formula used for redistribution (50% divided equally, 50% distributed on a population basis) there is no denying the change in principle.[20]

Neither these reforms nor the transfer of certain constitutional functions to the centre affected the budgetary powers of the State Governments. Decisions on capital as well as recurrent expenditure were in their hands and the Federal Government exercised very little effective control, irrespective of whether the revenue was independently collected or obtained from Federal sources. Revenue statutorily allocated to the States is revenue which the Federal Government is obliged to transfer to the States without conditions. Similarly, loans from the Development Fund (but not grants-in-aid) are allocated on a statutory basis: 50% is shared among the States on the basis of equality and the other 50% relative to population. Moreover the States are not accountable to the Federal Government.

Thus States, through their various ministries and executive councils prepare and approve their recurrent and capital budgets withou control from Lagos and in the confident expectation of revenue from the Federal Government. Furthermore, their accounts are audited internally by their own audit departments.

This is not to say, however, that there was no criticism of their financial management. The Third National Development Plan, while upholding the principle of State independence in budgetary matters

TABLE III
STRUCTURE OF REVENUE ALLOCATION

Revenue Source	Allocation to March 1975	Allocation from April 1975
Export Duties Produce, Hides and Skins Other exports	Approx. 87% to state of origin Approx. 13% DPA 100% to state of origin	100% DPA
Import Duties Tobacco Petroleum products	100% to state of consumption Approx. 91% to state of consumption Approx. 9% to DPA	100% to DPA
Mining Rents and Royalties 1. On-shore Production	45% to State of Derivation 50% to DPA 5% to Federal Govt.	20% to State of Derivation 80% to DPA
2. Off-shore Production	100% to Federal Govt.	100% to DPA;

Notes.
(1) Other revenue sources to the Distributable Pool Account (DPA) not affected by Decree No.6 of 1975 included 35% of the proceeds from 'unspecified imports' and excise duties.
(2) Allocation of the funds in the DPA remained on the basis of 50% equality and 50% relative population.
(3) Revenue collected and retained by the State Governments (Line 4 of Table 1 remained unaffected.
Source: Decree No. 13 of 1970; Decree No.6 of 1975; and Federal Ministry of Finance Lagos.

and in plan implementation, outlined new procedures for ensuring stricter control of capital projects and their implementation.[21] For example, it was noted that during the period of the Second National Plan 'projects which were never brought to the attention of the Central Planning Office, or which were rejected because they failed the usual viability tests' nonetheless masqueraded as 'Other Charges' in the estimates of recurrent expenditure. To prevent this practice, it was stipulated that

> the approved Recurrent and Capital Estimates of all the State Governments will henceforth be submitted to the Central Planning Office to be commented upon and placed before the Supreme Military Council for consideration.[32]

Such a procedure amounts to centralization of financial management through the backdoor and is likely to raise more problems for Federal-State relations than it intends to solve. It would mean that policy-decisions taken by State Executive Councils would be subject to scrutiny by Federal civil servants and, on their advice, to amendment or rejection. It assumes a capacity on the part of the Central Planning Office to collate nineteen (at that time twelve) State budgets with the Federal budget, between January and March of each financial year, before submitting them to the Supreme Military Council—an exercise likely to turn the Central Planning Office into the most politically lobbied department in the Federation. It would almost certainly give rise to conflict between the administrative-technical tidiness of the Central Planning Office and the dynamics of federal politics—a conflict-situation unlikely to be successfully managed within the existing walls of closed politics, and still less plausible if conducted within the open arena of Nigeria's civilian politics. It is the kind of procedure more likely to be honoured in its breach than in its observance, as was indeed the case during the 1976/77 financial year when neither the Federal nor the State Governments took cognizance of it.[25]

Thus the State Governments have retained virtually intact their budgetary autonomy but there is no denying the profound transformation in the structure of revenue allocation in the direction of rationality and equity—changes which will no doubt contribute to a more balanced economic and political system. These reforms were made easier, indeed possible, by the buoyancy of Federal revenue. We turn therefore to a consideration of its size, composition and distribution.

Section 2: Federal Government Revenue

The most significant trend has been the phenomenal increase in
Federal revenue: it has multiplied over fourteen times in a single
decade. This is due largely to the tremendous rise in revenue directly
attributable to oil production. Table IV indicates the share of oil in
total revenue between 1966 and 1976.

TABLE IV
SHARE OF OIL IN TOTAL FEDERAL REVENUE: 1970–1975 (N millions)

Year	Total Federal Revenue	Revenue from Petroleum*	% of Total
1969/70	633·2	166·4	26·3
1970/71	1,169·0	510·2	43·6
1971/72	1,404·8	764·3	54·4
1972/73	1,695·3	1,016·0	59·9
1973/74	4,537·0	3,726·7	82·1
1974/75	5,514·7	4,271·5	77·5

Note: *Components are petroleum profits tax, mining royalties, rents, fees, etc.
Source: Central Bank of Nigeria, Economic and Financial Review, Vol.13 (December,
1975), p.81.

As oil production built up in the 1970s, tax on petroleum profits
(retained wholly by the Federal Government) became the largest single
source of revenue. Table V sets out the percentage share of this and
other major taxes.

The growth and changing composition of Federal revenue affected
its allocation between the two levels of Government. Before States
were created in 1967 a fairly steady proportion of Federal revenue had
been allocated to the Regions—about 40% excluding loans and
grants—and the revenue of the Regions roughly equalled that retained
by the Federal Government for its own purposes.[24] But the proportion
allocated to State Governments fell to 23% in 1972/73 and to 16·5% in
1974/75.[25].

A fall in percentage terms did not however constitute a fall in actual
revenue received. Using 1966/67 as a base year, Table VI shows the
percentage increases in total recurrent revenue allocated to the States,
(statutory and non-statutory allocations combined.)

The phenomenal growth in Federal revenue allocated to the States
quite outmatched the growth in the State revenue from independent

TABLE V

SHARE OF MAIN TAXES IN FEDERAL GOVERNMENT REVENUE ON A PERCENTAGE BASIS: 1970-1975

Year	Direct Taxes			Indirect Taxes			
	Company Tax	Petroleum Profits Tax	Others [1]	Import	Export	Excise	Others [2]
1970	7·2	15·4	0·2	34·0	6·5	17·8	18·9
1971	5·4	32·8	0·4	24·4	3·2	14·4	19·4
1972	5·7	38·5	0·3	19·5	1·9	12·8	21·3
1973	4·5	45·4	0·5	18·2	0·7	11·6	19·1
1974	3·2	63·3	0·3	7·2	0·1	3·6	22·3
1975	4·7	49·1	0·4	11·4	0·1	2·3	32·0

Notes: (1) includes 'personal income tax, capital gains and airport taxes'.
(2) includes 'interests and repayments, mining royalties, rents, fees, etc. and miscellaneous'.

Source: Computed from Central Bank of Nigeria, *Economic and Financial Review*, Vol. 13, (December 1975), p. 81.

sources with the result that the ratio of the one to the other changed considerably; from 3:2 in 1968/69 to 3:1 in 1974/75. Table VII shows the trend. The sharp decline in independent revenue in 1974/75 was as a result of the reform of the marketing board system. The figures for subsequent years are bound to show a further decline because of the abolition of produce sales tax and cattle tax and the reduction in personal income taxes to levels now fixed by the Federal Governments.

TABLE VI

PERCENTAGE INCREASES IN FEDERAL RECURRENT APPROPRIATIONS
TO STATE GOVERNMENTS: 1969-1977

Year	Amount N million	%
1968/69	86·5	100
1969/70	164·1	190
1970/71	302·0	349
1971/72	334·2	386
1972/73	312·4	361
1973/74*	331·5	383
1974/75*	589·9	682
1975/76*	1,053·6	1,218
1976/77*	1,361·7	1,574

Note: *Estimates.
Source: Computed from *Digest of Statistics,* Lagos, Vol. 24 (Jan. 1975), p. 81 and *Federal Government Approved Estimates,* Federal Ministry of Information, (1973/74 to 1976/77).

TABLE VII

COMPOSITION OF STATE GOVERNMENTS' REVENUE: 1968–1975 (N million)

Year	Total Amount	Federal Source		Internal Source	
		Amount	%	Amount	%
1968/69	144·5	86·5	60	58·0	40
1969/70	232·2	164·1	70	68·1	30
1970/71	393·0	302·0	77	90·0	23
1971/72	454·1	334·2	73	119·8	27
1972/73	545·8	312·4	67	142·3	33
1973/74*	525·8	331·4	63	194·4	37
1974/75*	839·6	589·9	72	249·7	28

Note: *Estimates
Source: *Digest of Statistics,* Lagos, Vol. 24 (January 1975), p. 81 and *Approved Estimates of the State Governments: 1973/74 and 1974/75,* Federal Ministry of Finance, Lagos.

TABLE VIII

STATUTORY ALLOCATIONS TO STATES 1973/74-1976/77

States	1973/74 Nm	1974/75 Nm	1975/76 Nm	1976/77 Nm	% Differential between 1974/5 and 1976/77
Midwest: (Bendel)	54·9	139·9	135·9	121·1	− 13·4
Rivers: (Rivers)	34·2	101·0	113·0	123·6	+ 22·3
East Central: (Imo, Anambra)	31·9	58·3	108·7	144·7	+148·2
Western: (Ogun, Ondo, Oyo)	31·8	47·3	113·8	197·4	+317·3
North Eastern: (Bauchi, Borno, Gongola)	29·7	41·7	100·4	183·8	+340·7
North Western: (Niger, Sokoto)	24·7	34·9	83·7	126·4	+262·1
Kano: (Kano)	31·9	35·0	84·0	94·2	+169·1
Bonue-Plateau: (Bonue, Plateau)	20·0	30·0	70·6	119·2	+297·3
North Central: (Kaduna)	21·4	29·1	70·5	76·1	+161·5
South Eastern: (Cross River)	21·7	28·1	66·6	70·9	+152·3
Kwara: (Kwara)	15·4	23·9	57·3	56·8	+137·6
Lagos: (Lagos)	13·9	20·7	49·1	47·5	+129·4

Source: Federal Government Approved Estimates, Federal Ministry of Information, Lagos.

In addition, the Federal Government provided the States with loans and grants for development purposes. During the 1970-75 Development Plan period loans for this purpose amounted to N403·6 million on repayment schedules of between 5-15 years.[26] Grants-in-aid amounted to only N70·5 million in the period 1970-1974, but in the single year 1974/75 N49·3 million was provided, largely for the universal primary education programme as well as for the construction of roads and hospitals.[27]

The post-1967 reforms of the system of revenue allocation were designed to bring about a more equitable distribution among the States. This is particularly true of the 1975 reforms which clamped down heavily on the principle of derivation. Table VIII shows the distribution for the two financial years before and after the reform.

The effect of the reform is seen in the final column. Bendel, which received in 1974/75 about 60% more than in 1973/74, suffered a loss of over 13% by 1966/77. The other oil-producing State (Rivers) still gained, but only 22%. The greatest beneficiaries of the new system of allocation were the more populous States (the North East with over 340% and the Western with 317%).

Three things emerge clearly from the foregoing account. First, as a result of the 'oil bonanza', the Federal Government is financially in a much stronger position. Secondly, the States obtain a much larger share of their total revenue from the centre in ways which make them more dependent. Thirdly, the system of allocating funds from the centre to the States is more equitable. The political aspects of these developments is discussed in the next two sections.

Section 3: The Politics of Revenue Sharing

In establishing the twelve States in 1967, Gowon had promised to appoint a commission to 'recommend an equitable formula for revenue allocation taking into account the desires of the States.'[28] The eight-member committee, appointed in July 1968, was the sixth of its kind but the first composed solely of Nigerians. Its chairman was Chief I. O. Dina (the committee is henceforth referred to as the 'Dina Committee' and its report the 'Dina Report') an economist who had been a senior public administrator.[29]

The Committee's terms of reference were as follows:—

'in the light of the creation of twelve states, charged at present with the functions formerly exercised by the Regional Governments, to:

(a) look into and suggest any change in the existing system of revenue allocation as a whole. This includes all forms of revenue going to each Government besides and including the Distribution Pool;

(b) suggest new revenue sources both for the Federal and the State Governments; and

(c) report findings within four months.'

The Dina Committee was fully aware of the forces which had led to the civil war and the issues involved. It concluded a review of its predecessors' reports with this statement:

> We believe that fiscal arrangements in this country should reflect the new spirit of unity to which the nation is dedicated . . . . It is in the spirit of this new found unity that we have viewed all the sources of revenue of this country as the common funds of the country to be used for executing the kinds of programme which can maintain this unity.[30]

With this conviction and motivation, the Dina Committee proceeded to interpret its terms of reference so as to take into account fundamental constitutional and political questions:

> . . . . we felt that, as Nigerians, our work should be as comprehensive as possible . . . . [and] . . . . have been guided by the principle that revenue allocation must be seen as the essence of an overall financial and economic settlement in which all the governments [of the Federation] are motivated and geared to the development of one strong and fully integrated national economy within the context of a truly united Nigeria.[31]

Though noble, the motivation of the Committee was clearly at variance with Federal Military Government expectations. The Committee acknowledged that the terms of reference set by the Government 'were by design restrictive' in that no constitutional change in Federal-State relations was contemplated 'until a Constituent Assembly had met.' This notwithstanding, the Dina Committee attempted to provide what is called 'a useful basis' for the federation. To a much greater degree than is the usual practice of commissions appointed to enquire into some specific question within a given political context, it began with a conception of a new political order—in the spirit of a 'new-found unity'.[32]

The Dina Committee began with a powerful indictment of the existing revenue allocation system and, taking into consideration 'the overall national goals' of fiscal federalism, identified five problems.[33] First there had been a 'growing asymmetry between the functions of, and resources available to, the various component governments in the federation'. This was said to be true not only between the Federal and State Government but among the different State governments—a situation that was aggravated in 1967 by the arbitrary nature of Decree No. 15. Secondly, the existence of a multiplicity of taxing and spending authorities with regard to the same revenue source or expenditure function had generated major administrative problems and reduced effective fiscal co-ordination. 'This weakness', said the Committee, 'is particularly manifest under planning conditions which require a positive integration of development planning and fiscal administration.' Thirdly, the existing revenue allocation system was said to contain 'an unduly large gap between the allocation principles enunciated . . . . and the extent to which [they] were given operational interpretation'. Fourthly, the Dina Report castigated past fiscal review commissions for not making clear their theoretical approach. Finally, the Committee condemned the weight assigned to the principle of derivation in the existing allocation system.

The Committee conceived fiscal federalism in Nigeria as a process of adjustment whereby the revenue of each unit of Government is brought into line with its expenditure. As the Federal Government is in the best position to make such adjustments it should be given greater financial responsibilities. The Dina Committee recommended, therefore, that the Federal Government should assume responsibility for a number of matters on the Concurrent Legislative List of the Constitution, eg higher education; public safety and order; scientific and industrial research. The Federal Government was also recommended to embark on a policy of 'conditional grants' for health and road transport and to 'play a more vigorous policy and fiscal role in the industrial development activity of the States.'

These recommendations were followed by a detailed critical review of the various sources of revenue, of the problems of public debt management, and of the principles that should govern a new revenue allocation system. The Committee recommended a number of 'revolutionary and controversial measures'.[34] These included uniform rates of income tax, a reform of the Marketing Board system, a distinction between off-shore and on-shore oil revenues and an allocation of revenues as set out in Table IX.

The States Derivation Account was to be distributed according to the principle of derivation. The States Joint Account was the Distributable Pool Account, renamed so as to give it a different image, one less evocative of 'the divisive aspect of distribution of national esources' and more indicative of 'the initial need to increase the size of the national cake by joint productive effort.'[35] The Joint Account was to be shared on the basis of several criteria, namely, 'basic need or nominal budget gap, minimum national standards and balanced development'. The Committee indicated how these criteria were to be measured and recommended the formula to be applied for the first two years, 1969/70 and 1970/71. Table X sets out how it would have applied compared with the scheme later adopted by the Federal Military Government (Decree No. 13 of 1970).

TABLE IX

SYSTEM OF REVENUE ALLOCATION
RECOMMENDED BY THE DINA COMMITTEE

Accounts	Excise duty	Import duty	Export duty	On-shore rents	Mining On-shore royalties	Off-shore rents and royalties
Fed. Govt.	60	50	15	—	15	60
States Derivation	—	—	10	100	10	—
States Joint	30	50	70	—	70	30
Special Grants	10	—	5	—	5	10
Total	100	100	100	100	100	100

Source: The Dina Report, chapter 8.

The Special Grants Account, designed 'to meet the principle of national interest' and promote 'national cohesion', was to finance special development projects and special emergency and contingency needs.' It was to be administered by a Planning and Fiscal Commission, a permanent body 'endowed with effective executive power.' This Commission was also 'charged with the constitutional responsibility for a continuous study and review of revenue allocation and the changing problems of fiscal federalism'.

The Committee's report submitted in late January 1969, was circulated to the States for their consideration but when the Federal and State Commissioners of Finance met in April it was rejected. The

TABLE X

PERCENTAGE DISTRIBUTION OF THE DISTRIBUTABLE POOL
ACCOUNT (STATES JOINT ACCOUNT)

States	1 Government Scheme (effective from April '69)	2 Dina Committee's Recommendation (Rejected)	3 Difference between 1 and 2
Benue-Plateau:	7·8	7·7	+0·1
Kwara:	6·3	8·3	−2·0
Kano:	9·3	6·0	+3·3
North-Central:	7·8	7·7	+0·1
North-East:	11·3	9·8	+1·5
North-West:	9·3	8·8	+0·5
East-Central:	10·6	11·0	−0·4
South-East:	7·4	6·9	+0·5
Rivers:	5·6	1·6	+4·0
West:	12·7	19·3	−6·6
Lagos:	5·5	5·9	−0·4
Midwest:	6·4	6·9	−0·5
Criteria	50% on equality 50% on relative population	Quantification of need balanced development, etc.	

Source: Column 1 from Table II above.
Column 2 is the average of columns 3 and 6 of Table X in the *Dina Report,*
84.

Committee was said to have 'exceeded its powers and in many respec
ignored its terms of reference.'[35] The States had all emphasised whe
submitting their views to the Committee that the principle c
derivation was an essential and desirable feature of revenu
allocations.[36] The 'new spirit of unity' which was the basis of the Din
Committee's recommendations was still too new and had yet to b
consolidated by victory in the civil war. The Dina Report, in it
implications for the existing political order, was clearly to
controversial and too far ahead of its time.[37]

Yet, within the year and only three months after the end of the civ
war, the Supreme Military Council had decided on substanti
reforms. As shown in Table X the Distributable Pool Account came t
be shared among the States in proportions close to those recommende
by the Dina Committee. Indeed it can be said that by 1975 most of th
Dina Report had been implemented, and in some respects surpasse

g in the allocation of customs and excise duties and of mining
:venues, and in the Federal Government's increased responsibilities
>r education.

Furthermore, the Supreme Military Council's decision in October
)74 that the system of revenue allocation should be reviewed
eriodically as part of the process of preparing National Development
lans, was similar to the recommendation of the Dina Committee for
ie establishment of a permanent Planning and Fiscal Commission.
.nnouncing the Supreme Military Council's decision, Gowon had
aid:

> .... revenue allocation should be properly conceived not as a constitutional
> exercise but as a means of financing development programmes; that being
> the case, plan periods as approved from time to time by the Government,
> and not constitutional reforms and review, should be adopted as a logical
> time frame for reviewing the sharing of revenues among the Governments
> of the Federation. The Supreme Military Council is also of the view that
> revenue allocation in the Federation has to be regularly reviewed to ensure
> at all times that all levels of Government are enabled to perform their
> allotted development and governmental functions subject only to the
> totality of the resources available to Government.[38]

ection 4 The post-1970 reforms: an explanation and a concluding point f view

: may seem strange that the rejection of the Dina Committee's
roposals should have been followed shortly afterwards by reforms
ot very dissimilar. The answer lies in the rapid change of
ircumstances. Two factors interacted to produce a situation more
onducive to reform: the oil revenues and the civil war. Prior to 1971,
e. before oil became the outstanding source of revenue (see Table IV)
ie major taxes (export and import duties, customs and excise) were
iose to which the principle of derivation applied. Depending on the
ature and level of economic activity in a Region, its Government
ould at times staunchly defend the principle of derivation and at
ther times the principle of 'national interest'. In this way inter-
egional rivalry and conflict were exacerbated and a sense of national
nity inhibited. The Federal Government for its part had no surplus
evenue and so could not augment some Regional revenues so as to
ring them all into better balance. It was an inflexible situation. There
as always one or other Region unwilling to reform the system and the
ederal Government was incapable of making any change.

The oil revenue transformed the situation in two ways. First th principle of derivation began to produce quite unprecedente disparities in State revenues. The two States producing oil (Midwe and Rivers) began to accumulate huge surpluses and were the envy all the other States.[39] Secondly, the Federal Government, benefitin from the petroleum profits tax, also began to run a surplus which gav it the means of effecting changes in the structure of revenue allocatio It was able to abolish export duties and make compensating grant introduce uniform rates and allowances for income tax, and increa the size of the DPA. The two oil producing States were in no position t justify their anomalous situation. The principle of derivation ha become indefensible. Their Military Governors had instead to speak making 'sacrifices' for the sake of national unity. In the words of th Governors of the Mid-West:

> The new allocation formula was agreed upon by Nigerian rulers in th overall interest of the country . . . . the nation's interest should tak precedence over that of the States.[40]

The other contributory factor was the civil war and the changes engendered in the structure of consensus and conflict. Victory in th civil war did not merely keep Nigeria intact: it put the Federation o quite a different footing. The pre-war political system wa characterised by a weak centre denuded of authority and vitality by conflicting set of Regional interests. The configuration of forces in th post-war situation was quite different in a number of ways.

The most obvious change was the enhanced status of the Feder Government, which had undertaken the mobilization of the country resources during the war and initiated thereafter a programme reconstruction and rehabilitation. The most obvious manifestations the growth of central power were the much higher levels of Feder expenditure,[41] the many matters which had been brought within th ambit of Federal jurisdiction by Decree and administrative practic and the range of State activities for which the Federal Government ha begun to provide financial assistance. The system remained federal i character but the Federal Government had assumed an unprecedente authority of its own.

The federal structure was affected just as fundamentally by th abolition of the Regions and their replacement by twelve States i 1967, although it was only at the end of the civil war that the chang began to make itself felt. The old Regional mentality, that is th assumption of self-sufficiency, of a capacity to survive a break-up c the Federation, still lingered until banished by the Federal victory of January 1970. Only thereafter did the States quite definitely become sure of themselves as the new units of the Federation i.e. as States much more conscious than the former Regions of their insufficiencies, both in absolute terms and in relation one to another, of their subordinate status compared with that of the Federal Government and of their interdependence in matters of economic planning, manpower and general development. The twelve-State structure facilitated the emergence of a more autonomous Federal authority in a position to arbitrate and to provide effective leadership. The exercise of this authority depends of course on the ability to act cohesively and decisively, that is, on the Federal Government's own sense of purpose. In this respect, the civil war again proved a catalyst. The military, which had by its own divisions led the country into civil war, proved after the war to be a source of unity and strength, at least for the first few crucial years. The Federal Military Government, endowed with the prestige of victory, an extended range of powers and a financial surplus, provided the leadership that was necessary if the 'new spirit', embodied prematurely in the Dina Committee's Report, was to have its effect.

Conclusion

The testing time for the new arrangements will come with a return to open competitive politics under a new Constitution, but the changes effected between 1970 and 1975 seem likely to hold. The Constitutional Drafting Committee has endorsed the view expressed by the Federal Military Government in October 1974 that revenue allocation must be seen as a continuous process of adjustment (see above p. 243). It proposed a permanent Fiscal Review Commission to keep the federal fiscal system under constant review and to propose from time to time a formula for the allocation of revenue among the States and between the Federation and the States, having regard to population, equality of status among the States, the principle of even development of the entire country, the national interest and such other factors as the National Assembly may prescribe.[42]

The CDC's restatement of earlier views may be taken as confirmation of their validity in the changed circumstances of the post-war period. Indeed the increase in the number of States from twelve to nineteen has made even more essential a flexible system of revenue allocation over which the Federal Government has decisive influence.

This is not to say, however, that the States have lost or are likely to lose all financial autonomy. As have already been mentioned they retain ample discretion over their own budgetary appropriations and if any attempt were made to centralise, this would certainly be opposed. There are several reasons for believing this would be so. Although the centre is likely to attract aspiring politicians keen to foster a Nigeria-wide political culture, the country lacks an ideology and also the trained manpower which could sustain an efficient system of centralised administration—forces without which political centralization would be illusory. Moreover, the sheer size and diversity of the Federation requires that the political units below the level of central government retain considerable autonomy over essentially local issues and problems. In its development, the country is still very much locally orientated in the sense that so much of socio-cultural and economic life is still local in character. The majority of people perceive the structure of politics (the conflict, consensus, resources, institutions and underpinning values) in non-national local terms. Emergent political leaders, however deeply committed they may be to preserving the dominant and pre-eminent role of the Federal Government, are still likely to be mindful of the more limited horizons; conscious, that is, of their socio-cultural and family groups. The overall effect may well be a healthy federal system, a federation in which the Federal authority and the State authorities co-exist in an interaction of dependence and autonomy.

NOTES

1. See for the pre-civil war experience in fiscal federalism: A. Adedeji, *Nigerian Federal Finance,* (London, Hutchinson, 1969); and O. Teriba, 'Nigerian Revenue Allocation Experience, 1952–1965; A Study in Inter-Governmental Fiscal and Financial Relations,' *Nigerian Journal of Economic and Social Studies,* Vol. 8 (November 1966).

2. For a view of their cumulative impact in ordering federal-state relations, see the author's 'Federalism in Nigeria with particular reference to the Midwestern State: 1966–75,' *Unpublished Ph.D. Thesis,* University of Manchester, (July 1976).

3. The Midwestern Region Government pointed this out to the Fiscal Review Commission of 1964: see Nigeria, *Report of the Fiscal Review Commission* (K. J. Binns), Federal Ministry of Information, Lagos, (1965).

4. See the 1963 Constitution for the allocation of responsibilities between the federal and state (regional) governments; and Decrees No.14 and 15 of 1967.

5. Adedeji, *op. cit.* p. 254.

6. The creation of states in May 1967 was not a carefully studied operation. Although the agitation for it had a long history, the exercise was a crisis measure, albeit well conceived, to offset the declaration of secession in the Eastern Region.

7. *Constitution (Financial Provisions) Decree No.15 of 27 May, 1967.*

8. See the memoranda of the State Governments to the Revenue Review Committee of 1968/69 in Nigeria, *Report of the Interim Revenue Allocation Review Committee,* Federal Ministry of Information, Lagos, (1969).

9. *Constitution (Distributable Pool Account) Decree No.13 of 1970.*

10. *Off-shore Oil Revenue Decree (No. 9) of 1971.* There were obvious difficulties in attributing off-shore production to any particular State and disputes had already arisen.

11. The 1973 reform completed measures taken in 1968/69. In the Budget Speech of that year, the Federal Government announced that the Central Bank would take full responsibility for the financing of the sale of export crops controlled by the Marketing Boards because: 'it has been amply demonstrated to the nation during the present crisis [civil war] that the financing of our export crops is a weapon of high economic, political and social significance.' [Text of the 1968/69 Broadcast, Federal Ministry of Information, Lagos, 1968]. By *Decree No.50 of 1968* amending the Central Bank of Nigeria Act, the Central Bank became the only bank to grant advances and loans to the Marketing Boards; it gave the Bank the authority to decide the amount of loan which a Marketing Board would need for its operation at the beginning of each crop season; and the Decree stipulated that the Marketing Boards could fix prices they would pay to farmers only after consultation with the Central Bank.
    For the operation of the Marketing Board system see G. K. Helleiner, *Peasant Agriculture, Government and Economic Growth in Nigeria,* Homewood, Illinois: Irwin, (1966), pp. 152–200.

12. 'The Nigerian Produce Marketing Company Limited'—Annexure 'A' to a correspondence dated 29/9/75 between the Chairman of the Company, Mr. H. A. Ejueyitche, and Federal Commissioner for Trade, Brigadier (later General) M. Shuwa: Documents in author's possession.

13. The important distinction was between the 'southern states'—producers of cocoa, palm oil and palm kernel—and the 'northern states'—producers of groundnuts, cotton products and soya beans. The disagreement over 'equal pricing' and 'particularly in respect of groundnuts' led to the dissolution of the Board of the NPMC under the chairmanship of Mr. Ejueyitche on 17/10/75. Documents in author's possession; personal interviews with Mr. Ejueyitche, Ikoyi, 18/10/75.

14. See the *Text of Budget Broadcasts: 1973/4 and 1974/75.* Federal Ministry of Information, Lagos.

15. *Income Tax Management (Uniform Taxation Provisions, etc.) Decree No. 7 of 1975,* Text of Budget Broadcast, 1974/75, op. cit., p. 6. The States could adapt or modify certain rates of tax and could continue to levy a number of personal taxes such as community, capitation and development taxes [Section 21 A(a) and Table 1 of Schedule VII].

16. Text of 1975/76 Budget Broadcast, Federal Ministry of Information.

17. 14th Independence Anniversary Speech by Gowon—Full Text in *Nigeria Today,* No. 50, October 1974. The changes were made by *Constitution (Financial Provisions etc.) Decree No. 6 of 1975.*

18. See, among others, *Nigeria: Report of the Interim Revenue Allocation Review Committee* (Chairman: I. O. Dina, 1969), op. cit. Adedji, *Nigerian Federal Finance,* op. cit., (last chapter).

19. Such argument was fashionable among spokesmen for the State Governments who wished to stress the 'independence' of the states *vis-à-vis* the Federal

Government. For an example, see Text of a Lecture by E. K. Clark, Midwest Commissioner for Finance, on 'The Financial Relationship between the Federal Government and the State Government' to the 1974 National Youth Service Corps Members (Midwest Contingent) at Auchi—*Military Governor's Office* Benin (National Youth Service Corps Division).

20. Senior officials of the Federal Ministry of Finance, Lagos, could not explain the basis for this allocation (personal interviews October 1975). The FMG gave no reasons for allowing 20% of mining rents and royalties to continue to accrue to the State of origin and there is no obvious basis for it. It was believed perhaps that the State Governments could use the revenue for the social needs of the localities from which the oil is extracted, eg rehabilitation of the landscape. If this were so, the Federal Government could just as well have made such provision directly or through some special agency financed by the Federation, especially as past experience suggested that State Governments might not use such revenue for the special needs of the 'oil areas' and no means existed for ensuring such use.

21. See *Third National Development Plan 1975–80,* Vol. 1, (Federal Ministry of Information, Lagos, 1975) Ch. 33 Plan Implementation and Control p. 397–404.

22. *Ibid,* p. 398.

23. Personal communications with two senior officials: Federal Ministry of Finance (Capital Budget Division), and Central Planning Office, Lagos (October, 1976).

24. Derived from *Digest of Statistics:* Lagos, (various years).

25. Derived from Federal Revenue and Capital Estimates, (1966/67 to 1975/76), and Digest of Statistics, (Jan. 1975).

26. Figures obtained from the Treasury and Capital Budget Divisions of the Federal Ministry of Finance. Short-term Treasury Loan Assistance which helped the States to overcome cash deficits on capital budgets amounted to N.99·0 million.

27. Ibid.

28. Broadcast to the Nation on the Declaration of National Emergency and Creation of States, 27 May, 1967. Text in *The Struggle for One Nigeria,* (Lagos, Federal Ministry of Information, 1967).

29. The Committee was made up of 4 administrators and 4 academics. Four were economists— Prof. O. Aboyade and T. M. Yesufu, Chief I. O. Dina and Mr. A. E. Ekukinam. The other members were Dr. P. O. A. Dada, Malam Ahmed Talib and Ibrahim Tahir and Mr. F. M. C. Obi.

30. Dina Report, p. 27.

31. Dina Report, p. 2–3.

32. See the Committee's assertion: 'We have also examined the different interpretations the Governments in their various memoranda have given to our terms of reference, and where they have been incompatible with our interpretations, we have rejected them'—The Dina Report, p. 3.

33. Dina Report, p. 28–29.

34. Personal Interview with Mr. H. A. Ejueyitche who was, at the time, Secretary to the Federal Military Government: Ikoyi, 13 October, 1975.

35. 12 April 1969—*Daily Times.* No formal Government statement was made on the Report.

36. See Dina Report Appendix AIII 'Summary of Proposals submitted by Governments.'

37. Opinion expressed by Ayida, A. A., 'The Nigerian Revolution', *Proceedings of the (1973) Annual Conference of the Nigerian Economic Society,* p. 8.

38. 14th Independence Anniversary Broadcast: Text in *Nigeria Today* No. 50, October 1974.

39. See, for example, Budget Speech of the Governor of the Western State—*Approved Estimates* 1974/75, (Ministry of Information, Ibadan); *Daily Times* (Lagos, 20th and 29th April 1974; and *New Nigerian* (Kaduna), 10th April, 1974.

40. *New Nigerian* (Kaduna), 15th March, 1975.

41. Two good accounts and analyses so far are: O. Awolowo, 'The Financing of the Nigerian Civil War and its implication for the future Economy of the Nation', *Text of a Public Lecture* (University of Ibadan: 6/5/70); and O. Aboyade and A. Ayida,'The War Economy in Perspective', *Nigerian Journal of Economic and Social Studies,* Vol. 13, (1971). The end of the war did not end enormous expenditure on external affairs and diplomacy. On the contrary it made for the need to promote the country's new strength and image. The army was not demobilized and expenditure in defence and security has continued to grow. See the two post-1970 *National Development Plans* and *Federal Government Approved Estimates* (1970 to 1976).

42. *Report of the Constitution Drafting Committee containing the Draft Constitution,* Vol. I, (Federal Ministry of Information, Lagos), 1976, p. XXXII.

Part Four

LOCAL GOVERNMENT REFORM

9

Introduction

Keith Panter-Brick

In a Foreword to the *Guidelines for Local Government Reform* the Federal Military Government set out the purposes of this ambitious undertaking and the process of consultation which had preceded its announcement in August 1976. The following extracts from the Guidelines serve to introduce the following two chapters, each of which is a commentary with a particular geographical emphasis. Drs. Gboyega and Oyediran write from the vantage point of Ibadan; Dr. Aliyu portrays the reform as seen from Kaduna.

On the purpose of the reform, the Foreword states:

> The defects of previous Local Government systems are too well known to deserve further elaboration here. Local Governments have, over the years, suffered from the continuous whittling down of their powers. The State Governments have continued to encroach upon what would normally have been the exclusive preserves of Local Government. Lack of adequate funds and appropriate institutions had continued to make Local Government ineffective and ineffectual. Moreover the staffing arrangements to ensure a virile local government system had been inadequate. Excessive politicking had made even modest progress impossible. Consequently, there has been a divorce between the people and government institutions at their most basic levels.

> . . . . to stabilise and rationalise Government at the local level . . . . must, of necessity, entail the decentralisation of some significant functions of State Governments to local levels in order to harness local resources for rapid development. The Federal Military Government has therefore decided to recognise Local Governments as the third tier of governmental activity in the nation. Local Government should do precisely what the word government implies i.e. governing at the grass roots or local level.

The preparation of the reform 'began in late 1975 through the establishment of a small coordinative Committee' in the Cabinet office of the Federal Government. Initially, State governments were 'charged with the task of reorganising their respective local government systems' but for various reasons the Federal Government was obliged to take matters much more into its own hands. The reasons are stated to have been that 'an unco-ordinated approach to local government reform would result in considerable chaos and repetitive agitation from various localities for one model or the other' and that many of the proposals submitted by state governments did not show sufficient appreciation of the need for clear financial responsibility. So that the state governments could benefit from 'a cross-fertilization of ideas which a co-ordinated approach would compel', the country was divided into three zones. Zonal meetings were held to prepare papers on the definition and functions of local government, its financing, the role of traditional authorities within any proposed local government structure, and staffing arrangements. The zonal reports were discussed at conferences held in Enugu, Kaduna and Ibadan. A final coordinating conference was held in Ibadan. Thereafter the Supreme Military Council met jointly with the National Council of States (a body consisting of all State Governors) and in July 1976 was held a 'national conference of Traditional Rulers' attended by all the most senior Emirs, Obas and Chiefs.

The Foreword, in a somewhat ambivalent fashion, stressed not only the fundamental nature of the reform which made its inclusion in the draft constitution desirable, but also the freedom of action allowed to state governments by the Guidelines.

> The Federal Military Government does not intend to impose any solutions or indeed any structure on the country at the Local Government level. It accepts the principle that Local Government is primarily the responsibility of State Governments. It merely wishes to emphasise that these responsibilities should be clearly defined and that the Local Government should have adequate financial resources to meet their obligations which are mainly to stimulate development at the grassroots. Nothing in these reforms could be construed to mean an attempt at reducing or abolishing the traditional functions of our Emirs, Obas and Chiefs. On the contrary, the reforms recognise the crucial nature of the position of the traditional authorities and care has been taken to preserve the organic unity of our traditional institutions and societies.

The manner chosen to preserve traditional authority is complex. The

Guidelines permit State governments to choose from among five possibilities. These, reformulated, are:

1. If within the area of traditional authority several local councils are created, the overall traditional council remains in being with limited powers (see below). The Emir or Paramount Chief is President of the traditional council and he is consulted in the appointment of Chairmen of local government councils in his area.

2 & 3. Where the area of a traditional authority is coterminous with that of a new local government authority there are two alternatives
—a single council, if it is desired that the Emir or Paramount Chief should be an 'active President'.
—separate local government and traditional councils, if it is 'more consonant with local tradition or opinion that the Emir or Paramount Chief should be Ceremonial President only'.
[A single council is also permitted if one very large and one or more much smaller areas of traditional authority are encompassed by the area of a new local government authority. The minorities must agree to the Emir or Paramount Chief of the largest part being the 'active President' and the lesser chiefs are included as members of the Council].

4 & 5. Similar possibilities exist where a multiplicity of traditional authorities are encompassed by the area of a new local government. There may be
—a single council, the active Presidency rotating among the chiefs all of whom sit in the Council.
—separate councils, the chiefs taking it in turn to be the ceremonial president of the traditional council.

The traditional councils 'shall consist of traditional title holders, one or two representatives of each Local Government Council if this is deemed appropriate, and any other persons who may be desired to make the Council broadly representative of the major facets of life in the area. The precise composition of each Council shall be determined by State Governors after appropriate consultation within the area'.

The functions of a traditional council should be:—

(a) To formulate general proposals as advice to Local Governments.
(b) To harmonise the activities of Local Government Councils through discussion of problems affecting them generally, and giving advice and guidance to them.
(c) Co-ordination of development plans of Local Governments by joint discussion and advice.
(d) Community Tax Assessment within the area as a whole in consultation with Local Government Councils, and announcement of tax. Also to aid, as is the usual practice, in collection of tax.

(e) Determination of religious matters where appropriate.

(f) Support for Arts and Culture.

(g) Chieftaincy matters and control of traditional titles and offices, except where these are traditionally the exclusive prerogative of the Emir or Chief in which case the Council's function shall be advisory to the Emir or Chief.

(h) Determination of customary law and practice on all matters including that relating to Land;

(i) Making representations or expressing opinions to Government or any other organisation on the collective behalf of the Local Governments in the area.

(j) Deliberating on or making representations or expressing opinions to Government or any other organisation on any matters which it deems to be of importance to the Emirate or Chiefdom as a whole, or which may be referred to it by Government or other organisations.

Elections to the new local government councils were held in December 1976. The Constituent Assembly is recommended to underwrite the reform by including in the new Nigerian constitution a requirement that States must establish democratically elected local government councils, having regard to 'community of interest, traditional association and administrative convenience' (S.13 of the draft constitution). The draft constitution also specifies, in a schedule, what are to be the functions of local government councils. The *Guidelines* had tentatively made two lists, one of functions which were to be the responsibility of local councils 'save under exceptional or temporary circumstances', the other of functions which were to be 'regarded as Local Government responsibilities although it was recognised that initially they might have to be shouldered by state governments and other organisations'—a more flexible arrangement which accords with the advice of K. C. Wheare (see Ch. 12 p. 337).

10

A View from Ibadan

A. E. Gboyega and O. Oyediran

Since the early 1950s when indigenous regional governments were installed in Kaduna, Enugu and Ibadan, local government has been a subject of perennial concern, particularly in the southern part of the country, which, as a result, has witnessed several futile reforms. The Federal Military Government's *Guidelines For Local Government Reform* constitutes a watershed as far as local government reform is concerned. In place of isolated, piecemeal and regional endeavours to improve local government, it lays down a national framework within the context of which state reforms can take their bearings.

The Public Service Review Commission which reported in September, 1974 presaged a national framework for local government reforms when it recommended, *inter alia,* that all states should consider adoption of a single-tier system of local government and redefine the functional and financial relationship between them and their local authorities.[1] It was partly because of this recommendation and partly because of the obvious need for reform that the Federal Government enjoined State Governments to set up preparatory Commissions to recommend the necessary re-organisation. Meanwhile, a panel was at work in Lagos seeking means by which the Federal Government could render concrete and useful, yet unobtrusive, assistance to the state authorities. This federal panel, which consisted of senior officials of the Cabinet Office, collated the reports of the various states and attempted to reconcile the proposals with Federal Government objectives. The Federal Government's concern boiled down to two things: (a) how to avoid a confusing multitude of systems; and, (b) how to locate a authority accountable for the huge sums of money that it was prepare to grant to local authorities. The two were considered interdependen and, from the outset, federal officials strongly favoured a single-tie system of local government on the grounds that it minimised th problems of determining to which level of authority to provide feder grants and from whom to expect results.

The states differed, not unexpectedly, in their opinions of the mo suitable structure of local government. The Western State, by th reforms of 1973–74, had adopted a variant of the American Counc Manager Plan and though it had not yielded any remarkable, indec noticeable results, this was thought due to deficiencies in operation ar scanty resources rather than to the system as such. The view taken t the Western State was that it could be improved and should t maintained.[2] The eastern states—East Central, Rivers and Sou Eastern—and the Midwest had all abandoned local government in th form of local governance by elected councillors in favour of th administration of local affairs by state officials, acting in consultatic with local representatives. Some of these states wanted a continuatic of this system. The northern states, for their part, had made certa structural changes in the old system of Native Authorities witho however displacing to any great extent the Emirs as the tradition rulers, who continued to exercise an effective authority over a wic area of the North.

Thus, although there were significant differences within the souther part of the country, the most delicate issue was how to devise representative system, national in conception but offering meaningful role to traditional rulers, notably those of the larg northern Emirates. Their support, if not leadership, was essential to th success of the reform and they therefore needed assurance that it wou not be the demise of their long and powerful rule.

The diversity of existing practices and the delicacy of such issu made a process of nation-wide consultation doubly necessary. It was process required by the more open democratic style of administratio by which the new Federal Military Government distinguished itse from its predecessor, but it was also the only way of discovering wha would be generally acceptable. At the three zonal conferences held a Kaduna, Enugu and Ibadan local council officials, traditional rule and intellectuals all contributed to the discussions. The role of th federal officials was to coordinate the zonal deliberations so that ommon set of proposals could be submitted to a final meeting to be eld at national level in Ibadan. The task of harmonizing the eculiarities and interests of all the states with national objectives roved however not easy and the final version of the Guidelines was greed only after further deliberations at the highest level—of the iilitary themselves, in joint meetings of the Supreme Military Council nd National Council of States (in which sat the State Governors), and f the traditional rulers.

The importance accorded to traditional authority was symbolised y a gathering of all the most senior Emirs, Obas and Chiefs at Ibadan n July 7th. In addressing them the Head of State was at pains to recall heir participation in the preparation of the Guidelines. He reminded hem: 'I have had several opportunities of consulting some of you both ormally and informally. I have also had the benefit of the views of lany of you through emissaries sent to sound your opinions'. The lead of State also stated emphatically two things that the reforms were ot intended to achieve. Firstly, the Government did not want to isturb the traditional political structure or community. Secondly, it id not want to enforce uniformity all over the country. The reforms vere designed primarily 'to standardise the functions and financial esources of local governments and therefore their effectiveness for evelopment at local levels'.[3]

Considerable flexibility is provided by the five alternative rrangements for reconciling traditional authority with elected ouncils. The role of a traditional ruler may range from that of a assive non-partisan observer of local administration to that of an ctive leader involved in local affairs. The choice lies with State jovernments and it calls for a careful appreciation of local political lignments and predispositions. Not surprisingly therefore there is ome tardiness in the creation of traditional councils especially in the outhern part of the country. Some states have gone ahead omparatively rapidly e.g. Oyo which has established fifteen raditional councils, Ondo (nine) and Ogun (four). The Local jovernment Edicts of Bendel and Cross River make provision for raditional councils to be established but this has still to be done. That f Rivers State makes no such provision.

A closely related question which also called for flexibility is the size f the new local government authorities. In the Guidelines reference is iade to some 'sample analysis', said to have shown 'that where total opulation is significantly less than 150,000—300,000 overhead costs

as well as trained manpower problems are considerable' and tha
'above this range there appear to be few economies of scale', merely th
danger of a 'large and sluggish bureaucracy' which would also b
remote. This is a very dubious observation to make, for the pas
performance of local councils has been dictated not so much b
question of size as by state governments holding them on a short leas
and denying them adequate finance. Be that as it may, the Guideline
recommend a range of 150,000 to 800,000, except that towns and citie
are not to be divided even if over the upper limit.[4] Exceptions belo
150,000 required permission of the Chief of Staff, Supreme HQ, wh
was in charge of the reform. The higher maximum allowed more of
correspondence with traditional communities and urban areas.

It is interesting to compare the new local government units with pre
existing areas of administration. There have been some cases of
readjustment to smaller units, e.g. in Oyo, Ogun and Ondo (formerl
the Western State). The changes are summarised in Table I.

TABLE I

State	Number of local authorities		
	pre 1972	1972–76	1976 reform
Oyo	37	19	24
Ogun	42	7	10
Ondo	34	13	17
Western State	113	39	51

The reason for making the changes is not so much economic o
administrative as one of political expediency. For example the splittin
into two of Ijesha South Division in Oyo State reverses the merger o
Ijesha Urban District Council and Ijesha Southern District Counc
which took place at the end of 1972. The Inspector/Divisional Office
had reported at the time that the merger 'though economically wise i
politically inexpedient and fraught with difficulties.'[5] The opportunit
has now been taken to separate the two. It is the promise of adequat
grants-in-aid which has permitted some reversal of the consolidatio
that took place in the Western State in 1972. A similar sub-division ha
occurred in Bendel; whereas fourteen Divisional Developmen
Councils were established in the reforms of 1974, that of 1976 ha
resulted in the creation of nineteen local governments—presumably t
preserve the political identity of some small traditional communities
In the eastern states—Imo, Anambra, Cross River and River

states— where local government in the traditional sense has been abandoned in favour of 'development' administration by state officials, the administrative areas used for that purpose were taken over by the new local government councils. Thus Cross River State has utilized its seventeen administrative divisions and Rivers State its eighteen administrative divisions as the basis for the new local government areas.

Perhaps the most profound change provided by the new reforms at the local level is the disappearance of the famed Divisional Officer. The Guidelines directive on this issue was very emphatic. 'The Divisional Administration should have no responsibility for Local Government and play no part in it'. Divisional administration is regarded as 'essentially colonial', which must be abandoned now that a genuine effort is being made to give the local governments internal strength, and their sizes have been considerably reduced.

But the disappearance of the Divisional Officer who had an all-pervading influence in the localities does not imply that the Government will not supervise local governments. The various State Governments are to appoint Local Government Inspectors who have access to local government meetings and records in order to discharge the State Government's duty of oversight. In addition there is a reserve power to dissolve any council which is judged not to have performed satisfactorily. The only limitation on this power is that a Management Committee appointed by a State government in place of a local council may not remain in place for more than three months or, if its authority is renewed, for more than one year in the aggregate. Thus no state government may dissolve an elected local government and avoid holding an election in the area for more than a year.

The powers of oversight and the ultimate one of dissolution pale in the face of the powers previously enjoyed by the Divisional Administration. Consequently a great deal more responsibility falls on the executive secretary of the local governments. In order to ensure that the office does not prove unequal to the task, middle-level administrative officers (Senior Assistant Secretaries and Principal Assistant Secretaries) have been seconded to the local governments. It is the hope that these government officials will ultimately be replaced by local government staff. This hope is, no doubt, too sanguine; as yet the image of the local governments remains poor and it does not seem likely that men of the calibre of the government officials currently on secondment to the local governments will be found to replace them.

If the new local authorities are to be a real 'third tier of government' adequate financial resources must be provided. In the preparatory stages it was assumed that their needs could be calculated fairly precisely. In the end an arbitrary sum of N.100 million was provided by the Federal Government to be distributed among the States—and within each State—25% in equal shares and 75% proportional to population. A further N.250 million has been allocated for the financial year 1977/78. The large size of the grant is taken as evidence of the Federal Military Government's strong desire to make local government effective. In the past inadequate financial resources have severely restricted the activities of local authorities, especially in promoting local socio-economic development. But as the Public Service Review Commission observed, the most serious difficulty in the past has been 'the unilateral determination by state governments of the limits of income and of the income group local authorities can tax'. The present grants are generous but they have been determined unilaterally by the Federal Military Government and there is no certainty of their continuation, although if the new local government authorities do demonstrate their capacity to use effectively the present sums, their claim to a more secure source of revenue will be undeniable.

In his speech launching the Guidelines on 19 August 1976 the Chief of Staff, Supreme Headquarters, announced (a) that by October all states in the Federation would have promulgated the Local Government Edicts; these would embody the necessary electoral regulations, and (b) the adoption of direct elections into local government councils in Bendel, Benue, Imo, Kwara, Lagos, Ogun, Ondo, Oyo and Rivers; and the choice of indirect elections by the other ten states. [7]

Choice of direct or indirect elections became an issue soon after the announcement for two reasons: (a) the absence of uniformity in all states of the federation in the system of election and (b) the fact that local government councils were to be the electoral colleges for the Constituent Assembly.

Those who supprted a uniform system of direct elections were of the view that indirect election is not only full of serious abuses but also that it is undemocratic. Alhaji Aminu Kano whose state opted for indirect election, announced publicly that he would not vote, primarily on account of this decision. Like many who argued for direct elections all over the country, Aminu Kano felt that the Kano State government had taken a retrogressive step by opting for indirect elections. As the

Daily Times put it, 'part of the confusion in Nigeria is that indirect election brings to mind some of the abuses of the system when it was practised during the civilian regime and even before independence'.[8]

Supporters of indirect elections were very vocal as well. The main spokesmen for this group were the *New Nigerian* and Professor Odenigwe, the Commissioner for Local Government in Anambra State. In an editorial the *New Nigerian* observed that most of the critics of states that opted for indirect election had not studied the process carefully. Voters at both the primary and electoral college stages, the paper pointed out, would cast their votes secretly and not by show of hands. Since the primary units are small, the voters will be casting their vote for the people they know well and whom they can trust. There was moreover insufficient time to organise direct elections properly. It concluded, 'there is nothing undemocratic in the indirect system. It is in fact the best way for a community to elect its representatives. The issues to be dealt with by the local government councils are clear and straightforward, roads, sewerage etc. What is needed are men of integrity to supervise these projects. The communities know the people who have served them in good and bad times'.[9]

Professor Odenigwe, defending the Anambra State Government's adoption of indirect election, pointed to the absence of a proper electoral register and to the ban on party political activity which was incompatible with campaigning. But he also defended indirect elections on principle. They gave each local community an opportunity to be represented (at the primary level) and so respected local political tradition.

Each State, having decided its own mode of election, appointed a standing committee with responsibility for registering voters, receiving nominations, conducting the elections and announcing the results.

The various problems which confronted Lagos State during its registration exercise served as warnings to the other states. The initial response to the invitation to register was very disappointing and the closing date was twice extended. The period of registration, originally scheduled to last one week, September 13–18, was at first extended to September 24. Much publicity was given to the registration of the Head of State, Lt. General Olusegun Obasanjo, at Ward 2 Obalende on September 22. In a centre where 6,000 voters had been expected to register the Head of State was the 56th person to do so. A further extension to September 30 permitted a total registration of less than half a million.[10]

Several reasons may be suggested for this rather low response. First, there were too few registration centres, particularly in metropolitan Lagos; those fortunate enough to know where exactly they had to register complained of spending too much time queueing. This led the Governor to direct that more registration centres be opened. Secondly, there was insufficient publicity on radio, television and in the newspapers. It was stepped up after the first week and the military governor made several appeals to people to go out and register. Thirdly, it has been suggested that there was indifference because of the decision to make local elections non-partisan; if party politics had been allowed, the parties would have worked hard to see that people registered in larger numbers. The experience of the other states where the turn-out was most encouraging does not support this view. Probably a more important reason is the peculiar nature of Lagos. People had to register in wards where they live and not in their places of work. Most workers, market-women and even self-employed leave their homes before sunrise because of transport difficulties and they do not return until well after sunset. It was therefore extremely difficult for them to register within the stipulated hours of 8.30 a.m. and 6 p.m. Since the population of metropolitan Lagos is more than two-thirds the total population of Lagos State, it is no wonder therefore that the registration exercise was most discouraging.

The other states did much better not only in their preparations but also their results. Ogun State for example opened about 4,000 registration centres, each centre being expected to register an average of 500 voters. Ondo State devoted two weeks to registration. In Oyo State, a total of 3,277,632 people were registered during the exercise which lasted ten days, October 4–13.

Nomination of candidates took place in all states November 15–30. Two important announcements had been made, the one concerning the qualifications required of those seeking election and the other concerning the remuneration of those elected to office. A candidate had to be at least eighteen years of age and be resident for two years continuously in his local government area or be an indigene of the area. Anybody who had been found guilty of corruption or abuse of office by a judicial inquiry, was disqualified. Chiefs and any person in public employment, including teachers in grant-aided schools, were precluded from standing for election. There is no doubt that the exclusion of teachers was an unpopular decision and, as many observers pointed out, the ban on teachers and public servants opened the way to less qualified persons; the self-employed, the retired and even those without gainful occupation. The payment of salaries to councillors was an innovation which stimulated nominations and some of the lower paid public servants resigned in order to stand for election.[11] Councillors are to receive N.1,200 a year, Chairmen of councils N.6,000. (N.7,200 if the population is over 300,000) and supervisory councillors (chairmen of committees) N.4,500 (N.4,800 in the larger areas).

The following table summarizes the number of nominations received in seven of the states where direct elections were held.

1976 LOCAL GOVERNMENT ELECTION
IN SEVEN STATES OF NIGERIA

	Total No. of Seats	Unopposed	Seats Contested	No. of Candidates
Kwara	214	62	141(a)	266
Oyo	436	108	328	967
Ondo	251	123	119(b)	303
Imo	342	122	220	561
Lagos	171	40	131	414
Bendel	186	23	163	542
Ogun	134	64	70	175

(a) No candidates for eleven seats.
(b) 9 bye-elections were scheduled due to irregularities in nomination process.

Ondo State had the highest percentage of unopposed candidates (49%), followed by Ogun (47·9%). Lagos State returned only 23% of its candidates unopposed and in Bendel State the figure was 12·5%. In Anambra State which chose indirect election the electoral colleges returned over 70% unopposed. In Enugu, capital of the state, 22 of the 28 seats were uncontested and in Abakaliki, 22 out of 27. The contests during the second stage of the election were concentrated in Onitsha (where only 8 of the 23 seats were filled unopposed) Njikoka, Aguata and Nsukka.

The large number of candidates returned unopposed all over the country was questioned in some quarters. Some attributed this to the absence of political parties. As one columnist put it, 'here is a situation in which a more influential candidate can talk it down to a less influential one who owes no political party any obligations. Some of the candidates who have been returned unopposed have definitely bribed their ways through.'[12]

One of the problems which faced candidates and the electorate generally was the non-availability of electoral regulations. The Chief of Staff had said that these were to be published by the end of October. By the middle of December, less than two weeks before the election, only two states, Kwara and Oyo had gazetted their regulations. In most parts of the country candidates and voters had to rely on statements by state or federal officials published in the press. This could have given room to serious malpractices on the part of officials willing to frustrate candidates.

In the second place the voters list in some states, (for example Rivers) did not contain any addresses. Only names and registration numbers were given. This could have given room to impersonation. There were also allegations of Obas, Emirs and other traditional rulers in various parts of the country openly canvassing for candidates, contrary to the law. As the *New Nigerian* observed, however, 'All over the world, no election is ever conducted without complaints of election irregularities. It is in anticipation of these complaints that election appeals committees have been set up all over the country. The essential thing is that these committees should be made up of reliable and honest people who can be depended upon to give impartial judgment'.[13]

On the eve of election day the Head of State appealed to all Nigerians to go out and vote, underlining the importance of the elections. Until the official voting figures are published, it is difficult to know the exact turnout. Newspaper reports, however, give the impression that the response was reasonably good all over the country. In some states the election results shocked some old time politicians and former ministers and commissioners but the headlines of some of the newspapers appear exaggerated. The *Nigerian Observer* boldly stated 'It's "No" to old Guards: New Breed steps in'. The *Daily Sketch* of 30 December wrote 'Shocker for Old Politicians' and the *Daily Times* of the same date announced 'Fall of the mighty'. Some of them were successful however, even in Oyo, where the list of defeated politicians and former commissioners was longer than in any other state: it included four who had served as Commissioners in the Western State Military Government—Chief Mojeed Agbaje (Ibadan) Gabriel Fagbure and Alade Lamuye (Iwo) and Chief Kola Balogun (Osogbo); four former Ministers in Governments of the Western Region—Okunola Adebayo (Oluyole) S. A. Yerokun (Iseyin) K. O. Owonikoko and Saka Layonu (Ede): and several former Western Region parliamentarians—A. Adedeji (Ibarapa) J. A. Akintoba and N. A. Adibi (Ogbomoso). Michael Omisade (ex-Action Group) lost at Ife.

In Bendel State defeated candidates included Lawrence Borha, trade unionist and former Commissioner, and Dan Peacock Ogbebor, a former politician. In Kwara State the list included Alhaji Idi-Aro.

Former politicians who were successful included in Ogun State, Bisi Onabanjo (Ijebu) Tunji Otegbeye (Ilaro) Ade Oyalowo (Abeokuta) and Niyi Adegbenro son of late Alhaji D. S. Adegbenro (Abeokuta); in Oyo State, Victor Lajide former federal minister (Ogbomoso), Akinbowale Akintola cousin of late premier S. L. Akintola (Ogbomoso); in Ondo State, Olu Akinfosile and G. B. Akinyele; in Kwara State, J. S. Olawoyin and P. Dada: in Lagos State, Wole Awolowo son of Chief Obafemi Awolowo (Apapa).

From all these it would appear that the success or failure of a candidate depended on local factors. Therefore no generalisation can be made on the results of the election.

As expected, several appeals have been made and for various reasons: lateness in opening the polling station, voting by children under the age of 18, open canvassing at the polling station, use of loud speakers, tampering with ballot boxes while in transit from the polling station to the counting centres, inefficiency and ignorance of electoral regulations on the part of electoral officials and the stuffing of ballot boxes. In Anambra State a defeated candidate alleged that a policeman snatched a ballot paper from a voter and cast it without his consent. The policeman gave as his reason that 'the voter appeared rather indecisive and was wasting time in the booth'. In Ekanu Local Government the defeated candidate lost by only one vote. With the exception of Chief Agbaje no front line politician is known to have carried his allegation of electoral malpractices to the High Court. They all appear to have accepted Kola Balogun's position that defeat at the local government election is only round one in the electoral battle and that 'round two is just around the corner keeping in mind that the race is not always for the swift'.

In general very few women stood for election. There was however provision in the Guidelines for nomination of councillors (up to 25%). In Oyo State, the proportion is 10% and the opportunity has been taken to appoint twenty five women councillors, one for each council except Ibadan Municipal Council.

Conclusion

What are the chances that the present reform of local government in Nigeria will not go the way of previous attempts? The federal government's preference for local government rather than local administration is not in doubt. For the first time since the introduction of popularly elected local government councils in Nigeria the federal government has allocated a large sum of money to ensure effective government at the grass roots. This is not a one time allocation. Moreover, a federal Centre for Local Government Studies is planned for the training of local government officials. Yet these efforts need the positive support of state officials who have the basic responsibility for local government. This is where the danger lies. Even if finance ceases to be a problem and qualified staff are appointed and regularly trained, if state officials refuse to change their attitude all the federal government efforts will be in vain. From all available evidence state officials still look at local governments as mere agents of state government and of the state civil service. As the *New Nigerian* observed, 'Some state military governors have recently spoken to some of these councils in a manner more suited to a drill major's address to raw recruits on their first day on parade . . . . if the new system does not start off with the clearest understanding of the limits of everybody's competence, much will be lost of the intentions of the reforms and their contribution to future good democratic government.'[14]

NOTES

1. Federal Republic of Nigeria, *Public Service Review Commission,* Main Report Chapter 12 Para. 544 (1), (2). September 1974.
2. The reference to the Western State is appropriate because the consultations leading to the 'Guidelines' preceded the splitting of the State into Oyo, Ondo and Ogun States. Other references to states with respect to the preparation of the 'Guidelines' shall be to the pre–1976 states.
3. For the full text of Lt-General Olusegun Obasanjo's speech, see the *Daily Times* (Lagos) July 8, 1976 p. 11.
4. Subordinate councils may be established by the new local government authorities and powers delegated to them. Such subordinate councils will not however constitute a separate tier of government; they will not have any power to raise money nor will they be in direct receipt of grants from the federal or state government. None has as yet been created but provision has been made in e.g. The Local Government Edict, 1976, (No. 5) Supplement to Oyo State of Nigeria Gazette Extraordinary No. 27 Vol. 1, 4th October, 1976; and Ogun State Local Government Edict, No. 9, 1976.
5. Western State of Nigeria, *Proposals for the Reorganisation of Local Government Councils in the Western State of Nigeria.* (Western State Official Document No. 4 of 1971) Ibadan, Government Printer, 1971.
6. Public Service Review Commission op. cit. Chapter 12 Par. 509.

7. Soon after the announcement, Plateau State changed to direct election. It is interesting to note that of the remaining 9 that chose indirect election, only two, Anambra and Cross River, are Southern States. The other seven are Northern States.

8. *Daily Times* November 23, 1976. p. 3.

9. *New Nigerian* October 27, 1976 p. 1. The position taken by the *New Nigerian* is partly supported by the invalidation of the election of Alhaji Inuwa Wada in Kano primary municipal election. Inuwa Wada who is the uncle of the late Head of State, General Murtala Muhammed and who had widely publicised his presidential ambition was found guilty of election malpractices. He was fined ₦.100 and banned from local government elections for 5 years. This incident provided another opportunity for the paper to further educate those who opposed indirect election. 'Those rabid ideologues who have blindly condemned the indirect system of election as being undemocratic ought now to sit up and re-examine the issue. It is by no means a reactionary 'corrupt' system as they will like us to believe'. *New Nigerian* 15 December, 1976.

10. Estimated population for Lagos state (1976) is 3,514,107; that of metropolitan Lagos is 3,002,243.

11. In Kwara State for example, 115 teachers and other public servants were reported to have resigned their jobs. *New Nigerian* 4 December, 1976.

12. *Nigerian Observer* December 21, 1976 p. 5. After winning the petition against Inua Wada during the primary, Malam Tango announced his withdrawal from the final competition scheduled for December 28 on the basis of series of demands made on him 'to bribe his way' to the council.

13. *New Nigerian,* 15 December 1976, p.1. See footnote 9.

14. *New Nigerian,* 25 January, 1977, p. 1.

11

As Seen in Kaduna

Abubakar Yaya Aliyu

I wish to express my gratitude to Mallam Yaya Abubakar, Permanent Secretary, Political Division, Cabinet Office, Lagos and Alhaji Sani Sambo, Permanent Secretary, Ministry of Local Government, for helping me in preparing this chapter.

The reform of local government which the Murtala Muhammed Government initiated, as part of its political programme for a restoration of democratic civilian rule by October 1979, is both radical in conception and careful in its implementation. Since the imposition of colonial rule and the amalgamation of Nigeria in 1914, the system of local government had varied so much from region to region, province to province or even within provinces, owing no doubt to the nature of pre-existing historical conditions, that it was difficult if not impossible to discern in them a common structure, function, goal and philosophy. Moreover, past experience has clearly shown that, given the prevailing social, political and economic structure of the country as a whole, the success of democracy and nation-building, the maintenance of a stable social and political order and the establishment and consolidation of a terminal political community would depend ultimately on the reform of local government and the resolution of issues at the grass-root level. [1]

The Federal Military Government in taking the initiative in September 1975 directed each State Government to set up a Commission to appraise the problems involved in reorganisation and to submit proposals that would increase the responsibilities of local authorities and encourage participation at the grass-root level. They were also to indicate what staff and finance would be needed to carry out any proposed decentralisation. Furthermore, the Federal Government let it be known that the reports of all the States would be considered together with a view to discovering a common approach, that State governments were left free to choose their own method of election and that traditional rulers were to be accorded due recognition. [2]

The division of the country into zones for consultative purposes was to ensure a certain uniformity of approach. The reports from State Governments were collated and embodied into a document entitled 'Suggested Framework for a National System of Local Government'. [3] This was to form the subject of exhaustive discussion and consultation among all interested parties before emerging in its final form as 'Guidelines' for implementation by State governments. Thus, although the initiative, direction and necessary co-ordination came from the Federal Government, the Guidelines, as eventually formulated and approved, were the outcome of consultation at all levels. This process of consultation was necessary in order to ensure that whatever reform was finally approved took into account not only the varying conditions that exist throughout the country but also the practical difficulties involved in its execution—particularly in the North. The purpose of this chapter is three-fold: first to indicate the Northern Zone's response to the initial proposals; secondly, to report on the implementation of the reform in one of the Northern States (Kaduna); and thirdly to explore the prospects of success in the future.

The proposals differed from all preceding reforms, at least in the Northern part of the country, in two fundamental respects. Firstly, the term local government was itself clearly defined in such a way as to make it a third tier of Government and to emphasise the principles of representativeness, participation, devolution and autonomy. Secondly, the new local government authorities were to serve a population of between 150,000 and 600,000 (subsequently raised to 800,000). [4] These two elements carried far-reaching implications for most of the Northern States. It meant that Emirs and Chiefs could no longer administer their areas as sole authorities, neither could they determine the membership of the councils since the majority of the members were to be elected by a democratic process. Far more serious, the emirates in the north would be broken up, since each had a population, even on the basis of the 1963 census figures, well beyond the upper limit. This would obviously pose a threat to any organic unity and in turn undermine if not completely eliminate the institutional and symbolic basis of the emirate, as epitomised in the person and position of the Emir and District Heads. Thus these two elements of the reform formed a direct challenge to the Emirs and Chiefs both in structural and functional terms.

The Suggested Framework was, however, by no means insensitive to or unconscious of these implications and took them into account by outlining five alternative ways in which the new Local Government Councils and the Emirate or Traditional Council could be harmonized.[5] State governments were left to determine which of them would best suit local conditions.

In view of the radical departure from pre-existing practice and the need to explore all channels of communication and consultation, the Suggested Framework was discussed at a conference of Emirs and Chiefs of the northern states, held in Kaduna 25th—26th June 1976. The conference expressed qualified support, observing that the proposals were appropriate 'for the differing needs and circumstances of the various parts of this diverse country provided that:—

(i)   the choice of the right alternative in structural pattern is made in the case of each Local Government Authority;
(ii) certain improvements and modifications are made in different parts of the guidelines.'[6]

In amplification of the above general observation, the conference declared its preference for the institution, wherever possible, of a single council rather than separate local government and traditional councils. Of the five alternatives the first, second and fifth would best 'cater for all the different sizes of the Local Government Authorities in the Northern States', satisfy 'the strong and well-established customs and traditions in these states' and enable the Emir or Chief 'to play his role as father of all his people'. The conference also argued that because of the historical circumstances surrounding the creation of Emirates and Divisions, the reform should not involve any change in their boundaries.

The conference expressed great concern regarding the functions of Emirate Councils. Their role vis-à-vis the Local Governments in the 'Suggested Framework' was largely confined to the giving of guidance and advice, harmonizing, making representations and expressing opinions.

It was argued that if the preservation of the organic unity of the

Emirate was to be guaranteed and safeguarded, 'functional Emirate Councils' should be established and their terms of reference widened both in scope and range. To this end, the conference resolved that Emirate Councils should have additional functions, namely:

(i) Community Tax Assessment within the Emirate as a whole.
(ii) Determination of all religious matters.
(iii) Support for Arts and Culture.
(iv) Chieftaincy matters and maintenance of Traditional Titles and Offices.
(v) Any other matter that the State Government may delegate or hand-over to the Emirate Council or which the Local Government Authority Councils in their discretion may wish to hand-over to the Emirate Council.

Furthermore, the conference stressed that conferment of traditional titles in northern States is the prerogative of the Emir or Chief which he should exercise at his own discretion. This meant that neither the Emirate Council nor the Local Government Council should have a say in appointments to traditional offices even though their incumbents may be employees of Local Government.[8] It was also felt that all District Heads should be appointed as ex-officio members of the Local Government Council, and all title holders 'who by custom are members of the Emir's or Chief's Councils should be automatically members of the Emirate Council'.

The conference also questioned the procedures for the appointment of Local Government Chairman and the recruitment of senior Local Government Staff. The Suggested Framework had recommended that Council Chairmen be elected by the Councils subject to the approval of Military Governors, while all matters of recruitment promotion and discipline be dealt with at State level by an autonomous Local Government Service Boards should not be `set up, as they had not ensure a good working relationship between the two councils, Emirate Councils should be allowed to nominate several candidates for the Chairmanship of the Local Government Councils who could then be considered by the State Governor. It was felt also that Local Government Service Boards should not be set up, as they had not worked well in the past and that instead the Emirate Council should handle the appointment of all senior staff, including that of the Secretary.[10]

All these counter-proposals were designed so that special

recognition should be accorded to the position of Emirs and Chiefs and so that Emirate Councils should have the means of regulating more closely the activities of Local Governments in the northern States.

A careful analysis of the final guidelines, as adopted by the Federal Government in consultation with the Council of States, shows clearly the extent to which the Government was prepared to go to meet the wishes of the traditional rulers and in alleviating some of their fears and anxieties. Thus Emirate Councils were accorded virtually all the additional functions requested at the conference. Such offensive provisions as would enable the Emirate Council determine appointments to traditional titles and offices and the Local Government Service Board to determine the suitability of persons for appointment as District Heads were notably absent from the final guidelines. Though the maintenance of law and order was excluded from the new list of Emirate Council functions, Emirs and Chiefs have been given the responsibility of 'assisting Government in the maintenance of peace'.[11] How this is to be done remains a moot question since, with the take-over by Government of the Native Authority Police, Prisons and Courts since 1966, they would appear to lack the necessary resources.[12] However, they still have a responsibility for the essential institutional setting within which social order is maintained, for they have the right to appoint District and Village heads, albeit in consultation with Local Government Councils and subject to any regulations that may be imposed, also to tour any part of their Emirate or Chiefdom, to visit any Local Government institution and submit such observations as they may deem fit either to the Local Government concerned or to the State Government. Furthermore, Emirate Councils may designate some of their members as 'overall Co-ordinators of the various functions of the Local Government such as education and natural resources', with powers to inspect and report formally to their council, thus affording the Local Government a valuable source of second opinion'.[13] On the other hand Local Government Service Boards have been retained and all senior appointments are to be channelled through them.

The Guidelines in themselves have no legal force. This comes from enactment by State Governments. We examine briefly their implementation in one of the Northern States, Kaduna, (formerly North Central). The Kaduna State Government decided to rationalise as far as possible the new reforms with pre-existing administrative arrangements. Fourteen Local Governments have been established, corresponding to the former Administrative Areas, or Divisions, of which there were ten in 1969 and fourteen in 1975. With one exception, the population of these Areas (1963 figures) fell within the range specified in the Guidelines (150,000— 800,000). Birmin Gwari Local Government, with an estimated population of 50,000 (1963 figure 29,798), was treated as an exceptional case because of its geographical size (one of the largest in the State) and of its long historical existence as a separate unit of local government.[14]

The decision to adopt the fourteen former Administrative Areas as the new units of Local Government was a very wise one. Although the powers of the Area Councils had been in practice rather limited by their continued deference to traditional authority, they had the necessary infrastructure. They had had their own treasuries, secretariats, development projects etc, and were comparatively well endowed with high level manpower.

The application of the reform to the traditional authorities was in accordance with the first and third of the alternatives specified in the Guidelines. The large Emirates of Katsina and Zaria each extend over several local government units (six and four respectively) and there is therefore an overall Emirate Council in both cases. The smaller Emirates of Daura and Birmin Gwari are each coterminous with the area of a single unit of local Government and in both cases the decision was in favour of separate Emirate Councils. Similarly in Jema'a there is a separate Traditional council in which the presidency will rotate among local chiefs. Table 1 sets out the new pattern of authority.

All existing councils were dissolved on July 19, 1975 and replaced, as an interim measure pending the election of the new Local Government Councils, by caretaker committees composed mostly of officials. Their task was to maintain services, to assess the staffing needs of the new authorities, to deploy and reassign staff, to re-distribute the assets of the former Local Authorities and to help in the holding of elections.

The new Local Government Councils are composed of 75% elected and 25% nominated members, the maximum permitted by the Guidelines. Membership varies from ten to thirty (See Table III, p.280).

The Governor had declared that election would be 'indirect but by secret ballot using the electoral college system'.[15] Although no direct explanation was given for the adoption of the indirect system of election in the State, the rationale behind it lay in the fact that the ban on political parties had yet to be lifted; consequently candidates could

TABLE 1

KADUNA STATE: LOCAL GOVERNMENT COUNCILS AND EMIRATE/TRADITIONAL COUNCILS (1963 POPULATION)

Overall Emirate Council	Local Government Council		Total No. of Councillors
	Datsin-Ma	(412,767)	27
	Funtua	(420,606)	28
	Kankia	(380,193)	26
Katsina	Katsina	(424,721)	30
(2,286,032)	Malumfashi	(278,090)	19
	Mani	(369,655)	24
	Ikara	(295,908)	20
	Kachia	(296,570)	20
Zaria	Saminaka	(190,525)	13
(1,153,284)	Zaria	(370,911)	30
Separate but Coterminous Councils			
	Daura	(258,973)	17
	Birmin Gwari	(29,798)	10
	Jema's	(220,300)	14
Local Government Council only			
	Kaduna*	(149,910)	(455,000 projected)	26

(Total population 4,098,297)

*In the case of Kaduna Local Government the figure of 455,000 has been projected from the 1963 census figures, and is being used for all practical purposes. It is alone in this.

not campaign for votes but had to rely on their own image. As the Governor stated 'elections will not be based on any political party representations. Members will be elected on personal merit and ability to contribute to the development of the local governments. It will be easier for the members to make personal judgements on local issues rather than succumb to the forces of political parties, personalities, pressure-groups or even the press'.[16] One wonders on what basis the electorate could form an impression of the 'personal merit and ability' of the candidates or assess the relative potentiality of their individual contributions, when candidates were not permitted to organise and campaign for votes nor issue a manifesto or programme setting out the issues at stake and their own proposals for dealing with these. This, however, was not a matter on which the State government had any choice since the Supreme Military Council had already decided not to lift the ban on political parties until September 1978, after the new Constitution had come into force. In the circumstances, a system of indirect elections was held to provide better representation since the electorate could vote for persons known to them on a personal face-to-face basis.[17]

An Election Committee was appointed in mid-October to organise and conduct the elections, fixed for November 30th and December 28th. The Permanent Secretary, Military Governor's Office, was Chairman and the Committee had ten other members, of whom eight were state civil servants.[18] The government also appointed an Appeals Committee for each Local Government area to deal with any electoral complaints or petitions that might arise in the course of the elections. Unfortunately, it was only on January 6th 1977 that the Local Government Edict and the Electoral Regulations were officially approved and published, that is not until after the elections had been held. This meant that throughout the election period both the Committee and all other Electoral officers had to be guided by the draft provisions of the Edict and the Regulations. These were subject to all kinds of alterations and modifications, with the result that everybody concerned, including the Election Committee, had frequently to refer to the Ministries of Local Government and of Justice for a decision on certain specific issues.

Since the government had opted for a system of indirect elections, the Election Committee's first task was to break up each Local Government Area into primary units and to group these into electoral colleges from which the councillors would subsequently be elected. It was decided that the primary units should consist of about 2,000 electors. The figure was not uniformly applied and certain areas, where the communication system was very poor and villages far apart, were allocated a seat at the primary level even though the population, on the basis of the 1963 census figures, was less than 2,000. This was to ensure easy access to polling booths and to generate a sense of participation among all communities. The number to be elected at the primary level throughout the State turned out to be 2,289.

Nomination of candidates took place between 17th and 23rd November. The Governor had earlier announced that all adult tax-payers, including women, who produced tax receipts would have the

right to vote and be voted for. All employees in the public sector
including those in Local Government and other statutory
corporations, had to resign their appointments if they wished to
contest elections. Every primary election candidate was to deposit a
non-refundable sum of money (subsequently fixed at N.50 but later
abolished) and was to be free to use a symbol (subsequently disallowed)
or a photograph for identification purposes.[19] Thus under the draft
regulations, any person was qualified to vote and be voted for provided
he was not a public servant and 'had been directly assessed by the
revenue division of the State Ministry of Finance or . . . had had tax
deducted from his salary by his employer during the year immediately
preceding the election.'[20] Since, in the Northern States generally, the
vast majority of women traditionally do not pay tax, this automatically
excluded them from the election, unless they were able immediately to
pay a tax on their declared income and obtain a receipt. This was
precisely what several of them had to do.[21] The requirement that
candidates pay a non-refundable deposit of N.50—an amount too high
for most people—was an additional constraint.

A number of directives from the Federal Government eventually
brought about a revision of these regulations. Following the meeting of
all State Commissioners of Local Government with the Chief of Staff,
Supreme Headquarters, Lagos, it was decided to exempt all those
contesting the elections at the primary level from payment of any
deposit, to fix the voting age at 18 years, to disqualify from standing for
election any person who had been adjudged by a Tribunal of Enquiry
to be corrupt or who had been dismissed from public service. However,
it was only on 30th November, the very day fixed for the primary
elections, that the Federal Government issued another directive
removing the tax qualification in respect of women. The net result of all
these modifications and directives was to confuse the general public
and to create considerable difficulty for the administrators of the
election.

In the circumstances it is not surprising that nominations fell below
expectations. Out of the 2,289 elected, as many as 891 (approximately
39%) were returned unopposed.[22] In several areas, there were
widespread allegations of interference on the part of traditional rulers
who wished to have their own candidates returned unopposed. Indeed,
some had to be officially warned against interfering in the elections.
The situation was particularly bad in the rural areas, where some
district and village heads attempted with varying degrees of success to

have relations or nominees returned unopposed. Another serious problem was the tendency in many areas to view candidates in terms of their membership or association with the old political parties, namely the N.P.C. and N.E.P.U. or in terms of their identification with rival villages or communities. Communities tried to get their own representative into the council and rival politicians sought to settle old scores.

Most notable was the returning of 30 unopposed candidates for a total of 31 electoral seats in Birmin Gwari Local Government Area and 33 out of 34 in Doka District of Kaduna Local Government Area. Generally the number of contestants ranged from 2 to 10 with an average of about 3 to 4 per primary electoral unit. Only eight women were nominated in the whole State, of whom one was returned unopposed. Although polling continued until 9.00 p.m. to allow for women in purdah to cast their vote, the general turn out was far below expectations. Table II sets out the results for each Local Government Area:

TABLE II
KADUNA STATE: LOCAL GOVERNMENT PRIMARY ELECTIONS
NOVEMBER 30, 1976

Local Govern- ment Area	No. of electoral seats	Estimated Ballot Papers	Seats Declared Unopposed	Seats Contested	Votes Cast Total	Votes Cast per contes- ted election
Birmin Gwari	31	60,000	30	1	495	495
Funtua	229	420,000	75	153	52,698	344
Ikara	143	300,000	56	87	36,024	414
Jemaa	202	250,000	136	66	27,895	422
Kaduna	138	300,000	53	85	63,135	743
Katsina	179	400,000	51	128	56,896	444
Saminaka	117	100,000	63	54	24,290	450
Zaria	205	400,000	56	149	72,550	487
Malumfashi	135	280,000	24	111	47,550	428
Daura	121	200,000	43	78	36,162	463
Kachia	178	100,000	94	84	48,081	572
Mani	179	380,000	103	76	23,039	303
Kankia	230	400,000	83	147	57,431	391
Dutsen-Ma	202	60,000	24	178	101,056	568
Total	2,289	3,890,000	891	1,398	646,977	463

Source: Report on Local Government Elections 1976. Kaduna State of Nigeria. (unpublished) and Local Government Elections Vol. I.

The number of ballot papers was a very rough estimate of what might have been needed, based on projections of the 1963 figures. The State Government had decided not to compile an electoral register, although the draft regulations so provided. This, coupled with the subsequent decision to fix the voting age at 18, made it difficult if not impossible to determine with any degree of accuracy the number of people qualified to vote in any given constituency. It was not surprising therefore that widespread allegations were made of rigging in many primary constituencies. A total of 105 election appeals were registered with the various Appeal Committees, of which 50 were dismissed for lack of sufficient evidence; the rest were fully investigated, nullified and bye-elections held to the satisfaction of all the parties involved. Appeals were generally based on the grounds that people voted more than once or in areas where they did not reside, that persons under 18 were allowed to vote, that candidates used their own vehicles to convey supporters to polling stations and that they used their money to buy votes. It was of course difficult to substantiate or refute many of the allegations in the absence of an electoral register.

The electoral colleges were formed as single member constituencies, so as to facilitate the widest possible representation of districts. Nominations were to be received from the 20th–24th December, 1976 and 136 out of 235 councillors were returned unopposed. The distribution is shown in Table III.

The percentage of uncontested elections (57%) was even higher than for the primary elections (39%). Although no concrete evidence can be given to challenge the legitimacy or accuracy of the results, there were widespread allegations of malpractices. Large sums of money are said to have been spent in buying off votes. Since most of the electoral colleges were composed of not more than 18 members, and in many cases as few as five[24] it was very easy to influence the outcome of the election. In many instances, it was the size of the district in a particular Local Government area that determined not only the number of seats it had in the council but also the voting behaviour of the electorate. In areas where electoral colleges were composed of members from different villages, it was generally the candidate from the village with the larger number of voters in the college who won the election.[25] Thus one of the unfortunate consequences of the indirect system of elections was not only to maximise opportunities for rigging but also to generate or reinforce antagonism between villages and within districts.

TABLE III
KADUNA STATE. LOCAL GOVERNMENT SECONDARY ELECTIONS

Local Government Councils	Total of Elected Members	Unopposed	Contested	No. of nominated members
Birmin Gwari	8	8	—	2
Daura	13	9	4	4
Dutsen-Ma	21	12	9	6
Funtua	21	10	11	7
Ikara	15	8	7	5
Jemaa	11	3	8	3
Kachia	15	10	5	5
Kankia	20	13	7	6
Kaduna	21	13	8	5
Katsina	23	9	14	7
Malumfashi	15	11	4	4
Mani	19	11	8	5
Saminaka	10	4	6	3
Zaria	23	15	8	7
Total	235	136	99	69

Source: Report on Local Government Elections 1976 and Local Government Elections Vol. II.

By far the most striking feature of the elections was the social composition of those who ran for election, particularly at the primary level. They tended not to belong to what one might call the educated classes. This was no doubt due very largely to the Electoral Regulations, under which public officials, including school teachers, local government staff and members of care-taker committees—in effect most of the educated elements in the State—would have had to resign their offices in order to contest the elections. Many of them had put in many years of service, and resignation, which involved forfeiture of pension, gratuity and means of livelihood, was too risky a proposition. The risk was all the greater in view of the system of indirect election which made it often extremely difficult to predict the outcome, no matter how popular the candidate might be in any given primary unit or district. Table IV provides a rough idea of the educational and occupational backgrounds of those elected.

Thus of the 190 elected members whose educational and occupational backgrounds was known, only 61 (32%) had any formal

TABLE IV

SUMMARY OF THE EDUCATIONAL AND OCCUPATIONAL
BACKGROUND OF ELECTED COUNCILLORS

Local Government Council	No. of Elected Members	No. for whom background information is available	No. with Education beyond Primary level	No. employed in public sector	No. employed in private sector
Birmin Gwari	8	8	8	8	—
Daura	13	13	3	3	10
Dutsin-Ma	21	21	4	2	19
Funtua	21	?	?	?	?
Ikara	15	15	5	2	13
Jemaa	11	6	5	4	2
Kachia	15	9	10	11	4
Kaduna	21	19	2	—	19
Kankia	20	20	3	2	18
Katsina	23	23	5	5	18
Malumfashi	15	14	1	1	13
Mani	19	9	8	4	4
Saminaka	10	10	4	4	6
Zaria	23	23	3	2	21
Total	235	190	61	48	128

Source: Report of Local Government Elections 1976 p. 26–37.

education beyond primary level. As many as 128 (about 67%) came from the private sector, these being predominantly traders, contractors and big farmers, including a smaller proportion of commercial motor drivers and tailors. Within the public sector village scribes, health attendants, enumerators, court clerks and a few village and district heads outnumbered the higher paid civil servants, such as teachers, agricultural officers and administrative officers.

The general low level of educational attainment gave added importance to the twenty five per cent of nominated members when it came to selecting the chairmen of councils and chairmen of committees (called 'supervisory councillors' in the Guidelines). Two alternative procedures for election of Council Chairmen had been laid down in the Guidelines. The Kaduna State Local Government Edict favoured that which allowed the State Governor to select from a list of three drawn up by the Council in order of preference.[26] In many cases, Councils gave preference often by an overwhelming majority, to one of the nominated members, in virtue of educational qualifications and experience. In some instances the Governor preferred a second or third choice or referred the list back for the Council's reconsideration.[27] The State Government also tried to ensure that supervisory councillors were chosen from among those with the highest educational qualifications. There remain, nevertheless, many doubts in the minds of the educated classes generally, including members of the traditional elite, as to the ability of the councillors to exercise the responsibilities which have now been entrusted to Local Governments, not merely because so many of the councillors lack experience but also because of the conflict of interest that might develop in the case of those councillors who are traders and contractors. The divided attention that this might generate could weaken the effectiveness of the council or facilitate the emergence of a spoils system. This kind of speculation derives from the general observation that many of the councillors had contested the elections at great cost to their purse partly because of the enormous financial resources that were to be made available to the new Local Governments[28] and partly because election to a local Council could be the stepping stone to membership of the Constituent Assembly and thereafter to the Federal or State legislature.

Apart from the problems posed by the election, there are a number of other issues inherent in the new Local Government system which might jeopardise its chances of success. First, the creation of Local Governments, like the creation of States in 1967, might have a spiralling effect as more and more areas and communities compete for available resources and demand their autonomous authority as a means of achieving a higher level of socio-economic development. Even prior to the election some areas had begun to agitate for the creation of their own Local Government and the State Government was obliged to issue a strong warning reaffirming its decision to keep the number to fourteen.[29] Secondly, an overlap in powers allocated to the Emirate and the Local Government Councils might well bring them into conflict. One obvious area of friction relates to land. While section 61(1) of the Edict vests exclusive power for the control of land held under customary tenure in Local Government Councils, section 71(1) (k) of the same Edict allows Emirate/Traditional Councils 'notwithstanding any other provision of this Edict to determine customary law and practice on all matters governed by customary law including land tenure under customary law'. Another potential source of friction concerns village and District Heads. They are employees of Local Government but section 77(l) (j) permits

Emirate/Traditional Councils 'to determine questions relating to chieftaincy matters and control of traditional titles, and where such matters are within the exclusive prerogative of the Emir or principal chief, to give advice thereon where so requested'. This means that Local Government councils have no power to regulate chieftaincy affairs or discipline recalcitrant chiefs who are supposedly their own employees. Conflict might therefore arise over the question of loyalty where the demand of a Local Government Council on a District or Village Head is incompatible with the preferences or inclinations of an Emirate Council to whom, in the final analysis, he is answerable.

Thirdly, the allocation of powers to Local Government Councils, both in the Guidelines and in the Edict (Section 667), is to some extent conditional. There is one list of functions for which they have exclusive responsibility but another list of functions can only be exercised with the consent of the State Government. Almost all the exclusive powers have always been under local authorities even at the district level. The critical issue is therefore whether Local Governments will be allocated functions on the concurrent list so as to make them effective agents of socio-economic development at the grass-root level. Given the paucity of staff in most Local Governments and the low calibre of many of the councillors it is doubtful if the State government will allow them to exercise any of the concurrent functions in the near future. Finally it is not clear what measure of autonomy will be allowed by the prevailing staffing situation. At present, all the Secretaries of Local Government are civil servants seconded on a temporary basis and responsible to the Permanent Secretary of the Ministry of Local Government. They have therefore a dual role to play and in the eyes of the public are still seen as old style District Officers. Many of them are already experiencing a certain measure of frustration because they have to serve under councillors most of whom they consider intellectually inferior to themselves. The duality of their role tends therefore to militate against the autonomy of the new Local Governments. Moreover the Edict has provided for the appointment of Local Government Inspectors with power to attend all council and committee meetings, inspect all books, accounts and records of a council and advise local governments in regard to any of its functions (Edict Section 102). Although these powers have yet to be spelt out in an instrument, it is reasonable to suppose that Local Governments are not going to be as autonomous as would appear from the Guidelines. Indeed the tension that is likely to be generated in the relations between

Emirate/Traditional Councils and Local Governments is bound to strengthen the role of the Inspectorate, not only as a mechanism of supervision, standardization and co-ordination but, more important, as an effective channel of arbitration, conflict resolution and control, thereby reintroducing the problems of overcentralisation which the new national system of local government was supposed to prevent.

It must be emphasised in conclusion that although the State government is empowered to regulate and supervise the activities of Local Governments, the course which the new reforms have taken is in a sense irreversible. The results of the recent Local Government elections have demonstrated a sudden rise in the level of political and social consciousness, corresponding no doubt to the level of economic development generated by oil and the emergence of a new class of petty bourgeoisie which is increasingly challenging the old social and political order. The reforms also go a long way towards strengthening the supremacy of the Federal Government, a supremacy which it had begun to acquire since the coup of January 1966. It remains to be seen whether the Local Government reform exercise would stand the critical test of the first few years of civilian rule. Much will depend on three factors. First, there is still uncertainty as to the respective powers of Federal, State governments and local authorities. There will almost certainly be pressure in the Constituent Assembly to amend the draft in favour of more powers to the states and less autonomy to local authorities. Secondly, if the political parties find it expedient for electoral purposes to seek support of traditional rulers—and some such collaboration seems likely—the latter will expect some concessions favouring Emirate and Traditional Councils. This is all the more likely if the State government is in the hands of one party and another party wins control of some of the local government councils. Finally, only if the reform results in improved services at the local level will the new authorities gain the necessary support and self-confidence to survive. The resources that are being made available to them by the Federal and State governments could, if well spent, prove decisive in this respect.

NOTES

1. For an appreciation of the role of local authorities in the formation and operation of political parties and in the repression of opposition in Northern Nigeria, see R. L. Sklar, *Nigerian Political Parties,* Princeton, 1963; J. Coleman, *Nigeria: Background to Nationalism,* Berkeley 1963; C. S. Whitaker, *Politics of Tradition: Continuity and Change in Northern Nigeria,* Princeton, 1970.

2. Interview with the Cabinet Office, Lagos.

3. *Suggested Framework for a National System of Local Government,* Federal Ministry of Information, Printing Division, Lagos, 1976. Quoted hereafter as *Suggested Framework*.

4. Ibid, p. 6. The Guidelines raised the upper limit to 800,000 in order to maintain as much as possible the organic nature of existing districts, divisions and towns.

5. See above p. 255. The alternatives are stated in the Suggested Framework (p. 7–9) and in the Guidelines (p. 6–7) in terms that are virtually identical.

6. This and the following quotations are taken from the Minutes of the 'Conference of Emirs and Chiefs held in Kaduna on 25th and 26th June, 1976 on Local Government Reforms'.

7. They were accorded functions corresponding to items a, b, c, h, i of the functions mentioned on p. 255–6, together with the maintenance of law and order.

8. Ibid. The 'Suggested Framework' had stated that 'it would have to be borne in mind that District Heads have duties to Local Government Authorities, which should pay them, and that to ensure their suitability for their "functional" duties their appointments should need the approval of the Local Government Service Board'.

9. Suggested Framework, p. 10. These are of two types (as provided in Appendix B, p. 21), the first giving greater powers to the individual Local Government in the recruitment of its staff and the second concentrating all such powers in the Local Government Service Board. The Kaduna State Local Government Edict has adopted the latter type. (Kaduna State of Nigeria Gazette. Vol. II, 6 January 1977).

10. Minutes of Conference. The appointments were to be subject to the approval of the State government.

11. *Guidelines* p. 8. According to the *Guidelines* the Nigerian Police will be organised so that each Local Government Area is covered by a single unit of command; that most of the police in the area would be 'conversant with its language(s) and social background' and that a senior police officer would be designated to liaise with the local government council. There will also be a Police Committee for the area, in which the chairman of the local government council would sit, together with a traditional leader and two or three local dignitaries. Other members would be drawn from the police.

12. It should be noted that since the coup of January 1966, the Federal Military Government had taken over control of Police and Prisons: Native Courts had been redesignated Area Courts and transferred to the newly created State Governments in 1967–8.

13. *Guidelines,* p. 8. Note however that this provision was omitted from the Local Government Edict of Kaduna State. The President of an Emirate Council has only the right to receive copies of all agenda and minutes of the Local Government Council meetings as well as all information relating to the proceedings of the Councils.

14. *The Guidelines* allowed the 150.000—800.000 limits to be 'varied in exceptional geographical circumstances', moreover there was 'no upper limit to the size of Local Governments covering major towns so as to ensure that each town is within a single unit'.

15. Address by His Excellency, The Military Governor of Kaduna State at the launching ceremony of Local Government Reform, 23rd August 1976. Ministry of Information. Cited hereafter as Address of 23 August 1976.

16. The state government directed that not even symbols should be used by any candidate.
17. The November 4th to 11th editions of The *New Nigerian* carried reports of these arguments as expressed by the Military Governors of Borno and Niger and by various State Commissioners of Local Government.
18. *Report on Local Government Elections 1976, Kaduna State of Nigeria,* Unpublished, p. 1. Five were secretaries of Local Governments. Cited hereafter as *Report Local Government Elections.*
19. Address of 23 August 1976.
20. Draft Electoral Regulations, Kaduna State Government.
21. Communication with the Secretary of Kaduna Local Government.
22. Report Local Government Elections p. 10.
23. Ibid p. 20.
24. Ibid. p. 22.
25. Local Government Elections, 1976, Volume II, Annex II, Electoral Colleges and Voters Lists for Secondary Elections.
26. Guidelines p. 8 paragraph 26. The two alternatives are
    (a) The Council will elect three candidates from its own membership listed in order of preference. From the list the State Governor will nominate the Chairman. Once chosen, the Chairman shall normally hold office for the life of the Council.
    (b) The Council will elect a Chairman from its own membership but such election will be subject to ratification by the State Governor. 'In either case, the State Governor may refer such nominations to the Emirate or Traditional Council, where appropriate, for their comments.'
27. Communication with the Permanent Secretary, Ministry of Local Government.
28. The salaries of Chairman, Supervisory Councillors, Council members and Secretaries have been made very attractive. The Federal Military Government had also granted the sum of ₦.100 millions as aid to Local Government in addition to grants from state governments.
29. Statement from the Military Governor's Office, *New Nigerian,* November, 1976, p. 24.

Part Five

CONSTITUTIONAL REFORM

12

The Constitution Drafting Committee

Keith Panter-Brick

Military rule may share some of the characteristics of colonial rule, not least in the manner of departure. Both normally involve the preparation of a successor regime and no set procedures govern the manner in which this is done. A military regime that has assumed responsibility for correcting the deficiencies of its predecessor may act like a colonial government, exercising the power of tutelage, and reserving for itself the right to insist upon certain constitutional provisions. It will almost certainly give itself a period of grace, ruling by decree until certain conditions are fulfilled, and it may pre-empt future decisions by its own unilateral action.

Yet circumstances too set limitations to what might otherwise be quite discretionary and it is of interest to note the contrast between the discussions of the ad hoc constitutional conference which met in September 1966 with the work of the constitutional drafting committee (CDC) a decade later in 1975-76. In September 1966, the Federation and the army had virtually disintegrated and the ad hoc constitutional conference was convened so as to discover the terms of a modus vivendi. In each of the four regions of that time 'leaders of thought' had met and mandated a handful of delegates. Each delegation arrived with its own proposals, the terms on which agreement might be reached were quite open-ended and in the absence of unanimous agreement nothing was achieved. The process had been one of negotiation. The nature of the procedure was very different in October 1975 when Gowon's successor appointed the CDC. The break-up of Nigeria had been averted and the federal government had established its supremacy both administratively and financially. The number of states was shortly to be increased to nineteen and the local government system reformed. Moreover the Murtala Mohammed government had come to office to sweep clean, give direction and provide the constitutional foundations of good government. The CDC was not to carry out negotiations, nor even to discover what would be acceptable to entrenched interests: its task was more technical, and it worked to parameters set by a new found unity and purpose.

It was quite a large committee of forty-nine members, with a predominance of academics and lawyers. Almost a third of its members were or had been civilian commissioners in the Federal military government or in one of the State governments. A few had had experience of pre-1966 politics, either as ministers, parliamentarians or civil servants. Each of the States (twelve at the time of its convening) was represented by at least two members. The military's sole presence was that of an Army Chaplain; the Chairman was Chief Rotimi Williams, one of Nigeria's foremost lawyers and a former Minister in the Western Region.[1] The Committee was given a year in which to complete its task. Thereafter, but not until September 1977, a Constituent Assembly was to be convened and also allowed a year for its deliberations. Thus no less than three years were set aside for the completion of the exercise (it was none the less an improvement on Gowon's six) and no party politics were to be allowed. The ban on parties was to be lifted only in time for the first elections under the new constitution, scheduled for some time after October 1978.[2]

The terms in which Murtala Mohammed addressed the Constitution Drafting Committee (CDC) at its inaugural meeting on October 18th, 1975 seemed to confer upon it an importance equal to that of the future Constituent Assembly itself. Although he declared that the Committee's main task was 'to produce a first initial draft Constitution . . . . for public comment and discussion before submission to the Constituent Assembly', he ended by saying

> Distinguished Members of the CDC, you are at the bar of history. Your deliberations during the forthcoming months will be crucial as to whether or not we can create a political arrangement which will sustain us for many years to come. Nigerians everywhere will be looking up to you for a sound and enduring Constitution. (Vol. 1 p. xliii)*

Murtala Mohammed insisted moreover, that the Committee was

* Reference to the report of the committee and to the draft constitution will be given in the text rather than in footnotes. The report is in two volumes. Volume I contains

particularly well qualified for the task, asserting that it was both representative and expert.

In stressing the crucial importance of the CDC's deliberations Murtala Mohammed was no doubt indirectly seeking the cloak of authority for the Supreme Military Council's own proposals which were recommended to the Committee for its 'careful consideration'. The Supreme Military Council clearly pinned its hopes on 'a good constitution'. Behavioural factors were not entirely discounted but the emphasis throughout Murtala Mohammed's address was on a transformation of behaviour through wise constitutional provision.

> This Administration believes strongly that the provisions of the Constitution can be used for removing or minimizing some of our basic problems.

Murtala Mohammed gave an example

> The fear of the predominance of one Region over another has, for instance, been removed to a large extent by the simple constitutional Act of creating more States.

This deceptively simple illustration served to suggest that other problems might be resolved in similar fashion. The Supreme Military Council had discussed these and had come to certain conclusions. The main objective was clear; 'Politics must be transformed from its previous scenario of bitter personal wrangles into a healthy game of political argument and discussion.' The CDC was therefore asked to 'explore how to create a new parliamentary system which will not arouse tribal frenzies such as were characteristic of the previous political atmosphere'. A little more specifically the Committee was told that 'any constitution devised should seek to:

(i)   eliminate cut-throat political competition based on a system or rules of winner-takes-all. As corollary, it should discourage electoral malpractices;

(ii) It should also discourage institutionalised opposition to the

---

an explanatory report and the draft constitution. Volume II contains the recommendations of various sub-committees and decisions taken on these in plenary session. The reference to the explanatory report will be to paragraphs and sub-paragraphs (e.g. Report 2.2 or 3.2-1), to the draft constitution by section and sub-section (e.g. S66.2 or S116.2b) and to the sub-committees' reports and the decisions taken on these by volume and page (e.g. Vol. II 89). The Head of State's address is to be found in Volume I p. xli-xliii. The Committee is sometimes referred to in the text as the CDC.

Government in power and, instead, develop consensus politics and Government, based on a community of all interests rather than the interest of sections of the country;

(iii) firmly establish the principle of public accountability for all holders of public office. All public office holders must be seen to account openly for their conduct of affairs;

(iv) eliminate over-centralisation of power in a few hands, and as a matter of principle decentralise power wherever possible, as a means of diffusing tension. The powers and duties of the leading functionaries of Government should be carefully defined.'

The Committee was also informed that the Supreme Military Council had carried its deliberations a stage further 'to see how some of these principles could be implemented in practice'. In referring to its conclusions Murtala Mohammed touched on one major pre-occupation, the restraints that should be imposed on political parties. He repeated the requirement that parties be 'genuine and truly national' and added

. . . . in order to avoid the harmful effects of a proliferation of national parties, it will be desirable for you to work out specific criteria by which their number would be limited. Indeed the Supreme Military Council is of the opinion that, if during the course of your deliberations and having regard to our disillusion with party politics in the past, you should discover some means by which Government can be formed without the involvement of Political Parties, you should feel free to recommend.

This invitation somehow to raise the government above party was combined with a firm indication as to the type of government required. This was an

'. . . . Executive Presidential system of Government in which:

(a) the President and Vice-President are elected, with clearly defined powers and are accountable to the people. We feel that there should be legal provisions to ensure that they are brought into office in such a manner as to reflect the Federal character of the country; and

(b) the choice of members of the Cabinet should also be such as would reflect the Federal character of the country'.

The preference was clear: a President and a Government which draw support from the country as a whole. But the number and role of political parties was obscure. It was for the CDC to work out the connexion.

The Head of the State listed three other requirements:

An independent Judiciary to be guaranteed by incorporating appropriate provisions in the Constitution as well as by establishing institutions such as the Judicial Service Commission.
Provision of such corrective institutions as the Corrupt Practices Tribunal and Public Complaints Bureau.
Constitutional restriction on the number of States to be further created.

Finally, he referred to an issue which was then being much discussed and which was proving highly controversial, the inclusion in the Constitution of some statement of ideology. Precisely because of its controversial nature, it was to be excluded, since

.... we cannot build a future for this country on a rigid political ideology. Such an approach would be unrealistic. The evolution of a doctrinal concept is usually predicated upon the general acceptance by the people of a national political philosophy and, consequently, until all our people, or a large majority of them, have acknowledged a common ideological motivation, it would be fruitless to proclaim any particular philosophy or ideology in our Constitution.

The work of the CDC, as Murtala Mohammed said in his concluding remarks, was to be 'central' to the Government's programme and his address might properly be construed as the Committee's informal terms of reference.

The CDC did not consider itself bound by these directives. In any case it had been given in some respects an exploratory role. It also remained to be seen how far one requirement could be made consistent with another. The limitations on parties and on 'institutionalised opposition' had to be reconciled with 'a free democratic and lawful system of Government which guarantees human rights', with 'viable political institutions which will ensure maximum participation and consensus and orderly succession to political power' and with 'a free and fair electoral system which will ensure adequate representation of our peoples at the Centre'—all mentioned by Murtala Mohammed as features of a good Nigerian constitution. Similarly if the CDC was to eliminate 'over-centralisation of power in a few hands' it might think that a presidential system of government was not the best means of achieving it. Moreover, the large membership and its hybrid composition—a mixture of independent experts and opinion leaders—made its proceedings more open-ended. In taking into consideration the wider range of opinion represented by its own membership the CDC inevitably found it necessary to form its own conclusions, on matters of principle as well as detail, and to report openly the disagreements which arose in the course of its deliberations.

Indeed the Committee's deliberations should be seen as a stage in the wider public debate on Nigeria's future constitution, which had been in progress intermittently for a number of years prior to the Committee's appointment and which, once the report was published, burst forth in the press and elsewhere.

The general public was invited to submit its views either of a general kind or on particular matters: for example on 'The desirability or otherwise of having political parties' and 'Ceremonial or Executive Presidency' (Vol. 2, p. 9). Nearly 350 memoranda were received, mostly from individuals (Vol. 2, p. 10-26). Some were from public authorities (three State Governments and twelve local authorities, mostly in the North) and some from associations (eg the Social Reformers Movement, the National Joint Muslim Organisation, the National Council of Women Societies.) A number of the individual submissions came from prominent citizens, eg ex-President Azikwe and ex-Prime Minister Osadebay, and three came from members of the CDC itself. A surprisingly large number (nearly twenty) were submitted by religious bodies, both Christian and Muslim, and an equally large number by judges, including the Chief Justice of Nigeria and the Chief Justices of over half the States. Some of the titles were as arresting as the signs on mammy-wagons, eg 'Forward to a New Nigeria, Virile, Prosperous and Indivisible', 'Ode Replete of Illustration', 'Mixed-up', 'Correction Notice', 'Contribution of a widow's mite'. There were memoranda on 'Provisions against cheating' (from a Ministry of Finance official), on 'Plans to eliminate habitual criminals', (from a member of the Nigerian Prisons Service), and on 'The need to give Traditional medicine a place in our new Constitution' (from the Nigerian Association of Traditional Medicine Practitioners). A dozen memoranda were in Hausa. The Committee did not however take oral evidence and there is little reference in its Report to the views expressed by the wider public apart from the general acknowledgement of some 'very useful' memoranda.[3] It seems that the Committee members considered themselves sufficiently numerous and diverse to be the advocates of any worthwhile proposal.

To facilitate its deliberations the Committee divided itself into six sub-Committees, each to deal with a particular set of topics (Vol. 2, p. 29-31). Their recommendations, after consideration and sometimes amendment by the full Committee, were put into legal language, and at the same time co-ordinated, by a legal drafting sub-committee composed of all the lawyers (of whom there were twelve). This manner of proceeding was adopted in order to expedite the Committee's deliberations but it was not without disadvantages. Apart from the first two meetings, there was little opportunity for seeing how everything pieced together. The inaugural meeting was devoted to a general discussion of 'the basic causes of instability in Nigeria during the civilian regime and possible constitutional remedies' and to deciding the apportionment of topics to sub-committees. (Report 1-3) The second meeting discussed the Head of State's address. The next four plenary sessions were taken up with discussing sub-committee recommendations, very largely on a piece-meal basis, with occasional reconsideration of previous decisions. Thereafter the legal sub-committee began its final drafting but, because of the Chairman's illness, it was not until August 9th, a few weeks before the report was due to be submitted to the Government, that the CDC had an opportunity of considering its work as a whole. Only at this very late stage did two members of the Committee signify their total disagreement and desire to submit their own report. It had however been assumed that the recording of disagreements in the Report itself would be sufficient. The Committee had scarcely the time to consider afresh any issues of principle or of overall conception and no alternative but to proceed on the basis of what had been prepared for its final consideration as an agreed document. The dissenting report and alternative draft was treated as a memorandum which its authors could submit to the government privately.

Three of the Committee's conclusions—those in favour of a mixed economy, a competitive party system and a presidential system of government—stand out as perhaps the most fundamental. The first was a prominent issue in the discussion of ideology, a discussion which proved unavoidable, despite the Head of State's warning that it was 'fruitless'. The second was almost taken for granted and received surprisingly little attention. The decision in favour of a presidential system of government was a basic innovation and one which still causes some apprehension. Each is discussed more fully below as part of a wider-ranging discussion of the draft constitution as a whole. It has very many interesting features and for the purposes of its discussion we shall deal in succession with:

I   Ideology, national integration and political parties

II   The Presidency, checks and balances, the executive
III Federalism, Islamic law and local government

I. Ideology, National Integration and Political Parties

1. IDEOLOGY

A Constitution, either explicitly or implicitly, enshrines certain values or establishes a hierarchy of values and some conflict of opinion over their formulation is almost inevitable. In any case, there was strong public demand for some constitutional commitment of an ideological nature and the Committee decided in its very first meeting to consider including a statement of national objectives and directive principles of state policy. The Constitutions of India, Pakistan and the French-speaking African States served as models. (Vol. 2, p. 37 and p. 39) Conflict arose, however, not only over the formulation or wording of any such statement but also on the question of its enforcement in the courts. The two matters are clearly inter-related. There is a considerable difference between long-term political objectives to which one aspires, directive principles which indicate the policies to be pursued, and individual rights enforceable in the courts. To some extent it is a technical matter—it may be argued that some objectives or principles are not amenable to judicial proceedings—but it is also a question of the extent of one's political commitment.

The Committee's Report argues the need for a constitutional statement of national objectives and directive principles in sociological and behavioural terms:

> Governments in developing countries have tended to be pre-occupied with power and its material perquisites. Given the conditions of under-development, power offers the opportunity of a lifetime to rise above the general poverty and squalor that pervade the society. It provides a rare opportunity to acquire wealth and prestige, to be able to distribute benefits in the form of jobs, contracts, scholarships and gifts of money and so on to one's relatives and political allies. (Report 3.2-1)

The report continues:

> Perhaps the Constitution is in part to blame for this. Our 1963 Constitution like its predecessors spoke only in terms of power and of rights, but never of duties . . . . Our experience has shown this to be an inadequate approach to constitution making. . . . . the Constitution should cast on the State definite duties towards its subjects. (Report 3.2-2)

Thus a trust in constitutional norms as regulators of behaviour is expressed, despite the explicit recognition of powerful sociological pressure on individuals. The report indeed becomes quite eloquent in this respect:

> Unless the goals and the fundamental attitudes and values that should inform the behaviour of its members and institutions are clearly stated and accepted, a new nation is likely to find itself rudderless, with no sense of purpose and direction. By defining the goals of society and prescribing the institutional forms and procedures for pursuing them, a statement of fundamental objectives and directive principles in our Constitution seeks to direct and concert the efforts and actions of the people towards the achievement of those goals. In this way it seeks to unite the society into one nation bound together by common attitudes and values, common institutions and procedures, and above all an acceptance of common objectives and destiny. The need for such provisions in the Nigerian Constitution is all the greater because of the heterogeneity of the society, the increasing gap between the rich and the poor, the growing cleavage between the social groupings, all of which combine to confuse the nation and bedevil the concerted march to orderly progress. Only an explicit statement of objectives and directive principles which clearly sets the parameters of government and informs its policies and actions can generate a spirit of co-operation, peace, unity and progress. If the fundamental objectives and directive principles are enshrined in the constitution, then this may make them appear less of political slogans, investing them with the quality of constitutional, albeit non-justiciable norms, and thereby making it easier for political leaders and all public functionaries to establish and show the desired identification with them. (Report 3.2-3)

There was no full agreement on objectives and principles, still less on the assertion that the norms should be non-justiciable.

To some members the original statement of objectives as prepared in sub-committee, read like a socialist manifesto. The sub-committee had in fact not hesitated to speak in terms of ideology and had declared one of the fundamental objectives to be that:

> Within the context of a participatory democracy informed by the ideals of Liberty, Equality and Justice, the state shall, as a long-term goal, strive towards a socialist order based on public ownership and control of the means of production and distribution. (Vol. II, p. 37)

The majority in plenary session however considered that the only ideology acceptable to Nigerians as a whole was a 'Mixed Economy'. The two contending views were supported by well-worn arguments. The advocates of a 'positive and categorical' statement of socialist ideology claimed that it would ensure that the country knows where it is going, that it is the 'only solid foundation upon which the happiness and prosperity of the people can be based' and that it is 'the only effective answer to the conditions of under-development, inequality and exploitation.' (Report 3.7-1). The proponents of a mixed economy warned that wealth must first be created before it can be distributed and that it would be a mistake to arouse expectations that cannot be fulfilled. They argued that 'it is difficult to pursue the two goals of rapid development and the extreme forms of income equality at the same time' and they believed socialist economies to be less efficient (Report 3.7-2). The draft, as finally agreed, left the future open.

Thus 'major sectors of the economy' as determined by the federal legislation 'from time to time' (S10) are definitely to be run as public enterprises. All use of Marxist phraseology is avoided and so are the sort of difficulties encountered by one of the other sub-committees. It had been asked to 'examine and recommend constitutional provisions for protecting the people and the resources of this country from foreign exploitation'. It endeavoured to draw up a list of activities which should be under state management and of resources which should be in Nigerian hands. It could not agree, however, whether the government should (for example) hold a majority share in any company exploring for and extracting minerals or whether it would be sufficient if Nigerians held the majority of shares. (Vol. II, p. 131). The Committee, by using the sibylline phrase 'major sectors of the economy' and by letting the federal legislature determine what these are, avoided having to make any decisions other than one of principle, namely that there could be a mixture of public and private enterprise. This having been established, the State was then enjoined to 'direct its policy towards ensuring' certain objectives. There should be planned and balanced economic development; the community's material resources should be harnessed and distributed so as to serve the common good; and there should be no concentration of economic power in the hands of a few individuals or a group (S10.3). The legislature is empowered to set up a body to review from time to time the ownership and control of business enterprises, to make recommendations to the President, and to administer any law for the regulation and ownership of such enterprises. (S10.4). State policy should also be directed towards ensuring a whole range of desiderata characteristic of the welfare state, such as suitable and adequate food and shelter, a minimum living wage, adequate medical and health facilities, unemployment benefit, just and humane working conditions, adequate facilities for leisure and for social, religious and cultural life, the protection of the young and aged against exploitation and against neglect, equal and adequate educational opportunities (S11.3, S12.1). To these ends both public and private enterprise may make their respective contributions—an arrangement considered to be more congruent with the political objective of an open and participatory democracy and hence more conducive to stability. (Report 3.7-4).[4]

In one important respect, however, there was to be incongruity. Whereas political rights, such as that of peaceful assembly and association, and also the right to private property, (subject only to the State's right of compulsory purchase on payment of prompt and adequate compensation), are all given the status of individual constitutional rights enforceable in the courts, the economic and social objectives are made dependent on future legislation. They are enumerated in a separate chapter of the draft constitution (Chapter II) and are not justiciable.

It had been suggested by the sub-committee that any person should be able to apply to a court for a declaration that a law or some government action was not in accordance with a directive principle. Such a declaration was not to render the law or action invalid but it was to be 'a ground for the impeachment of the appropriate functionaries'. This proposal lacked majority support in the full committee, on the familiar grounds that it would impose inappropriate responsibilities on the judiciary.

> By their nature, the provisions relate to policy goals or directions rather than to the existence or extent of legal rights vested in any individual or group normally subject to the jurisdiction of courts of law. It is a field in which professional lawyers who preside over courts of law are not necessarily the most competent judges. (Report 3.3)

It was also argued that such provisions

> are new and no one can be too confident of the most appropriate method of ensuring their observance. If provisions are made for that purpose in the Constitution and it turns out to be unsuitable or ineffective, it would require a constitutional amendment to deal with the situation. (ibid)

Chapter II of the draft is then simply

> a yardstick for judging the performance of any government . . . . a constitutional directive to the organs of state to guide their actions . . . . a reminder to Government functionaries that their position is one of trust involving powers as well as duties. (Report 3.2-3)

It has 'a pre-eminently educative, emotive and psychological value for the governors as well as the governed'. (Vol. 2, p. 38).

The distinction which the majority of the Committee wished to make is brought out most forcibly in another passage defending the decision not to include a list of social and economic rights in Chapter IV (which enumerates fundamental rights enforceable by the courts.) It was argued that they were not strictly rights at all.

> By their nature, they are rights which can only come into existence after the government has provided facilities for them. Thus, if there are facilities for education or medical services one can speak of the 'right' to such facilities. On the other hand, it will be ludicrous to refer to the 'right' to education or health where no facilities exist. If one has in mind the right of an individual to insist on the provision of these facilities then it is a 'right' which depends upon the availability of resources and in the final analysis one is really referring to the obligation or duty of the government to provide the facilities . . . . Most of the fundamental rights are in a sense natural rights vested in every individual and to which he is entitled without any obligation or duty on the part of the government to provide facilities for their enjoyment. Thus, the rights to freedom of expression or to liberty of a person are rights which do not depend upon the provision of any facilities by the government. Moreover, all fundamental rights are in the final analysis, rights which impose limitations on executive, legislative or judicial powers of the government and are accordingly easily justiciable. By contrast, economic and social 'rights' are different. They do not impose any limitations on governmental powers. They impose obligations of a kind which are not justiciable. To insist that the right to freedom of expression is the same kind of 'right' as the 'right' to free medical facilities and can be treated alike in a constitutional document is, the majority of us feel, basically unsound. (Report 4-2)[5]

The emphasis is on the availability of resources and the possibility that the State might not be able to provide, rather than on the individual's right to demand State provision. But behind this argument may be detected a certain antipathy to welfare socialism, or at least scepticism about its cost. It was made most explicit in education, a matter on which some members showed particular concern. Some wanted to see a State monopoly of education with the emphasis on equal educational opportunities at all levels, and by implication, free education. Others wanted to preserve the right of voluntary agencies to establish, own and operate private schools, and by implication an individual right to pay for a higher standard of education (Vol. II, p. 55). The issue was not entirely resolved but the draft does make free education 'subject to the availability of resources'—a rather ironic decision, since the military government was in the very process of introducing a system of free universal primary education and of abolishing most tuition and boarding fees at higher levels.[6] Present costs are, however, well below what they will be when the system is fully expanded and it remains to be seen what resources will be judged available for this particular purpose.

The Committee's refusal to make any of the directive principles or social and economic 'rights' justiciable in any way meant that questions such as the precise mixture of public and private enterprise, and the level of welfare expenditures, would not be constitutional issues but matters for the political parties and the electorate to determine. As stated in the Report— rather obliquely—'The Nigerian Constitution should be flexible and should enable a popularly elected government to pursue policies which have been put and explained to the electorate.' (Report 3.7-2). Even so, a further precaution was written into the draft. In the section on political parties it is stated that, while 'the programme, as well as the aims and objects of a political party shall conform with the provisions of Chapter II' (the Chapter containing the fundamental objectives and directive principles of State policy), this does not prohibit a party from 'advocating or canvassing for an alteration in the provisions of any part of this Constitution, including Chapter II.' (S174).

This ideological division was not one which the Committee was able to bridge, despite the belief of most of its members that Chapter II, as finally drafted, gave some satisfaction to all shades of opinion. It was the more extreme left which declared itself dissatisfied, thus giving itself the task of presenting counter-proposals for deliberation by the Constitutional Assembly. The objection expressed most vociferously and vigorously relates to the non-justiciability of social and economic rights on a par with political rights. The criticism is a telling one. If a Constitution proclaims that among its fundamental objectives and principles of State policy are certain standards of welfare for all its citizens, then it would seem consistent that any aggrieved individual should have the means of redress in the courts. The politicians should not be free to disregard the obligation. Of course, the State must have the means of so providing but this is difficult to deny convincingly when there is so much public and private conspicuous consumption. On the other hand the argument which prevailed in the Committee is equally pertinent. Although vastly increased, the resources of Nigeria are certainly not unlimited and the precise allocation of scarce resources is a question on which opinion can justifiably differ. How to provide for the welfare of the citizens in the most effective manner is necessarily a matter not of law but of politics, and to say this is not to deny the responsibility: it is merely to place it where it is most appropriate.

The Constitutional Assembly will have to decide how far to make such matters a question of right—or perhaps find some middle way of the kind suggested by one of the sub-committees. It recommended that at least a right to education (to levels within the nation's resources) and to free health services should be included among the rights enforceable in the courts. Moreover, it favoured specific constitutional authorisation for the implementation, 'as soon as possible', of rights to social security. These were considered too vital to relegate to a non-justiciable Chapter II.

> The fact that National Objectives are broad objectives for the long term raises the issue that in the long run we might all be dead. (Vol. 2, p. 176)

In addition it recommended (although it was readily admitted that this was not a constitutional point) that the Government set up 'task forces' to 'produce concrete social security proposals which could be implemented . . . . as . . . . circumstances and resources permit.' (Vol. 2, p. 210)

Awolowo, who declined to serve on the CDC but who offered his comments soon after the publication of the draft, went further. He suggested that the Constitution should set a definite time limit for implementation—five years for all objectives including the abolition of unemployment and the provision of unemployment benefit, pensions for the old, free education, adult education, free medical care and fifteen years for the modernisation of agriculture and the construction of one mile of all-season road per two square miles of territory—a list of grandiose proportions.[7]

These attempts to impose upon possibly recalcitrant authorities a constitutional obligation in such matters may appear vain but they are rooted in a profound Nigerian mistrust of office-holders, including parliamentarians. A court declaration would of course be no substitute for legislative and executive action but it would certainly be a political embarrassment.

2.   NATIONAL INTEGRATION

The preoccupation with ideology was in part a concern for national unity, but equally strong among Nigerians is their consciousness of ethnic and cultural diversity. The CDC wished therefore to define the fundamental objective of national integration in such a way as to take this into account, especially in the making of appointments.

The general objective is set out in S9 of the draft where it is stated that

'(1) . . . . national integration shall be actively encouraged whilst discrimination on the grounds of place of origin, religion, sex, status, ethnic or linguistic association or ties shall be prohibited.

(2) For the purpose of promoting national integration it shall be the duty of the State to—

(a) provide adequate facilities for and encourage free mobility of people, goods and services throughout the country;

(b) secure full residence rights for every citizen in all parts of the country;

(c) encourage intermarriage among persons from different places of origin, or of different religious, ethnic or linguistic association or ties; and

(d) promote or encourage the formation of associations that cut across ethnic, linguistic, religious or other sectional barriers.

(3) The state shall foster a feeling of belonging and of involvement among the various peoples of the country, to the end that loyalty to the Nation shall override sectional loyalties.'

The mention of ways in which to promote national integration is interesting. The exact wording of any final draft could be important. The obligation to secure residence rights implies some action in cases of discrimination, especially of the kinds experienced in the past.[8] The obligation to 'encourage' intermarriage is offensive to some Muslims, for a girl of that faith cannot marry a non-Muslim. The sub-section refers mainly to private conduct and the manner in which the state chooses to exercise its duty could be highly controversial.

The major issue however was how to ensure impartiality in the making of appointments and in the conduct of government and it gave rise, according to the Report, to 'very sharp differences'. Three alternative formulations were proposed. One prescribed quite explicitly a policy of ethnic arithmetic, stating that

(i)   The predominance in the Federal Government or any of its agencies of persons from some states, ethnic or other sectional groups to the exclusion of persons from other states, ethnic or other sectional groups, or the monopoly of the office of the President by persons from any state or ethnic group shall be avoided.

(ii)   The affairs of every government in the Federation shall be conducted so as to ensure a fair and just treatment for all ethnic groups within the area of authority of such government. (Draft 3.5-4)

A second left out any mention of particularistic identities, since the objective was to treat these as irrelevant. It stated quite boldly

> The composition of every government in the Federation and the conduct of its affairs shall be carried out in such manner as to recognize the need for national integration and the promotion of national unity. (Draft 3.5-5)

A third formulation struck a middle course: it was thought desirable to require 'fair and equitable treatment for all the component states and ethnic groups,' but unwise to insist on comprehensive representation because 'impracticable or unwieldy.'

Eventually a compromise was reached by having recourse to a phrase used by Murtala Mohammed in his address to the Committee when referring to the manner of electing the President and Vice-President, namely that this should reflect the federal character of the country. Thus section 8 of the draft states

> The composition of the Federal Government or any of its agencies and the conduct of their affairs shall be carried out in such manner as to recognise the federal character of Nigeria and the need to promote national unity and to command loyalty. Accordingly, the predominance in that Government or in its agencies of persons from a few states, or from a few ethnic or other sectional group shall be avoided. (sub-section 2).

Similar provision is made for state and local government.

> The composition of a government other than the Federal Government or any of the agencies of such government and the conduct of their affairs shall be carried out in such manner as to recognise the diversity of the peoples within their area of authority and the need to promote a sense of belonging and loyalty among all the people of Nigeria. (sub-section 3).

The phrase 'federal character of Nigeria' is defined. It 'refers to the distinctive desire of the peoples of Nigeria to promote national unity, foster national loyalty and give every citizen of Nigeria a sense of belonging to the nation notwithstanding the diversities of ethnic origin, culture, language or religion which may exist and which it is their desire to nourish and harness to the enrichment of the Federal Republic of Nigeria.' (Ch. X Definition and Short Titles S210).

The draft is not content with making this general statement of principle in S8 of Chapter II. The requirement that appointments shall reflect the federal character of Nigeria is repeated in other parts of the draft, e.g. S146 which gives the President the power to appoint to the highest ranking positions in the civil service. Moreover, in the section that deals with the appointment of Ministers, a reference to S8 is considered insufficient, for it adds 'at least one Minister of the Government of the Federation shall be appointed from among Nigerian citizens who belong to each of the States comprising the Federation.' (S123.2). A person is said to 'belong to' a state if either of his parents is 'a member of a community indigenous to that State'. (S210).

3. POLITICAL PARTIES

The draft accepts a plurality of parties as the unavoidable concomitant of a democracy in which the individual has a right to 'hold opinions and to receive and impart ideas and information without interference' (S.32), and the right 'to assemble freely and associate with other persons' (S.33). The malpractices of political parties in the past, which had provoked the intervention of the military in 1966 and to which the Head of State did not fail to refer in his address to the CDC, certainly stood in need of correction—but not to the extent of regimentation. It is true that the sub-Committee that dealt with political parties (along with fundamental rights and the electoral law) was asked to consider 'whether there should be no party, one party or multiple parties' and that the public also had been invited to submit views on 'the desirability or otherwise of having political parties' but this was not an issue on which the sub-Committee had many doubts.

It was fortified in this approach by a 'cursory reading' of the memoranda submitted by the public. Of the twenty eight memoranda which referred specifically to party, only one favoured a one-party system and five a no-party system. The remaining twenty-three supported two or more parties. (Vol. II p. 177).

The notion of a single-party regime—a feature of so many African countries—is dismissed in a few sentences.

Nothing much needs to be said about this. Our society is too heterogeneous and the apparent necessity for the creation of a successful one-party state is too ill developed to be a viable option. Besides it seems clear that few people would want to see a one-party state imposed—and for it to exist it would have to be imposed and by the Military regime and that would not be consistent with the declared aim of the regime to foster an open democratic system. (Vol. II p. 177).

In short, if any of the military leadership leaned in that direction, it would have to be their responsibility. As far as the sub-Committee was concerned there was simply no case for it.

The no-party state received almost as short shrift. Ethiopia, Haiti and Saudi-Arabia were cited as examples, 'hardly countries Nigeria would want to emulate.' It was pointed out that any organised representation of opinion or interests would have to take a 'syndicalist or corporativist' form, stigmatised as 'a fascist system of government.' The alternative was the emergence of factions, 'more difficult to control and manage than a party system of government' (ibid).

Having decided without much difficulty that there was no acceptable alternative to a multi-party system (which might in practice be a two-party system), the sub-Committee was left with the task of formulating the regulations to be observed if parties were to be accepted as 'genuinely national' and democratic. The criterion of a 'genuinely national' party echoes that imposed on public authorities in the name of national integration, that is, a party must be seen to reflect the federal character of the country. Thus no association may function as a political party unless its membership is open to every Nigerian citizen irrespective of his place of origin, religion, ethnic group or sex. Its name, emblem or motto must not have any ethnic or religious connotation and must not give the appearance that the association's activities are confined to a particular part of Nigeria. Its headquarters must be in the federal capital. Its leadership must be 'federal', meaning that not less than two-thirds of the executive Committee or other governing body must 'belong to' different States. (S172.b,c,f.)

In one respect the draft may have gone too far, for in seeking to avoid identification of a political party with interests or sentiments that are in any way particularistic, it has prohibited associations from canvassing in an election (S171). Much will no doubt depend on the meaning given to 'canvass for votes'. Some restraint may be necessary, (e.g. on the endorsement of particular candidates or parties by ethnic associations or religious bodies) but an imposition of silence on all associations during an election campaign, even when the interests of their members are clearly at issue, would be excessive and very difficult to enforce.

To ensure conformity with democratic practice there are provisions concerning the election of officers, finance and illegitimate methods of persuasion. First, the executive committee or governing body may not remain in office for more than four years without being re-elected on a democratic basis (S173). Secondly a party has to declare its assets, revenues and expenditures and is allowed virtually only two sources of revenue: individual contributions and a grant out of public funds. Any other financial support is forbidden, either from abroad or from any association within Nigeria, including presumably business associations, trade unions and ethnic associations (S175). The federal legislature is expected to provide an annual block grant for distribution to parties 'on a fair and equitable basis' (S178C). Finally parties (and associations generally) may not resort to the most obvious forms of intimidation, that is, they may not 'retain, organise, train or equip any person for the purpose of enabling them to be employed for the use or display of physical force or coercion in promoting any political object or interest, or in such a manner as to arouse reasonable apprehension that they are organised and either trained or equipped for that purpose' (S177). This last provision may not be sufficient to banish all fear of intimidation and it may be difficult to attribute actions of a mob, e.g. the burning of houses, or the subtlety of traditional pressures to party organisation, but S178 does authorise the legislature to pass a law which would hold party leaders responsible for the actions of their followers in contravention of S177 and this could possibly be a deterrent.[9]

The administration of these regulations is entrusted to the Electoral Commission, a body composed of one member from each State and up to five additional members, none of whom may be less than 50 years old. They are appointed by the President but only after he has consulted a Council of State and obtained the approval by both Houses of the Federal legislature. Once appointed they can only be removed with the consent of two-thirds majority of the Senate (S137, 129.1, 129.4, 131.4, 132).[10]

The Electoral Commission prescribes the form in which parties must submit their accounts and it has powers of inspection (S175) (4). The Commission has to submit to the legislature an annual report on party finances, drawing attention to any breach of the regulations or failure by the parties to supply the necessary information (S176). It is the Commission which will distribute the block grant to the parties (S178c) and it is most likely to be in accordance with a formula fixed by the legislature e.g. the number of votes obtained at the previous general election, as suggested by the Committee (Vol. II p. 215). It is not clear from the draft where lies the authority to rule that a party has failed to comply with the requirements mentioned earlier—e.g. to rule that the name is unacceptable or that party leaders have not been properly elected, but presumably it would lie with the Commission; nor what would be the consequences of any such ruling— e.g. on a party's legal status.[11] Punitive powers, e.g. disqualification from holding public office, are envisaged only for breaches of the rules concerning foreign financing and organisation of party thugs (S178 a and b). The legislature is to pass the necessary legislation and conviction will presumably be a matter for a court of law rather than the Commission.

The Commission's other function is the administration of elections. It is made responsible for the registration of electors, the delimitation of constituencies (subject to approval by the legislature) and the conduct of elections at both federal and state level (S136 and S67–79).

The drafting of an electoral law has been left to the Constituent Assembly, the Legal Sub-Committee having had insufficient time to deal with the matter. The draft does, however, prescribe eighteen as the minimum age for exercising the vote; twenty-one and thirty-five years for election to the House of Representatives and Senate respectively. A sub-Committee favoured proportional representation with a system of party lists (Vol. II. p. 182) but the Committee as a whole preferred single-member constituencies (Vol. II p. 213). Public employees are required to have resigned at least four months before the election, if they wish to stand as candidates (S64 f)—but it is not clear whether teachers are included. There are the usual disqualifications from membership of a legislature including a conviction of dishonesty. The disqualification of those dismissed by the military since January 15, 1966 is made dependent on whether the due process of law had been observed. Those found guilty of corruption, unjust enrichment or abuse of office by any ad hoc tribunal or enquiry, provided they were given an opportunity of defending themselves, are disqualified from standing in the *first* of the elections held under the new constitution. The Committee undoubtedly had in mind the extensive and summary purges of the Murtala Mohammed regime in which many were dismissed or retired without any hearing. It is a subtle compromise between the corrective measures of a military regime and concern for justice and, if accepted by the Constituent Assembly, would avoid the long and often acrimonious debate that took place in the Ghanaian

Constitutional Assembly.[12] It is also a telling reflection on the importance attached to the first election following a return to civilian rule.

II. The Presidency, Checks and Balances, The Executive

1. AN EXECUTIVE PRESIDENT

The Report presents a straight choice between cabinet government of the Westminster type and presidential government on the American model and weighs the scales very heavily in favour of the latter, mainly because of the manner in which executive power is constituted in the Westminster system. A ceremonial head of state and a collegiate executive, dependent upon a parliamentary majority for its continuation in office, is declared to be an inappropriate arrangement for Nigerian purposes.

The Report rejects a bicephalous executive as both meaningless and impractical, at least in Africa.

> The separation of the Head of State from Head of Government involves a division between real authority and formal authority . . . In the context of Africa the division is not only meaningless, it is difficult to maintain in practice. No African Head of State has been known to be content with the position of a mere figurehead. The experience of Nigeria, Uganda, Lesotho and Swaziland testifies to this . . . . the lesson of African experience with the system is that if non-political Heads of State are not already in existence, mere constitutional provisions alone will not bring them into being . . . The clashes and conflicts inherent in the system produce instability in government and in society and also endanger national unity. The system of separation clearly fails to provide a clear focal point of loyalty, which is indispensable to national integration. (Report 7.1—3 and 4).

This argument is also used to reject a proposed 'middle way', which would have avoided a concentration of power in the hands of a single person, whereby a President might be invested with those functions which 'sustain the State' and a Vice-President would have responsibility for day-to-day government. This was considered by the majority of the Committee to be 'fraught with the same dangers of clash of personalities and interests, and of conflict of authority.' (Report 7.1—11).

A second argument rejects any form of responsibility which is necessarily shared.

The dangers of separation are complemented by the disadvantages of plurality. The single executive has the merit of unity, energy and despatch . . . . it is essential to effective leadership in Government that there should be a single individual in the capacity of a chief executive who can decide and act promptly . . . . and who can impose his will . . . .
Another demerit of the plural executive is that it undermines responsibility . . . first, through the weakened authority of the prime minister to enforce collective responsibility and . . . . secondly, by making it difficult to determine on whom the blame or punishment for error should fall . . .
The Westminster system hampers effective government in yet another respect . . . . the right of the executive to govern derives from the legislature . . . . Under the presidential system . . . . the President will be elected directly by the people, a fact which gives him an independent right to govern. (Report 7.1—5, 6 and 7).

Apart from a general and not very well founded allusion to difficulties which prime ministers 'in the developing countries of the Commonwealth' are said to have had in controlling ministers and enforcing collective responsibility, this second argument is un-supported by any empirical evidence. Certain defects are attributed to the Westminster system and the presidential system is credited with the corresponding virtues in quite a priori fashion. There are, after all, valid arguments in favour of both cabinet government and presidential government and neither the one nor the other can be said to be inherently superior, nor even manifestly more suitable at some particular time or place.[13] A country may, however, experience the one and prefer the other, in the hope of improvement and as a symbol of change. In Ghana and Nigeria reactions were similar but contrary; a rejection of the preceding regime, presidentalism in the case of Ghana, prime ministerial/cabinet government in the case of Nigeria.

It was as if Nigerians felt out of step with the rest of Africa (though not with Asia). Unlike most other new African Commonwealth countries, it had preserved a ceremonial head of state when it became a republic in 1963. In the very different climate of the 1970s, a bicephalous executive had come to be seen as an anachronism and doubly so. It was a colonial legacy and its continuance had been due entirely to regional divisions. These were now deemed to be a thing of the past. The office of executive president had therefore acquired irresistible symbolic importance, apart from its alleged functional advantages. It was required in order to express more emphatically the aspiration for national unity and to project more effectively Nigeria's image abroad. The report of the relevant sub-committee set out these requirements in more positive and succinct terms than did the main Report:

> ... a Chief Executive must perform and be seen as performing the following functions:
> (a) that of being a symbol of national unity, honour and prestige;
> (b) being a national figure—a political leader in his own right; and
> (c) that of being an able executive—someone who can give leadership and a sense of direction to the country (Vol. 2 p. 67).

The functions are multiple but the office has to be single and only an executive president fits the bill.

The preference expressed for an executive president was axiomatic, in the sense that many other decisions were regarded as consequential. The presidency is made the centre piece of the political system, the overall design is conceived in terms of checks and balances and the remaining institutions are designed accordingly. The legislature, the judiciary and the various consultative bodies are thus seen primarily as procedural and substantive restraints upon presidential powers. Moreover, certain instrumentalities, essential to the state, the judges, the civil servants, the electoral machinery and the census officials—are protected from the abuses of executive power even more than they are from prime ministerial power in the Westminster system. Much of the ensuing discussion of the draft constitution has been from this same perspective, questioning whether the proposed checks and balances on presidential power are sufficient or effective. Some criticism goes further—it challenges the initial decisions to establish any such office as that of executive president, which is seen as altogether too powerful, whatever may be the checks and balances. Some members of the Committee were themselves hesitant, being of the opinion that 'a President with such wide powers and armed with the organised forces of the State could easily become a dictator' (Report 7.1—8). They had in mind however, some unconstitutional action e.g. dismissal of the legislature.

The possibility that power will be usurped can scarcely be used to criticise some particular constitutional arrangements, for it is a danger that spares none. A coup is a coup and it could be encouraged just as readily by a distribution of power that proves restrictive as by a concentration of power that incites the appetite for more. As stated in the Report itself 'the ultimate sanction against usurpations of power is a politically conscious society jealous of its constitutional rights to choose those who direct its affairs' (7.1—9). The precise distribution of authority among the various holders of office is, in this respect, not decisive. This is not, however, to say that it is unimportant and immune from criticism. We need, therefore, to examine what is proposed and to consider the suggested arrangements, not merely as a system of checks and balances but also as elements of a political system resting ultimately on the support of the electorate.

2. EXECUTIVE/LEGISLATIVE RELATIONS

The draft provides for a President and Vice-President elected jointly in a nation-wide poll (S111). The degree of support necessary for elections was a matter of considerable discussion (Vol. II p. 68–9, 187, 212) (Report 7.1— 12). There was agreement in principle that support needed to be widespread and not just an overall majority but it was not easy to be agreed on a precise formula. One sub-Committee recommended a division of the country into zones and a system of rotation so that there would be a combined North-South representation on every ballot paper and, over the years, a circulation of the two offices among all the states. After considering numerous proposals, the Committee finally decided in favour of two different sets of rules, depending on the number of presidential candidates. In an election contested by more than two candidates the highest overall number of votes is sufficient, provided it is not less than a quarter of the vote in two-thirds—*thirteen*—of the states. Otherwise there is a second ballot, contested by the candidate with the highest overall vote and by whichever of the other candidates won most states (in the event of two or more winning the same number of states, the one with most votes). In an election contested by only two candidates—whether on first or second ballot—the highest number of votes is sufficient provided it is a majority in half—*ten*—of the states, failing which the choice is exercised by the federal and state legislatures jointly and by simple majority.

The President and Vice-President are elected for a fixed term of four years and may not serve more than two terms (S114b). The legislature, also elected for four years (S62.1) and from single member constituencies, consists of a Senate, in which each State is represented by five Senators, and a House of Representatives elected from constituencies of roughly equal population. The two Houses have equal powers, even over finance. The President and the members of the two Houses are thus independent of one another, each holding its authority directly from the electorate.

A majority on the Committee took the view that 'an executive presidency of the type proposed . . . implies a somewhat rigid separation of powers between the executive and the legislature' (Report 7.2—1). Others, less concerned with checks and balances, stressed the need for co-operation. 'Modern government should be a co-operative, co-ordinated effort and not a tug-of-war between the principal organs of Government' (Report 7.2—2). The issue which brought out this difference of opinion most sharply was the role of ministers in relation to the legislature and in particular whether or not they should be members of the legislature.

The draft makes ministerial office incompatible with membership of the legislature but permits ministers to attend and take part in the proceedings of either House. No further indication is given of what should be the role of ministers in the legislature. They would, of course, be acting on behalf of the President, who has appointed them, and clearly a great deal would depend upon the relationship that obtains between President and legislature. This could be, if the draft is to be any guide in this matter, one in which each keeps his distance or one of friction based on mutual mistrust, not at all conducive to the necessary degree of co-operation. There is certainly an imbalance in the draft provisions. The emphasis is on the legislature's powers to censure rather than to support. Thus provision is made for impeachment of the President (S117), the holding of enquiries or investigations backed by the power of subpoena (S80 and 89), the appointment of a Public Complaints Commission (S81) and the audit of public accounts (S90). All are necessary but all are corrective. They are ex post facto counter-measures. The contribution which the legislature can make to executive action while it is still in its formative stages, through constructive discussions with Ministers who are present when the legislature is formulating the law or debating public issues, is almost overlooked. Indeed an unfortunate impression is given by the section on powers of enquiry and investigation that the attitudes and procedures needed for exposing corruption and inefficiency are the same as those required in the legislative process. These powers are conferred for the purpose of:

(a) enabling the Legislative House to make laws with respect to any matters within its legislative competence and to correct any defects in existing laws, and

(b) to expose corruption, inefficiency or waste in the execution or administration of laws within its legislative competence and in the disbursement or administration of funds appropriated by it. (S 80.2)

The notion that legislation and public policy generally require the constructive collaboration of executive and legislative lacks any proper recognition in the draft. There is provision for each House to establish committees but no suggestion that one of the functions of a committee is to assist in maintaining a close and fruitful co-operation between President and legislature. For instance, in matters of foreign policy, the draft is silent except on one point, the procedure for the implementation of treaties which require domestic legislation (S104). It might be thought that the legislature has no other role. It is perhaps taken for granted that the President, through his Minister of Foreign Affairs, will keep the legislature informed and seek an exchange of views not merely on the subject of a treaty but also on the conduct of foreign affairs generally. There are however, no specific constitutional norms requiring this kind of co-operation in the exercise of joint, albeit separate, responsibilities for the making of treaties.

The deliberations in the relevant sub-committee were rather more balanced. Although also somewhat inquisitorial in outlook and tone, its report does view the political process as one in which the executive, legislature and public are jointly engaged in an exercise of mutual persuasion. For instance, it refers to the functions of providing information, of conveying the expectations of constituents, of educating and persuading the public.[14] The recommendations of the sub-committee (Vol. II p. 82) are not in fact reflected adequately in the draft. Its proposal that the President should address the legislature at the opening of each session, in order to outline legislative proposals for the coming year and give an account of the previous year's administration, and its proposal that the Government should have the right to introduce its own Bills are both omitted from the draft. The recommendation that Ministers must consider it a duty to attend, when requested to explain Government policies or answer questions, is given a rather unfelicitous formulation; S65.1 states that Ministers *may* attend which almost suggests that they might choose not to attend, while S89 d states that they are subject to a warrant compelling them to attend any enquiry which the legislature or Public Complaints Commission may hold. The procedure for impeachment also differs in the draft from that which had been recommended by the sub-committee. The motion which initiates investigation into alleged 'misconduct in the performance of the functions of his office' on the part of the President or Vice-President may be moved in the House or in the Senate by only one-quarter of the members instead of one-third.

Impeachment is generally employed when all else has failed and should not be a procedure that a disgruntled minority can set in motion, even if the actual impeachment requires a two-thirds majority. The Constituent Assembly may deem it prudent to place some more stringent limitation, either by requiring greater initial support or by restricting the frequency with which any individual member may move such a motion (as in France in the case of a motion of censure on the government of the day) or by defining more restrictively the grounds for impeachment. It might bear in mind Burke's reply to Dr. Price when he claimed that the people of England had acquired the right not only to choose their own governors but also 'to cashier them for misconduct'. 'No government' said Burke, 'could stand a moment, if it could be blown down by anything so loose and indefinite as an opinion of "misconduct" '.[15]

The Committee none the less seems to have assumed that the necessary co-operation and co-ordination between executive and legislature would be forthcoming. It realised that there might be a deadlock over proposed legislation but it suggested that

. . . . the government and the leaders of the legislature would have to meet and work out a compromise. In the case of the budget . . . . the Constitution provides that the last budget passed by the legislature shall operate and the services of the government will have to be financed within the limits of that budget. Although this is the legal position, we feel that in practice the President or a Governor would normally have some form of understanding with a party or group of parties in the legislature which will ensure that its major bills are passed. Prudence and common sense require such a course (Report 6.5).

This general approach, which relies on behavioural characteristics to override an institutionalised system of checks and balances, is valid only in so far as such conflict is intermittent. As Burke has said one should not make the 'extreme medicine of the constitution its daily bread'.[16]

A presidential system can only work satisfactorily if the conflict inherent in the system is itself kept in check. The prescribed procedures must strike a balance between supportive and supervisory functions. While this is as much a matter of practice as it is of prescription, there is need for prudence and common sense in the formulation of the rules just as in the operation of them. The onus is all the greater if among the paramount objectives are stability, national integration and economic development. There must be means whereby executive leadership can bridge the gap of potential conflict. Whether the Committee has produced an adequate draft from this point of view is doubtful.

A minority of the Committee certainly had doubts about the decision that ministers should not be members of the legislature. It is stated in the report that

> Some members felt that membership of the legislative House by ministers has a cardinal merit in bringing the government and the legislature into close and regular contact. The real value of this is not just that their membership enables them to participate in the work of the legislature, to answer questions from members and generally to explain the actions of the government; it lies more importantly in the fact that, since the ministers are the leaders of the parliamentary parties, their legislative membership and participation enable them to rally to the government the support of the majority of members of the legislative House. Their ministerial offices give them the authority which the legislative party leaders in America do not have. Together the ministers give guidance and leadership to the members of the legislative House thereby maintaining the parties' authority over them and checking an undue assertion of independence, such as characterizes American congressmen. (Report 7.2— 2).

The statement opens up quite a different perspective, that of close collaboration brought about by party organisation. The majority view keeps party also entirely out of the picture. The only reference to party is in the suggestion, quoted earlier, that the executive 'would normally have some form of understanding with a party or group of parties in the legislature'. This is a vague phrase: in any case the understanding is said to owe its existence not to party but to 'prudence and common sense'. It presumably would be ad hoc, restricted to each issue as it arose and there is no suggestion of any prior commitment between President and members of the legislature to a party programme. The reference to party is, in this passage, pointless if not actually misleading.

The Committee, in insisting on a 'rigid separation', was in fact rejecting three possible alternative arrangements which need to be distinguished, especially as there has been considerable pressure since the publication of the draft constitution for some amendment of the proposed incompatibility rule.

First, ex-officio membership could be conferred on whomever happened to be appointed to ministerial office by the President. This is not so very different from the proposed provision that Ministers may attend and take part in discussion, except that it would also confer a right to vote. It would not in itself provide a party following.

Secondly, the President could be obliged to appoint Ministers exclusively from the legislature. It is a possibility that appeals to those who see it as a desirable restraint on the President's discretion (subject to State representation and Senate approval) to appoint whomever he please. This limitation might ensure the President a following in the legislature but not necessarily, for it does not oblige him to appoint party leaders and he may prefer not to do so.

Finally, there is the possibility of a prior electoral pact which links the election of President with that of the legislature and thereby gives some assurance of mutual co-operation. Joint simultaneous election is in fact the hidden premise in the minority point of view; otherwise, to assert that 'Ministers are the leaders of the parliamentary parties', is to beg the question. This pre-condition is hidden only because the Report leaves it out. The view attributed to the minority is in fact a verbatim but unacknowledged quotation from a book written by a member of the Committee, Professor Nwabueze. It is reproduced, out of context, from a paragraph which begins:

> By linking the elections of the President and the legislature under a single ballot, the element of popular support in the choice of the organs of government is maintained, simplicity is achieved and expense reduced; above all, the President is guaranteed an almost certain chance of a legislative majority. But the cardinal merit in this connection is the establishment of a cabinet composed of members of the legislature, thus bringing the government and legislature into close and regular contact.[17]

Had the Committee favoured 'close and regular' contact between the executive and legislature it might have considered an electoral arrangement of this kind. Its merits, for Prof. Nwabueze (and some others on the Committee?) are that it helps to override the separation of powers by instituting a hybrid presidential-parliamentary system. To the rest of the Committee, however, this was obviously enough to disqualify it from consideration. They were not looking for any half-way measures. Having concentrated executive powers into the hands of a single person, the Committee considered itself committed to 'a somewhat rigid separation of powers'. It was not even prepared to confer on Ministers an ex-officio membership.

The Committee's concern for arrangements which would unquestionably institute a system of checks and balances is understandable but it accounts for a concomitant blindness to the role of the legislature in support of presidential policies and perhaps also for a failure to give explicit consideration to the role of party in providing that support. The Report avoids any mention of the role of party in the election of the President. The question of parties and that of the presidency were dealt with by separate sub-committees but that cannot be accepted as an explanation. A shortage of time prevented the Legal Sub-Committee from drafting an electoral law, which might have been an opportunity to consider the role of party, but this is doubtful, for although the Committee had decided in favour of holding simultaneous presidential and legislative elections (Vol. II p. 213) the possible party political implications seem to have been ignored. It was considered simply as a question of 'mechanics', i.e. administrative feasibility, on which the advice of the Electoral Commission was needed (Report 6.9 and p. xxxviii). Clearly very little weight was given to elections as a mechanism for bringing a party to power. It is perhaps a lawyer's perception of elections that they are the affair of individual candidates and individual electors. Individual electors return a President, a Senate and a House of Representatives. This is true but can a constitution drafting committee leave the party connection to the imagination—or to practice, which is of course decisive but which might be anticipated. Presidential candidates might possibly stand independently of party, perhaps in the manner of de Gaulle who refused to be identified with a particular party although he was supported by one. One might make the assumption that, in a presidential system, party organisation, while vital for the purpose of an election, is of relative insignificance between elections, for representatives and senators will use their own individual judgment when roll-calls are held, as is the tendency in the USA. The Report does not indulge in such speculations, which is a pity for the question of party is one of the major preoccupations of those who await a return to civilian rule and the fact that the presidential system depends less on party than the Westminster system could be a decisive argument in its favour. A reading of the Report gives the impression that the Committee avoided the issue as far as possible, or looked at it only peripherally.

The only parts of the draft touching on this question require members elected independently of parties to remain independents, at least until the following general election (S336) and party members to retain any party label used at the time of their election (on pain of losing their seats) (S66.9). Was the Committee trying to make elected representatives remain faithful to those who elected them? And was it trying to outlaw the practice of climbing on the bandwagon of a victorious party, a feature of the period 1960–1966? If the latter, then the Committee showed itself more concerned with the probability of collaboration between the executive and the legislature—based on patronage—than with the possibility of deadlock; but it also seemed surprisingly unaware—or unwilling to consider—that the dynamics of party politics may, in a presidential system, be quite unlike those of parliamentary parties whose support is needed for maintaining the government in office.

One is tempted to say that the Committee's report is myopic in two inter-related respects. It avoids the question of organised opposition just as much as the question of party majorities. A notable omission from the Committee's indictment of the Westminster system is any reference to its most distinctive feature, the counterpoise to Government that is provided by the official Opposition. This is also its major defect from many an African point of view, it being thought to create opposing loyalties at a time when a common allegiance requires to be reinforced. The argument was to hand but the Committee chose not to use it. The Report is in fact altogether silent on the question of 'institutionalised opposition' which was singled out by the Supreme Military Council as something to be discouraged. One is left wondering how the Committee's proposals are to be assessed from this point of view, especially as it so clearly rejected the notion of a no-party or a one-party state. Constitutional provisions which permit a multi-party system might be thought conducive to 'institutionalised opposition', or was the Committee thinking that it is only in the Westminster system of government that opposition is 'institutionalised'? Had the Committee given more systematic consideration to the role of party in a presidential system it might also have faced up to the question of opposition and asked itself whether parties, in their competition for the presidency, were or were not likely to be engaged in a zero-sum type of party politics, in which a victorious party is in office and a defeated party is relegated to being in opposition. It might then also have dealt with another of the problems raised by Murtala Mohammed in his Inaugural address to the Committee—that of eliminating 'cut-throat political competition based on a system or rule of winner-takes-all'. These are all vital questions which the Report passes over in silence.[18] It would be prudent for the Constituent Assembly to consider carefully whether or not the draft in its endorsement of an executive presidency does not constitute a prize for which parties might compete even more ruthlessly than they ever did in the past. The Supreme Military Council favoured an executive presidency but in a political environment that is non-partisan. The draft on the contrary envisages a system of competitive politics.

3. THE EXERCISE OF EXECUTIVE POWER

Although the Committee looked to the separation of powers as its main safeguard against an abuse of presidential power, it did not neglect other means of achieving the same end. It was of the opinion that in some matters the President should be obliged to seek, and possibly follow, the advice of some body specially constituted for the purpose and that, in some other still more sensitive matters, the President should be restricted to appointing persons who would act on his behalf but on their own authority without any outside direction whatsoever.

Provisions of this kind are commonly held to be different from the separation of powers. Nevertheless if the constitution specifies that in certain matters the President shall act in conjunction with a wide range of other persons, many of whom act ex officio, then the executive authority is to that extent distributed and subjected to a measure of internal restraint. Provisions of this kind may presuppose and in a sense complement a separation of powers between the executive and legislature, for the latter may be given a voice in the appointment and dismissal of some of those designated to assist the President. Such a distribution of authority within the ambit of an executive presidency, no less than the separation of the executive from the legislature, may be a contribution to good government and is certainly a characteristic feature of constitutional government, the exact opposite of Machiavelli's precept that 'A prince ought always to take counsel, but only when he wishes, not when others wish'.[19] It provides a check prior to the actual exercise of executive powers, a factor all the more important if the other 'powers' (legislature and judicature), are firmly restricted to an ex post facto scrutiny.

This is to state the matter in very general terms and it is the task of constitutional lawyers—and legislators—to prescribe what exactly are the limitations, whether these be procedural or more substantive. The CDC thought it expedient to establish quite a number of councils or commissions with specified responsibilities of this kind but the discretion which the president retains is not always expressed with sufficient clarity.

Potentially one of the most important bodies is likely to be the

Federal Executive Council, especially if the Constituent Assembly decides to restrict the appointment of Ministers to members of the legislature. It is stipulated that

> (3) The President shall hold regular meetings with the Vice President and all Ministers of the Government of the Federation (which meetings shall be known as meetings of the Federal Executive Council) for the purpose of—
>
>> (a) determining the general direction of domestic and foreign policies of the Federal Government:
>> (b) co-ordinating the activities of the President, the Vice-President and the Ministers of the Government of the Federation in the discharge of their executive responsibilities; and
>> (c) advising the President generally in the discharge of his executive functions other than those functions with respect to which he is required by this Constitution to seek the advice or act on the recommendation of some other body. (S.124.3)

The language is not free of ambiguity but practice will no doubt provide the meaning. The various constitutional requirements that the President must give representation to every State in his appointment of Ministers, that the Senate must confirm the appointments, that the President must have fairly widespread electoral support, together with the various political unknowns such as the nature of party connexions and the degree of pluralism in the political culture, could combine to bring about a form of cabinet government, which would give scope not only for the exercise of presidential authority but also for the practice of more collective responsibility. On the other hand, it is equally conceivable that none but the Presidency can provide the authority called for in a political system that is fragmented by federalism and by a separation of powers. In that case the President could claim sole executive responsibility and act accordingly, both in and outside of the Federal Executive Council. The draft proposes fourteen other councils or commissions at federal level—and five within each State (S128). It is a heterogeneous lot ranging from bodies such as the National Population Commission and the National Defence Council to the various Commissions for making appointments to the civil service, the judiciary, and the police. The only common feature is that each in its own way is a restraint on the President's exercise of discretionary power in matters considered to be of supreme importance or sensitivity. The restraint may be no more than an obligation to consult a small group of high ranking officials whom the President has the power to replace if he so chooses e.g. the National Defence Council. At the other extreme, the council or commission is not subject to any higher executive authority whatsoever and its word is law e.g. the Electoral Commission.

Some of these bodies have a relatively long and continuous history, having been first established as part of the constitutional system of 1960 and left in place by the military in 1966, e.g. the Public Service and Police Commissions. Others are the outcome of developments since 1966 and are constitutionally reinforced versions of administrative arrangements first established by the military, e.g. the present National Universities Commission would become the National Commission on Higher Education and be entrusted with a wide range of functions, executive as well as advisory.

Some old problems are poured into new bottles, such as the National Population Commission and the Electoral Commission, and one may hope that they do not break under the pressures that in the past have prevented the conduct of an accurate census and of free elections. The extreme sensitivity of such matters is reflected in the triple consent that is required for appointments to these two bodies and also to the Judicial Service Commission (see above p. 309). Security of tenure is provided for most Commissions—that is, members serve for five years, may be reappointed for a further term of five years and may only be dismissed by the President if a two-thirds majority in the Senate has so requested on the grounds of incapacity or misbehaviour (S131) (S132). There is a novel provision in the case of the National Population Commission. If the President is advised by the Council of States that there are 'demonstrable perversities or manifest inaccuracies' in the Commission's report following a national census, he has to reject the report and ipso facto all the members of the Commission are dismissed (S132 and S158). This is certainly to hang the sword of Damocles over the heads of the Commissioners but a reasonably accurate assessment of Nigeria's population would be impossible without certain other precautions. The Commission is given authority to appoint and train its own staff and to publish its own reports. It may carry out sample surveys and is to provide machinery for the registration of all births and deaths. Provided adequate means are put at its disposal and it is not required to rush into the taking of a census, the Commission is unlikely to be guilty of perversities which are demonstrable and of inaccuracies which are manifest.

The Council of States would be a totally new body of considerable prestige composed of the President and Vice-President, any former Presidents, retired Chief Justices and Grand Muftis, the President of the Senate and Speaker of the House of Representatives, the Attorney General, the State Governors and a representative of each State Council of Chiefs, a total of some forty to fifty members. The occasions on which the President would have to consult this august body are very varied: when awarding national honours or exercising the prerogative of mercy, and when exercising his powers in relation to the Electoral Commission, Judicial Service Commission and National Population Commission (in effect the nomination of Commissioners). The President may consult the Council of States on the maintenance of public order and on any other matter he thinks fit. It is not a body which could be convened speedily and this could prove a handicap. A consensus of opinion in the Council would certainly add authority to any Presidential decision but whether its consultation would have much symbolic effect in the event of real disagreements may be doubted.

4. DEFENCE AND SECURITY

There cannot be a consitutional defence against a coup by the armed forces. A constitution can, however, do two things. It must, at the very least, provide for the exercise of lawful authority. This could conceivably take the form of a civilian-military dyarchy but if full civilian control is preferred it needs to be established in a manner that does not detract from the efficiency of the armed forces as a profession and guards against use of the army for partisan purposes. Secondly, a constitution may seek to identify the armed forces with the civilian population in various ways, for instance by imposing a period of national service on all citizens, or by giving the armed forces duties of a civilian nature or by making sure that recruitment is not restricted to some particular part of the country.

The Committee addressed itself to both questions but its Report makes very little comment. It draws attention, in a single paragraph, to only one issue, the allocation of responsibilities for the maintenance of public order and security between the federal and state authorities and in particular the problem of defining the circumstances which would justify intervention by the federal authorities in matters which are normally a state responsibility—an echo of the 1962 crisis in the Western Region, and an important issue, but one that concerns a division of responsibility among civilian authorities, not the issue of civilian control over the military.[20] The report of the sub-Committee does however provide a more general background explanation to its several recommendations although it amounts to only a page (Vol. II p. 224–5).

It begins with the briefest of references to the long-standing debate on whether or not to recognise an inevitable military involvement in politics by instituting a civilian-military dyarchy. After this fleeting observation the sub-committee simply goes on to assume that the military can definitely be at the service of the civilian authorities. This is not explicitly stated but it is implicit in its recommendations and in a passage that stresses the importance of giving the political authorities decisive control. It concerns the position of the police but is indicative of a more general point of view.

> The Sub-Committee counsels caution in drawing constitutional provisions regulating the Police, especially its insulation from political influence, so as not to harmstring (sic) the Government in the performance of its law and other (sic) functions. While constitutional provisions could check abuses on the part of those who would subvert the constitution, the same provisions might inhibit performance by good-intentioned people (Vol. II p. 224).

Having made an assumption of loyalty the sub-committee passed on quickly to say that 'the objective of the Armed Forces should be to constitute themselves into an integral part of the society rather than being a miniature and independent community divorced from the rest of society'—an odd statement if one remembers that the Armed Forces had long ceased to be miniature and that the problem is not their divorce from society but their involvement. The sub-committee then refers to a second objective, the need for open as opposed to selective recruitment, so that 'no particular tribe should be dominant in the forces or a particular arm of it'. The means suggested for achieving these joint objectives is two-fold, military service for 'secondary school leavers' and 'military participation in the economic development of the nation'. The limitation to secondary school leavers seems to be based on the idea that economic development would be a task for 'units of trained technicians and qualified men'. Mingled with this proposal is the argument that military service will provide the youth with both discipline and employment (Vol. II p. 228–229).

There is no confirmation that the military authorities were consulted. It is stated that 'the co-operation of individuals and bodies interested in its work' was sought and that 'a number of memoranda were received in the process' (Vol. 2, p. 219) but since the sub-committee was responsible for making proposals concerning the public services generally it cannot be assumed that any military authorities gave their opinion. Col. Pedro Martins sat on the sub-committee but an Army Chaplain could hardly be taken as a spokesman for the interests of the military. Murtala Mohammed in his address to the Committee had given no guidance and indeed had not even listed civilian-military relations among the questions requiring the CDC's particular attention. It was a nettle that the sub-committee and the Committee had to grasp by making their own unaided suggestions. They were quite clear on some points, prudent on others by simply authorising the legislature to decide and altogether silent on one important matter.

The clear subordination of the armed forces to the civilian authority is prescribed by making the President Commander-in-Chief, with 'powers to determine the operational use of the Armed Forces', and by giving him the right to appoint the Head of the Combined Armed Forces and the Heads of all the Services (S167). The President is to be advised in 'matters relating to the defence of the sovereignty and the territorial integrity of Nigeria' by a Defence Council in which sits the Vice-President, the Minister of Defence and the military heads whom the President has appointed (S137). Likewise a National Security Council, its membership also entirely ex-officio, is to advise the President on matters of 'public security'.

A long list of matters was left over for determination by the legislature, notably the possibility of an armed police force (S161c), the conditions and circumstances in which the armed forces may be used by the President to aid the civil authorities, whether the armed forces should have additional responsibilities other than for defence and internal security (the sub-committee had proposed 'shall participate in the development of the nation as an organ of the State'—Vol. II p. 229), and the question of compulsory military service (until the necessary legislation is passed 'The President shall maintain adequate facilities in all secondary and post-secondary educational institutions in Nigeria for giving military training to all Nigerian citizens in such institutions which desire to have such training—S169).

The draft is silent on the question of recruitment and appointments other than those made by the President under S.167. The Committee had agreed to establish an Armed Forces Commission for the purpose and a body with this name is listed in the 'Arrangement of Sections' of the draft constitution (S.168). The text itself passes over this section—later explained as a deliberate omission.[21] According to the sub-committee report, the Commission was to consist of 'a chairman and nine other members including the service Chiefs', and the composition of the armed forces was to 'reflect the federal character of the country' (Decisions 5A and 5B). An Armed Forces Commission would be an innovation. None existed under the 1963 Constitution and the regional quota system, which was introduced in 1950 for men and in 1961 for officers, had no other authority than ministerial instruction.[22] The draft does not require either the Police Service Commission or the Civil Service Commission to maintain this kind of balance when making appointments (although it was recommended in sub-committee for the civil service (Vol. 2 p. 223)). It would be extraordinary and quite unacceptable if the military were singled out, along with Ministers, for such treatment. The Constituent Assembly may well decide to drop all references to 'the federal character of the country' in the matter of appointment, even though it may still insist on an Armed Forces Commission which includes civilian members.

All told, it is not surprising that the part of the draft which deals with the armed forces is the most open-ended and inconclusive. It may well be that the Constituent Assembly itself will find it difficult to be any more definitive.

5. POLICE AND PUBLIC ORDER

The Committee had a much easier task in determining authority with respect to the police, if only because flexible and workable arrangements had already been set out in the 1960 constitution. These are reproduced in almost identical terms in the Committee's draft. (S.161–165).

There are only minor changes in the membership and functions of the Police Council and the Police Service Commission. The Council, its ex-officio membership in future dominated numerically by nineteen state governors (out of 23 members), has a general supervisory power over organisation and administration—but not operational control. If the President rejects any of the Council's recommendations, the federal legislature has to be informed. Appointments, dismissals and disciplinary control are the responsibility of the Police Commission, a body of eight to ten persons appointed by the President. Their appointment requires Senate confirmation and none may be dismissed unless a two-third majority in the Senate requests it on grounds of incapacity or misbehaviour. The only appointment and dismissal not entirely in the hands of the Police Commission are those of the Inspector-General, who is in overall command, and of the Commissioners of Police who are appointed to command in each of the States. In the case of the Inspector-General there is some confusion in the draft for it is stated in S.137 that the President appoints on the advice of the Commission whereas S.163(2) stipulates that the Commission appoints after consulting the President.

Operational control of the police is on the lines stated in the 1960 constitution. The Inspector-General of Police is in overall command but is obliged to comply with any directives given by the President. Similarly a Commissioner of Police in command in a State could receive a directive from the State Governor but he may request that it be referred to the President for approval (S.162.4). The sub-committee had wanted to extend this arrangement down to local authorities—a demand which has some support in the North—but this was not accepted in plenary session (Vol. II p. 226.)[23]

These provisions need to be considered together with those which set out the respective responsibilities of federal and state authorities for the maintenance of public order and security. The Committee was concerned lest the federal authorities usurp or 'take over' that which was clearly considered to be primarily a state responsibility, save in exceptional circumstances (Report 6.7). Federal action is authorised in the draft in separate ways. The first is an assumption by the Federation of legislative power in time of war or whenever meetings of a State legislature become impossible (S.101.4–101.5). The federal legislature may then make 'laws for the peace, order and good government of that State with respect to matters not included in the Exclusive Legislative list'. The second is an assumption of executive power at the request of a State Governor unable to maintain public order or essential supplies and services. (S.120.2)[24] The third is the proclamation of a state of emergency which may be requested by a State Governor if supported by a two-thirds majority of the State legislature or imposed by the President if within a reasonable time no such request is made. Such action by the President requires the support of the House of Representatives and of the Senate, within two to ten days (depending on whether the Houses are in session or not) (S.39.8). There is no specific mention made of a power to remove a State Governor but this may be implied.

6. THE CIVIL SERVICE

The notion of a civil service serving impartially on a permanent basis the political authorities of the day and so itself non-political, is one that has been much contradicted in practice but it is still regarded as the norm in Nigeria. The only innovations in the draft are mainly provisions which seek to reinforce the norm within the context of a new and in some respects rather different, political system. It is proposed that an independent Commission should continue to be responsible for the appointment and dismissal of civil servants and for exercising disciplinary control over them. The President is given discretion in the choice of those who are to occupy the highest positions, such as Permanent Secretaries and Ambassadors, or to serve as his personal staff. In one respect his discretion is greater than that enjoyed by the Prime Minister in the 1960 Constitution for he is not obliged to consult the Civil Service Commission, but in another respect it is less since in making these appointments he has to have regard to 'the federal character of Nigeria' (S.146). The Civil Service Commission is not governed by the requirement although it was recommended in sub-committee and approved in plenary session (Vol. 2 p. 223 and p. 238). That the Commission itself should be 'as representative of the country as possible' was recommended by the sub-committee but not accepted in full committee (Vol. II p. 222).

One may detect the anxieties of civil servants in this pronounced concern for balanced representation on the Commission—in addition to the autonomy that would derive from the rule that its members be removable only for incapacity and misbehaviour on an address supported by a two-thirds majority in the Senate. It reflected perhaps a belief that the constitutional and political environment had changed in ways that could threaten their careers. There is reference in the sub-committee's report to 'the common ambivalence of views on the civil service and the need to bolster morale which has been shaken as a result of the recent purge in the public services' and it sees the requirement that the civil service conforms with national objectives as entailing 'more public scrutiny'. (Vol. II p. 220). The institution of an executive presidency separate from the legislature is also seen as a change which could affect the rights of civil servants. The sub-committee looked to the legislature no less than to the Civil Service Commission for guarantees. This concern certainly explains one new constitutional provision, the protection of any acquired right to a pension or gratuity (S.149). The sub-committee had also recommended—and it was approved in plenary session but excluded from the draft—a Civil Service Tribunal that would have given civil servants a speedy and economical redress against administrative decisions affecting their rights and entitlements (Vol. II p. 221 and p. 238).

7.   CODE OF CONDUCT

The Committee, noting that 'corruption and abuse of office has eaten deeply into the fabric of the public service' (Report 7.5) proposed a code of conduct, in the hope that this would prove a more effective restraint than the criminal code or the Civil Service Rules. In considering how wide to cast the net and what to catch, the Committee looked to the Tanzanian and Zambian examples but kept Nigerian experience in mind.

It was decided to cast the net over all public employees and not just those in leading positions, although the legislature may decide that those below a certain rank should be exempted from certain provisions, such as periodic declaration of one's assets. Thus the draft specifies a long list of offices to which the code shall apply. It ranges from the President down to employees of local authorities and includes all elected representatives, university teachers, military personnel and the staff of 'companies in which the State has a controlling interest'. Consideration was given to extending the coverage even wider to take in private business, lest a code restricted to public officers deprived the public service of those with the greatest talent. This particular problem can of course only arise in a thriving mixed economy. The opportunity is lacking in Tanzania but the experience of Zambia shows the danger.[25] The Committee must have thought that on balance the evident difficulties of applying the code to the private sector outweigh the potential loss to the public service. The radical alternative—the abolition of the private sector—had little support.

It is perhaps for this reason that the net, although cast wide, has not too fine a mesh. The code contains an admirable and essential statement of principle. 'A public officer shall not put himself in a position where his personal interest conflicts with his duties and responsibilities' (Code S.2). More specifically but 'without prejudice to the generality' of S.2, a public officer is precluded from holding two public offices simultaneously and may not

engage or participate in the management or running of any private business profession or trade to such extent as to make it impracticable or difficult for him to perform the duties and responsibilities of a specified office; or in such manner as to enable him to advance the interest of such business, profession or trade through his position as a public officer.

This does not absolutely preclude all business or professional activity and certainly does not exclude giving a guiding hand to business activities undertaken by others, especially spouses and children.

Thus personal enrichment, beyond what might reasonably be saved from one's official salary, will still be possible if it derives from some spare time activity; and the members of one's immediate family may grow rich on their own account—unless there is some actual or potential conflict of interest of a specific nature. The most important parts of the Code could therefore be those which envisage public inspection of any declaration of assets (S 15.1b) and which place on the public officer the onus of proving that what is declared is 'attributable to income, gift or loan approved' by the Code. (S11.3)

The declaration has to include the property and assets of one's spouse and unmarried children under the age of twenty one, with the result that any notable improvement in the family fortunes will have to be explained although the exclusion of children who have grown up or married early could prove a loophole. The only gifts permitted are those 'from relatives or personal friends to such extent and on such occasions as are recognised by custom' (S6.3) and borrowing is restricted, in the case of public officers of the highest rank, to loans from recognised financial institutions (S7a).

The Code, as finally drafted, falls short of what was recommended by the sub-committee, in several respects. The sub-committee suggested that it should be illegal for

> a leader or his spouse to draw more than one salary, to employ workers in connection with any trade, business, profession or vocation, including the running of a hotel, boarding house or like establishment for gain or profit; to own a house let out on rent to others; to be shareholder or director in a privately-owned enterprise.

Thus it was provided in the sub-committee's draft that no leader may 'engage in any private business, trade or profession'; nor may he be in receipt of any earned income other than his salary and whatever might be derived from his own labour on land owned and occupied by him personally; nor may he have any investment income other than from bank deposits, government stock or shares in registered companies. (Vol. 2, p. 42-3). This might be thought an onerous restraint on some of the categories covered by the code, e.g. elected representatives who, not being sure of re-election, need some alternative means of livelihood and who in any case are unlikely to be in continuous session (they must sit for at least half a year—S61). This is one of the difficulties of trying to impose a uniform code on widely varying categories of public servants. It is worth noting that a separate code of conduct had been suggested for judges, imposing a particular high standard. They were to avoid *inter alia:*

(e) Membership in any voluntary association of a non-national character including local self-development clubs. The prohibition extends to international organisations like the Red Cross, the St. John's Ambulance Brigade, the Britain-Nigeria, Afro-Arabian, Nigeria-USSR and Nigeria-China friendship societies, etc. Contributions of funds to the activities of local voluntary associations or development clubs are permissible.

(g) Association with women of easy virtue and versatile talent such as the so-called 'society ladies', the seduction or enticement of other peoples' wives or minors and general sexual immorality.

(h) Chronic indebtedness.

(i) Drunkenness and/or the use of drugs. (Vol. II, p. 107-8)

The sub-committee's draft was rejected in two other respects. It required an annual declaration whereas the full Committee considered a declaration every four years more appropriate. Secondly, it wanted to prohibit the ownership of more than one plot of state land. This limitation was to apply not just to holders of public office but generally to all 'persons' and the state was to recover any holdings in excess of a single plot (after compensation). The proposal was said to have 'evoked very heated controversy'. The Report devotes more space to it than to any other issue (3.6-3.9). It was conceived in part as a corrective measure aimed at those who made enormous gains through the allocation of plots in select areas, e.g. Victoria Island, Lagos, and in part as a measure to equalise opportunity—which for some was a concession in that they preferred outright nationalisation of all land (Vol. II, p. 236). The majority of the Committee however was of the opinion that a limitation of this kind would place unnecessary obstacles to economic development and legitimate aspirations and without any public benefit—they had in mind the difficulties it would create for businessmen, shopkeepers and those who plan an eventual return to their home areas. The retrospective aspects of the proposal were condemned as 'obnoxious, immoral, unethical and wholly unjusticiable.' (Report 3.6-1)

The Code of Conduct is to be enforced by two special bodies, a Bureau and a Tribunal. The Bureau is to receive and check all declarations of assets, on such terms and conditions as the legislature may prescribe, and receive complaints about non-compliance. The Tribunal hears any disputed cases referred to it by the Bureau. The penalties which it may impose include dismissal, disqualification for up to 15 years and forfeiture of property. There is a right of appeal to the Supreme Court but the prerogative of mercy may not be exercised. Both the Bureau and the Tribunal enjoy security of tenure and are appointed, in the case of the Bureau, by the Senate and in the case of the Tribunal, by the President on the recommendation of the Judicial Service Commission. The Bureau is made responsible to the legislature.

The Code of Conduct has been made part of the Constitution (as one of the Schedules). The Sub-Committee recommended this as a means of giving it a higher status than that of the ordinary law without, however, making it too difficult to amend.

III. Federalism, Islamic Law and Local Government

1. FEDERALISM

A federal Nigeria was so much taken for granted that it had no need to be mentioned in Murtala Mohammed's address to the Commission, except for the laconic statement 'We are committed to a Federal system of Government' (Report p. xlii). The draft differs from the constitution of 1960 (but follows that of 1954) by being a constitution for each of the States as well as for the Federation. This is one of the reasons why it is so long. While it would be possible to extract from it separate Federal and State constitutions if so desired, a conjoint constitutional instrument was considered 'more convenient when there are as many as nineteen States' and also to have the 'advantage of minimising the drafting work involved in the creation of a new State within the Federation' (Report 2.2). These are scarcely weighty reasons and one suspects that there was really no desire to let each State set up its own Constituent Assembly and act as if it had some sovereign authority of its own. The States were not coming together to form a Federation: the Federation was reconstituting itself in its own sovereign (and centralising) fashion and Murtala Mohammed's address assumes that the Commission would be acting for the States as well as the Federation.

The possibility that the process of creating more States might be continued, after the enactment of the new Constitution, was not one that the Supreme Military Council encouraged. It had appointed a Committee to make recommendations for the creation of additional States and it regarded that exercise as final, for Nigeria could not afford to undergo a repetition of the destabilisation engendered by the agitation for the creation of States in the 1970-1975 period.[26]

The draft does not rule out altogether the possibility of altering the present division into nineteen States but the procedure for amendment is such that it will be very difficult to make any change. It would require the support of two thirds of the members of both Houses of the Federal legislature and of two thirds of the State legislatures (a requirement that is itself entrenched even more rigidly). Some members of the Commission argued strongly in favour of more flexible arrangements on the grounds that it would be unwise to deny all hope of change when the demand for it was likely to be strong and persistent. Their case is set out at some length in the Report (6.11-2). It is pointed out that there is nothing 'sacrosanct' about a particular number of States and it is claimed many Nigerians continue to regard state boundaries as transitional. For instance 'It is inconceivable, almost bordering on naivety, to think that people in the Calabar-Ogoja Area, will suddenly turn sweet under a civilian political government and be quiet when, even under the present firm military administration which has come out unequivocally against further creation of more states, they and their chiefs have defied apparent reproof and have continued canvassing openly, loudly and petitioning for the creation of their new State. Such peoples and communities will certainly be more open and aggressive under a civilian government.' It is argued that too rigid a procedure for effecting a change in the future will only create the impression that the door is permanently closed, with the result that people will resort to extra-constitutional means to secure their demands. The Tiv riots of the early 1960s are cited as an example of what could occur.

The two attitudes are thus diametrically opposed. Some, especially the military, believe that it is possible to say 'enough is enough' and therefore it should be said (outright or in effect). Others do not believe this to be practical politics. It seems inevitable that the Constituent Assembly will be under some pressure to create even more states in addition to the existing nineteen and this may have to be the price for a rigid amendment procedure.[27]

The institutions which the draft prescribes for the States are virtually identical to those recommended for the Federation. There are just three notable points of divergence. A State legislature is unicameral (S46). A State Governor (minimum age 35) is elected by simple majority (S111.5). A State Council of Chiefs advises the Governor on 'customary or cultural affairs, intercommunal relations, chieftancy matters' (S137). It had been recommended in sub-committee and accepted in plenary session that 'the Governor would need to be elected by an absolute majority, if necessary, after a second ballot' (Vol. II, p. 73 and p. 90). It is not clear whether the change made in the final drafting was by design or by accident. An absolute majority would be more in line with the concern expressed elsewhere in the draft for safeguards against unbalanced representation.

There is no provision for State citizenship in addition to Nigerian citizenship, although the phrase 'citizens who belong to a state' is used in S123 to ensure that no State shall be without a Federal minister. It was suggested in sub-committee that the Governor also should be an 'indigene of the State', defined as an ability 'to show that any of his grandparents or their forebearers were born in that State' (Vol. II, p. 73). This was not accepted by the full Committee and the electoral law, to be drafted by the Constituent Assembly, will presumably require no more than a residence qualification.

The allocation of legislative powers between the Federation and the States takes the form of a single list of subjects for which the former has exclusive jurisdiction (S100 and Second Schedule). There is no list of concurrent powers, that is, subjects on which both the Federation and the States may legislate. Thus recognition is given to a process of centralisation, in the sense that many of the concurrent powers of the 1963 Constitution have become exclusively federal. In practice, of course, what is concurrent is always potentially exclusively federal, since as soon as the federal legislature exercises its concurrent powers, to that extent state legislatures are excluded. Indeed a concurrent list may come to be emptied of meaning by action of the federal legislature. But this had not happened prior to 1966. Many of the concurrent powers were in practice exercised by the Regions. Only under military rule have the federal authorities acted to the exclusion of the regional and later state authorities in such matters as higher education, television, marketing of produce, income tax and trade unions. The decision of the Committee to put these on an exclusively federal list is therefore the recognition of a de facto but quite constitutional centralisation, of developments which have taken place under a decade of military rule.

The decision to omit from the draft a list of concurrent powers is said to have been taken for reasons of simplicity (Report 6.4). Wheare is quoted at some length in support but the Committee is again selective in what it chooses to quote. Wheare does indeed say that 'undoubtedly the simplest form of division is obtained by having one list only and that actually exclusive' (which leaves open the question whether it be a federal or a states list and some members of the Committee strongly urged the latter). But Wheare also goes on to discuss the merits of a concurrent list and concludes

> it is better always, if possible, to admit concurrent jurisdiction, if only perhaps as a transitional measure. In most cases it will be unavoidable. But what is likely to work best is a short exclusive list and a rather long concurrent list.[28]

'Simplicity' refers to the problem of judicial interpretation which is easier if there is but a single list. This may have been the overriding consideration in the mind of the Committee but some mention needs to be made of the consequences. The decision not to include in the draft a list of concurrent powers cuts two ways. An exclusive list unaccompanied by any concurrent list confines the authority in question to those matters listed. This could prove restrictive if the list is not worded generously. Yet if it is worded generously it could prove restrictive in the opposite sense—what remains is very little. A concurrent list provides an opportunity for both the federation and the states to legislate. The federal authority need only act to the extent that it is considered necessary to ensure desirable uniformity or to safeguard the national interest and states have room to act within those limits. It is a flexible arrangement suitable for the taking of joint cooperative action but requiring negotiation.

The Committee appears on the contrary to have been of the opinion that its exclusive federal list, although generously worded, might still prove insufficient. It included therefore a clause which gives the Federal legislature jurisdiction for

> The establishment and regulation of authorities for Nigeria or any part thereof—
>
> (a) to promote and enforce the observance of the fundamental objectives and directive principles contained in the Constitution (Second schedule, item 61).

The report discounts the fears that such a clause could be used to 'take over the powers and functions of a State Government' arguing that it can only be used for a defined purpose and that 'properly interpreted there is no danger' (Report 6.4). Such a purpose however is capable of almost infinite expansion and there is no knowing what will be its interpretation; so much will depend on the courts.

The Committee also contends that an allocation of legislative power—either as exclusive or as residual—is not an allocation of executive power. The argument is stated more clearly in a sub-committee report than in the main Report where it is in parts almost incomprehensible and in any case incomplete. According to this sub-committee

> It is very easy to misinterpret the establishment of an exclusive legislative list for the Federation as if it excludes the States from executive action in relation to the subjects so covered. For example, if industrial development is on the exclusive list, the State Governments can nevertheless initiate, establish or engage in industrial development but they must do so within the regulations or laws or policy established by the Federal Government. In addition, the Federal Government can delegate to the State Governments the executive authority over a subject on which the State legislatures have no competence. This is often the case where ease of administration so recommends. (Vol. II, p. 141).

Even this statement is confusing. The reference to the possibility that the Federal Government may delegate executive authority pre-supposes that exclusive executive authority does lie with the Federation—which is the contrary of the opening sentences. The supposition that the States could, through executive action, engage in activities over which the Federation has exclusive legislative powers—as if they were individuals free to act within the law[29]—is not in line with the general understanding of how federal systems operate. States in a federation do not have an implied general executive power and this is in fact made clear in the draft itself by S122 where it is stated:

> Subject to the provisions of this Constitution the executive authority of a state shall extend to the execution and maintenance of the constitution, all laws enacted by the legislature of the State and to all matters with respect to which the Legislature of the state has for the time being powers to make laws . . . . (S122)

This is a limited power and S.122 shuts the states out completely from any of the matters listed in the Second Schedule, not only in the making of the law but also by the way of administrative action. However, if one consults the Second Schedule one sees that in certain matters it does actually give the States a concurrent power. Thus, not only industrial development, the example used by the sub-committee, but also commercial and agricultural development is allocated to the Federation without prejudice to the right of the Government of a State or its agency to initiate or participate in such development—a clause that could prove as important to the States of the Nigerian Federation as the inter-state commerce clause of the constitution of the United States of America is to the US Federal Government. In a similar way concurrent powers are given to the State Governments in respect to broadcasting and television, museums and libraries, the incorporation, regulation and winding up of bodies corporate and statistics.[30] Furthermore, in many matters the legislative power is allocated to the Federation only to the extent that the federal legislature claims it, e.g. price control is a federal matter only in respect to 'goods and commodities designated by the National Assembly as essential'. This leaves open the right of state legislatures to impose price controls on other goods. Similarly worded provisions apply to antiquities and monuments, roads, river shipping and navigation, ports, parks, marketing of agricultural produce, education, (professional, technological, technical and vocational) and water. The list is not so exclusively federal as would appear. The Report is certainly a confused guide in this matter and the Constituent Assembly may well turn directly to Wheare and restore a concurrent list.

Of crucial importance to any federation is the allocation of sources of revenue. The Committee gave the matter 'anxious consideration' and consulted the Federal Ministry of Finance on a number of ideas for amending the existing system which was said to be 'unsatisfactory and undoubtedly unfair to some of the states with large populations' (Report 7.4-1). None proved acceptable and the attempt to write into the constitution a formula for revenue allocation was postponed. Nonetheless certain revenues are ear-marked for the states on the basis of derivation (S139), these being 'taxes and duties on capital gains, incomes and profits of persons other than companies and on documents or transactions by way of stamp duties' (S103). A Distributable Pool Account is also to be established, whereby certain revenues will be distributed among the states (S138). In addition the federal legislature, guided by recommendations from a permanent Fiscal Review Commission (S137), has authority to decide which revenues shall be paid into this Account and how they shall be distributed. The Committee, anticipating a possible deadlock in the federal legislature, recommended that the Federal Military Government should work out and enact a formula, in consultation with the states. This would then become a Schedule to the Constitution and remain operative until the federal legislature decided otherwise. The Committee urged that this exercise be completed before the Constituent Assembly convenes (Vol. I, p. 101). In short, as in the case of the creation of new states, the military is treated as a *deus ex machina,* alone capable of taking the necessary decision. The Federal Military Government has since announced the appointment of a Technical Committee on Revenue Allocation to assist it in this task.[31]

2.   ISLAMIC COURTS

The deliberations of the Committee ran into considerable difficulty of a doctrinal nature as soon as it became necessary to define the status of Islamic law and Sharia courts within the overall legal system.

The fundamental question of principle is stated in Ch. II, where it is declared that 'every citizen shall have equality of rights, obligations and opportunities before the law' (S11 (1) (a)). This is qualified, however, for it 'shall not invalidate a rule of Islamic law or Customary law' (S11 (2)). The disagreement that arose is explained in the Report:

> Some members do not agree with the reservation about Islamic or customary law and they argued that nothing should be allowed to qualify the statement of what, after all, is a statement of the ideal which we wish to attain and it ought to be expected that rules of Islamic or customary law would or should eventually give way to the ideals of equality enshrined in that rule. The majority however maintained that ideas which have been embodied in rules of Islamic law or customary law are part of the religious or cultural heritage of the various people concerned and have been accepted as binding for a very long time. It would unnecessarily outrage the religious or cultural ideas of most Nigerians not to recognize the need for the suggested reservation. (Report 3.4-1)

The Committee's report states quite frankly why some members found difficulty in giving constitutional recognition to Islamic law. It says:

> There was some argument to the effect that the reservation about Islamic and customary law may turn out to involve constitutional protection for rules of conduct which may be wholly indefensible and which do not deserve to be so protected (Report 3.4-2).

Such criticism—reiterated in subsequent debate—is clearly offensive to Moslems and they tend to treat it as ill-informed comment emanating from persons who speak not with an authentic Nigerian voice but in borrowed tones, those of the English law.

One can recognise in this quarrel all the prejudices that have caused so much disunity in the past. That they rose to the surface in the Committee and continue to animate public debate is perhaps inevitable. The majority of the Committee were able however to agree on the principle that in some matters the law may vary, depending on the religious or ethnic community into which one is born and with which one continues to be identified, bearing in mind that 'throughout Nigeria Islamic law as well as customary law has always been enforced and observed only to the extent that they are not repugnant to natural justice, equity and good conscience' (ibid).

Agreement on the principle was vital but the Committee had also to decide whether any changes were needed in the existing system of courts. A pattern of divided jurisdiction had been instituted in the Northern Region on independence in 1960 so that Muslims resident in the North could be certain of living under their own civil law (the Sharia) administered by their own learned judges. A Sharia Court of Appeal had been established to hear appeals from the so-called native courts in all matters of family law (including wills and gifts) and in any other case of civil law should the parties specifically request to have their case dealt with under Islamic law. There was no further right of appeal to the Supreme Court of Nigeria, except on questions involving interpretation of the constitution or of fundamental human rights. On the other hand the criminal code was unified and all cases involving the criminal law went on appeal to the High Court of the Northern Region; but, when hearing appeals from the native courts (for these dealt also with criminal matters), the High Court included a judge of the Sharia Court of Appeal.

When the Northern Region was sub-divided in 1967, each of the six Northern States established its own Sharia Court of Appeal thus maintaining the established system of divided jurisdiction. In 1975-76 further sub-division was imminent but there was also a new emphasis on national integration and some restructuring of the judicial system was more or less inevitable, even if the principle of divided jurisdiction was still retained.

There are several inter-related issues. First, the several State Sharia Courts of Appeal need to be brought under the jurisdiction of a higher court, in the same way as the High Court of each State is under the

jurisdiction of the Supreme Court. But to give the Supreme Court—a
court versed primarily in English law and procedure—jurisdiction over
the Sharia would be unacceptable to Muslims. On the other hand there
is resistance to the idea of a Supreme Court sitting in separate divisions
when the function of a Supreme Court is to be the apex of a unified
legal system. This dilemma was avoided by creating two separate
courts of appeal below the level of the Supreme Court; a Federal Court
of Appeal, to hear appeals from the High Court of each State and a
Federal Sharia Court of Appeal to hear appeals from any State Sharia
Courts of Appeal. This was decided despite the acute lack of qualified
persons to man two federal appeal courts in addition to the Supreme
Court. Some of the Committee thought that instead, the strengthening
of the Supreme Court should have first priority (Report 8.1-2). This
duality of intermediate Appeal Courts is however essential to preserve
the present practice whereby all cases decided under Sharia law go on
appeal to a separate system of Sharia Courts, with an ultimate right of
appeal to the Supreme Court, only if a 'substantial question' of
constitutional law is at issue (S184 (5)).

The Committee was also faced with the question whether Sharia
courts should remain confined to the former Northern Region or be
extended to other States of the Federation inhabited by Muslims. This
is not quite the simple matter it looks. Most of the non-Northern
Muslims are Yoruba who have their own customary courts. Their
spokesmen in the Committee saw little need for a Sharia Court of
Appeal and indeed some disadvantages. This question was therefore
left for each State legislature to decide (S180.2b).

Finally, certain difficulties arose in the course of deciding
qualifications for appointment, notably to the Supreme Court. To the
extent that the system of courts remains divided there is no difficulty,
for each legal tradition provides its own qualified judges. Thus, for
appointment to the Federal Court of Appeal and to the High Court of
each State the relevant qualification is admission to the Nigerian Bar
on the basis of British-type qualifications, whereas appointment to the
Federal and State Sharia Courts of Appeal depends on possession of a
recognised qualification in Islamic law combined with considerable
practical experience or distinction as a scholar. It is the combination of
the two traditions at the apex of the system which causes difficulty.
Either those appointed would need to possess both sets of
qualifications (and it is said that there are no more than two or three
considered eligible in this respect) or the Court would need to be

composed of persons whose qualifications differ. Although the Sub-Committee recommended that up to one-third of the Supreme Court judges could be persons with qualifications solely in Sharia law, the full Committee insisted on a uniform qualification. Those appointed must be 'qualified legal practitioners'—i.e. qualified in the Western tradition and of not less than 15 years standing (S150.6) but the President, when making appointments to the Supreme Court (on the recommendations of the Judicial Service Commission and subject to confirmation by the Senate) is to include 'persons learned in Islamic Law and persons learned in Customary law' (S150.5).

There was also a difference of opinion as to whether those appointed to the Sharia court should be 'professed Muslims'. To some this was an essential qualification for sitting in judgment on the Sharia law. Others considered a knowledge of Islamic law sufficient and religious practice to be entirely a personal matter. The Sub-Committee had included this additional qualification (Vol. 2, p. 113) but it was deleted in plenary session.

A settlement of these delicate issues involved the Committee in several days of debate and required the moderating influence of some of the older members. More than any other issue with which the Committee had to deal, it was a touchstone for testing the degree of tolerance and the will to unite. Meanwhile, the more extreme proponents of the respective traditions have voiced their discontent with the settlement reached by the Committee. The demand for an unqualified declaration of equality before the law and a fully secular State is countered by the demand that Islamic law and its custodians, the Mufti, be given equality of status in the Supreme Court and priority in all States where Muslims predominate.[32]

3. LOCAL GOVERNMENT

By including a section on local government the CDC was in effect underwriting action taken by the Federal Military Government in the course of the Committee's own deliberations.[33] The military clearly set great store on its reform of the system of local government and the Committee reciprocated by making 'a system of local government by democratically elected local government councils' one of the directive principles of state policy listed in Ch. II of the draft (S13). Moreover it is one of the only two justiciable sections of that controversial chapter.[34] Thus the question of local self-government, as one of principle, is taken out of the hands of the states. Three criteria are laid down for determining the areas of local authorities—community of interest, traditional association and administrative convenience— criteria which might be thought no more amenable to judicial action than some of the other national objectives and directive principles which have been excluded from the jurisdiction of the courts, e.g. social and economic rights. Special mention is made—a comment on past practice—of a state government's obligation to ensure respect for universal suffrage. A schedule to the draft Constitution sets out the minimum functions of local authorities and they are to participate in 'economic planning and development'.

Conclusion

A committee appointed to draft a constitution may expect its work to be assessed from many different points of view. Its conclusions may be thought politically biased, or perhaps too favourable to some particular interest, and the CDC has certainly not escaped such criticism for it has been attacked on the grounds that it seeks to preserve the interests of a capitalist class and of a privileged elite—a view expressed, for example, by the two members of the Committee who dissented from the official report.[35] A draft may also be judged on stylistic grounds and on this score also the committee's work has been considered by some as unnecessarily long, far too technical and largely incomprehensible to the general body of citizens. Yet, however defective a draft may appear to be from a political or stylistic point of view, it is, after all, only an interim report and not the final document. Being but a draft, its main value may lie as much in the clarification of what is at issue as in the presentation of specific proposals.

The interval of a whole year between publication of the Report and the first meeting of the Constituent Assembly has allowed plenty of time for public discussion. The *Daily Times* sponsored and reported on a series of public meetings held throughout the country. Many of the Universities organised conferences which were also reported in the press. Although some members of the CDC expressed their views, including dissent on particular recommendations, most of them left the task of explanation and advocacy to others. How far the general public was enlightened it is difficult to say. There were many complaints that the Report was difficult to obtain, especially when first published, and that it was available only in English. When a translation in Hausa did appear it was only of the draft constitution: it omitted that part of the report which explains the innovations and the extent of disagreement within the committee.[36] There was however plenty of coverage on radio and TV and in the vernacular press. The major difficulty most probably lay in the technicality of the language used in the draft. The Constituent Assembly is the intended beneficiary of all this debate, a special unit in the Federal Cabinet office having been established to receive comments and monitor the public discussion. What sort of reports it presents to the Constituent Assembly remains to be seen. They are unlikely to assess the weight of opinion or the cogency of the particular arguments but may serve as a supplement to the CDC Report, especially on those issues which have become the focus of public attention, such as the means whereby some of the fundamental objectives are to be achieved, the exercise of Presidential power, what position is to be accorded Islamic law and whether the freedom of the press is sufficiently guaranteed.[37]

The CDC entrusted some important issues, e.g. concerning the military, to subsequent legislation and left others to the course of events. The Constituent Assembly may or may not conclude that it has no alternative but to do the same. For instance there is no attempt in the draft to limit the number of parties but there are advocates of a limitation to but one or at most two parties—one capitalist, the other socialist.[38] The implementation of many fundamental objectives is likewise left in the Report to the operations of a competitive party system, but the Constituent Assembly may find itself under considerable pressure to make the outcome less open-ended. Whatever the arrangements preferred, the practice will be experimental. Moreover watching the experiment is likely to be the military, another subject on which the Constituent Assembly may or may not choose to be more explicit than was the CDC.

Members of the Constituent Assembly will not be able to claim any mandate conferred directly by the electorate itself, for about ten per cent are to be nominated by the Federal Military Government and the rest elected by local government authorities. Additional members are the Chairman of the CDC and the rapporteurs of the six sub-committees. The Government is to appoint the Chairman and Deputy Chairman of the Assembly. The local authorities have been grouped for the purpose of this election; five seats have been allotted to each State plus a share of one hundred and eight other seats according to population. This gives the highest number of seats to Kano (16) and the lowest to Niger (7). Whether those elected will prove suitable for the task has been questioned on two grounds: it is alleged that they will have only a remote connexion with the electorate and will lack the necessary intellectual capacity. Even if such criticism is exaggerated, it is unfortunate that it can be made with a great deal of plausibility. The charge that they are remote and therefore unrepresentative is based on their mode of election. In half the states the local councils themselves were elected only indirectly with the result that many members of the Constituent Assembly find themselves twice removed from the electorate they are supposed to represent. In any case, turn out in the local elections was disappointingly low: very many councillors were returned unopposed and the conduct of the election was far from perfect.[39] The charge of intellectual incapacity also arises from the circumstances of the election. Public employees including teachers were discouraged from standing because they would first have had to resign from the public service and few were willing to take the risk. The effect was to leave the way open to people of little education. These facts may however come to be outweighed by other events. Those elected to the Constituent Assembly may establish a more direct relationship with the electorate in the course of the proceedings and thereby establish a valid claim to be representative. Moreover, many of those elected will be eminently qualified. No less a person than the Governor of the Central Bank resigned in order to represent 'his people' in the Constituent Assembly. Many of the candidates are of similar standing; there should therefore be no complaint of intellectual incapacity.[40]

It is presumably hoped that there will emerge from the Constituent Assembly a constitution that has secured near unanimous approval in much the same way as the CDC gave virtually unanimous approval to the draft constitution. It could then be claimed to have the necessary degree of consent. But if serious divisions of opinion do emerge, difficulties could arise. No referendum has been envisaged.[41] It is not even certain whether the military intends that the Constituent Assembly shall enact the constitution on its own authority. This question may be left open until the last minute, as happened in Ghana, thereby safeguarding for the military government an ultimate power of veto.[42]

Finally it should not be assumed that the constitution due to be enacted in 1978 will be the last word. Constitutions evolve through amendment or usage and they may be written afresh. The drafting of a constitution for Nigeria, after a decade in which so much has changed, is bound to have been something of an act of faith.

NOTES

1. The Head of State explained how the Committee was chosen. They 'were selected first on the basis of two per State, (so) as to obtain as wide a geographical coverage as possible and secondly from our learned men in disciplines considered to have direct relevance to Constitution-making, namely, history, law, economics and other social sciences, especially political science. Eminent Nigerians with some experience in Constitution-making were brought in to complete the spectrum' (Report p. xliii). No fewer than fourteen were academics and five others had taught in universities. Twelve were lawyers, six held appointments as civil commissioners in state governments and eleven others had served at one time or other as federal or state commissioners. (These categories overlap but they account for 39 out of 49 members). The list of members is given in Volume II, p. 5-7.

2. Announcement by General Murtala Mohammed. October 1st, 1975 (*West Africa*, 6 October 1975, p. 1166).

3. The only references to memoranda from the public are to be found in Vol. I, p. ii, and Vol. II, p. 175, 177 and to solicited memoranda on Vol. II, p. 219.

4. The Report attributes this perceptive insight to members said not to be in agreement with either the sub-committee or the overriding majority of the Committee. Their manner of stating the respective contributions of public and private enterprise was however adopted in the final draft.

5. Compare the distinction between 'positive rights' and 'human rights' in M. Cranston, *What are Human Rights?* 1973, Ch. 1.

6. See 'National Policy on Education' Government Printer 1976 and the announcement by the Head of State at Ibadan University 17 November 1976.

7. *Daily Times* 9 December 1976.

8. For example, some of the Ibos displaced during the Civil War are still trying to return to their homes in Port Harcourt. (*West Africa* 20 June 1977, p. 1242). Reference is made to this problem in other chapters. See Ch. 3, p. 81, Ch. 4, p. 135, note 20.

9. A law, known familiarly as 'la loi anti-casseurs' was introduced in France after the troubles of 1968. It made organisers of demonstrations responsible for damage done by those ostensibly under their orders.

10. An Electoral Commission was appointed in November 1976, headed by Chief Michael Ani, a retired civil servant. Its membership was said to reflect the 'federal character of the nation' (*West Africa* 29 November 1976, p. 1826). The formal decree establishing the Federal Electoral Commission was not published until June 1977. Each State appoints a member.

11. S33 of the draft qualifies the right of association in a sub-section which refers to the 'powers conferred by this Constitution on the Electoral Commission with respect to political parties to which that Commission does not accord recognition'. There is no clarification of what would amount to a refusal to recognise a party and strictly speaking no such power is conferred on the Electoral Commission by S137 and S171-S178.

12. D. Austin and R. Luckham (eds) *Politicians & Soldiers in Ghana 1966-1972,* Cass, London 1975, p. 109-111.

13. For a comparative analysis of the powers of the US President and UK Prime Minister, see R. E. Neustadt *'White House and Whitehall'* in A. King (ed). *The British Prime Minister,* London 1969, p. 131-150. He shows that both are obliged to win support from colleagues.

14. A sub-committee report states that public hearings, on bills that are being considered in committees of the legislature, 'help to diffuse potential opposition to the law'. There is presumably a misprint: 'diffuse' should read 'defuse' (Vol. 2, p. 77).
15. Edmund Burke. *Reflections on the Revolution in France,* Everyman Library, London 1910, p. 25. In France, the signatories to an unsuccessful motion of censure may not move another in the same session of parliament. Impeachment in the USA can only be for 'treason, bribery, or other high crimes and misdemeanours' (Article 11. S4).
16. Edmund Burke. Ibid, p. 60.
17. *Presidentialism in Commonwealth Africa,* London 1974, p. 432-3. This is not the only acknowledged quotation from this book. Compare the arguments quoted earlier from paragraphs 7.1-4 to 71-6 of the Report with Nwabueze, p. 89-91 and p. 433-4.
18. The only reference to 'opposition' is that quoted above in note 14. The report of the two dissenting members does however venture an opinion as to how the institutions of president etc., as proposed by the CDC, would be related to political forces and what manner of consensus politics would prevail—it would be a 'shabby consensus among the representatives of different factions of the Nigerian bourgeois elite'. The various bourgeois elite factions are those of business, the bureaucracy and the professions (see note 35) but the dominant elite at state level is expected to be ethnic because of the manner in which the draft constitution reserves certain offices at state level for those who ethnically 'belong to' the state, (see p. 21). 'There will only be bargaining among the various ethnic elites to maximise their own share of the loot of public funds: a bargaining process which would periodically degenerate into violent squabbling'.
19. Machiavelli. *The Prince,* Ch. 23.
20. For an account of the 1962 crisis see J. P. Mackintosh, *Nigerian Government and Politics,* London 1966, Ch. x.
21. The strange omission of S168 went largely unnoticed until March 1977. A not altogether clear statement by the CDC's Chairman, reported in the *New Nigerian* 1st April 1977, referred to the omission as the decision of a majority on the Committee. S168 is not in fact the only omission: S39 which deals with a state of emergency is short of sub-section 8(c). No explication has been given for this.
22. See N. J. Miners. *The Nigerian Army 1956-1966,* London 1971, p. 116.
23. A Police Committee is to be established for each local government area. See p. 286, note 11.
24. This provision could be abused by a State Governor in collusion with the Federal Government.
25. See B. O. Nwabueze, op. cit, p. 380-1 for comments on the 'Leadership Code' in Tanzania, and *Africa Confidential* Vol. 18, No. 10, May 13, 1977 for difficulties concerning the Zambian code.
26. See Ch. 7. In his address to the CDC, the Head of State referred to this matter in almost note-like and not very precise language. There was a need for 'Constitutional restriction on the number of States to be further created. This could be done either by creation or by total proscription after the current exercise' (a reference to the increase to nineteen states announced a few months later) Report p. xlii-xliii.
27. Aminu Kano, a member of the CDC, called upon the military to create more states before handing over power (*West Africa* 13 June 1977, p. 1178). That same

month Haliru Abdullahi called for the splitting of Kaduna State into two—a Zaria and a Katsina State, (*New Nigerian* 4 June 1977).

28. K. C. Wheare. *Federal Government* 4th ed. Oxford 1963 p. 79.

29. The Report makes in fact no distinction between private and public persons. It states: 'if any person or authority wishes to engage in activities relating to that subject, he can do so in accordance with laws and regulations made by the appropriate government over that subject' (Report 6.3).

30. Item 60 reads 'Statistics for the purpose of a State Government . . . .' This should obviously read 'Statistics other than . . . .' The Constitution itself confers concurrent legislative powers for 'the maintaining and securing of public safety and public order' and of essential supplies and services (S.101).

31. *New Nigerian* 9th July 1977. It is to report by November 30, 1977.

32. A demand made in a meeting held at the Centre of Islamic Legal Studies, Institute of Administration, Zaria, 11–15 April 1977 (*New Nigerian* 18 April 1977).

33. For the reform in question, see Chapters 9–11.

34. The other section which is enforceable in the courts is that which prohibits the adoption of 'any religion as the State religion' (S.17).

35. Their own unpublished 'report' states:
'A recurrent strand in the intellectual and moral outlook of the bulk of CDC members . . . . is a basic commitment, sometimes thinly disguised and sometimes blatantly expressed, to the consolidation and perpetuation of the neo-colonist capitalist social and economic order in Nigeria . . . .decisions were made with the clear intention and purpose of safeguarding and even enhancing the control of the various bourgeois elite interests . . . . these bourgeois interests range from those of the bureaucratic and administrative bourgeoisie to those of the professional (especially legal) and business bourgeoisie.'
Their alternative draft formulates in very general terms six fundamental principles, a long list of individual rights and duties, and seven fundamental economic and social objectives. Among the seven fundamental objectives is 'national control of the key resources . . . (and) . . . key sectors of the economy . . . (especially) . . . minerals, extraction and processing industries, including petroleum . . . (and) commercial tanking' (S.35). Protection is given to 'legitimately acquired private property . . . so long as it is beneficial to the country's economy and to the interests of the Nigerian people' (S.37). All political parties must comply with the six principles and seven objectives which are enforceable by the courts. Only parties recognised by a National Electoral and Parties Commission would be allowed to put up candidates (S.43). The judiciary would be reformed so that it gave less weight to 'technical arguments' of a law built around the defence of private property'.

36. The Chairman of the CDC announced in April that translations into Hausa, Ibo and Yoruba would be available in May, i.e. nine months after the English version (*West Africa* 11 April 1977, p. 732). See also *New Nigerian* 18 May 1977.

37. The provisions of S.32 which guarantee 'freedom of expression, including freedom to hold opinions and to receive and impart ideas and information without interference' and which give everyone the right 'to own, establish and operate any medium for the dissemination of information, ideas and opinions' (except for radio and television broadcast) are considered by some as an inadequate safeguard of the right of the press to deal freely with all matters of public interest. The greatest danger to press freedom lies however in pressure from newspaper proprietors, especially if the proprietor is government. The *New*

Nigerian is publicly owned and the Government took over a majority shareholding of the *Daily Times* in autumn 1975.

Several State Governments own newspapers, e.g. Kwara State owns the *Nigerian Herald*. The Nigerian Guild of Editors called on the Federal and State governments to dispose of their holdings in newspapers (*West Africa* 18 April 1977 p. 782).

38. The suggestion that electors should have a choice between a capitalist and a socialist party was made by Dr. Ali Yahaya in a paper entitled 'The party system and the Nigerian polity' given to a conference on the draft constitution held at the Institute of Administration, Zaria, 21st–22nd March 1977. At the same conference, the Commissioner for Education in Borno State, Alhaji Hassan El-Badawy, made a strong plea for a one-party state.

39. See Chapter 10 and 11, esp. p. 265–7 and p. 278–81.

40. Adamu Ciroma, the Governor of the Bank, was unopposed, as were over sixty others (out of a total of 202). Candidates included the Vice-Chancellor of Ahmadu Bello University (Iya Abubakar), the Pro Vice-Chancellor of Jos University (R. A. O. Akinjide), several members of the Constitution Drafting Committee (e.g. Ibrahim Tahir, Dr. I. D. Ahmed, Abubakar Usman, Babu Audu, Paul Belabo, Chief Murphy), several former leading politicians (e.g. Tarka, Fani-Kayode, Kola Balogun, Yahaya Gusau, Shehu Shagari, Ibrahim Nock and Shettimo Ali-Monguno), and some prominent officials or ex-officials (e.g. Kem Salem, the former Inspector-General of Police and S. A. Awoninyi, Federal Permanent Secretary). The number of unopposed candidates was most striking in Niger (all seven seats) and Borno (nine out of the eleven seats). The competition was keenest in Anambra, Bendel, Imo, Lagos and Oyo—an average of three to four candidates per seat. A very high proportion of those contesting were lawyers—over a quarter rising to a half in Ogun and Ondo. Very few of the councillors were themselves candidates.

41. The question of a referendum began, however, to be raised in June 1977. See, for instance, a series of four editorials in the *New Nigerian* 18th to 21st May 1977.

42. D. Austin and R. Luckham op. cit p. 115–6.

MAPS

FIGURES

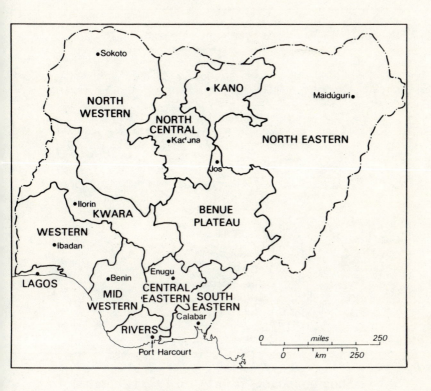

State boundaries before 1976 (12 States)

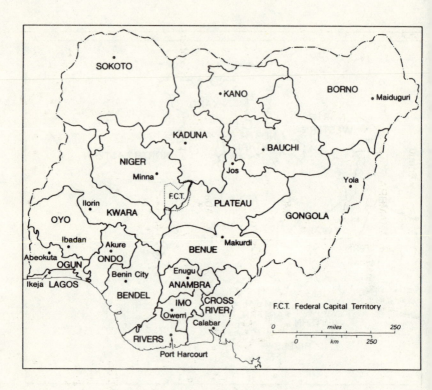

State boundaries from April 1976 (19 States)

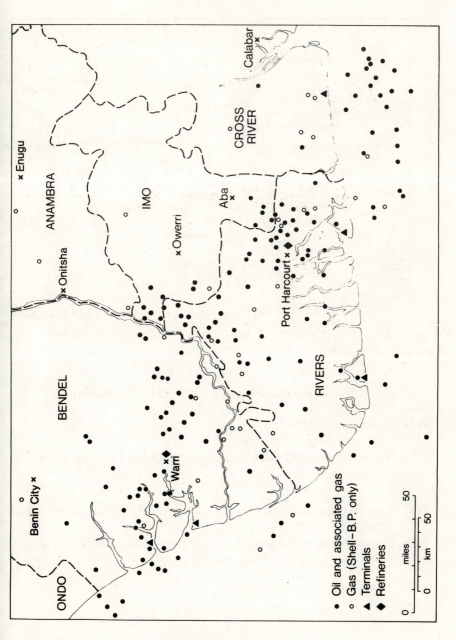

Oil and Gas Fields

FIGURE 1.

OIL REVENUE AS PERCENTAGE OF FEDERAL REVENUE

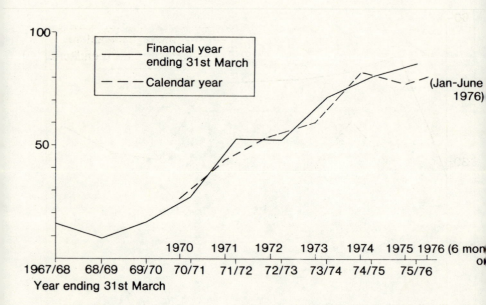

Note. Oil revenue is
 (1) Petroleum profits tax.
 (2) Fees, rents and royalties.
 (3) Nigerian National Oil Corporation supplies (as from 1974–75).

Sources
 (1) Recurrent estimates of the Government of the Federal Republic of Nigeria 1967/68 to 1976/77.
 (2) Central Bank of Nigeria: Economic and Financial Review. Vol. 14 No. 1 December 1975, No. 2 June 1976.

FIGURE 2.

DEFENCE EXPENDITURE AS PERCENTAGE OF FEDERAL EXPENDITURE

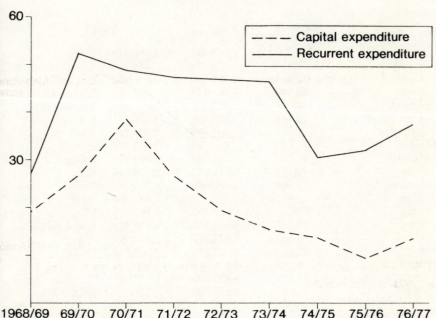

Notes
  (1) Recurrent expenditure excludes statutory and non-statutory appropriations to States.
  (2) Capital expenditure excludes loans-on-lent to States.
  (3) 1972/73 recurrent expenditure is omitted for 1972–73 because of manifest omissions from the published figures.
  (4) Figures up to 1971–72 are actual expenditure. Recurrent expenditure 1973–76 is the approved estimate. Capital expenditure 1973–1976 is the probable expenditure.
Sources. Recurrent and Capital Estimates of the Government of the Federal Republic of Nigeria.

FIGURE 3.

THE NINETEEN STATES

State	Estimated Area Sq. Kms.	Estimated Population (i)	(ii)	Capital
Anambra	15,770	2,943,483	3,596,618	Enugu
Bauchi	61,814	2,193,674	2,431,296	Bauchi
Bendel	38,061	2,435,839	2,460,962	Benin City
Benue	69,740	3,041,194	2,427,017	Makurdi
Borno	116,589	2,990,526	2,997,498	Maiduguri
Cross River	29,164	3,600,000	3,478,131	Calabar
Gongola	102,067	3,002,808	2,605,263	Yola
Imo	13,032	3,280,340	3,672,654	Owerri
Kaduna	70,293	4,098,305	4,098,306	Kaduna
Kano	42,123	5,774,842	5,774,840	Kano
Kwara	73,404	2,309,338	1,714,485	Ilorin
Lagos	3,535	1,443,567	1,443,568	Ikeja
Niger	73,555	1,271,767	1,194,508	Minna
Ogun	20,241	1,557,946	1,550,996	Abeokuta
Ondon	18,165	2,272,675	2,729,690	Akure
Oyo	42,862	5,158,884	5,208,884	Ibadan
Plateau	56,245	2,026,657	2,026,657	Jos
Rivers	21,172	1,800,000	1,719,925	Port Harcourt
Sokoto	94,588	4,538,808	4,538,787	Sokoto

(i) According to Federal Government White Paper on the Report of the Panel on Creation of States, Federal Ministry of Information 1976.
(ii) As agreed at meeting of Secretaries to State Military Governments May 17, 1977. Figures prepared by Federal Office of Statistics (*West Africa* 4 July 1977 p. 1,386).

SELECT BIBLIOGRAPHY

1. Official Reports, Documents and Legislation

2. Books and Articles

    PART ONE. THE MILITARY IN OFFICE

    PART TWO. POLITICAL ECONOMY

    PARTS THREE, FOUR AND FIVE. FEDERAL, LOCAL GOVERNMENT
    AND CONSTITUTIONAL REFORM

3. Papers and Unpublished Material

BIBLIOGRAPHY

1. Official Reports, Documents and Legislation

NIGERIA FEDERAL GOVERNMENT. MINISTRY OF INFORMATION, LAGOS

Report of the Constitution Drafting Committee, 2 Vols. 1976
Federal Military Government Views on the Report of the Panel on Creation of States 1976.
Federal Military Government Views on the Report of the Industrial Enterprises Panel 1976.
Guidelines for Local Government Reform 1976
Report of the Public Service Review Commission, Main Report 1974
Suggested Framework for a National System of Local Government 1976
Report of the Fiscal Review Commission 1965
Report of the Interim Revenue Allocation Review Committee 1969

NIGERIA FEDERAL GOVERNMENT. MINISTRY OF ECONOMIC DEVELOPMENT. CENTRAL PLANNING OFFICE

Third National Development Plan 1975–80, 2 Vols.
Second National Development Plan 1970–74. First progress report n.d.

WESTERN STATE GOVERNMENT

Report of the Commission of Inquiry into the Civil Disturbances which occurred in certain parts of the Western State of Nigeria in the month of December 1968. Ibadan 1969.
The Truth about Tax Riots: Governor Adebayo speaks. Ibadan 1969.

U.K. COLONIAL OFFICE

Report of the Commission appointed to enquire into the fears of Minorities and the means of allaying them. Cmd 505 1958.

2. Books and Articles

PART ONE—THE MILITARY IN OFFICE

Akinsanya, A. A. 'The Military Regime, Top Bureaucrats and What Next? The Nigerian Case' (*Geneva-Africa* XV.1. 1976).

Akinsanya, A. A.   'The Machinery of Government during the
                          Military Regime in Nigeria".
                          (*International Review of Administrative Sciences*
                          1976).

Bebler, A.   *Military Rule in Africa: Dahomey, Ghana, Sierra
                          Leone and Mali.* New York 1973.

Bennett, V. P.   'Patterns of Demilitarisation in Africa'
                          (*Quarterly Journal of Administration,* Ife 1974).

Bienen, H.   *The Military and Modernisation,* Chicago 1970.

Bienen, H.   'Military and Society in East Africa'
                          (*Comparative Politics* 6.4.1974).

Bienen, H. & Morell, D.   *Political Participation under Military Regimes,*
(eds)   Beverly Hills, Sage, 1976.

Cox, T. S.   *Civil Military Relations in Sierra Leone,*
                          Cambridge, Mass 1976.

Dare, L. O.   'The Patterns of Military Entrenchment in
                          Ghana and Nigeria' (*Africa Quarterly* XVI.III.
                          1977).

Decalo, S.   *Coups and Army Rule in Africa: Studies in
                          Military Style.* New Haven, Yale University
                          Press 1976.

Decalo, S.   'Military Coups and Military Regimes in Africa'
                          (*Journal of Modern African Studies* 11.1.1973).

Dent, M. J.   'The third military coup in Nigeria' (*World
                          Today,* September 1975).

Dowse, R.   'The Military and Political Development' (in
                          Leys, C. ed.) *Politics and Change in Developing
                          Countries.* Cambridge 1969).

Feit, E.   *The Armed Bureaucrats.* Boston 1973.

Feit, E.   'Military Coups and Political Development:
                          some lessons from Ghana and Nigeria.' (*World
                          Politics* XX.2. 1968).

Feit, E.   'The Rule of the "Iron Surgeons": Military
                          Government in Spain and Ghana.' (*Comparative
                          Politics* 1.4. 1969).

Finer, S. E.   *The Man on Horseback.* London 1967.

Huntington, S. P. (ed.)   *Changing Patterns of Military Politics,* New
                          York 1962.

Johnson, J. (ed.)   *The Role of the Military in Undeveloped
                          Countries,* Princeton 1962.

Kirk-Greene, A. H. M.   *Crises and Conflict in Nigeria: a Documentary
                          Source Book 1966–1970.* 2 Vols. London 1971.

Luckham, R.   *The Nigerian Military,* Cambridge 1971.

Miners, N. J.   *The Nigerian Army 1965–1966,* London 1971.

Ollawa, P. E.	'The Political and Social Setting of Military Government in Nigeria: Problems of Political Instability Revisited.' (*Geneva-Africa* XV.2.1976).
Olorunsola, V. A.	*Soldiers & Power: The Development Performance of the Nigerian Military Regime.* Stanford 1977.
Olowu, E. O.	*The Legislative Process in a Military Regime: The Nigerian Experience.*
Panter-Brick, S. K. (ed.)	*Nigerian Politics and Military Rule: Prelude to Civil War.* London 1970.
Peil, M.	'A Civilian Appraisal of Military Rule in Nigeria' (*Armed Forces and Society* 2.1. 1975).
Van Doorn, J.	*Armed Forces and Society.* The Hague 1968.
Welch, C.	*Soldier and State in Africa.* Evanston 1970.

PART TWO—POLITICAL ECONOMY

Aboyado, O. & Ayida, A.	'The War Economy in Perspective' (*Nigerian Journal of Economic and Social Studies* Vol. 13. 1971).
Adedeji, A.	*Nigerian Federal Finance,* London 1969.
Akeredolu-Ale, E. O.	*Underdevelopment of Indigenous Entrepreneurship in Nigeria.* Ibadan 1973.
Amin, S.	*Neo-colonialism in West Africa.* London 1973.
Bauer, P. T.	*West African trade: a study of competition, oligopoly and monopoly in a changing economy.* London 1954.
Blair, J. M.	*The Control of Oil.* New York 1976.
Collins, P. et al	*The Policy of Indigenization in Nigeria.* Special issue of *Quarterly Journal of Administration* (Ife) IX.2. January 1975.
Cohen, R.	*Labour and politics in Nigeria.* London 1974.
Cronjé, S., Ling, M. & Cronjé, G.	*Lonhro: portrait of a multinational* London 1976.
Eicher, C. K. & Liedholm, C. (eds.)	*Growth & development of the Nigerian economy.* East Lansing 1970.
Helleiner, G. K.	*Peasant Agriculture, Government and Economic Growth in Nigeria.* Homewood 1966.
Jackson, E. F.	*Economic Development in Africa.* Oxford 1965.
Kilby, P.	*Industrialisation in an Open Economy: Nigeria 1945–66.* London 1969.
Madujibeya, S. A.	'Oil and Nigeria's Economic Development' (*African Affairs* Vol. 75, 1976).

Mayall, J. 'Oil and Nigerian Foreign Policy' (*African Affairs* Vol. 75 1976).

Meyer, R. K. & Pearson, S. R. 'Contributions of petroleum to Nigerian economic development' (*in* Pearson & Cownie (eds.). *Commodity Exports and African Economic Development.* London 1974).

Mummery, D. R. *The protection of international private investment: Nigeria and the world community.* New York 1960.

Nafziger, E. Wayne *African Capitalism: a case study in Nigerian entrepreneurship.* Stanford 1977.

National Industrial Conference Board *Unusual foreign payments: a survey of the policies and practices of US companies.* New York 1976.

Oyejide, T. A. *Tariff Policy and Industrialization in Nigeria.* Ibadan 1975.

Pearson, S. R. *Petroleum in the Nigerian Economy.* Stanford 1969.

Perham, M. (ed.) *Mining, commerce and finance in Nigeria.* London 1948.

Proehl, P. O. *Foreign Enterprise in Nigeria: laws and policies.* Chapel Hill, North Carolina 1965.

Robbins, L. *The Economic Basis of Class Conflict and Other Essays in Political Economy.* London 1939.

Sampson, A. *The Seven Sisters.* London 1975.

Schatzl, L. H. *Petroleum in Nigeria.* Ibadan 1969.

Seidman, A. 'Changing theories of political economy in Africa'. (*in* Fyfe, C. (ed.) *African studies since 1945: a tribute to Basil Davidson.* London 1976.)

Stolper, W. F. *Planning Without Facts: Lessons in resources Allocation from Nigeria's Development.* Cambridge Mass. 1966.

Teriba, O. 'Nigerian Revenue Allocation Experience 1952–1965.' (*Nigerian Journal of Economic and Social Studies* Vol. 8 1966).

Tiffen, M. *The Enterprising Peasant: Economic Development in Gombe Emirate 1960–1968.* HMSO London 1976.

Vallenila, L. *Oil: The Making of a New Economic Order.* McGraw-Hill 1975.

Wilson, C. *The History of Unilever.* London 1954.

Williams, G. (ed.) *Nigeria: Economy and Society.* London 1976.

Yesufu, T. M. *An Introduction to Industrial Relations in Nigeria.* London 1962.

Yesufu, T. M. (ed.)   *Manpower Problems and Economic Development in Nigeria.* Ibadan 1969.

PARTS THREE, FOUR AND FIVE—FEDERAL, LOCAL GOVERNMENT AND CONSTITUTIONAL REFORM

Adedeji, A. & Rowland, L. *Local Government Finance in Nigeria: Problems and Prospects.* Ife 1972.

Akinyemi, B. *Federalism and Foreign Policy: the Nigerian Experience.* Ibadan 1974.

Aluko, Olajide 'The 'New' Nigerian Foreign Policy' (*Round Table,* October 1976).

Ahmadu Bello, Alhaji Sir *My Life.* Cambridge 1962.

Atta, A. A. 'The development of Nigeria's political personality'.
(*Quarterly Journal of Administration,* Ife October 1971).

Awolowo, O. *Thoughts on the Nigerian Constitution.* Ibadan 1966.

Beer, C. E. F. *The Politics of Peasant Groups in Western Nigeria.* Ibadan 1976.

Campbell, I. 'The Nigerian Census: an Essay in Civil-Military Relations.'
(*Journal of Commonwealth and Comparative Politics,* XIV. 3. 1976).

Coleman, J. *Nigeria: Background to Nationalism.* Berkeley 1963.

Dudley, B. J. *Instability and Political Order.* Ibadan 1974.

Eleazu, Uma O. *Federalism and Nation-Building: the Nigerian Experience 1954–1964.* Ilfracombe 1977.

Gambari, I. A. 'Nigeria and the World: a growing internal stability, wealth and external influence'. (*Journal of International Affairs* 2, 1975).

Idang, G. J. *Nigeria: Internal Politics and Foreign Policy (1960–66).* Ibadan 1972.

Kirk-Greene, A. H. M. *Lugard and the Amalgamation of Nigeria: a documentary record.* London 1968.

Mackintosh, J. P. *Nigerian Government and politics.* London 1966.

Melson, R. & Wolpe, H. (eds.) *Nigeria: Modernisation and the Politics of Communalism.* Michigan 1971.

Nwabueze, B. O. *Presidentialism in Commonwealth Africa.* London 1974.

Ojo, Olatunde J. B. et al. *Federalism and State Administration* (Special issue of *Quarterly Journal of Administration.* Ife X.2 January 1976).

Peil, M.	*Nigerian Politics: the People's View.* London 1976.
Plumb, J. H.	*The Growth of Political Stability in England 1675–1725.* London 1967.
Post, K. W. J. & Vickers, M.	*Structure and Conflict in Nigeria 1960–65.* London 1973.
Tamuno, T. N.	'Separatist Agitations in Nigeria since 1914.' (*Journal of Modern African Studies.* 8.4.1970).

3. Papers and Unpublished Material

Asiodu, P. C.	*Some aspects of Nigerian Oil Policy 1971–75* Lagos 1977.
Asobie, H. A.	*Domestic Political Structure and Foreign Policy. The Nigerian Experience 1960–74.* (Ph.D. thesis University of London, July 1977).
Atta, A. A.	*The role of the civil service in the development process,* Lagos 1972.
Ayida, A. A.	*The Nigerian Revolution* (Proceedings of the Annual Conference of the Nigerian Economic Society 1973).
Campbell, I.	*Nigeria: Prologue to a Coup.* (University of Warwick, Department of Politics, Working Paper No. 7, October 1975).
Madujibeya, S. A.	*Economic enclaves, technology transfer and foreign investments in Nigeria.* (School of Oriental and African Studies, University of London. Paper given to seminar on Urban Culture, November 1975).
Oyovbaire, S. E.	*Federalism in Nigeria with particular reference to the Midwestern State 1966–75.* (Ph.D. thesis. University of Manchester 1976).
Turner, T.	*Oil and Government: the making and implementation of petroleum policy on Nigeria* (Ph.D. thesis, University of London 1977).
Wrigley, C. C.	*The development of state capitalism in late colonial and post colonial Nigeria* (African Studies Association of the U.K. Paper presented to 1974 Conference).

Index

(Reference to footnotes is selective)

203, 216, 218, 220, 270, 297, 317, 335, Ch. 6 passim; balanced Federation, 204, 211–12, 214, 218, 227–8, 243, 246

Regionalism, 4, 14, 15, 18, 23, 144, 147–8, 227, 243–5, 293, 312

Representation—on advisory councils, 38–9; informal representation, 40–1; the military seen as representatives, 51; the representative principle, 106; through interest groups, 109; of states in federal institutions, 294, 306–7, 323, 336; in Constituent Assembly, 345–6

Revenue allocation, 2, 3, 5–6, 19, 110–11, 216–17, Ch. 8 passim; principles of derivation, 3, 147, 163n, 225, 227–30, 231, 238, 240, 242–4, 339; formula, criteria for allocation, 20, 23, 164n, 216–17, 241, 245, 339–40; planning and fiscal commission (proposed) 214; technical committee on Revenue Allocation, 340

Revenue Allocation Review Committee (Dina Committee), 225, 228, 238–43, 245, 248n

Rights, 298, 300–4, 307, 340–1, 349n. (See also Ideology)

Rivers State, 111, 135n, 228, 229, 244, 258–9, 260–1, 262, 266

Rotimi, Brigadier, 44, 47, 65

Rufas, Alhaji, A. D., 206

Sardauna of Sokoto, 105, 117

Sardauna State (proposed), 209, 218

School boards (committees), 35, 40

Self-help committees, 39–40

Shehu Shagari, 77

Shell-B.P., 179, 182, 184, 186, 192, 195n

Shuwa, Mohammed, 96n, 108, 134n

Social mobilisation, 14, 205, 216

Socialism (socialist revolution), 9, 36, 118, 128, 299–300, 302, 345

Sokoto State, 207

Sokoto Province, 214

Sole administrators, 34–5, 36, 38

Somolu Commission, 30, 54n

Sotimi, Major, 34

South East State (See Cross River State)

State governments, budgetary autonomy, 225, 231–3, 246, 248n; independent sources of revenues, 3, 226, 229, 231, 234, 236, 247n; relations with local authorities, 253–4, 259, 260, 261, 268, 274, 283–5

State Governors (military), 24, 29ff, 65, 67, 69, 71, 99n, 106, 109, 111–13, 114–15, 116, 119, 121, 126, 201, 254, 283; removal, 53, 72, 76, 114, 121; membership of Supreme Military Council, 71–2, 112; relegation to Council of States, 115; corrupt, 122, 123

State Governors (future), 325, 328–9, 336

State monopoly, 142–3, 172, 154, 178, 185, 191, 302

Stolper, W. 160, 163n, 165n

Students, 86, 88, 102, 110, 118, 120, 206

Suke Kolo, 118

Sule Katagum, 119, 205

Supreme Military Council, 17–18, 31, 67, 89, 113, 125, 233, 242–3, 254, 259, 277, 293–5, 321, 335; composition, 71–2, 80, 89, 115, 116; attendance by Secretary, Federal Military Government, 118

Tai Solarin, 196

Taiwo, Ibrahim (Colonel), 87

Tanko Yakasi, 77

Tarka, J., 69, 70, 115

Taxation, 35–7, 75, 154, Ch. 8 passim, esp. 226, 230, 240, 245, 255, 339

Technocrats, defined, 176–77; role of, in making of oil policy, 179ff; technocratic state, 193

Temple C. L., 202

Tether, C. G., 173–4, 194n

Tinubu, K. O., 56n

Tiv, 66, 98n, 113, 126–7, 136n, 207, 211, 215, 335

Trade Unions, 49, 74, 128, 153, 155, 165n

Traditional rulers (leaders), 4, 28, 32, 35, 38, 39, 55n, 116, 126–7, 254–6, 258–9, 264, 266, 271–6, 278–9, 283–5

Udoji, Chief J. O., 205 (See also Public